INDIAN ENGLISH LITERATURE

STUDY GUIDE: COVERS ALL IMPORTANT TOPICS WITH PREVIOUS YEAR QUESTION PAPERS

RACHANA AMARNATH
@HAPPYLITERATURE

Contents

Acknowledgements   vii

Block 1 - Non-Fictional Prose

1. Non-Fictional Prose: A Survey   3
2. Swami Vivekananda, Sri Aurobindo, And Ananda Coomaraswamy   5
3. Gandhi   19
4. Jawaharlal Nehru   29
5. Nirad C. Chaudhuri   41
6. Vikram Seth And Amitav Ghosh   46

Block 2 - Untouchable

7. About Mulk Raj Anand: Career And Works   61
8. Overview Of The Novel "Untouchable"   62
9. Questions & Answers   63

Block 3 - Kanthapura

10. About Raja Rao: Career And Works   81
11. Overview Of The Novel "Kanthapura"   83
12. Questions & Answers   84

Block 4 - Clear Light Of Day

13. About Anita Desai: Career And Works   101
14. Overview Of The Novel "Clear Light Of Day"   102
15. Questions & Answers   103

Block 5 - Midnight's Children

16. About Salman Rushdie: Career And Works   119
17. Overview Of The Novel "Midnight's Children"   120
18. Questions & Answers   121

Block 6 - Short Stories

19. About Short Story   145
20. R.K. Narayan: An Astrologer's Day & Engine Trouble   150

Contents

21. Arun Joshi: The Only American From Our Village — 174

22. Manoj Das: A Trip Into The Jungle — 186

23. Subhadra Sen Gupta: The Fourth Daughter — 196

24. Shashi Despande: Miracle — 208

25. Raji Narasimha: A Toast To Herself — 217

26. Githa Hariharan: Gajar Halwa — 232

27. Ruskin Bond: No Room For Leopard & Copperfeild In Jungle — 245

Block 7 - Poetry

28. Background To Indian English Poetry — 257

29. Henry Derozio — 259

30. Toru Dutt — 264

31. Sri Aurobindo — 274

32. Sarojini Naidu — 280

33. Kamla Das — 290

34. Nissim Ezekiel — 297

35. A.K Ramanujan — 306

36. Arun Koltakar — 314

37. Jayanta Mahapatra — 320

38. Keki Nasserwanji Daruwalla — 326

39. Rajgopalan Parthasarathy — 333

Block 8 - Tara

40. About Mahesh Dattani: Career And Works — 343

41. Overview Of "TARA" — 344

42. Questions & Answers — 346

IGNOU Previous Years' Question Papers

43. June 2020 — 367

44. Dec 2020 — 369

45. June 2021 — 371

Contents

46. Dec 2021	373
47. June 2022	375
48. Dec 2022	377
49. June 2023	379
50. Dec 2023	381
51. June 2024	383

Acknowledgements

Creating a book is a journey that cannot be undertaken alone, and likewise this book "Indian English Literature - Study Guide" is the result of the collective effort and support of many wonderful individuals.

I am deeply grateful to my family for their unwavering encouragement and understanding during the countless hours I spent immersed in literature. Your belief in me fuels my passion.

To my students, past and present, thank you for being my constant source of inspiration. Your curiosity and enthusiasm for learning remind me daily of the profound impact education can have.

A heartfelt thank you to my colleagues, mentors, and fellow educators who have shared their knowledge and insights, shaping my approach to teaching and the content of this book.

I extend my appreciation and respect to the literary community, including the authors of the Indian Literature discussed within these pages. Your creativity and vision continue to enrich our lives.

Lastly, I would like to express my gratitude to the team at Notion Press, whose expertise and support, both direct and indirect, have been instrumental in bringing this book to life.

Thank you all for being a part of this endeavour.

Warm regards,
Rachana Amarnath

Disclaimer :

The information and opinions presented in "Indian English Literature - Study Guide" are intended for educational and informational purposes only. While diligent efforts have been made to ensure the accuracy and reliability of the content, the author and publisher make no representations or warranties regarding the completeness, suitability, or validity of the information provided. Readers are encouraged to refer to reference materials and consult their respective universities or educational institutions for comprehensive and up-to-date information on the subject.

The author respects copyright laws and encourages readers to do the same, if any material used in this book infringes upon copyright or trademark, it is unintentional. The author and publisher disclaim any liability for actions taken based on the information contained herein. It's important to note that different educational institutions may have specific requirements, curriculum changes, or variations in their syllabus. Therefore, readers are responsible for verifying and complying with the guidelines set forth by their respective institutions.

This disclaimer applies to all versions of the book, whether in print or electronic format.

Block 1 – Non-Fictional Prose

Scan the QR code to watch video

CHAPTER ONE

Non-Fictional Prose: A Survey

1. Introduction

The unit traces the evolution of Indian English non-fictional prose, emphasizing its literary merit and role in documenting India's sociocultural and political history. It highlights the need to analyse prose as rigorously as poetry, focusing on style, diction, and structure.

2. Key Historical Writers (Pre-Independence)

Dean Mahomet: First Indian author in English; wrote The Travels of Dean Mahomet (1794), an epistolary memoir describing colonial India. His work blends Indian observations with European literary influences.

Raja Rammohun Roy: Pioneer of expository prose; advocated social reforms (e.g., abolition of sati). Notable works include A Defence of Hindu Theism (1817) and essays promoting English education.

Swami Vivekananda: Renowned for speeches at the 1893 Parliament of Religions. His prose combined spiritual idealism with social critique, using simple, impactful language.

Rabindranath Tagore: Nobel laureate whose lectures (e.g., Nationalism) critiqued Western imperialism and celebrated Indian humanism.

Sri Aurobindo: Philosopher and critic; works like The Life Divine blended spirituality with literary criticism, advocating a synthesis of Eastern and Western thought.

3. Post-Independence Prose

Nirad C. Chaudhuri: Controversial essayist and autobiographer (The Autobiography of an Unknown Indian), critiquing Indian society with dense, allusive prose.

Ved Mehta: Blind author of autobiographical works (Continents of Exile series), blending sensory detail with introspective narratives.

Others: Notable memoirs by R.K. Narayan (My Days), biographies by S. Gopal (Jawaharlal Nehru), and travelogues by Salman Rushdie (The Jaguar

Smile).

4. Forms and Varieties of Prose

Essays:

- Formal: Scholarly articles (e.g., Raja Rammohun Roy's treatises).
- Personal: Light, anecdotal pieces (e.g., R.K. Narayan's humorous essays).
- Biography/Autobiography: Chronicles lives with subjective or objective lenses (e.g., Nehru's introspective Autobiography).
- Travelogues: Blend cultural observation with personal reflection (e.g., Dean Mahomet's Travels).
- Expository Prose: Academic writing on philosophy, history, and criticism (e.g., Sri Aurobindo's The Renaissance in India).

5. Literary Analysis of Prose

Style: Examined through diction, sentence structure (e.g., Chaudhuri's complex syntax vs. Tagore's lyrical simplicity).

Narrative Techniques: Use of descriptive, narrative, and expository modes.

Themes: National identity, colonialism, spirituality, and social reform.

6. Conclusion

Indian non-fictional prose reflects the nation's intellectual and cultural journey, from colonial encounters to post-independence self-reflection. Despite its functional origins, it achieves literary depth through masterful use of language and form. The unit underscores its significance alongside fiction and poetry in Indian English literature.

CHAPTER TWO

Swami Vivekananda, Sri Aurobindo, and Ananda Coomaraswamy

Swami Vivekananda

Swami Vivekananda (1863–1902), born Narendranath Datta, was an Indian Hindu monk, philosopher, and disciple of Ramakrishna. He introduced Vedanta and Yoga to the West and helped globalize Hinduism.

Born into a wealthy Bengali family in Calcutta, he was drawn to spirituality from a young age. After Ramakrishna's passing, he traveled across India, witnessing the struggles under British rule.

In 1893, he gained worldwide recognition at the Chicago Parliament of Religions with his speech on religious unity and tolerance. He later lectured across the U.S. and Europe, founding the Vedanta Society. In India, he established the Ramakrishna Math and Mission for social service.

A key figure in India's nationalist movement, Vivekananda is honored as a patriotic saint, and his birthday is celebrated as National Youth Day.

Question and Answer

Q.1) Distinctive Features of Hinduism Emphasized by Swami Vivekananda in His Addresses.

Ans: Introduction: Swami Vivekananda's addresses at the 1893 Parliament of Religions sought to redefine Hinduism as a dynamic, universal philosophy rooted in India's ancient spiritual heritage. Drawing from the provided material, his portrayal of Hinduism revolves around seven key features, each aimed at countering colonial and missionary critiques while asserting India's civilizational identity.

1. Sanatana Dharma: The Eternal, Inclusive Truth

Vivekananda framed Hinduism as Sanatana Dharma—an eternal, universal tradition transcending rigid dogma. In his Paper on Hinduism, he described it as a "pre-historic religion" whose essence lies in the Vedas and Vedanta. Unlike Abrahamic faiths, Hinduism, he argued, is not confined to a single prophet or text but evolves through diverse paths (yogas)—jnana (knowledge), bhakti (devotion), karma (action), and raja (meditation). This inclusivity allows it to absorb Buddhism and Jainism as complementary philosophies rather than rivals, reflecting a "harmony of religions."

2. Tolerance and Inclusivity

In his Response to Welcome, Vivekananda highlighted Hinduism's historical tolerance, contrasting it with religious persecution in other cultures. He noted India's sheltering of persecuted communities like Jews and Parsis, asserting that Hinduism "has welcomed all faiths" and "given them asylum." This pluralism, he argued, stems from the belief that all religions are valid paths to the "Supreme Lord," a principle he encapsulated in the Bhagavad Gita's teaching: *"Whoever comes to Me, through whatsoever form, I reach him."

3. Unity in Diversity

Using the parable of frogs in a well (Why We Disagree), Vivekananda illustrated the futility of religious exclusivity. Each frog (religion) claims supremacy, yet none grasps the vastness of truth. Hinduism, he stressed, acknowledges diverse perspectives as fragments of a unified reality. This metaphor underscored his call for interfaith harmony, urging listeners to move beyond sectarian "fanaticism" and embrace a global spirituality.

4. Spirituality Over Ritualism

Vivekananda distanced Hinduism from ritualistic caricatures. While defending idol worship as symbolic (Paper on Hinduism), he clarified that idols are mere aids to focus on the formless Divine. True Hinduism, he asserted, prioritizes self-realization—realizing the soul's (atman) identity with Brahman (universal consciousness). He dismissed ritual orthodoxy, stating, "It is an insult to a starving man to teach him metaphysics" (Religion Not the Crying Need), emphasizing spirituality's social relevance.

5. Compatibility with Science

Vivekananda bridged Hinduism with scientific inquiry, asserting that Vedantic concepts like Brahman and karma align with modern science. He likened religious truths to hypotheses requiring verification, declaring, "Verification is the perfect proof of a theory" (Paper on Hinduism). The law of karma mirrored cause-effect principles, while the soul's immortality resonated with energy conservation. This rational approach aimed to position Hinduism as a "science of the spirit," adaptable to evolving knowledge.

6. Social Responsibility

In Religion Not the Crying Need, Vivekananda prioritized India's material upliftment, urging missionaries to replace proselytization with famine relief. He linked spirituality to social justice, condemning the exploitation of the poor and advocating for seva (service) as a spiritual duty. His founding of the Ramakrishna Mission institutionalized this ethos, blending monasticism with education and healthcare.

7. Buddhism as Fulfillment

Vivekananda viewed Buddhism not as a break from Hinduism but its logical progression. He noted that Buddha's disciples were often Brahmins and that Hindu texts later absorbed Buddhist ethics (Buddhism, the Fulfillment). By framing Buddhism as a reform movement within Sanatana Dharma, he reinforced Hinduism's capacity for self-renewal and inclusivity.

Conclusion: Vivekananda's addresses redefined Hinduism as a rational, inclusive, and socially engaged tradition. By stressing its tolerance, scientific temper, and ethical core, he sought to revive India's self-respect and position it as a global spiritual leader. His vision remains a cornerstone of modern Hindu identity, advocating a balance between ancient wisdom and contemporary challenges.

Q.2) Discuss Swami Vivekananda's Views on Buddhism

Ans: Introduction: Swami Vivekananda's engagement with Buddhism reflects his broader mission to synthesize India's spiritual heritage with modern rationalism while advocating for religious pluralism. His nuanced perspective on Buddhism—marked by admiration for its ethical rigor and critique of its philosophical limitations—reveals his commitment to positioning Hinduism as a universal, inclusive tradition. Below is an expanded exploration of his views:

1. Buddhism as a Reform Movement Within Hinduism

Vivekananda contextualized Buddhism within the evolution of Hindu thought, framing it as a reformist response to Vedic ritualism and social inequality. During the Buddha's era (6th century BCE), Hinduism had become entangled in rigid caste hierarchies and elaborate sacrificial rites (yajnas), which marginalized lower castes and prioritized ritual over ethical living. The Buddha, according to Vivekananda, emerged as a "protestant" reformer who sought to purify religion by:

Rejecting Caste: The Buddha's teachings openly opposed Brahminical supremacy, advocating equality and merit over birth.

Simplifying Spirituality: He replaced complex rituals with a focus on moral conduct (sila), meditation (dhyana), and wisdom (prajna).

Emphasizing Personal Experience: The Buddha urged followers to verify truths through self-effort ("Be lamps unto yourselves"), aligning with Vivekananda's emphasis on empirical spirituality.

Vivekananda admired this reformist zeal, noting that Buddhism's rise mirrored Hinduism's capacity for self-correction. However, he insisted that Buddhism was not a break from Hinduism but a natural evolution within the Sanatana Dharma (eternal truth) framework.

2. Ethical Praise and Philosophical Critique:

Vivekananda lauded Buddhism's ethical framework, particularly its emphasis on:

Ahimsa (Non-violence): The Buddha's rejection of violence resonated with Hindu ideals of compassion.

Compassion (Karuna): The Bodhisattva ideal of selfless service for others' liberation paralleled Vivekananda's karma yoga.

Alleviation of Suffering: The Four Noble Truths and Eightfold Path provided a pragmatic roadmap to transcend dukkha (suffering).

However, he critiqued Buddhism's metaphysical foundations:

Denial of the Soul (Anatman): Buddhism's doctrine of anatman (no permanent self) conflicted withVedanta's assertion of the eternal atman (soul) united with Brahman (universal consciousness). Vivekananda argued that denying the soul's immortality stripped spirituality of its ultimate goal—moksha (liberation).

Neglect of the Divine: The Buddha's silence on God and the afterlife, while pragmatic, left a philosophical void. For Vivekananda, Hinduism's embrace of both personal (saguna) and formless (nirguna) aspects of divinity offered a more complete spiritual framework.

3. Buddhism in the Context of Universalism

At the 1893 Parliament of Religions, Vivekananda positioned Buddhism as a vital thread in Hinduism's pluralistic tapestry. He declared:

"Buddhism is the fulfillment of Hinduism."

This statement underscored his belief that:

Syncretism: Hindu texts like the Bhagavata Purana later integrated Buddha as an avatar of Vishnu, symbolizing Hinduism's absorptive capacity.

Shared Ethos: Both traditions emphasized dharma (righteousness) and ahimsa, though through different lenses.

Global Relevance: Buddhism's spread across Asia demonstrated the universal applicability of Indian spirituality, a theme central to Vivekananda's vision of India as a Vishwa Guru (world teacher).

4. Historical Trajectory: Decline in India, Global Spread

Vivekananda lamented Buddhism's disappearance from India but attributed it to:

Monastic Elitism: The monastic focus (Sangha) alienated laypeople, creating a disconnect between ascetics and society.

Hindu Reforms: Post-Buddhist Hindu thinkers like Adi Shankara incorporated Buddhist critiques (e.g., anti-ritualism) into Advaita Vedanta, revitalizing Hinduism and reducing the need for a separate Buddhist identity.

Conversely, he celebrated Buddhism's global reach:

Cultural Adaptation: In countries like Sri Lanka, Tibet, and Japan, Buddhism adapted to local contexts, proving its versatility.

Ethical Legacy: Its emphasis on compassion influenced global humanism, aligning with Vivekananda's ideal of a "religion of humanity."

5. Practical Spirituality vs. Holistic Synthesis

While Vivekananda admired Buddhism's focus on ethics and mindfulness, he believed Hinduism offered a broader synthesis:

Integrative Paths: Hinduism's yogas—jnana (knowledge), bhakti (devotion), karma (action), and raja (meditation)—catered to diverse temperaments, whereas Buddhism primarily emphasized sila and dhyana.

Social Engagement: Vivekananda's Ramakrishna Mission mirrored Buddhist sanghas but integrated service (seva) with Vedantic philosophy, addressing both material and spiritual needs.

6. Legacy and Contemporary Relevance

Vivekananda's views on Buddhism remain influential in interfaith dialogue and Hindu revivalism:

Interfaith Harmony: His framing of Buddhism as a "fulfillment" of Hinduism prefigured modern efforts to bridge Eastern traditions.

Critique of Dogmatism: By celebrating Buddhism's ethical core while critiquing its metaphysical gaps, he modeled constructive interreligious engagement.

Modern Hinduism: His emphasis on practical Vedanta—combining meditation with social service—reflects Buddhist influences, showcasing synthesis over sectarianism.

Conclusion

Swami Vivekananda's engagement with Buddhism was neither uncritical nor dismissive. He honored its ethical contributions and reformist role while asserting Hinduism's metaphysical completeness. For him, Buddhism exemplified the dynamic, self-correcting nature of Sanatana Dharma, capable of integrating diverse truths without losing its essence. His vision—rooted in pluralism and universalism—remains a guiding light for fostering global spiritual solidarity, where diverse traditions coexist as complementary paths to truth.

Q.3) Discuss Swami Vivekananda's Vision of Hinduism and Science.

Ans: Introduction: Swami Vivekananda, a key architect of modern Hinduism, consistently emphasized the profound alignment between Hindu philosophy and scientific inquiry. He argued that Hinduism, particularly Vedanta, shares foundational principles with science, making it uniquely suited to coexist with and even complement modern scientific advancements. His perspective sought to dismantle colonial-era stereotypes of Hinduism as "superstitious" and position it as a rational, universal tradition. Below is an exploration of the key similarities he identified:

1. Unity of Existence: Brahman and Universal Consciousness

Vivekananda equated the Vedantic concept of Brahman (the ultimate, formless reality) with the scientific understanding of a unified cosmic field. Just as science posits that all matter and energy originate from a singular source (e.g., the Big Bang or quantum fields), Vedanta asserts that Brahman is the substratum of all existence. He stated:

"The universe is a manifestation of the Eternal One, as modern science also shows that all forces are manifestations of one universal energy."

This "unity in diversity" mirrors scientific theories about the interconnectedness of subatomic particles and ecosystems.

2. Law of Karma and Cause-Effect Relationships

Vivekananda drew parallels between the Hindu law of karma (action and consequence) and the scientific principle of causality. He explained karma not as fatalism but as a dynamic system where every action generates a corresponding reaction, akin to Newton's Third Law. For him, karma was a moral and spiritual equivalent of the physical laws governing the universe:

"The law of karma is the law of causation applied to the moral and spiritual world."

This framework aligns with scientific determinism, where observable phenomena are governed by immutable laws.

3. Immortality of the Soul and Conservation of Energy

Vivekananda linked the Vedantic belief in the soul's immortality (atman) to the scientific law of energy conservation. He argued that just as energy cannot be destroyed but only transformed, the soul transcends physical death:

"The soul is not a compound; it cannot be dissolved. It is the same today and tomorrow, eternally."

This analogy bridged spirituality with physics, suggesting that consciousness, like energy, is a fundamental, indestructible aspect of reality.

4. Empirical Approach: Verification Over Dogma

Vivekananda emphasized that Vedanta, like science, prioritizes direct experience and verification over blind faith. He often quoted the Upanishadic injunction "Neti, Neti" (Not this, Not this)—a method of inquiry to discard falsehoods and arrive at truth—as akin to the scientific method. In his Paper on Hinduism, he declared:

"Religion, like science, must submit to verification. Verification is the perfect proof of a theory."

This empirical spirit, he argued, made Hinduism a "science of religion," where truths are discovered through meditation and self-realization rather than imposed doctrines.

5. Rational Inquiry and Rejection of Dogmatism

Vivekananda criticized ritualistic dogma in Hinduism, aligning himself with the Buddha's rational critique of superstition. He saw Vedanta's focus on jnana yoga (the path of knowledge) as compatible with scientific skepticism. For instance, he dismissed literal interpretations of mythologies, urging followers to seek their symbolic meaning:

"The stories of the gods are psychological truths clothed in poetic imagery."

This approach mirrored scientific demystification of natural phenomena.

6. Cosmology and Cyclic Time

Vivekananda highlighted Hinduism's cosmological parallels with modern science. The Puranic concept of cyclical time—where universes undergo endless cycles of creation (srishti), preservation (sthiti), and dissolution (pralaya)—resonated with theories of an oscillating universe or multiverse. He noted:

"Hinduism's cosmic cycles are not mere myths but intuitions of a deeper truth science is yet to fully grasp."

7. Evolution and Spiritual Progress

Vivekananda interpreted Darwinian evolution as a material counterpart to Hinduism's spiritual evolution. He posited that biological evolution culminates in human consciousness, which then evolves toward self-realization (moksha):

"Evolution is not merely physical; it is the unfolding of the soul toward perfection."

This teleological view aligned with Teilhard de Chardin's later concept of the "Omega Point" but was rooted in Vedantic thought.

Conclusion: Hinduism as a "Science of the Spirit"

Swami Vivekananda's synthesis of Hinduism and science was revolutionary. By framing Vedanta as a rational, empirically verifiable system, he countered colonial narratives of Hindu "backwardness" and positioned it as a complement to scientific inquiry. His vision emphasized that:

Science and spirituality are complementary: While science explores the external world, Hinduism investigates inner consciousness.

Truth is universal: Both seek to uncover the same reality through different lenses.

Adaptability is key: Hinduism's timeless truths can evolve alongside scientific discoveries.

For Vivekananda, this synthesis was not mere analogy but a call to harmonize material progress with spiritual growth, ensuring humanity's holistic advancement. His ideas remain foundational to dialogues on science and religion, underscoring Hinduism's enduring relevance in a technologically driven world.

Q.4) Aspect of Indian culture figure in the writing of Swami Vivekananda or Shri Aurobindo

Ans: Introduction: The writings of Swami Vivekananda and Sri Aurobindo are deeply interwoven with the spiritual, philosophical, and cultural fabric of India, reflecting their shared mission to reinterpret and revitalize the nation's heritage amid colonial and modern challenges. Both thinkers drew extensively from India's ancient traditions, such as Vedanta, Yoga, and the epics, to articulate a vision of Indian culture that harmonized spiritual depth with pragmatic relevance. Their works emphasized the universality of Hindu philosophy while asserting its unique capacity to address global existential and ethical dilemmas.

Swami Vivekananda anchored his philosophy in Vedanta, which he presented as the essence of Hinduism and a universal religion transcending sectarian boundaries. In his iconic 1893 address at the Parliament of Religions, he framed Hinduism as a tradition of Sarva Dharma Sambhava (equal respect for all religions), a principle rooted in India's pluralistic ethos. He popularized Yoga as a scientific discipline, systematizing practices like Raja Yoga to demonstrate their alignment with rational inquiry. Vivekananda also reinterpreted Indian epics like the Ramayana and Mahabharata as allegories for inner spiritual struggles, transforming figures like Ravana into metaphors for ego and ignorance. His emphasis on seva (selfless service) through the Ramakrishna Mission reflected the Indian cultural ideal of integrating spirituality with social action, urging Indians to revive self-respect through education and ethical living.

Sri Aurobindo, meanwhile, fused Vedantic thought with evolutionary philosophy, envisioning a future where humanity's spiritual and material progress converged. His concept of Integral Yoga sought to elevate human consciousness toward a divine life on Earth, synthesizing Upanishadic ideals like Brahman (universal consciousness) and Shakti (creative energy) with modern scientific insights. In Essays on the Gita, he reinterpreted the Bhagavad Gita as a guide to spiritualized action, emphasizing Karma Yoga as a means to align duty with inner growth. Aurobindo's epic poem Savitri reimagined the Mahabharata's tale of Savitri and Satyavan as a cosmic allegory of humanity's quest for liberation, illustrating his belief in mythology as a vehicle for profound psychological and spiritual truths. His defense of Indian civilization in Foundations of Indian Culture countered Western critiques by asserting the superiority of India's spiritual ethos over Europe's materialistic paradigm.

Both thinkers championed cultural nationalism, though through distinct lenses. Vivekananda positioned India as the world's spiritual guru, arguing that its ancient wisdom could remedy the moral bankruptcy of Western materialism. He urged Indians to embrace their heritage with pride, advocating for "man-making education" that combined traditional values with modern knowledge. Aurobindo, initially a revolutionary nationalist, later shifted focus to spiritual evolution as the key to societal transformation. He envisioned India synthesizing Eastern spirituality with Western rationality, creating a culture where Dharma (moral order) guided material progress. His experimental township, Auroville, embodied this ideal, aiming to harmonize diversity with unity.

On social issues, Vivekananda critiqued caste-based discrimination while respecting India's traditional structures, advocating merit over birth. His Ramakrishna Mission institutionalized seva as a spiritual practice, blending charity with cultural revival. Aurobindo emphasized holistic education, prioritizing the "education of the soul" to nurture physical, mental, and spiritual growth. Both saw India's future in balancing tradition and modernity—Vivekananda through global spiritual leadership, and Aurobindo through a consciousness-driven evolution of society.

Their legacies endure as cornerstones of India's cultural identity. Vivekananda's portrayal of Hinduism as a rational, universal tradition reshaped global perceptions, while his call to "Arise, awake!" inspired generations of nationalists. Aurobindo's vision of a spiritually awakened humanity continues to influence thinkers and movements worldwide, underscoring the timeless relevance of India's cultural and philosophical heritage. Together, their works illuminate the dynamic interplay between tradition and modernity, offering a roadmap for a civilization rooted in spiritual wisdom yet engaged with the challenges of a changing world.

Sri Aurobindo

Life and Work

Sri Aurobindo was born in Calcutta on 15 August 1872. When he was seven, he was sent to England for his education. He studied at St. Paul's School in London and later at King's College, Cambridge. After returning to India in 1893, he worked in Baroda for thirteen years, serving the Maharaja and teaching at Baroda College. During this time, he also joined a revolutionary group and helped plan a secret uprising against British rule.

In 1906, after the Partition of Bengal, he left his job in Baroda and moved to Calcutta, where he became a leader of the nationalist movement. He was the first Indian political leader to openly demand full independence in his newspaper Bande Mataram. He was arrested multiple times for sedition and conspiracy but was released due to a lack of evidence.

Sri Aurobindo started practicing Yoga in 1905, and in 1908, he had a deep spiritual experience. In 1910, he left politics and moved to Pondicherry to focus entirely on his spiritual life. Over the next forty years, he developed a new path of Yoga, called Integral Yoga, which aimed not just at spiritual liberation but also at transforming human nature.

In 1926, with the help of his spiritual companion, the Mother, he founded the Sri Aurobindo Ashram. He wrote many important books, including The Life Divine, The Synthesis of Yoga, and Savitri. Sri Aurobindo passed away on 5 December 1950.

Q.1) How does Sri Aurobindo make case of Indus Civilization?

Ans: Introduction: Sri Aurobindo's defense of India's civilization, articulated in his essay Is India Civilized? (1918–19), challenges Western critiques of Indian culture by redefining the very notion of civilization. Responding to British critic William Archer, Aurobindo argues that true civilization is not measured by material progress or technological dominance but by its ability to harmonize the physical, mental, and spiritual dimensions of human life. He positions India as a unique civilization rooted in spiritual idealism, contrasting it with Europe's materialistic ethos. Aurobindo's case rests on India's ancient philosophical traditions, its emphasis on inner growth, and its potential to guide humanity toward a higher consciousness.

Aurobindo asserts that India's civilization is anchored in spirituality as the "leading motive" of life. Unlike Europe, which prioritizes material prosperity, India's cultural ethos revolves around realizing the Eternal Spirit (Brahman) immanent in all existence. This spiritual focus is reflected in its ancient texts, such as the Vedas and Upanishads, which explore the soul's journey toward self-realization (atman) and liberation (moksha). For Aurobindo, India's greatness lies in its ability to integrate spirituality into daily life through practices like yoga, meditation, and dharma (moral duty). He contrasts this with Europe's "predatory" materialism, which, despite technological advancements, fosters discontent and existential voids.

Aurobindo condemns Europe's civilizational model as inherently flawed. He describes post-Renaissance Europe as "material, predatory, and aggressive," citing colonialism, ecological exploitation, and spiritual bankruptcy as its hallmarks. While acknowledging Europe's medieval religious traditions, he critiques their intolerance and rigidity, contrasting them with India's inclusive spirituality. For instance, India's acceptance of diverse paths to truth—from atheistic Jainism to devotional Bhakti—demonstrates a maturity absent in dogmatic Western frameworks. Aurobindo argues that Europe's obsession with external progress neglects the inner self, rendering its achievements hollow.

Aurobindo envisions a global struggle between India's spiritual idealism and Europe's materialism. He predicts three stages of interaction: conflict, concert (cooperation), and sacrifice (self-transcendence). While Europe's current dominance stems from its aggressive material pursuits, Aurobindo insists that India's spiritual resilience will ultimately prevail. He advocates "aggressive spirituality"—revitalizing India's cultural forms to project its ideals globally. This does not mean rejecting modernity but synthesizing it with ancient wisdom. For example, India's spiritual practices like yoga and Vedanta, when dynamically reinterpreted, could address modern anxieties and offer holistic solutions to global crises.

Aurobindo positions India as a future "world-Guru," guiding humanity toward a harmonious, spiritually awakened society. He cites historical precedents, such as Swami Vivekananda's global impact, to argue that India's ideals—non-violence, pluralism, and self-realization—hold universal relevance. Even if India faces temporary setbacks, its civilizational ethos, rooted in sanatana dharma (eternal truth), ensures its enduring contribution to human progress.

Conclusion

Sri Aurobindo's case for India's civilization transcends defensive posturing; it is a visionary call to reclaim and project India's spiritual heritage as a remedy to global ills. By defining civilization through the lens of inner harmony rather than external conquest, he challenges Eurocentric narratives of progress. His emphasis on synthesizing tradition with modernity—reviving India's spiritual dynamism while engaging constructively with the West—remains profoundly relevant. Aurobindo's faith in India's civilizational mission underscores its potential to lead humanity toward a future where material advancement coexists with spiritual fulfillment, ensuring true and lasting progress.

Ananda Coomaraswamy

Life and Work

Ananda Kentish Coomaraswamy (1877–1947) was a geologist, art historian, philosopher, and curator. He was born in Sri Lanka to an English mother and a Tamil father, but after his father's early death, he was raised in England. He studied geology and became a respected scientist, discovering a new mineral called Thorionite. However, his visit to Sri Lanka changed his life. He became deeply interested in South Asian art, culture, and philosophy.

Coomaraswamy believed that India's true strength lay in its traditional arts and crafts, not in Western-style modernization. He saw that skilled craftsmen across India and Sri Lanka were preserving ancient artistic traditions, but colonial rule was destroying these practices. He argued that reviving traditional arts was key to India's national identity and criticized blind imitation of the West.

His book Essays in National Idealism (1911) emphasized that nations are built by artists and thinkers, not just by economic or political power. He defended Indian art against Western critics who dismissed it as primitive. He also challenged the idea that Greek influence shaped Indian sculpture, proving that Indian artistic traditions were independent and superior in many ways.

From 1907 to 1916, Coomaraswamy worked in India, trying to establish a museum but faced obstacles. Eventually, he moved to the Boston Museum of Fine Arts, where he spent the last 30 years of his life, preserving and promoting Indian and Islamic art. Despite living abroad, he remained connected to India and passed away after its independence. India lost a great scholar who had passionately fought for its cultural heritage.

Question and Answer

Q.1) What according to Anand Coomaraswamy does the bronze image of the dancing Shiva Symbolize Discuss.

Ans: Introduction: Ananda Coomaraswamy, a pioneering scholar of Indian art and philosophy, interprets the bronze Nataraja—the dancing form of Shiva—as a profound metaphysical and cosmological symbol. His analysis transcends superficial mythological readings to reveal the Nataraja as a synthesis of Hindu philosophical principles, artistic expression, and cosmic truths. The Nataraja embodies the eternal rhythm of the universe, representing the cyclical processes of creation (srishti), preservation (sthiti), destruction (samhara), veiling (tirobhava), and liberation (anugraha). The dynamic posture of Shiva captures the harmonious interplay of these forces, where creation and destruction are not opposing acts but complementary phases of existence. The flaming circle (Prabhamandala) surrounding Shiva symbolizes the boundless universe and the cyclical nature of time, emphasizing that life and death, birth and decay, are inseparable aspects of the divine dance.

Coomaraswamy delves deeply into the symbolic attributes held by Shiva in the Nataraja form. The drum (damaru) in Shiva's right hand represents the primal sound (nada) of Aum, the vibration from which the universe emerges. This connects to the Vedantic concept of Shabda Brahman, where sound is the essence of reality. In his left hand, the flame (agni) signifies transformative destruction, dissolving illusions (maya) to purify the cosmos and enable renewal. The dwarf (Apasmara Purusha) crushed under Shiva's foot symbolizes avidya (ignorance) and ego, illustrating the triumph of divine wisdom over unconsciousness. Shiva's raised palm in the abhaya mudra reassures devotees of liberation from fear and suffering, while his flowing hair and serene face embody both cosmic energy and inner stillness.

Central to Coomaraswamy's interpretation is the Nataraja's representation of the unity of opposites. Shiva's androgynous form blends masculine vigor and feminine grace, reflecting the union of Purusha (spirit) and Prakriti (matter). The raised leg signifies liberation (moksha), transcending earthly bonds, while the grounded leg represents engagement with the material world, symbolizing the coexistence of transcendence and immanence. This duality mirrors the Advaita Vedantic principle of non-duality (Advaita), where apparent opposites dissolve into a unified reality. The dance itself is both dynamic and meditative, embodying the paradox of motion within stillness and destruction within creation.

Philosophically, Coomaraswamy links the Nataraja to the Upanishadic concept of Sat-Chit-Ananda (Being-Consciousness-Bliss). The dance expresses the divine joy (ananda) inherent in existence, where the cosmos arises from Shiva's ecstatic play (lila). The rhythm of the dance reflects the interconnectedness of all life, contrasting with Western art's static ideals by emphasizing cyclical time and perpetual transformation. Coomaraswamy critiques colonial-era scholars who dismissed the Nataraja as a "primitive idol," arguing instead that it is a sophisticated allegory of universal truths. For him, the image is not merely a religious icon but a visual treatise on the nature of reality, designed to convey abstract philosophy through symbolic art.

Conclusion: Coomaraswamy elevates the Nataraja from a cultural artifact to a universal emblem of cosmic harmony. The bronze encapsulates the essence of Hindu thought, where art, philosophy, and spirituality converge. It serves as a reminder of the individual's potential to transcend ignorance through divine wisdom and participate in the eternal dance of existence. His interpretation underscores the timeless relevance of Indian artistic traditions in articulating profound metaphysical truths.

CHAPTER THREE

Gandhi

Revered as India's "Father of the Nation," Mahatma Gandhi pioneered non-violent resistance (Satyagraha), influencing global civil rights movements. Trained as a lawyer in London, he fought racial injustice in South Africa (1893–1914) before leading India's struggle for independence.

Returning in 1915, he championed Swaraj through the Non-Cooperation, Civil Disobedience, and Quit India movements, using boycotts, fasting, and moral defiance to weaken British rule. Beyond politics, he fought caste discrimination, promoted women's rights, and encouraged self-reliance through khadi.

Assassinated in 1948, Gandhi's legacy lives on through his autobiography The Story of My Experiments with Truth and his influence on leaders like Martin Luther King Jr. and Nelson Mandela. His principles of truth and non-violence remain guiding forces in social justice worldwide.

Importance of Swaraj

Hind Swaraj (1909), Gandhi's critique of modernity, remains strikingly relevant today, offering solutions to 21st-century crises. It challenges unchecked industrialization and consumerism, advocating instead for sustainability, ethical living, and decentralized systems.

The importance of Hind Swaraj in today's context lies in its profound critique of modernity and its timeless call for moral and spiritual renewal. Written over a century ago, Gandhi's ideas in Hind Swaraj resonate deeply with contemporary challenges, offering a roadmap for addressing issues like environmental degradation, consumerism, inequality, and the erosion of ethical values.

Environmental Crisis: Gandhi warned of ecological harm from exploitative industrialization. His vision of village-centric economies, manual labor, and harmony with nature aligns with modern calls for renewable energy and reduced consumption.

Consumerism & Alienation: He decried materialism's erosion of moral-spiritual values—a prescient critique amid today's mental health crises and social fragmentation. His Swaraj (self-rule) prioritizes inner growth, simplicity, and community over relentless technological progress.

Inequality & Globalization: Gandhi's Swadeshi (local self-reliance) counters corporate exploitation, inspiring fair trade and equitable resource distribution. His decentralized governance model addresses wealth disparities and empowers marginalized communities.

Non-Violence in Conflict Resolution: Amid global polarization, Gandhi's Satyagraha (truth-force) offers a path to peace through compassion and dialogue, rejecting violence as a tool for change.

A blueprint for ethical modernity, Hind Swaraj urges a shift from profit-driven excess to a society rooted in justice, ecological balance, and human dignity.

Question & Answer

Q.1) Discuss Hind Swaraj as a post-colonial text.

Ans: Introduction: Hind Swaraj by Mahatma Gandhi, written in 1909, is a seminal text that can be analyzed as a postcolonial work, even though it was written decades before the formal establishment of postcolonial studies as an academic discipline. The book critiques colonialism, modernity, and Western civilization while envisioning an alternative path for India's future. It challenges the dominant narratives of progress and development imposed by colonial powers and offers a radical rethinking of freedom, self-rule, and cultural identity. Here's a discussion of Hind Swaraj as a postcolonial text:

1. Critique of Colonialism and Modernity

At its core, Hind Swaraj is a powerful critique of British colonialism and the modern civilization that underpins it. Gandhi argues that colonialism is not merely a political or economic system but a cultural and moral one that dehumanizes both the colonizer and the colonized. He rejects the idea that Western civilization represents progress, instead calling it a "disease" that promotes materialism, greed, and violence. This critique aligns with postcolonial theory, which questions the Eurocentric narratives of modernity and development imposed on colonized societies.

Gandhi's assertion that "the English have not taken India; we have given it to them" is a profound postcolonial insight. It shifts the focus from blaming the colonizer to examining the complicity of the colonized in their own subjugation. This idea resonates with postcolonial thinkers like Frantz Fanon and Edward Said, who emphasize the psychological and cultural dimensions of colonialism. Gandhi's call for self-purification and moral regeneration as a path to freedom reflects a postcolonial desire to reclaim agency and redefine identity outside the framework of colonial domination.

2. Rejection of Mimicry and Westernization

One of the central themes of Hind Swaraj is Gandhi's rejection of the uncritical imitation of Western culture and institutions. He criticizes Indians who admire British systems like railways, courts, and modern education, arguing that these institutions perpetuate inequality and moral decay. This critique aligns with postcolonial concerns about mimicry, a concept explored by Homi Bhabha, where colonized societies imitate the colonizer's culture, often losing their own identity in the process.

Gandhi's vision of Swaraj (self-rule) is not about replicating Western models of governance but about creating a uniquely Indian form of self-governance rooted in tradition, spirituality, and simplicity. He advocates for a return to village-based economies, decentralized governance, and self-reliance, challenging the centralized, exploitative systems of colonial rule. This emphasis on cultural authenticity and self-definition is a hallmark of postcolonial thought.

3. Alternative Vision of Freedom

Hind Swaraj offers an alternative vision of freedom that goes beyond political independence. Gandhi's concept of Swaraj is not just about driving out the British but about achieving self-rule at the individual and collective levels. He emphasizes moral and spiritual development, arguing that true freedom requires self-discipline, non-violence, and a rejection of materialism. This holistic approach to freedom challenges the narrow, Eurocentric definitions of liberty and progress.

Gandhi's critique of modernity and his advocacy for a simpler, more sustainable way of life resonate with postcolonial concerns about the destructive impact of globalization and industrialization. His ideas anticipate later postcolonial critiques of development, which argue that the Western model of progress often exacerbates inequality and environmental degradation in formerly colonized nations.

4. Resistance and Non-Violence

Gandhi's philosophy of Satyagraha (non-violent resistance) is a cornerstone of Hind Swaraj and a key postcolonial strategy for challenging oppression. Unlike revolutionary movements that seek to overthrow colonial powers through violence, Gandhi's approach emphasizes moral strength, self-sacrifice, and the power of truth. This method of resistance aligns with postcolonial efforts to dismantle oppressive systems without replicating their violence.

Gandhi's emphasis on non-violence also reflects a postcolonial concern with the psychological and cultural dimensions of resistance. By rejecting violence, he seeks to preserve the humanity of both the oppressor and the oppressed, fostering a sense of shared dignity and mutual respect. This approach has inspired countless postcolonial movements, from the civil rights struggle in the United States to anti-apartheid activism in South Africa.

5. Cultural Revival and Identity

Hind Swaraj is deeply concerned with the revival of Indian culture and identity, which had been eroded by colonialism. Gandhi critiques the Westernization of Indian society and calls for a return to traditional values, such as simplicity, self-reliance, and spirituality. This emphasis on cultural revival is a central theme in postcolonial literature, which often seeks to reclaim and celebrate indigenous traditions that were suppressed or devalued under colonial rule.

Gandhi's vision of India as a spiritual civilization contrasts sharply with the materialistic, industrial model of the West. He argues that India's strength lies in its moral and cultural heritage, which can serve as a foundation for a more just and equitable society. This celebration of cultural identity and resistance to cultural imperialism is a key aspect of postcolonial thought.

6. Relevance to Postcolonial Theory

While Hind Swaraj predates the formal development of postcolonial theory, its themes and ideas anticipate many of the concerns explored by postcolonial scholars. Gandhi's critique of colonialism, his rejection of mimicry, his alternative vision of freedom, and his emphasis on cultural revival all align with postcolonial efforts to challenge dominant narratives and reclaim agency.

Moreover, Gandhi's holistic approach to freedom—encompassing political, social, and spiritual dimensions—offers a valuable framework for postcolonial studies, which often seeks to move beyond narrow definitions of liberation. His emphasis on non-violence and moral strength provides a powerful alternative to the cycles of violence and oppression that characterize much of colonial and postcolonial history.

Conclusion

As a postcolonial text, Hind Swaraj is both a critique of colonialism and a visionary blueprint for a decolonized future. Gandhi's ideas challenge the Eurocentric assumptions of modernity and progress, offering an alternative vision rooted in tradition, morality, and non-violence. His emphasis on self-rule, cultural revival, and ethical living resonates deeply with postcolonial concerns about identity, agency, and justice. In a world still grappling with the legacies of colonialism, Hind Swaraj remains a vital and inspiring text that calls us to rethink our values and strive for a more equitable and compassionate world.

Q.2) Comment on Gandhi's view on education and their relevance in the age of globalization.

Ans: Introduction: Gandhi's views on education, as articulated in Hind Swaraj and other writings, are deeply rooted in his philosophy of holistic development, self-reliance, and moral upliftment. He critiqued the colonial education system imposed by the British, which he believed alienated Indians from their cultural roots and created a class of individuals disconnected from the realities of their society. Gandhi's vision of education emphasized character-building, practical skills, and cultural rootedness, rather than mere literacy or rote learning. In the age of globalization, his ideas remain profoundly relevant, offering a counter-narrative to the commodification of education and the homogenizing effects of globalized culture.

Gandhi's Vision of Education

Education for Life, Not Just Livelihood:

Gandhi believed that education should prepare individuals not just for earning a living but for living a meaningful and ethical life. He emphasized the development of moral values, self-discipline, and social responsibility over the mere acquisition of degrees or technical skills. In his view, true education should cultivate the mind, body, and spirit, fostering a sense of purpose and connection to society.

Critique of Colonial Education:

Gandhi sharply criticized the British education system in India, which he saw as a tool for cultural imperialism. He argued that it produced a class of "English-educated" Indians who were alienated from their own culture and traditions. This system, he believed, prioritized Western knowledge and values over indigenous wisdom, creating a sense of inferiority among Indians. Gandhi famously called this education system a "factory for clerks," designed to serve the colonial administration rather than empower the masses.

Focus on Practical Skills and Self-Reliance:

Gandhi advocated for an education system that emphasized practical skills and self-reliance. He believed that education should be closely linked to the needs of the community and the realities of everyday life. For instance, he promoted vocational training in crafts like spinning, weaving, and farming, which would enable individuals to contribute to their communities and reduce dependence on imported goods.

Cultural and Ethical Foundation:

Gandhi stressed the importance of grounding education in India's cultural and ethical traditions. He believed that learning should include the study of indigenous languages, literature, and religious texts, which would instill a sense of pride and identity in students. At the same time, he advocated for a multilingual and inclusive approach, encouraging Indians to learn each other's languages and cultures to foster unity and mutual respect.

Decentralized and Community-Based Education:

Gandhi envisioned a decentralized education system that would be accessible to all, especially the rural poor. He believed that education should be rooted in the local context, with schools serving as centers of community development. This approach would empower villages and reduce the urban-rural divide.

Resisting the Commodification of Education:

In today's globalized world, education is increasingly treated as a commodity, with a focus on profit-making and market-driven skills. Gandhi's emphasis on education as a tool for holistic development offers a powerful alternative. His vision reminds us that education should not merely serve economic interests but should also nurture ethical, social, and spiritual growth.

Preserving Cultural Identity:

Globalization often leads to the erosion of local cultures and traditions, as Western values and lifestyles dominate global discourse. Gandhi's call for culturally rooted education is particularly relevant in this context. It encourages societies to preserve their unique identities while engaging with the world, fostering a sense of pride and belonging among younger generations.

Promoting Sustainable Development:

Gandhi's emphasis on practical skills and self-reliance aligns with the growing need for sustainable development in a globalized world. His advocacy for vocational training and community-based education can help address issues like unemployment, rural poverty, and environmental degradation. By equipping individuals with skills that are relevant to their local contexts, education can become a tool for sustainable and inclusive growth.

Fostering Ethical Leadership:

In an era marked by corruption, inequality, and environmental crises, Gandhi's focus on moral and ethical education is more important than ever. His vision of education as a means to cultivate compassion, integrity, and social responsibility can help create leaders who prioritize the common good over personal gain.

Addressing Inequality:

Globalization has exacerbated inequalities, with access to quality education often limited to the privileged few. Gandhi's vision of decentralized and inclusive education offers a way to bridge this gap. By making education accessible to all, regardless of socio-economic status, societies can work towards greater equity and justice.

Balancing Tradition and Modernity:

Gandhi's approach to education provides a framework for balancing tradition and modernity. While he critiqued the blind adoption of Western models, he did not reject modern knowledge outright. Instead, he advocated for a synthesis of the best of both worlds, where traditional wisdom and modern science coexist harmoniously. This balanced approach is essential in a globalized world, where societies must navigate the tensions between preserving their heritage and embracing progress.

Conclusion

Gandhi's views on education challenge the dominant paradigms of globalization, offering a vision that is rooted in ethics, sustainability, and cultural pride. In an age where education is increasingly driven by market forces and global competition, his ideas remind us of the deeper purpose of learning: to cultivate well-rounded individuals who contribute to the well-being of their communities and the world. By embracing Gandhi's holistic and inclusive approach to education, societies can address the challenges of globalization while staying true to their values and traditions. His vision remains a beacon of hope and guidance in the quest for a more just, equitable, and compassionate world.

Q.3) How can Gandhi's views of Swaraj and Swadeshi, be relevant in present day India ?

Ans: Introduction: Gandhi's vision of Swaraj (self-rule) and Swadeshi (self-reliance) remains deeply relevant in present-day India, offering a moral and practical framework to address contemporary challenges. At its core, Swaraj is not merely political independence but a holistic idea of empowerment that begins with the individual and extends to communities and the nation. In today's context, Swaraj calls for decentralizing power and resources to ensure that governance is participatory, transparent, and accountable. For instance, grassroots movements advocating for local decision-making in environmental policies or land rights echo Gandhi's belief that true democracy flourishes when people closest to the ground shape their own futures. The push for strengthening Panchayati Raj institutions, empowering villages to manage their resources and needs, is a modern embodiment of Swaraj, ensuring that development is inclusive and rooted in local realities.

Swadeshi, meanwhile, emphasizes economic and cultural self-reliance, urging societies to prioritize local production, traditional knowledge, and sustainable practices. In an era of globalization, where India's markets are flooded with imported goods and foreign capital, Swadeshi offers a counter-narrative. It encourages support for indigenous industries, small-scale artisans, and farmers, reducing dependency on volatile global supply chains. The recent emphasis on "Vocal for Local" campaigns, promoting handmade products like khadi or millets, reflects Swadeshi's spirit. It is not about isolation but about creating resilient economies that value sustainability over mindless consumerism. For example, the revival of organic farming or renewable energy initiatives in rural areas aligns with Swadeshi principles, fostering ecological balance while empowering communities.

Moreover, Gandhi's ideas resonate in the fight against social and environmental crises. Swaraj's emphasis on ethical self-governance is critical in addressing corruption, inequality, and environmental degradation. A Swaraj-inspired approach would demand that development projects prioritize the well-being of marginalized communities over corporate interests, ensuring that industrial growth does not come at the cost of displacing farmers or polluting rivers. Similarly, Swadeshi's critique of unchecked industrialization urges India to rethink its development model, balancing technological advancement with ecological stewardship. The growing movements against single-use plastics or deforestation, for instance, reflect a Swadeshi-like consciousness about preserving natural resources for future generations.

Culturally, Swadeshi challenges the homogenizing forces of globalization, advocating for the preservation of India's diverse languages, crafts, and traditions. In a world where Western cultural norms often dominate media and education, Swadeshi calls for curricula that celebrate India's plural heritage and for policies that protect artisans and weavers from being erased by mass-produced goods. It also resonates in the digital age: promoting homegrown tech innovations and digital platforms that cater to India's unique needs, rather than uncritically adopting foreign models.

However, Gandhi's vision is not a rejection of progress but a plea to harmonize modernity with morality. In today's India, marked by rapid urbanization and technological disruption, Swaraj and Swadeshi remind us that development must be anchored in justice, equity, and compassion. They ask us to build an India where growth does not alienate the poor, where technology serves humanity rather than displacing it, and where globalization does not erase local identities. Ultimately, Gandhi's ideals are not relics of the past but guiding lights for a nation striving to balance its ancient wisdom with the demands of a complex, interconnected world.

Conclusion: Gandhi's vision of Swaraj and Swadeshi offers timeless principles that remain profoundly relevant in present-day India. Swaraj, with its emphasis on self-governance, ethical leadership, and decentralized power, provides a blueprint for creating a more inclusive and participatory democracy. It challenges us to ensure that development is not just about economic growth but about empowering individuals and communities to take charge of their own destinies. Swadeshi, on the other hand, calls for self-reliance, sustainability, and the preservation of local cultures and economies. In an age of globalization, it reminds us to value indigenous knowledge, support local industries, and prioritize ecological balance over unchecked consumerism. Together, Swaraj and Swadeshi inspire us to rethink India's path to progress. They urge us to build a society where technology and tradition coexist, where growth is equitable, and where development serves the needs of the many rather than the profits of the few. Gandhi's ideals are not about rejecting modernity but about harmonizing it with morality, ensuring that progress is rooted in justice, compassion, and respect for all life. As India navigates the challenges of the 21st century—be it inequality, environmental degradation, or cultural homogenization—Gandhi's vision remains a guiding light, calling us to create a nation that is not only prosperous but also humane, sustainable, and true to its deepest values.

CHAPTER FOUR

Jawaharlal Nehru

Jawaharlal Nehru (1889–1964), India's first Prime Minister (1947–1964), Nehru played a key role in the independence movement and led the nation's early years. Educated at Harrow, Cambridge, and Inner Temple, he was imprisoned multiple times for his nationalist activities.

Nehru's major works, written mostly in prison, include:

- An Autobiography (1936) – his personal and political journey.
- Glimpses of World History (1939) – letters to his daughter on global history.
- The Discovery of India (1946) – reflections on India's heritage, later adapted into Bharat Ek Khoj.

Question and Answer

Q.1) Do you agree that self-scrutiny and self-criticism play a large part in Nehru's An Autobiography? Substantiate your answer with examples from the excerpts you have read in this course.

Ans: Yes, I agree that self-scrutiny and self-criticism play a significant role in Jawaharlal Nehru's An Autobiography. Throughout the text, Nehru engages in deep introspection, critically examining his actions, thoughts, and motivations. This self-reflective approach is one of the defining features of his writing and adds a layer of honesty and humility to his narrative. Below are some examples from the excerpts that substantiate this claim:

1. Self-Deprecation and Honesty About His Early Life

In Chapter IV: Harrow and Cambridge, Nehru reflects on his time in England with a sense of self-criticism. He describes himself as a young man trying to imitate the lifestyle of a "man about town," which he later dismisses as shallow and pointless. He writes:

"I was merely trying to ape to some extent the prosperous but somewhat empty-headed Englishman who is called 'man about town'... This soft and pointless existence, needless to say, did not improve me in any way. My early enthusiasm began to tone down, and the one thing that seemed to go up was my conceit."

This candid admission shows Nehru's willingness to critique his younger self and acknowledge his flaws, such as vanity and superficiality.

2. Critical Reflection on His Role in the Freedom Struggle

In Chapter VII: The Coming of Gandhiji, Nehru reflects on his father Motilal Nehru's initial reluctance to support Gandhi's satyagraha movement. He does not shy away from questioning his own and his father's motives:

"What good would the gaol-going of a number of individuals do? What pressure could it bring on the Government? Apart from these general considerations, what really moved him was the personal issue. It seemed to him preposterous that I should go to prison."

Here, Nehru critically examines his father's hesitation and, by extension, his own privileged position, showing a nuanced understanding of the complexities of their involvement in the freedom struggle.

3. Self-Questioning in Prison

In Chapter XXX: In Naini Prison, Nehru reflects on his experiences in jail and his feelings of guilt for receiving better treatment than other prisoners. He writes:

"I felt a sense of guilt at having an easier time in the jail."

This statement reveals his self-awareness and empathy for fellow prisoners, as well as his discomfort with the privileges he enjoyed due to his social status.

4. Reflection on His Writing Process

In Chapter LXVIII: Epilogue, Nehru acknowledges the difficulty of capturing past moods and experiences accurately. He admits:

"It is difficult to recapture a past mood, and it is not easy to forget subsequent happenings. Later ideas must inevitably have coloured my account of earlier days."

This shows his awareness of the limitations of memory and the subjective nature of autobiography, further highlighting his commitment to self-scrutiny.

5. Critique of His Dual Identity

In the same chapter, Nehru reflects on his mixed identity as someone influenced by both Eastern and Western cultures. He writes:

"I am a queer mixture of the East and West, out of place everywhere, at home nowhere... I cannot get rid of either that past inheritance or my recent acquisitions."

This self-critical analysis of his identity reveals his struggle to reconcile his dual cultural influences, adding depth to his self-portrait.

6. Admission of Egotism

In the preface to the Autobiography, Nehru openly acknowledges the egotistical nature of his narrative:

"I must warn him [the reader], therefore, that this account is wholly one-sided and, inevitably, egotistical: many important happenings have been completely ignored, and many important persons, who shaped events, have hardly been mentioned."

This admission demonstrates his self-awareness and humility, as he recognizes the limitations of focusing on his own perspective.

Conclusion

Nehru's Autobiography is marked by a consistent thread of self-scrutiny and self-criticism. Whether reflecting on his early years, his role in the freedom struggle, his privileged position, or his cultural identity, Nehru approaches his life story with honesty and introspection. This willingness to critique himself not only adds credibility to his narrative but also makes his Autobiography a deeply human and relatable work. His self-reflective style invites readers to engage with his journey on a personal level, making it a timeless piece of literature.

Q.2) There is a great deal of self-scrutiny in Nehru's writing. Do you agree? Give a reasoned answer.

Ans: Yes, I agree that there is a great deal of self-scrutiny in Nehru's writing, particularly in his Autobiography. This introspective quality is one of the defining features of his prose and sets his work apart from many other political autobiographies. Nehru's willingness to critically examine his thoughts, actions, and motivations adds depth and authenticity to his narrative, making it not just a historical account but also a deeply personal and reflective journey.

One of the most striking examples of Nehru's self-scrutiny is his candid reflection on his early years. In Chapter IV: Harrow and Cambridge, he describes his time in England with a sense of self-deprecation, acknowledging his youthful attempts to imitate the lifestyle of a "man about town." He admits that this phase of his life was marked by superficiality and conceit, stating, "This soft and pointless existence, needless to say, did not improve me in any way. My early enthusiasm began to tone down, and the one thing that seemed to go up was my conceit." This honest critique of his younger self reveals Nehru's ability to look back at his past with a critical eye, recognizing his flaws and growth over time.

Nehru's self-scrutiny is also evident in his reflections on his role in India's freedom struggle. In Chapter VII: The Coming of Gandhiji, he examines his father Motilal Nehru's initial reluctance to support Gandhi's satyagraha movement, questioning both his father's motives and his own privileged position. He writes, "What good would the gaol-going of a number of individuals do? What pressure could it bring on the Government?" This introspection shows Nehru's ability to analyze not only his actions but also the broader implications of his family's decisions, demonstrating a nuanced understanding of the complexities of their involvement in the national movement.

Another powerful example of Nehru's self-scrutiny can be found in his reflections on his time in prison. In Chapter XXX: In Naini Prison, he expresses guilt over receiving better treatment than other prisoners, stating, "I felt a sense of guilt at having an easier time in the jail." This admission highlights his empathy for fellow prisoners and his discomfort with the privileges he enjoyed due to his social status. It also underscores his commitment to fairness and equality, values that were central to his political philosophy.

Nehru's self-scrutiny extends to his writing process itself. In Chapter LXVIII: Epilogue, he acknowledges the challenges of capturing past experiences accurately, noting, "It is difficult to recapture a past mood, and it is not easy to forget subsequent happenings. Later ideas must niinevitably have coloured my account of earlier days." This reflection on the limitations of memory and the subjective nature of autobiography demonstrates his intellectual honesty and his awareness of the complexities of self-representation.

Finally, Nehru's self-scrutiny is evident in his exploration of his dual identity as someone influenced by both Eastern and Western cultures. In the Epilogue, he describes himself as "a queer mixture of the East and West, out of place everywhere, at home nowhere." This candid admission reveals his struggle to reconcile his dual cultural influences and adds a layer of vulnerability to his self-portrait. By critically examining his identity, Nehru invites readers to reflect on their own cultural and personal complexities.

Conclusion: Nehru's Autobiography is marked by a profound sense of self-scrutiny. Whether reflecting on his early years, his role in the freedom struggle, his privileged position, or his cultural identity, Nehru approaches his life story with honesty and introspection. This willingness to critique himself not only adds credibility to his narrative but also makes his Autobiography a deeply human and relatable work. His self-reflective style invites readers to engage with his journey on a personal level, making it a timeless piece of literature.

Q.3) Delineate the features of Nehru s prose style as illustrated in the passage taken from Autobiography

Ans: Introduction: Jawaharlal Nehru's prose style in his Autobiography is marked by a combination of clarity, elegance, introspection, and a reflective tone. His writing is both personal and philosophical, blending historical narrative with self-analysis. Below are the key features of Nehru's prose style, as illustrated in the passages from his Autobiography:

1. Clarity and Simplicity

Nehru's prose is characterized by its clarity and simplicity. He avoids unnecessary complexity, making his writing accessible to a wide audience. For example, in Chapter IV: Harrow and Cambridge, he describes his early years in England with straightforward language:

"I was merely trying to ape to some extent the prosperous but somewhat empty-headed Englishman who is called 'man about town'... This soft and pointless existence, needless to say, did not improve me in any way."

This clear and direct style allows readers to easily follow his thoughts and experiences.

2. Introspection and Self-Criticism

A defining feature of Nehru's prose is his introspective and self-critical approach. He constantly reflects on his actions, motivations, and growth. In Chapter VII: The Coming of Gandhiji, he critically examines his father's reluctance to support Gandhi's satyagraha movement:

"What good would the gaol-going of a number of individuals do? What pressure could it bring on the Government?"

This self-questioning reveals his intellectual honesty and willingness to scrutinize his own and his family's decisions.

3. Reflective and Philosophical Tone

Nehru's writing often takes on a reflective and philosophical tone, as he contemplates broader themes such as history, identity, and human nature.

In Chapter LXVIII: Epilogue, he reflects on the nature of memory and the passage of time:

"It is difficult to recapture a past mood, and it is not easy to forget subsequent happenings. Later ideas must inevitably have coloured my account of earlier days."

This philosophical musing adds depth to his narrative, inviting readers to think beyond the immediate events.

4. Use of Humor and Irony

Nehru's prose is occasionally laced with subtle humor and irony, which adds a layer of wit to his writing. In Chapter IV: Harrow and Cambridge, he humorously describes his attempts to live like a "man about town":

"My early enthusiasm began to tone down, and the one thing that seemed to go up was my conceit."

This self-deprecating humor makes his narrative more engaging and relatable.

5. Vivid Descriptions and Imagery

Nehru's writing is enriched by vivid descriptions and imagery, which bring his experiences to life. In Chapter XXX: In Naini Prison, he describes the night sky from his prison cell:

"At night I imagined I was at the bottom of a well. Or else that part of the star-lit sky that I saw ceased to be real and seemed part of an artificial planetarium."

This poetic imagery not only conveys his sense of isolation but also highlights his ability to find beauty even in difficult circumstances.

6. Balanced and Objective Analysis

Despite the personal nature of his Autobiography, Nehru maintains a balanced and objective tone when discussing historical and political events. In Chapter LIV: The Record of British Rule, he systematically analyzes the impact of British rule in India, giving credit where it is due while also critiquing its shortcomings:

"We must be grateful to the British for the one splendid gift of which they were the bearers, the gift of science and its rich offspring. It is difficult, however, to forget or view with equanimity the efforts of the British Government in India to encourage the disruptive, obscurantist, reactionary, sectarian, and opportunist elements in the country."

This balanced approach demonstrates his ability to separate personal feelings from historical analysis.

7. Emotional Restraint

Nehru's prose is marked by emotional restraint, even when discussing deeply personal or painful experiences. In Chapter LXVIII: Epilogue, he reflects on his dual cultural identity with a sense of detachment:

"I am a queer mixture of the East and West, out of place everywhere, at home nowhere... I cannot get rid of either that past inheritance or my recent acquisitions."

This restrained expression of his inner conflict adds a layer of sophistication to his writing.

8. Use of Quotations and Literary References

Nehru frequently incorporates quotations and literary references into his prose, showcasing his erudition and love for literature. For example, in Chapter LIV: The Record of British Rule, he quotes the American poet E. Markham to highlight the plight of Indian peasants:

"Bowed by the weight of centuries he leans / Upon his hoe and gazes on the ground, / The emptiness of ages in his face, / And on his back the burden of the world."

These references enrich his narrative and connect his personal experiences to broader cultural and literary traditions.

9. Personal and Intimate Tone

Despite his intellectual and philosophical reflections, Nehru's prose often feels personal and intimate, as if he is speaking directly to the reader. In Chapter LXVIII: Epilogue, he writes:

"Sometimes we were fortunate enough to touch that fullness of life which comes from attempting to fit ideals with action."

This intimate tone creates a sense of connection between the author and the reader, making his narrative more engaging.

Conclusion

Nehru's prose style in his Autobiography is a blend of clarity, introspection, reflection, and elegance. His ability to combine personal narrative with philosophical musings, his use of humor and vivid imagery, and his balanced and objective analysis make his writing both engaging and thought-provoking. At the same time, his emotional restraint and intimate tone add a layer of sophistication and relatability to his work. These features not only make his Autobiography a compelling read but also establish Nehru as one of the finest prose writers of the 20th century.

Q.4) Make an assessment of Nehru's prose style on the basis of excerpt from his Autobiography.

Ans: Jawaharlal Nehru's prose style, as illustrated in the excerpts from his Autobiography, is a remarkable blend of clarity, introspection, elegance, and philosophical depth. His writing is both personal and universal, combining historical narrative with self-reflection, and it stands out for its intellectual honesty, emotional restraint, and vivid imagery. An assessment of his prose style reveals several key characteristics that make his work distinctive and enduring.

One of the most striking features of Nehru's prose is its clarity and simplicity. He writes in a straightforward and accessible manner, avoiding unnecessary complexity. For instance, in Chapter IV: Harrow and Cambridge, he describes his youthful attempts to imitate the lifestyle of a "man about town" with directness and simplicity: "This soft and pointless existence, needless to say, did not improve me in any way. My early enthusiasm began to tone down, and the one thing that seemed to go up was my conceit." This clarity allows readers to easily follow his thoughts and experiences, making his narrative engaging and relatable.

Another defining aspect of Nehru's prose is his introspection and self-criticism. He constantly reflects on his actions, motivations, and growth, demonstrating a willingness to scrutinize himself. In Chapter VII: The Coming of Gandhiji, he critically examines his father's reluctance to support Gandhi's satyagraha movement: "What good would the gaol-going of a number of individuals do? What pressure could it bring on the Government?" This self-questioning reveals his intellectual honesty and adds depth to his narrative, as he does not shy away from acknowledging his own and his family's flaws.

Nehru's prose is also marked by a reflective and philosophical tone. He often contemplates broader themes such as history, identity, and human nature, elevating his writing beyond mere autobiography. In Chapter LXVIII: Epilogue, he reflects on the nature of memory and the passage of time: "It is difficult to recapture a past mood, and it is not easy to forget subsequent happenings. Later ideas must inevitably have coloured my account of earlier days." This philosophical musing adds a layer of depth to his narrative, inviting readers to think beyond the immediate events and consider larger existential questions.

A subtle yet distinctive feature of Nehru's prose is his use of humor and irony. In Chapter IV: Harrow and Cambridge, he humorously describes his attempts to live like a "man about town": "My early enthusiasm began to tone down, and the one thing that seemed to go up was my conceit." This self-deprecating humor not only makes his narrative more engaging but also reveals his ability to laugh at himself, adding a touch of humility to his writing.

Nehru's prose is further enriched by vivid descriptions and imagery, which bring his experiences to life. In Chapter XXX: In Naini Prison, he describes the night sky from his prison cell: "At night I imagined I was at the bottom of a well. Or else that part of the star-lit sky that I saw ceased to be real and seemed part of an artificial planetarium." This poetic imagery not only conveys his sense of isolation but also highlights his ability to find beauty even in difficult circumstances, showcasing his literary sensibility.

Despite the personal nature of his Autobiography, Nehru maintains a balanced and objective tone when discussing historical and political events. In Chapter LIV: The Record of British Rule, he systematically analyzes the impact of British rule in India, giving credit where it is due while also critiquing its shortcomings: "We must be grateful to the British for the one splendid gift of which they were the bearers, the gift of science and its rich offspring. It is difficult, however, to forget or view with equanimity the efforts of the British Government in India to encourage the disruptive, obscurantist, reactionary, sectarian, and opportunist elements in the country." This balanced approach demonstrates his ability to separate personal feelings from historical analysis, adding credibility to his narrative.

Another notable feature of Nehru's prose is his emotional restraint. Even when discussing deeply personal or painful experiences, he maintains a sense of detachment. In Chapter LXVIII: Epilogue, he reflects on his dual cultural identity with a calm and measured tone: "I am a queer mixture of the East and West, out of place everywhere, at home nowhere... I cannot get rid of either that past inheritance or my recent acquisitions." This restrained expression of his inner conflict adds a layer of sophistication to his writing, making it more impactful.

Finally, Nehru's prose is characterized by its personal and intimate tone, which creates a sense of connection between the author and the reader. In Chapter LXVIII: Epilogue, he writes: "Sometimes we were fortunate enough to touch that fullness of life which comes from attempting to fit ideals with action." This intimate tone makes his narrative feel like a conversation, drawing readers into his world and making his experiences more relatable.

Conclusion: Nehru's prose style in his Autobiography is a masterful blend of clarity, introspection, reflection, and elegance. His ability to combine personal narrative with philosophical musings, his use of humor and vivid imagery, and his balanced and objective analysis make his writing both engaging and thought-provoking. At the same time, his emotional restraint and intimate tone add a layer of sophistication and relatability to his work. These features not only make his Autobiography a compelling read but also establish Nehru as one of the finest prose writers of the 20th century.

Q.5) Discuss an autobiographical element in Nehru 's Autobiography

Ans: Jawaharlal Nehru's Autobiography is a rich and multifaceted work that combines personal narrative, historical reflection, and philosophical musings. As an autobiography, it adheres to many of the genre's conventions while also transcending them to offer a broader commentary on India's struggle for independence and Nehru's own intellectual and emotional journey. Below is a discussion of the key autobiographical elements in Nehru's Autobiography:

1. Personal Narrative and Self-Reflection

At its core, Nehru's Autobiography is a personal narrative that chronicles his life from childhood to his role as a key leader in India's independence movement. He provides detailed accounts of his early years, education, political awakening, and experiences in prison. For example, in Chapter IV: Harrow and Cambridge, he reflects on his time in England, describing his attempts to imitate the lifestyle of a "man about town" and his eventual realization of its emptiness. This self-reflection is a hallmark of autobiographical writing, as it allows the author to explore their growth and development over time.

Nehru's narrative is deeply introspective, as he constantly examines his thoughts, motivations, and actions. In Chapter VII: The Coming of Gandhiji, he critically analyzes his father's reluctance to support Gandhi's satyagraha movement and his own privileged position in the freedom struggle. This self-scrutiny adds depth to his narrative, making it not just a recounting of events but also a journey of self-discovery.

2. Historical and Political Context

While Nehru's Autobiography is deeply personal, it is also firmly rooted in the historical and political context of his time. He uses his personal experiences as a lens to explore broader themes such as colonialism, nationalism, and social justice. For instance, in Chapter LIV: The Record of British Rule, he provides a systematic analysis of British rule in India, critiquing its exploitative nature while also acknowledging its contributions to science and technology. This blending of personal and historical narratives is a key feature of his autobiography, as it situates his life within the larger story of India's struggle for independence.

3. Emotional and Psychological Depth

Autobiographies often delve into the emotional and psychological dimensions of the author's life, and Nehru's work is no exception. He openly discusses his feelings of guilt, doubt, and conflict, adding a layer of vulnerability to his narrative. In Chapter XXX: In Naini Prison, he reflects on his experiences in jail and his discomfort with the privileges he enjoyed as a political prisoner: "I felt a sense of guilt at having an easier time in the jail." This emotional honesty makes his autobiography more relatable and human, as it reveals the inner struggles behind his public persona.

4. Philosophical Musings

Nehru's Autobiography is not just a recounting of events but also a platform for philosophical reflection. He frequently contemplates broader themes such as the nature of history, the passage of time, and the complexities of human identity. In Chapter LXVIII: Epilogue, he reflects on the challenges of capturing past experiences accurately: "It is difficult to recapture a past mood, and it is not easy to forget subsequent happenings. Later ideas must inevitably have coloured my account of earlier days." These philosophical musings elevate his autobiography, transforming it into a meditation on life, memory, and the human condition.

5. Use of Literary Devices

Nehru's Autobiography is enriched by his use of literary devices such as vivid imagery, humor, and irony. For example, in Chapter XXX: In Naini Prison, he describes the night sky from his prison cell with poetic imagery: "At night I imagined I was at the bottom of a well. Or else that part of the star-lit sky that I saw ceased to be real and seemed part of an artificial planetarium." This use of imagery not only conveys his sense of isolation but also highlights his literary sensibility. Similarly, his self-deprecating humor in Chapter IV: Harrow and Cambridge adds a touch of wit to his narrative, making it more engaging.

6. Balanced and Objective Tone

Despite the personal nature of his autobiography, Nehru maintains a balanced and objective tone when discussing historical and political events. In Chapter LIV: The Record of British Rule, he provides a nuanced analysis of British colonialism, acknowledging its contributions while also critiquing its exploitative nature. This balanced approach demonstrates his ability to separate personal feelings from historical analysis, adding credibility to his narrative.

7. Exploration of Identity

A central theme in Nehru's Autobiography is the exploration of identity, particularly his dual identity as someone influenced by both Eastern and Western cultures. In Chapter LXVIII: Epilogue, he reflects on this duality: "I am a queer mixture of the East and West, out of place everywhere, at home nowhere... I cannot get rid of either that past inheritance or my recent acquisitions." This exploration of identity is a key autobiographical element, as it reveals his inner conflict and adds depth to his self-portrait.

8. Intimate and Conversational Tone

Nehru's Autobiography is written in an intimate and conversational tone, as if he is speaking directly to the reader. This tone creates a sense of connection between the author and the reader, making his narrative more engaging. For example, in Chapter LXVIII: Epilogue, he writes: "Sometimes we were fortunate enough to touch that fullness of life which comes from attempting to fit ideals with action." This intimate tone invites readers to reflect on their own lives and experiences, making his autobiography not just a personal story but also a universal one.

Conclusion

Nehru's Autobiography is a rich and multifaceted work that combines personal narrative, historical reflection, and philosophical musings. Its autobiographical elements—such as self-reflection, emotional honesty, exploration of identity, and use of literary devices—make it a compelling and enduring work. By situating his personal story within the broader context of India's struggle for independence, Nehru transforms his autobiography into a meditation on history, identity, and the human condition. This blending of the personal and the universal is what makes his Autobiography a timeless classic.

CHAPTER FIVE

Nirad C. Chaudhuri

Nirad C. Chaudhuri (1897–1998), An Indian writer and intellectual known for his erudite, provocative critiques and Anglophilic views, Chaudhuri became a self-taught polymath after studying at Calcutta University. Denied academic posts for lacking a formal degree, he turned to journalism and broadcasting, growing disillusioned with Indian culture.

His breakthrough work, The Autobiography of an Unknown Indian (1951), along with later titles like The Continent of Circe (1965) and Scholar Extraordinary (1974), cemented his reputation as a divisive thinker. Celebrated for his rigorous, European-inflected prose yet critiqued for elitism and colonial sympathies, he spent his later years in Oxford until his death at 100, leaving a complex legacy.

Question and Answer

1) Discuss Nirad C. Chaudhari's Prose style in reference to The Autobiography of An unknown Indian.

Ans: Introduction: Nirad C. Chaudhuri (1897–1998) was a prominent and controversial Indian writer known for his intellectual rigor, Anglophilic tendencies, and unsparing critiques of Indian society. Nirad C. Chaudhuri's prose style in The Autobiography of an Unknown Indian is unique and easily recognizable. It is marked by his deep knowledge, formal tone, and frequent references to Western literature, history, and culture. His writing reflects his admiration for European intellectual traditions, which can be seen in the way he uses classical allusions and foreign phrases. He often includes Latin, French, and German words without explanation, assuming that his readers are familiar with these languages. For example, he compares the boats in Kishorganj to "triremes," which were ancient Greek warships, and describes the river as "our Nile," drawing a parallel to the great river of Egypt. Similarly, he uses phrases like des mémoires d'outre-tombe (French for "memoirs from beyond the grave") and Civis Britannicus Sum (Latin for

"I am a British citizen") without providing translations.

Another major characteristic of his prose is the complexity of his sentences. He often writes long, detailed, and somewhat convoluted sentences, filled with multiple clauses and digressions. For instance, when he describes how his childhood town would appear from an airplane, he writes, "Had there been aeroplanes in our boyhood, the small town would have looked like a patch of white and brown mushrooms from a height of five hundred feet." This kind of writing, full of excessive details and formal phrasing, can sometimes feel overly complicated. Critics like C.D. Narasimhaiah have criticized his style, calling it "Accountant's English" or the writing of a "village chronicler," suggesting that it lacks the grace and flow of more imaginative prose.

Chaudhuri's writing is also known for its detached and analytical tone. He observes and describes events and people with an almost clinical precision, rather than engaging with them emotionally. This detachment is evident in how he describes his hometown, Kishorganj, as "one among a score of collections of tin-and-mat huts." Instead of painting a warm or nostalgic picture of the place, he reduces it to an impersonal and ordinary settlement. In contrast, writers like Raja Rao in Kanthapura create a deep emotional connection between the reader and the Indian landscape by using local imagery and traditions. Chaudhuri's distant tone reflects his colonial mindset, where he often judges India using European standards rather than embracing its own cultural uniqueness.

Despite his formal and sometimes rigid style, Chaudhuri is also known for his sharp irony and satire. He does not hesitate to criticize Indian society, especially its hypocrisy and conservatism. His observations can be witty and biting, such as when he mocks the custom of ritualized weeping by newlywed women during Durga Puja. He notes how these women would continue wiping their eyes even when they were miles away from their parental home, simply to maintain social expectations. Similarly, he sharply criticizes India's obsession with skin color in marriage, exposing how people prefer fair-skinned brides. In these moments, his writing becomes more direct and impactful, free from his usual long-winded explanations.

At times, Chaudhuri's writing achieves great vividness, particularly when he describes sensory experiences. His description of the monsoon in Bengal is an excellent example. He writes, "Everything was wet to the marrow of the bone. Neither we nor our clothes were ever properly dry. When we were not slushy, we were damp." Here, the short, rhythmic sentences and strong sensory details make the reader almost feel the dampness in the air. In such moments, his prose comes alive with striking clarity, proving that despite his tendency for complexity, he is capable of creating powerful and evocative descriptions.

One of the most controversial aspects of Chaudhuri's prose is his choice of words and phrases, which often reveal his admiration for British rule and his Eurocentric worldview. The most famous example of this is the dedication at the beginning of The Autobiography of an Unknown Indian, where he writes, "To the memory of the British Empire in India..." This led to widespread criticism, with many accusing him of being overly loyal to the British and lacking patriotic sentiment. His use of phrases like Civis Britannicus Sum and his later writings, such as The Continent of Circe, further reinforced the perception that he viewed India through an Orientalist and colonial lens. In The Continent of Circe, he even describes India as a "sorceress" that dehumanizes its people, a statement that many found offensive and dismissive of the country's rich history and culture.

Because of his unique prose style, Chaudhuri has received mixed reactions from critics. Some, like C.D. Narasimhaiah, have dismissed his writing as "ossified academic" prose, meaning that it is rigid, overly intellectual, and full of snobbery. Others, like Nissim Ezekiel, have acknowledged his deep scholarship and originality but criticized him for being too self-absorbed and moralistic. While his writing is undoubtedly rich in intellectual depth and originality, it also suffers from verbosity, elitism, and an over-reliance on European frameworks to interpret Indian realities.

Conclusion: Chaudhuri's prose in The Autobiography of an Unknown Indian is a reflection of his complex identity as an Indian intellectual deeply influenced by Western traditions. His vast knowledge and sharp analytical mind make his writing engaging for those who appreciate intellectual depth. However, his formal tone, long-winded sentences, and excessive use of European references make his work less accessible to the common reader. His detached approach and controversial views further add to the complexity of his prose. Ultimately, his writing style is both a strength and a limitation—brilliant in its insights, yet often distant and difficult for readers unfamiliar with his worldview.

Q.2) Do you agree with the view there are two Nirad C Chaudhuri, a historical witness and a pseudo-historian give reason.

Ans: Introduction: Nirad C. Chaudhuri (1897–1998) was a prominent and controversial Indian writer known for his intellectual rigor, Anglophilic tendencies, and unsparing critiques of Indian society. His intellectual personality can be seen in two different ways: as a historical witness and as a pseudo-historian. This means that sometimes he writes about history in a detailed and accurate way, while at other times, he shapes history according to his own beliefs. This difference in his writing shows the inner conflict of a man who admired Western ideas but was also critical of India's social and cultural traditions.

As a historical witness, Chaudhuri is at his best in his autobiographical works like The Autobiography of an Unknown Indian and Thy Hand, Great Anarch!. In these books, he writes about his personal experiences growing up in early 20th-century Bengal. He describes events and everyday life with great detail, making his readers feel as if they are experiencing them too. For example, he talks about the monsoon floods in Kishorganj, the Durga Puja celebrations, and how women cried loudly during festivals, not because of real sadness but out of habit. His descriptions are so detailed that one can almost feel the dampness of the rainy season when he writes, "Everything was wet to the marrow of the bone. Neither we nor our clothes were ever properly dry." He also presents an interesting view of British colonial rule. On one hand, he criticizes the British for keeping Indians away from power; on the other hand, he admires their discipline and governance, calling it a "civilizing mission." In such moments, Chaudhuri acts like a historian, recording the details of a world that was changing and slowly disappearing.

However, there is another side to Chaudhuri, where he does not remain neutral and instead presents history in a way that supports his personal opinions. This can be seen in his book The Continent of Circe (1966). In this book, he puts forward a controversial idea that Hindus are not the true natives of India but are descendants of European Aryans. This idea ignores evidence of ancient Indian civilizations like the Indus Valley Civilization and the rich history of Dravidian cultures. In the same book, he compares India to Circe, a sorceress from Greek mythology who turns men into animals. By using this metaphor, he makes India look like a land that destroys human values, which is a very negative and one-sided view. Similarly, in Thy Hand, Great Anarch!, he criticizes Mahatma Gandhi, calling his leadership self-centered. He also dismisses India's freedom movement as nothing but chaos. Instead of using proper historical research, he relies on personal opinions and selective examples. He even tries to justify the actions of British colonial rulers like Robert Clive, saying that Clive's greed was not against the rules. This clearly shows that he sometimes changes historical facts to fit his own ideas rather than presenting an unbiased account.

The reason for these two sides of Chaudhuri's writing lies in his complex relationship with colonialism. He was deeply influenced by Western education and ideas, and he often looked at India through a Western perspective. When he wrote about his personal experiences, his writing was based on real observations and was mostly free from this bias. But when he wrote about history and politics, his frustration with post-independence India often made him write in a way that was unfair and overly critical. Many scholars, like Sudesh Mishra and C. Paul Verghese, have pointed out that this contradiction in Chaudhuri's writing reflects his struggle to balance his admiration for Western values with his Indian identity. For instance, he respected the achievements of ancient Vedic India but disliked modern Hindu practices. He praised British rule but at the same time complained about how the British treated Indians unfairly.

Conclusion: Chaudhuri's writing has two sides—one where he is an honest observer of history and another where he distorts history to support his personal beliefs. His autobiographical works are valuable because they give a detailed and rich picture of life in colonial India. However, his historical and political writings are often biased and based on his own frustrations rather than solid facts. This makes him a complex figure—highly intelligent, deeply conflicted, and caught between two worlds, unable to fully belong to either.

CHAPTER SIX

Vikram Seth and Amitav Ghosh

Vikram Seth

Vikram Seth, born in Calcutta and raised in Dehra Dun, is a celebrated Indian author whose academic journey took him from mathematics at St. Stephen's College to philosophy, politics, and economics at Oxford and economics at Stanford, followed by research in China. His diverse body of work spans poetry, travel writing, and novels, including the award-winning The Golden Gate (a novel in sonnet form) and the epic A Suitable Boy, which explores post-independence Indian life and is being adapted for television.

Question and Answer

Q.1) Does Vikram Seth writing lack depth Discuss offering your views.

Ans: Introduction: Vikram Seth is one of India's most famous writers. He has written books in different styles, including novels, travel stories, and poetry. Vikram Seth's writing in From Heaven Lake does not lack depth. Instead, his depth comes in a quiet and understated manner. His style is simple and clear, using short sentences and precise descriptions. This makes his travel narrative easy to read, but beneath this simplicity, there is a richness of thought and observation. His ability to notice small details and reflect on them gives the book a deep and meaningful quality.

One of the key ways Seth adds depth to his writing is through his interactions with the people he meets during his journey. He does not just describe them; he tries to understand their lives, emotions, and struggles. For example, the Uyghur man selling caps is not just a street vendor in

Seth's eyes—he represents a unique culture and way of life. Similarly, the Tibetan truck driver, Gyanseng, is more than just a fellow traveler. Through their conversations and shared experiences, Seth brings out themes of loneliness, connection, and the human need for companionship. He does not explain these themes directly, but they emerge naturally through his interactions.

Seth's descriptions of nature also show great depth. He does not just mention landscapes; he makes the reader feel them. He describes the vast, empty spaces of Tibet, the changing colors of the sky, the rough mountain roads, and even the yaks he encounters along the way. His comparison of yaks to Pekinese dogs or willow trees shows his poetic sensibility and makes the unfamiliar seem familiar. These descriptions are not just decorative; they reflect the challenges of his journey and the emotional impact of being in such a vast and isolated land.

Another aspect that adds depth to the book is Seth's reflections on his journey. He does not provide long political discussions, but his simple observations about the differences between India and China are thought-provoking. He notices the ways in which the two countries function differently, from government policies to the attitudes of ordinary people. Without making strong judgments, he encourages the reader to think about these cultural and political contrasts.

The inclusion of poetry throughout the book is another way Seth adds depth to his storytelling. His poems provide a more personal and emotional insight into his experiences. While his prose is often calm and restrained, his poetry expresses deeper feelings of longing, isolation, and reflection. These poems break up the narrative and allow the reader to connect with his inner thoughts in a different way.

Conclusion: Vikram Seth's writing in From Heaven Lake is not lacking in depth. His style is simple, but this simplicity allows the reader to focus on the essence of his experiences. Through his careful observations of people, his vivid descriptions of nature, his quiet reflections on cultural differences, and his use of poetry, he creates a travelogue that is both intellectually and emotionally rich. His book is not just about a physical journey across China; it is also about an internal journey of understanding, connection, and self-reflection.

Q.2) Discuss Vikram Seth's Prose Style.

Ans: Introduction: Vikram Seth is one of India's most famous writers. He has written books in different styles, including novels, travel stories, and poetry. His way of writing is special because it is both simple and beautiful. His words flow smoothly, making his books easy to read while still being deep and meaningful. He pays great attention to detail, describes places and people in a realistic way, and brings emotions to life through his words. Whether he is writing about love, travel, music, or society, his writing always feels natural and engaging.

Some of his most famous books include A Suitable Boy (1993), which is a long novel about post-independence India; From Heaven Lake (1983), a travel book about his journey through China; and An Equal Music (1999), which tells the emotional story of a musician. In all these books, Seth's writing is clear, elegant, and full of life. His ability to switch between different types of writing—fiction, travel writing, and poetry—shows how talented he is.

Clear and Elegant Writing Style

One of the most important things about Vikram Seth's writing is that it is clear and easy to understand. He does not use difficult words or complex sentences just to sound impressive. Instead, his words flow naturally, making his books enjoyable for all kinds of readers. Even when he writes about deep and serious topics, his style remains simple and graceful.

For example, in A Suitable Boy, he tells the story of families, politics, and romance in India after independence. The novel is very long, but because of his smooth and engaging writing, it never feels boring. His clear storytelling helps readers connect with the characters and their struggles.

Attention to Detail and Realism

Another reason why Seth's writing is special is that he describes things with great attention to detail. He carefully paints a picture of places, people, and emotions so that readers can easily imagine them. Whether he is describing the busy streets of Kolkata, the peaceful canals of Venice in An Equal Music, or the vast landscapes of China in From Heaven Lake, his descriptions are full of life.

Seth's background in economics and his love for music and travel influence his writing. This means that he not only tells good stories but also adds layers of reality to them. His characters talk in a way that matches their social background and culture, making them feel real. The way he describes emotions, nature, and daily life makes his books rich and immersive.

Poetic and Musical Flow

Vikram Seth is also a poet, and this is clear in the way he writes. Even when he is writing prose (regular sentences, not poetry), his words have a musical rhythm. His sentences are carefully crafted, making his writing pleasant to read.

One of his most unique books is The Golden Gate (1986), which is a novel written entirely in verse. This shows how comfortable he is with poetry and how he can blend it into storytelling. Even in his other books, his poetic sense is present, making his descriptions more beautiful and his emotions more powerful.

Different Tones for Different Stories

Seth has a great ability to change his writing style depending on what he is writing about. In From Heaven Lake, his tone is personal and thoughtful, as he shares his experiences of traveling through China. In An Equal Music, his writing is emotional and melancholic, capturing the feelings of a musician who has lost his love. In A Suitable Boy, he uses a mix of humor, irony, and warmth to tell a vast and complex story about Indian society.

This ability to adjust his tone and style makes his writing feel real and natural. Whether he is writing about history, love, travel, or music, he knows exactly how to set the right mood and engage the reader.

Use of Gentle Humor and Irony

Another special feature of Vikram Seth's writing is his use of humor. He does not rely on loud jokes, but instead, he includes quiet and intelligent humor in his storytelling. His way of looking at society, politics, and relationships often includes irony, making his writing both entertaining and meaningful.

For example, in A Suitable Boy, he gently makes fun of the rigid social rules of India after independence. He shows how people follow traditions, sometimes without thinking, and how families worry too much about things like marriage and status. His humor makes the story more enjoyable while also making the reader think about society.

A Perfect Balance of Simplicity and Depth

Seth's biggest strength as a writer is that he balances simplicity with deep meaning. His writing is not too complicated, but it is never shallow. His words are easy to understand, yet they carry strong emotions and important ideas. He does not over-explain things; instead, he lets the reader feel the depth of his characters and their journeys naturally.

Whether he is describing love, separation, travel, or personal struggles, his words always touch the heart. His ability to switch between different types of writing—whether fiction, travel writing, or poetry—proves that he is a master storyteller.

Conclusion

Vikram Seth's prose style is a wonderful blend of clarity, poetic beauty, and deep meaning. His attention to detail, his ability to create real and relatable characters, and his smooth, musical flow make his writing stand out. He can write about different subjects with ease, switching between humor, seriousness, and emotion effortlessly. His works reflect his deep understanding of human emotions, relationships, and cultural differences. Whether he is writing about the political and social landscape of India, the journey of a traveler in China, or the emotional struggles of a musician, his writing remains powerful and engaging. His prose proves that simple language can still be rich in meaning, making him one of the finest writers of his time.

Amitav Ghosh

Amitav Ghosh is one of the most celebrated contemporary writers, known for his richly layered novels, insightful travelogues, and thought-provoking non-fiction. Born in Calcutta (now Kolkata) in 1956, Ghosh spent his childhood in India, Bangladesh (then East Pakistan), and Sri Lanka, which exposed him to diverse cultures and histories from an early age. This multicultural upbringing deeply influenced his writing, as his works often explore themes of migration, identity, and the interconnectedness of human experiences across time and space.

After graduating from St. Stephen's College in Delhi, Ghosh pursued social anthropology at Oxford University, earning a D.Phil. His academic background is evident in his writing, which is meticulously researched and often delves into historical and cultural contexts. Ghosh's career has been marked by a unique ability to blend fact and fiction, creating narratives that are both intellectually stimulating and emotionally resonant.

Major Works and Themes

Ghosh's literary repertoire includes novels, travelogues, and non-fiction, each reflecting his deep engagement with history, culture, and global issues.

Novels:

The Circle of Reason (1986): Ghosh's debut novel, often compared to Salman Rushdie's Midnight's Children, is a sprawling tale that follows the journey of Alu, an orphan accused of terrorism. The novel explores themes of identity, migration, and the clash between tradition and modernity.

The Shadow Lines (1988): This novel, which won the Sahitya Akademi Award, examines the arbitrary nature of borders and the impact of historical events like Partition on personal and collective identities. It is a deeply introspective work that weaves together memories, history, and imagination.

The Calcutta Chromosome (1996): A genre-defying novel that blends science fiction, detective fiction, and the supernatural, it revolves around the discovery of the malarial parasite and a secret society manipulating history.

The Ibis Trilogy (2008–2015): Comprising Sea of Poppies, River of Smoke, and Flood of Fire, this epic trilogy explores the Opium Wars and their impact on India, China, and Britain. It highlights themes of colonialism, trade, and cultural exchange.

Travelogues and Non-Fiction:

In an Antique Land (1992): A blend of travel writing, history, and memoir, this book traces the journey of a 12th-century Indian slave mentioned in medieval manuscripts. Ghosh juxtaposes this historical narrative with his own experiences as a researcher in Egypt, exploring themes of cultural interconnectedness.

Dancing in Cambodia, at large in Burma (1998): This travelogue reflects on Ghosh's visits to Cambodia and Burma, capturing the resilience of societies recovering from political turmoil. It is a poignant exploration of history, memory, and cultural revival.

The Great Derangement: Climate Change and the Unthinkable (2016): In this non-fiction work, Ghosh addresses the urgent issue of climate change, critiquing the failure of literature and politics to adequately confront the crisis.

Writing Style and Contributions

Ghosh's writing is characterized by its lyrical prose, meticulous research, and ability to weave together multiple narratives and time periods. His works often challenge conventional boundaries between genres, blending history, fiction, and autobiography. Ghosh's deep empathy for his characters and his commitment to telling marginalized stories make his writing both compelling and humane.

One of Ghosh's most significant contributions is his ability to highlight the interconnectedness of cultures and histories. Whether through the lens of colonialism, migration, or environmental crisis, his works reveal how global forces shape individual lives and communities. His focus on historical events, such as the Opium Wars or the Khmer Rouge regime, underscores the enduring impact of history on contemporary societies.

Legacy and Impact

Amitav Ghosh's works have earned him numerous accolades, including the Jnanpith Award, India's highest literary honor, and the Dan David Prize. His novels and travelogues have been translated into multiple languages, reaching a global audience. Ghosh's ability to combine storytelling with profound social and historical commentary has cemented his place as one of the most important writers of our time.

Beyond his literary achievements, Ghosh is also an influential voice on global issues, particularly climate change. His non-fiction works, such as The Great Derangement, have sparked important conversations about the role of literature and art in addressing environmental crises.

Question and Answer

Q.1) Critically assess Amitav Ghosh as a travel writer.

Ans: Introduction: Amitav Ghosh is a highly regarded travel writer whose works blend meticulous research, vivid storytelling, and a deep understanding of cultural and historical contexts. His travel narratives, such as Dancing in Cambodia, At Large in Burma (1998), showcase his ability to weave together personal experiences, historical events, and socio-political commentary into compelling prose. Ghosh's travel writing is not merely descriptive; it is analytical and reflective, offering readers a nuanced perspective on the places he visits and the people he encounters. His work stands out for its ability to connect the past with the present, revealing the enduring impact of history on contemporary societies.

One of Ghosh's greatest strengths as a travel writer is his ability to juxtapose different historical periods and cultural narratives. In Dancing in Cambodia, for instance, he contrasts the grandeur of King Sisowath's visit to France in 1906 with the devastation wrought by the Khmer Rouge regime in the 1970s. This counterpoint technique allows Ghosh to highlight the resilience of Cambodian society, particularly through the revival of traditional dance, which becomes a symbol of cultural rebirth. His descriptions of the Cambodian people's determination to rebuild their lives after years of terror are both poignant and inspiring. Ghosh's focus on ordinary individuals, such as Kong Sarith, a worker dedicated to restoring Angkor Wat, adds a deeply human dimension to his narratives, making them relatable and emotionally resonant.

Ghosh's travel writing is also marked by his self-effacing style. Unlike many travel writers who place themselves at the center of their narratives, Ghosh often remains in the background, allowing the places, people, and histories he explores to take center stage. This approach lends authenticity to his work, as it emphasizes the voices and experiences of those he encounters rather than his own. For example, in Dancing in Cambodia, Ghosh's descriptions of Angkor Wat and its significance to the Cambodian people are vivid and immersive, yet he refrains from inserting his personal opinions or emotions. Instead, he lets the monument and its stories speak for themselves, creating a sense of immediacy and intimacy for the reader.

Another notable aspect of Ghosh's travel writing is his ability to blend fact and fiction seamlessly. In In an Antique Land (1992), for instance, he combines historical research with autobiographical elements, creating a narrative that is both scholarly and deeply personal. The book explores the interconnectedness of cultures through the story of a 12th-century Indian slave mentioned in medieval manuscripts, while also recounting Ghosh's own experiences as a researcher in Egypt. This interplay between past and present, fact and imagination, allows Ghosh to explore complex themes such as identity, migration, and cultural exchange in a way that is both intellectually stimulating and emotionally engaging.

Ghosh's travel writing is also distinguished by its rich, evocative language and attention to detail. His descriptions of landscapes, monuments, and people are vivid and immersive, drawing readers into the worlds he portrays. For example, in Dancing in Cambodia, his portrayal of Angkor Wat is not just a visual account but a multi-sensory experience that captures the monument's historical, cultural, and spiritual significance. Similarly, his depiction of the Cambodian people's struggles and triumphs is rendered with empathy and sensitivity, making their stories both compelling and unforgettable.

However, some critics argue that Ghosh's travel writing can be overly dense or academic at times, particularly when he delves into historical or anthropological details. While this depth of research adds richness to his narratives, it may also alienate readers looking for a more straightforward travelogue. Additionally, Ghosh's focus on broader socio-political themes sometimes overshadows the personal, experiential aspects of travel writing, which some readers might find less engaging.

Conclusion: Amitav Ghosh is a travel writer of exceptional skill and insight. His ability to intertwine history, culture, and personal narrative sets him apart from many of his contemporaries. While his work may occasionally lean toward the scholarly, it is ultimately this depth and complexity that make his travel writing so compelling. Ghosh's narratives not only transport readers to distant lands but also challenge them to think critically about the interconnectedness of cultures and the enduring legacies of history. Through his evocative prose and empathetic storytelling, Ghosh reaffirms the power of travel writing to illuminate the human condition and foster a deeper understanding of the world.

Q.2) Discuss Amitav Ghosh as a writer of travelogues.

Ans: Introduction: Amitav Ghosh is a distinguished writer of travelogues, known for his ability to blend historical depth, cultural insight, and personal reflection into his narratives. His travel writing, such as Dancing in Cambodia, At Large in Burma (1998) and In an Antique Land (1992), transcends the conventional boundaries of the genre, offering readers not just vivid descriptions of places, but also profound explorations of history, identity, and human resilience. Ghosh's travelogues are characterized by their meticulous research, evocative prose, and a deep empathy for the people and cultures he encounters.

One of the defining features of Ghosh's travel writing is his ability to connect the past with the present. In Dancing in Cambodia, for instance, he juxtaposes the grandeur of King Sisowath's visit to France in 1906 with the devastation wrought by the Khmer Rouge regime in the 1970s. This interplay between historical eras allows Ghosh to highlight the resilience of Cambodian society, particularly through the revival of traditional dance, which becomes a symbol of cultural rebirth. His narratives often reveal how historical events continue to shape contemporary realities, offering readers a deeper understanding of the places he visits. This historical consciousness sets Ghosh apart from many travel writers, as it adds layers of meaning and context to his descriptions.

Ghosh's travelogues are also notable for their self-effacing style. Unlike many travel writers who place themselves at the center of their narratives, Ghosh often remains in the background, allowing the places, people, and histories he explores to take center stage. This approach lends authenticity to his work, as it emphasizes the voices and experiences of those he encounters rather than his own. For example, in Dancing in Cambodia, Ghosh's descriptions of Angkor Wat and its significance to the Cambodian people are vivid and immersive, yet he refrains from inserting his personal opinions or emotions. Instead, he lets the monument and its stories speak for themselves, creating a sense of immediacy and intimacy for the reader.

Another hallmark of Ghosh's travel writing is his seamless blending of fact and fiction. In In an Antique Land, he combines historical research with autobiographical elements, creating a narrative that is both scholarly and deeply personal. The book explores the interconnectedness of cultures through the story of a 12th-century Indian slave mentioned in medieval manuscripts, while also recounting Ghosh's own experiences as a researcher in Egypt. This interplay between past and present, fact and imagination, allows Ghosh to explore complex themes such as identity, migration, and cultural exchange in a way that is both intellectually stimulating and emotionally engaging. His ability to weave together different narrative threads demonstrates his skill as a storyteller and his deep understanding of the human condition.

Ghosh's travelogues are also distinguished by their rich, evocative language and attention to detail. His descriptions of landscapes, monuments, and people are vivid and immersive, drawing readers into the worlds he portrays. For example, in Dancing in Cambodia, his portrayal of Angkor Wat is not just a visual account but a multi-sensory experience that captures the monument's historical, cultural, and spiritual significance. Similarly, his depiction of the Cambodian people's struggles and triumphs is rendered with empathy and sensitivity, making their stories both compelling and unforgettable. Ghosh's prose is often poetic, with a keen eye for detail that brings his subjects to life.

However, some critics argue that Ghosh's travel writing can be overly dense or academic at times, particularly when he delves into historical or anthropological details. While this depth of research adds richness to his narratives, it may also alienate readers looking for a more straightforward travelogue. Additionally, Ghosh's focus on broader socio-political themes sometimes overshadows the personal, experiential aspects of travel writing, which some readers might find less engaging.

Conclusion: Amitav Ghosh is a travel writer of exceptional skill and insight. His ability to intertwine history, culture, and personal narrative sets him apart from many of his contemporaries. While his work may occasionally lean toward the scholarly, it is ultimately this depth and complexity that make his travelogues so compelling. Ghosh's narratives not only transport readers to distant lands but also challenge them to think critically about the interconnectedness of cultures and the enduring legacies of history. Through his evocative prose and empathetic storytelling, Ghosh reaffirms the power of travel writing to illuminate the human condition and foster a deeper understanding of the world.

Q.3) Discuss Vikram Seth and Amitav Ghosh as a travel writer.

Ans: Introduction: Vikram Seth and Amitav Ghosh are both well-known Indian writers, and they have also written interesting travel books. While both authors describe their journeys in detail, their styles and approaches to travel writing are quite different. Seth focuses more on personal experiences and the beauty of the places he visits, while Ghosh explores history, culture, and politics alongside his travels.

Vikram Seth as a Travel Writer

Vikram Seth's most famous travel book is From Heaven Lake (1983), which describes his journey through China. His writing is simple, clear, and elegant. He does not use complicated language, and his descriptions of places and people feel real and natural. He notices small things—how the light changes in the mountains, how yaks move, and how people in different parts of China live their daily lives.

One of the best parts of Seth's travel writing is his ability to bring out emotions. He meets different people on his journey, like the Tibetan truck driver Gyanseng and a Uyghur cap seller. Through these interactions, he explores themes like loneliness, human connection, and survival. He does not explain these ideas directly but lets them emerge naturally from his experiences.

Seth also adds poetry to his travel writing, making his descriptions more beautiful. His personal reflections on India and China give the reader interesting insights into how these two countries are similar and different. He does not get into deep political discussions, but his simple observations make readers think. His writing is gentle, warm, and filled with a sense of wonder about the world.

Amitav Ghosh as a Travel Writer

Amitav Ghosh's travel writing is quite different from Vikram Seth's. Some of his well-known travel books include In an Antique Land (1992) and Dancing in Cambodia, At Large in Burma (1998). While Seth focuses more on personal experiences, Ghosh blends travel with history, culture, and politics.

One of the most important features of Ghosh's travel writing is his deep research. He does not just describe the places he visits—he connects them to their past. For example, in Dancing in Cambodia, he writes about King Sisowath's visit to France in 1906 and compares it to Cambodia's suffering under the Khmer Rouge in the 1970s. He shows how history continues to affect the present, making his travel writing more meaningful.

Another feature of Ghosh's writing is that he does not put himself at the center of the story. Instead of focusing on his own thoughts and feelings, he lets the people, history, and culture of the place take the spotlight. His writing is detailed and serious, and he often discusses big themes like migration, identity, and cultural exchange.

In In an Antique Land, he mixes history with his own travel experiences in Egypt, telling the story of a 12th-century Indian slave. This book is not just about a journey—it is also about how different cultures are connected across time. His writing is deep, intelligent, and thought-provoking.

Similarities Between Vikram Seth and Amitav Ghosh

Both writers have traveled to different parts of the world and written about their experiences. They are both skilled at describing places and people in a way that makes the reader feel like they are there. They also both explore themes like identity, cultural exchange, and human connections.

Another similarity is their poetic touch. While Seth includes actual poems in From Heaven Lake, Ghosh's writing has a poetic rhythm, even when he is writing about history. Both writers also bring a personal element to their travel books, though in different ways—Seth through his emotions and reflections, and Ghosh through his deep research and storytelling.

Differences Between Vikram Seth and Amitav Ghosh

The biggest difference between them is in their writing style. Vikram Seth's writing is simple, personal, and emotional, while Amitav Ghosh's writing is detailed, intellectual, and historical. Seth focuses more on his own experiences and the people he meets, while Ghosh focuses more on history, politics, and culture.

Seth's travel writing is light and easy to read, even when it touches on deep themes. On the other hand, Ghosh's writing can be more complex, as he includes a lot of historical and political information. Some readers may find Ghosh's work a bit dense, while others may find Seth's style too simple.

Another difference is their approach to storytelling. Seth's travel book is mainly about his personal journey and the places he sees, while Ghosh's books mix travel with historical research, showing how the past influences the present.

Conclusion

Both Vikram Seth and Amitav Ghosh are excellent travel writers, but their approaches are different. Seth's writing is personal, poetic, and focused on experiences, while Ghosh's writing is detailed, historical, and focused on culture and politics.

Block 2 - Untouchable

Scan the QR code to watch video

CHAPTER SEVEN

About Mulk Raj Anand: Career and Works

Mulk Raj Anand (12 December 1905 – 28 September 2004) was a pioneering Indian English writer renowned for his unflinching portrayal of marginalized communities and social injustices in colonial India. A key figure in Indo-Anglian fiction alongside R.K. Narayan and Raja Rao, he gained global acclaim for protest novels like Untouchable (1935), exposing caste oppression, and Coolie (1936), highlighting labour exploitation.

His works, including Two Leaves and a Bud (1937) and The Village (1939), blend gritty realism with Punjabi and Hindustani idioms, critiquing poverty, colonialism, and systemic inequities.

Educated in Amritsar and London, Anand's socialist ideals shaped his empathetic narratives. Honoured with the Padma Bhushan and Sahitya Akademi Award (1968), his legacy endures as a cornerstone of modern Indian literature, amplifying the voices of the oppressed and inspiring debates on caste, labour, and social reform.

CHAPTER EIGHT

Overview of the novel "Untouchable"

In 1933, 18-year-old Bakha, an untouchable sweeper in Bulashah, endures daily humiliation under a rigid caste system. His life revolves around cleaning latrines and streets, a job that isolates him and his family to a cramped, impoverished area. His day is marked by bitter encounters—from demeaning scoldings by figures like Havildar Charat Singh and public insults when a higher-caste man touches him, to the indignity his sister Sohini faces while fetching water, denied even the basic right due to her "polluted" status. Although moments of relief come when he learns to read with the help of higher-caste friends and receives a respectful gesture along with a new hockey stick from Charat Singh, the systemic injustice remains overwhelming. His distress deepens when he discovers a Brahmin priest falsely accusing Sohini of polluting him after a failed sexual assault. Amid personal setbacks, including being blamed for a violent altercation he did not incite, Bakha's day takes a hopeful turn when he hears Mohandas Gandhi speak out against the caste system—an inspiring message that contrasts with the skepticism expressed by educated bystanders. This single day in Bakha's life vividly portrays both the harsh realities of untouchability in colonial India and a glimmer of hope for societal change.

CHAPTER NINE

Questions & Answers

Scan to watch the video

Q.1) Write a critical note on plot construction in Untouchable.

Ans: Introduction: Untouchable is an important novel by Mulk Raj Anand, first published in 1935. It is one of the earliest and most influential works in Indian English literature that tackles the issue of caste discrimination and the struggles of untouchables in Indian society. The novel helped establish Anand as a major English author in India. The story was inspired by an incident involving Anand's aunt, who was shunned for sharing a meal with a Muslim woman. In this, Anand's debut novel, the plot focuses on the need to end the caste system. It portrays a single day in the life of Bakha, a young sweeper who is considered untouchable because his job involves cleaning latrines.

Main content:

Untouchable doesn't focus on telling a traditional story; instead, it is a strong argument against the social issue of untouchability. The book's main goal is to reveal the problems caused by untouchability and to examine its effects from social, moral, psychological, and religious angles. This clear focus gives the plot a strong sense of unity and purpose.

In fact, Untouchable is considered one of the most well-structured and consistent plots in Indian English literature. Anand made this structure even tighter by following Mahatma Gandhi's advice to cut the manuscript down to about half its original size, removing unnecessary details.

Even though it wasn't done on purpose, the novel follows the three Aristotelian unities by focusing on events that happen in just one day of Bakha's life. This single day reflects the sad reality of untouchables, who are at the bottom of the social hierarchy in the rigid caste system of Hindu society, particularly before the Partition of India.

The plot is carefully built to show the difficulties faced by people at the bottom of the social hierarchy. Here's a simple breakdown of how the plot works:

1. Realistic Daily Life

The story is set in one day of Bakha's life, showing his struggles and the unfair treatment he endures as an untouchable. By focusing on his everyday tasks, like cleaning latrines and getting water, Anand effectively illustrates the harsh realities of Bakha's life and the discrimination he faces.

2. Focused Narrative

The plot revolves around a single day, which helps keep the story intense and detailed. This approach allows Anand to dive deeply into Bakha's experiences and emotions, making the reader feel the impact of the caste system on his life.

3. Character Interactions

Bakha's interactions with other characters are central to the story. These include his father, Lakha, his sister, Sohini, and the priest, Pundit Kali Nath. Each character plays a role in showing different aspects of caste discrimination. For example, Lakha's strictness and the priest's abuse highlight the various ways that society mistreats untouchables.

4. Symbols and Themes

Anand uses symbols and themes to explore the caste system. For example, Bakha's job of cleaning latrines symbolizes the low status of untouchables. The hockey stick given to Bakha by Charat Singh represents a small chance for change and hope, contrasting with the overall harshness of

Bakha's life.

5. Conflict and Resolution

The story has several conflicts, both inside Bakha's mind and with the people around him. Internally, Bakha struggles with his self-worth. Externally, he faces unfair treatment from higher-caste individuals. The climax occurs when Bakha faces accusations of pollution and violence. The story ends with Gandhi's speech and a debate about social reform, suggesting that while change is possible, Bakha's personal issues remain unresolved.

6. Social Reform and Change

The plot also engages with ideas about social reform. Gandhi's speech and the debate between a lawyer and a poet reflect the wider discussions about ending the caste system. Anand uses these elements to show the broader context of Bakha's struggles and the ongoing fight for equality.

Conclusion

In Untouchable, Anand uses the plot to powerfully show the life of an untouchable and criticize the caste system. By focusing on one day of Bakha's life, detailing his struggles, and including important symbols and themes, Anand creates a story that highlights both personal hardship and the need for social change.

Q.2) 'Various themes have been explored, mirroring the social and political picture of colonial India in Anand's novel.' Enunciate.

Ans: Introduction: "for this section refer answer 1 of this chapter"

Main Content:

Mulk Raj Anand is known for being a novelist deeply committed to social issues. His books often compare the social problems faced by individuals with the attitudes of those in privileged parts of society. In Untouchable, Anand focuses on the terrible problem of untouchability in Hindu society before the Partition of India. He highlights how the caste system has long prevented many people in India from improving their lives.

In the novel, Anand clearly shows the harsh and difficult lives of the untouchables. He suggests that the only way to free them from the strict and harmful traditions is for people to develop compassion and kindness. He also believes that untouchables need to find the courage to live confidently and healthily despite their challenging situation.

Anand skillfully illustrates the harsh reality of Hindu society, which was becoming increasingly divided into rigid social groups. E.M. Forster, in his preface to Untouchable, comments on this aspect of the novel:

The untouchable sweeper is in a worse position than a slave. A slave might change masters or even gain freedom, but an untouchable is stuck in a fixed, unchangeable role. They are cut off from social interaction and the comfort of their religion. Because they are considered unclean, their touch is seen as polluting, forcing others to purify themselves and change their plans. As a result, untouchables are seen as both disturbing and repulsive by orthodox people. They have to announce their presence to avoid causing discomfort. It's no wonder that the constant rejection and harsh treatment affect the sweeper's self-image and sense of worth.

The opening paragraph of the novel highlights the clear separation between the untouchables and the rest of the town's residents:

The untouchables lived in a cluster of mud-walled houses, forming a separate area away from both the town and the military camp. This area was home to scavengers, leather-workers, washermen, barbers, water-carriers, grass-cutters, and other outcastes in Hindu society.

The several themes are explored that reflect the social and political situation in colonial India. Here's a breakdown:

1. Caste Discrimination

The novel highlights the severe discrimination faced by untouchables due to the caste system. It shows how this discrimination affects their daily lives and social interactions.

2. Social Inequality

Anand portrays the deep social inequalities between the untouchables and higher-caste individuals. The novel demonstrates how these inequalities impact every aspect of the untouchables' lives.

3. Colonial Influence

The book examines the impact of British colonial rule on Indian society. It contrasts British influences with traditional Indian practices, showing how colonial rule affects social structures and attitudes.

4. Social Reform

The novel discusses the need for social reform to address the injustices of the caste system. It reflects the growing movement for change and the efforts of reformers like Mahatma Gandhi.

5. Religious Critique

Anand critiques how religion is used to justify and maintain caste discrimination. The novel explores how religious practices and beliefs contribute to the oppression of untouchables.

6. Psychological Impact

The book also delves into the psychological effects of caste discrimination on individuals. It shows how being treated as inferior affects the self-esteem and mental health of untouchables.

7. Economic Exploitation

The novel touches on economic issues, illustrating how untouchables are economically marginalized and exploited. It reflects the broader economic disparities of the time.

Conclusion:

Anand's novel uses these themes to paint a detailed picture of the social and political landscape of colonial India, shedding light on the struggles and injustices faced by untouchables.

Q.3) Discuss the narrative technique used in Untouchable.

Ans: Introduction: "for this section refer answer 1 of this chapter"

Mulk Raj Anand has said that he was greatly influenced by James Joyce's writing style and techniques, even though he didn't do this on purpose. Anand describes a novel as a story that shows how people change through their conflicts within a specific time and place, unlike a recital that tells stories outside of time. Anand clearly states that while he was inspired by European techniques, it doesn't make his novel any less Indian or worse in any way. The novel's rich content, ideas, and the portrayal of human struggle and growth during Gandhi's time make it distinctly Indian and give it a strong sense of life and intensity.

Mulk Raj Anand once said that he started writing a long, complex story, influenced by the old Urdu epic Farsara-I-Azad by Ratan Nath Sarshar, in the early 1920s. This story was very lengthy and felt endless, like a river flowing from the Himalayas that hoped to eventually reach the ocean.

In Untouchable, Mulk Raj Anand employs several narrative techniques to effectively tell the story and convey its themes. Here's an overview of the key techniques used in the novel:

1. Stream of Consciousness

Anand uses stream of consciousness to provide a deep, intimate look into Bakha's thoughts and feelings. This technique allows readers to experience Bakha's internal struggles, anxieties, and reflections in real-time, making his experiences more vivid and relatable.

2. Realistic Portrayal

The novel is grounded in realistic details of everyday life for untouchables. Anand uses detailed descriptions of Bakha's daily routines, interactions, and environment to create an authentic representation of the harsh conditions faced by the untouchables in colonial India.

3. Third-Person Limited Narrative

The story is told from a third-person limited perspective, primarily focusing on Bakha. This approach allows readers to closely follow Bakha's experiences and emotions while maintaining some narrative distance. It helps in presenting Bakha's personal view of the world and his encounters with caste discrimination.

4. Social Commentary

Anand weaves social commentary throughout the narrative, using Bakha's experiences to critique the caste system and social inequalities. The novel doesn't just tell a story; it also serves as a vehicle for social and political critique, reflecting Anand's views on the need for reform.

5. Symbolism

The novel uses symbols to reinforce its themes. For example, Bakha's job as a sweeper and the constant reminders of his low status symbolize the broader social and moral issues related to caste discrimination. Symbols like the hockey stick gifted by Charat Singh represent hope and the possibility of change.

6. Dialogue and Character Interaction

The interactions between characters are crucial in revealing the social dynamics and prejudices of the time. Anand uses dialogue to illustrate the attitudes of higher-caste individuals and the struggles of the untouchables. These interactions highlight the conflicts and tensions between different social groups.

7. Historical and Cultural Context

The novel incorporates elements of historical and cultural context to enrich the narrative. By including references to historical figures like Mahatma Gandhi and discussing social practices of the time, Anand provides a backdrop that situates Bakha's personal story within a larger socio-political framework.

8. Episodic Structure

The plot unfolds in a single day, giving it an episodic structure. This structure helps in maintaining a focused narrative and intensifies the impact of each event. The day-in-the-life approach allows for a concentrated exploration of Bakha's experiences and the social issues he faces.

Conclusion

Mulk Raj Anand's use of these narrative techniques in Untouchable helps create a powerful and immersive portrayal of the life of an untouchable in colonial India. The techniques work together to bring out the novel's social critiques, deepen the reader's understanding of the protagonist, and vividly depict the harsh realities of caste discrimination.

Q.4) Discuss the appropriateness of the title, Untouchable.

Ans: Introduction:"for this section refer answer 1 of this chapter"

Main Content: The novel was originally called Bakha and was almost twice as long as it is now. While staying at Mahatma Gandhi's Sabarmati Ashram for three months, Anand shared his story with Gandhi and also read Gandhi's simple story about a sweeper-boy named Uka, published in Young India. In his article "On the Genesis of Untouchable: A Note," Anand explains that Gandhi advised him to remove parts of the novel that were overly dramatic and cluttered with comic and tragic elements. Gandhi also suggested cutting over a hundred pages, especially where Bakha was shown thinking and dreaming too much, like a "Bloomsbury intellectual." Following Gandhi's advice and focusing more on the story rather than just making a social statement, Anand published the novel in 1935 under the new title Untouchable.

The absence of the word "the" in the title makes the novel a symbolic representation of the suffering faced by millions of untouchables in India. These individuals are at the bottom of the caste system and victims of social injustice. Bakha, the main character, represents not just the untouchable sweepers but also all marginalized and deprived groups in society. He shows the hardships of those who live in self-pity and helplessness, treated as outcasts by higher castes both physically and emotionally. Therefore, the title Untouchable is very fitting and clearly reflects the novel's main theme.

The title Untouchable is highly appropriate for Mulk Raj Anand's novel for several reasons:

1. Direct Reflection of the Main Issue

The title directly addresses the central theme of the novel—caste discrimination. The term "untouchable" refers to those at the lowest level of the caste system in India, who are socially excluded and considered impure. By using this title, Anand immediately signals to readers that the novel will explore the harsh realities faced by this marginalized group.

2. Symbolic Significance

The title symbolizes the broader social and psychological impact of untouchability. It represents not just the physical touch, but the entire social distance and discrimination that untouchables experience. The title encapsulates the sense of exclusion, rejection, and dehumanization that

Bakha and others like him face daily.

3. Focus on the Protagonist

The novel follows the life of Bakha, an untouchable sweeper. By naming the novel Untouchable, Anand emphasizes Bakha's identity and the social position that defines his life and experiences. The title reflects Bakha's struggle with his caste identity and his quest for dignity and respect.

4. Critique of Social Norms

The title also serves as a critique of the caste system and its rigid social norms. It challenges readers to confront the unjust practices that uphold the untouchability doctrine. By highlighting this term, Anand draws attention to the need for social reform and greater empathy towards those who suffer due to caste discrimination.

5. Reflects the Historical Context

During the time Anand wrote the novel, untouchability was a significant social issue in India. The title captures the essence of this historical and cultural problem, making the novel a relevant and powerful commentary on the societal norms of that period.

Conclusion

Overall, the title Untouchable is fitting because it succinctly conveys the core issues of the novel, including the social, emotional, and systemic challenges faced by the untouchables. It provides an immediate understanding of the novel's focus and highlights the serious critique of the caste system that Anand seeks to address through his narrative.

Q.5) Discuss Mulk Raj Anand's novel "Untouchable as a novel of social criticism.

Or

Discuss Mulk Raj Anand's Untouchable as a social novel.

Or

How is the question of caste addressed in Mulk Raj Anand's Untouchable? Explain.

Ans: Introduction: "for this section refer answer 1 of this chapter"

Main Content: The novel is a social story about the problem of untouchability in India. It tells the story of Bakha, an eighteen-year-old sweeper, and shows his experiences over one day. Bakha's job is to clean the public toilets, which is both hard and degrading work.

Untouchable highlights Anand's concern for people who are treated poorly in society. The novel shows how Bakha, despite having dreams and hopes for his future, is kept apart from others because of the caste system.

This system assigns people fixed roles based on their caste, and Bakha's life is shaped by this unfair system.

Anand, as has been suggested by Prof.H.M. Williams, exemples the problem of 'untouchability', the treatment of the latrine-cleaning class condemned to isolation and deprivation as handlers of excrement; he exposes this is a social evil and suggests its remedy." There are many occasions in the novel which reveal the stark and naked realities in the society. One such occasion is when the untouchables are victimized, ravished and their morale shattered into pieces. The well incident in the novel poignantly describes how these ill-fated people are usurped by the so-called high class touchable. Bakha's sister once goes to the village well for fetching water. She waits to be given a little water from the well, as she is not allowed, being untouchable, to touch anything there. Ultimately, the village priest does the needful and asks her to come to his house for cleaning. But, seeing nobody around, when she goes to house, he tries to molest her. The priest tries to fish in the troubled waters. The cruller think is when people gather, the priest impenitently indicts the innocent girl that she has defiled his religion. He returns home desperately and tells his father Lakha about his insult and Sohini's molestation by the pandit' he says; "They think we are mere dirt, because we clean their dirt"; If we view the incident from humanitarian perspective, we must say that might is right. The untouchables, being weak, have no justice, we can see from the beginning of the novel the lives of Bakha and his sister were struggling for financial, identity and social, existence in the novel.

Anand criticizes the caste system because it isolates people like Bakha, calling them "Untouchable" and making them feel alienated from society. This sense of separation and unfair treatment is a central theme of the novel.

Key Aspects of Social Criticism in Untouchable

Caste System Critique: Anand's novel serves as a direct critique of the caste system and the oppressive practices associated with it. The protagonist, Bakha, is a representative figure of the untouchables, and his daily struggles underscore the systemic injustices and the dehumanization faced by people in this position. The narrative reveals how the caste system dictates every aspect of the lives of untouchables, from their social status to their treatment by others.

Empathy and Human Dignity: Anand employs a compassionate and empathetic narrative style to humanize Bakha and others in his community.

By focusing on Bakha's personal experiences, the novel challenges readers to see beyond the stereotypes and prejudices associated with untouchables. The detailed portrayal of Bakha's emotions, dreams, and frustrations elicits sympathy and prompts a reevaluation of entrenched social norms.

Social Injustice and Reform: Through Bakha's encounters and experiences, Anand highlights the social injustices perpetuated by both the traditional caste system and the colonial context of British India. The novel indirectly calls for social reform and justice, questioning the legitimacy of the caste-based discrimination and advocating for a more equitable society.

Symbolism and Allegory: Anand uses symbolism to enhance the novel's critique. For instance, Bakha's experiences can be seen as an allegory for the broader struggle against social oppression and inequality. The cleanliness and impurity themes symbolize the arbitrary nature of caste-based discrimination and underscore the need for societal change.

Representation of Social Hierarchies: Anand does not only focus on the untouchables but also depicts the various layers of the social hierarchy, including the middle and upper castes. By illustrating the attitudes and behaviors of individuals from different social strata, the novel critiques how these hierarchies contribute to and perpetuate discrimination.

Conclusion: Untouchable was groundbreaking in its time for its candid portrayal of caste discrimination and its call for social reform. Anand's work influenced Indian literature and social thought, bringing attention to the plight of untouchables and contributing to the discourse on caste and social justice. The novel remains a powerful example of how literature can serve as a tool for social criticism and change.

Q.6) Critically examine the ending of Mulk Raj Anand's novel Untouchable. What is your suggestion for ending untouchability?

Or

Does Mulk Raj Anand's Untouchable provide a viable solution to the eradication of untouchability ? Discuss.

Ans: Introduction: "for this section refer answer 1 of this chapter"

The novel Untouchable doesn't follow a typical structure with a clear beginning, middle, and end. Instead, it ends with an open-ended conclusion, presenting three possible solutions to ending untouchability:

Converting to Christianity.

Following Gandhi's advice for lower-caste people to improve their behavior and gradually integrate into mainstream Indian society.

Introducing modern sanitation systems like flush toilets.

Forster's note in the Preface helps explain this approach:

The book is simple in its design but still has a clear structure. It covers just one day in a small area. The big problem of untouchability happens in the morning, affecting everything that happens afterward, even the pleasant events like the hockey match and the country walk. After many ups and downs, the book concludes with three potential solutions. Bakha goes back to his father and his difficult life, thinking about Gandhi and modern sanitation. His day ends, and th The ending of Mulk Raj Anand's novel Untouchable is both poignant and thought-provoking. To critically examine the conclusion and discuss potential solutions for ending untouchability, let's consider the final moments of the novel and the broader implications of Anand's narrative.

Critical Examination of the Ending

The Climactic Moment:

The novel concludes with Bakha, the protagonist, experiencing a moment of personal despair after a series of humiliations and injustices. His day culminates in a series of events that reinforce his sense of social alienation. The climax involves Bakha's encounter with a high-caste Hindu, who represents the same systemic biases that Bakha has been subjected to throughout the novel.

The Moment of Hope:

Despite the grim reality faced by Bakha, the ending of the novel includes a glimmer of hope. Bakha encounters a young reformist who speaks about the possibility of change and equality. This moment introduces a more optimistic perspective, suggesting that there is potential for social reform and the abolition of untouchability.

Symbolism of Change:

Anand's ending uses Bakha's interaction with reformist ideas as a symbolic gesture towards potential social change. The novel ends on a note that, while not completely resolving Bakha's plight, opens up the possibility of a future where untouchability could be eradicated through collective effort and social reform.

Suggestions for Ending Untouchability

Education and Awareness:

Promoting education and raising awareness about the historical and social implications of untouchability can play a crucial role in dismantling caste-based discrimination. Educational programs should emphasize the importance of equality and human dignity, challenging stereotypes and prejudices.

Legal Reforms:

Strengthening and enforcing laws that prohibit caste-based discrimination is essential. While legal frameworks exist in many countries to combat untouchability, rigorous implementation and monitoring are necessary to ensure that these laws are effective and that violators are held accountable.

Economic Opportunities:

Providing economic opportunities and resources to marginalized communities can help address the socio-economic disparities that perpetuate untouchability. Initiatives aimed at improving access to employment, healthcare, and social services for marginalized groups can help reduce inequalities.

Social and Cultural Change:

Initiatives to promote social integration and cultural change are vital. This includes encouraging inter-caste marriages, fostering dialogue between different social groups, and celebrating cultural diversity. Changing social attitudes and breaking down caste-based barriers requires collective effort and a commitment to equality.

Community Engagement:

Engaging with community leaders, activists, and organizations that work on caste-based issues is important for creating grassroots movements and support networks. Collaborative efforts between different sectors of society can drive meaningful change.

Conclusion

Mulk Raj Anand's Untouchable concludes with a hopeful note, suggesting that change is possible even in the face of entrenched social injustices. To effectively address and ultimately end untouchability, a multifaceted approach involving education, legal reforms, economic opportunities, social and cultural change, empowerment, and community engagement is necessary. These efforts must be sustained and supported by collective will and action to achieve lasting social transformation.

Q.7) Discuss the Mulk Raj Anand's novel Untouchable as a modern novel.

Ans: Introduction: "for this section refer answer 1 of this chapter"

Main Content:

Mulk Raj Anand's Untouchable, is a significant work in the context of modern literature, particularly within the framework of Indian writing in

English. Its modernity can be examined through various aspects such as its thematic concerns, narrative style, and socio-cultural relevance.

1. Thematic Concerns

Social Critique: Untouchable is notable for its critical examination of the caste system and untouchability, which are central issues in Indian society. Anand's focus on the everyday struggles of the untouchable caste and their dehumanizing experiences reflects a modern approach to literature, as it addresses social injustices and systemic inequalities.

Humanism and Empathy: The novel is grounded in a deep sense of empathy and humanism. Anand's portrayal of Bakha, the protagonist, and his experiences, aims to evoke compassion and understanding from the reader. This emphasis on the individual's emotional and psychological landscape is a hallmark of modern literature.

2. Narrative Style

Stream of Consciousness: Anand employs a narrative style that delves into Bakha's inner thoughts and feelings, using techniques reminiscent of stream of consciousness. This approach offers readers an intimate view of the protagonist's psychological state and personal struggles, aligning with modernist trends in literature.

Realism: The novel's realistic portrayal of life for an untouchable is a key aspect of its modernity. Anand's detailed and unflinching depiction of Bakha's daily hardships reflects a commitment to realism and a departure from idealized or romanticized portrayals of Indian life.

Social Realism: Anand's focus on the socio-economic conditions of the untouchable community highlights his use of social realism. The novel does not shy away from depicting harsh realities, including discrimination and poverty, which aligns with modernist tendencies to confront and critique societal issues.

3. Characterization

Complex Characters: The characters in Untouchable are portrayed with depth and complexity. Bakha, for instance, is not merely a victim but is also depicted with personal dreams, aspirations, and frustrations. This nuanced characterization reflects a modernist interest in exploring the inner lives of individuals.

Symbolic Figures: Anand uses symbolic figures, such as Bakha, to represent broader social issues. Bakha's interactions with other characters, including those from different castes, serve to highlight the pervasive nature of caste-based discrimination and the challenges of overcoming it.

4. Social and Political Context

Historical Context: Untouchable is set against the backdrop of colonial India, a period marked by social and political upheaval. The novel's exploration of caste issues within this context provides insight into the complex interplay between colonialism and traditional social structures, reflecting modern concerns about power, identity, and reform.

Reformist Perspectives: The novel engages with contemporary reformist ideas, including those advocated by figures like Gandhi. Anand's depiction of Bakha's interactions with reformist ideas illustrates the tension between traditional practices and the push for social change, highlighting the modern struggle for social justice.

5. Innovative Structure

Open-Ended Conclusion: The novel's open-ended conclusion, presenting multiple potential solutions to untouchability, reflects a modern sensibility. Rather than offering a neat resolution, Anand leaves readers with unresolved issues and possibilities, encouraging reflection and continued dialogue.

Focused Narrative: The novel's focus on a single day in Bakha's life, with detailed attention to his experiences and thoughts, is a modern narrative technique that emphasizes the significance of individual moments and their broader implications.

Conclusion

Untouchable is a modern novel in its thematic exploration of social injustice, its use of realistic and innovative narrative techniques, and its complex characterizations. Mulk Raj Anand's work not only addresses critical issues of his time but also employs modernist methods to deepen the reader's understanding of the protagonist's experiences and the broader socio-political landscape.

Q.8) Discuss Mulk Raj Anand's novel Untouchable as a Gandhian novel.

Ans: Introduction: "for this section refer answer 1 of this chapter"

Main Content: In the early 20th century, many writers were strongly influenced by Gandhi. He stirred up a lot of thought and change among educated people. Gandhi urged Harijans (the untouchables) to avoid bad habits and gradually become part of mainstream Indian society. He saw the caste system as a group system based on specific roles and considered untouchability as a major problem for Hinduism. Gandhi even said that if he were to be reborn, he would choose to be an untouchable. He wanted to experience their struggles and try to help improve their difficult situation.

Mulk Raj Anand is a notable writer who pioneered a new style of realism and social protest in Indian English fiction. He focused on the difficult lives of the poor and oppressed in his books. His novel Untouchable is strongly influenced by Gandhi's efforts to end untouchability, a deeply rooted problem in Indian society. Anand was inspired by a moving story about a sweeper boy named Uka, which Gandhi had written in Young India. This story motivated Anand to write the first draft of his novel, originally calle While the novel does not explicitly present itself as a Gandhian work, it resonates with several aspects of Gandhi's vision for social change and reflects his influence in various ways.

1. Portrayal of Caste System and Untouchability

Critique of Untouchability: Gandhi was a vocal critic of untouchability and the caste system, advocating for the upliftment of the untouchables, whom he referred to as Harijans or "children of God." Anand's Untouchable addresses the brutal realities of untouchability and caste-based discrimination, aligning with Gandhi's concerns. The novel's depiction of Bakha's daily struggles highlights the dehumanizing effects of the caste system, echoing Gandhi's call for social reform.

Empathy and Human Dignity: Gandhi's philosophy emphasized the inherent dignity of every individual, irrespective of their caste. Anand's portrayal of Bakha as a complex and empathetic character reflects this Gandhian principle. The novel's detailed exploration of Bakha's emotional and psychological experiences underscores the idea that untouchables are deserving of respect and human dignity.

2. Gandhian Solutions and Reformist Ideas

Gandhi's Reformist Approach: Gandhi advocated for the moral and social reform of untouchables, encouraging them to adopt new ways of living that would help them integrate into mainstream society. In Untouchable, Anand indirectly engages with Gandhi's reformist ideas through the depiction of Bakha's encounters with different social attitudes. The character's experiences reflect the broader discourse on reform that Gandhi championed.

Integration into Mainstream Society: Gandhi's call for the gradual integration of untouchables into mainstream Indian society is reflected in the novel's portrayal of Bakha's interactions with various social groups. Although the novel does not provide a straightforward solution, it suggests that social attitudes must evolve for meaningful change to occur, aligning with Gandhi's vision of gradual and systemic reform.

3. Gandhi's Influence on Characters and Ideals

The Reformist Figure: Towards the end of the novel, Bakha encounters a reformist who speaks of Gandhi's ideas and the possibility of change. This character's dialogue about improving oneself and seeking social integration resonates with Gandhi's principles. The presence of this figure highlights Gandhi's influence on contemporary debates about untouchability and social reform.

Social and Moral Upliftment: Gandhi's emphasis on moral and spiritual upliftment is mirrored in the novel's underlying message. Anand's portrayal of Bakha's suffering and his eventual encounter with reformist ideas reflects a Gandhian concern for personal and social transformation. The novel suggests that addressing untouchability requires both individual and collective efforts, in line with Gandhi's holistic approach to social change.

4. Challenges and Critiques

Complexity of Solutions: While the novel engages with Gandhian ideas, it also presents a complex view of the challenges faced by untouchables. Anand does not provide a singular, ideal solution to untouchability but instead offers multiple possibilities, including Gandhi's approach and modern sanitation solutions. This nuanced portrayal reflects the difficulties in implementing Gandhian reforms in a deeply entrenched social system.

Modern vs. Traditional Approaches: Anand's novel also addresses modern approaches to social issues, such as the introduction of flush toilets as a solution to sanitation problems. This reflects a broader dialogue about the efficacy of traditional Gandhian methods versus contemporary solutions. The novel presents these ideas alongside Gandhian thought, suggesting that multiple strategies might be necessary for social reform.

Conclusion

Untouchable can be considered a Gandhian novel in its critique of caste discrimination and its engagement with Gandhi's ideas about social reform. Through its depiction of Bakha's struggles and its exploration of potential solutions, the novel aligns with Gandhi's emphasis on human dignity and moral upliftment. However, Anand also incorporates modern perspectives and acknowledges the complexity of social change, reflecting a broader dialogue about addressing untouchability. The novel, thus, serves as a bridge between Gandhian ideals and contemporary approaches to social justice.d Baka, which later became Untouchable.

Block 3 - Kanthapura

Scan the QR code to watch video

CHAPTER TEN

About Raja Rao: Career and Works

Raja Rao (November 8, 1908 – July 8, 2006) was an Indian-American writer who wrote novels and short stories in English. His work often explores deep, philosophical themes. His novel The Serpent and the Rope (1960), which is partly based on his own life and his quest for spiritual truth in Europe and India, made him a prominent writer and won him the Sahitya Akademi Award in 1963. In 1988, he received the Neustadt International Prize for Literature for his entire body of work. Rao's diverse writing is considered an important part of both Indian English literature and world literature.

Raja Rao's literary works are known for their exploration of philosophical and spiritual themes. Here are some of his most notable works:

The Serpent and the Rope (1960) – This semi-autobiographical novel delves into the search for spiritual truth. It follows the journey of a man who travels through Europe and India in his quest for understanding.

Kanthapura (1938) – Rao's first novel, set in a small Indian village during the Indian independence movement. It tells the story of how Gandhi's ideas impact the lives of the villagers.

The Cat and Shakespeare (1965) – A novel that blends modern and traditional themes, featuring a complex narrative about a man's philosophical journey and his encounters with different characters.

Comrade Kirillov (1976) – This novel explores the tensions between individual desires and collective political movements through the story of its protagonist, Kirillov.

A Passage to India (1984) – Not to be confused with E.M. Forster's novel of a similar name, this work by Rao is a reflective exploration of cultural and spiritual themes.

The Snake and the Rope (1960) – Often confused with his earlier work, this is actually an essay collection that discusses various philosophical ideas. Rao's works are celebrated for their poetic language and deep engagement with Indian philosophy and spirituality.

Overview of the novel "Kanthapura"

"Kanthapura" is a 1938 novel by Raja Rao that depicts the transformative impact of Gandhian ideals on a small South Indian village. Narrated by the elderly Achakka, the story centers on Moorthy, a young Brahmin who, inspired by Gandhi's teachings of non-violence and self-governance, returns to his village to awaken his community. As Moorthy spreads his message of unity and challenges traditional caste hierarchies—especially the mistreatment of the Pariahs—the villagers become increasingly divided, and tensions rise. The movement gains momentum as a local Congress Committee is formed, prompting brutal repression from British authorities led by figures like Bade Khan. Despite Moorthy's arrest and escalating violence at a British-owned estate, determined leaders such as the widow Rangamma step in to continue the struggle, urging non-violent resistance and civil disobedience. Ultimately, "Kanthapura" captures both the hope and the hardships of a community in the midst of a revolutionary fight against colonial oppression and entrenched social injustice.

CHAPTER TWELVE

Questions & Answers

Q.1)Discuss the role of women characters in Kanthapura.

Or

In what manner do the women characters in 'Kanthapura' contribute to the progress of the

novel ? Discuss

Ans: Introduction: "Kanthapura" is a novel by the Indian author Raja Rao, first published in 1938. Raja Rao was an Indian-American writer who wrote novels and short stories in English. His work often explores deep, philosophical themes. Kanthapura is considered one of the finest examples of Indian writing in English and is often regarded as a significant work in the realm of Indian literature. The story centers around the character Moorthy, a young Brahmin who becomes an ardent follower of Mahatma Gandhi after being influenced by his teachings of non-violence and civil disobedience.

Main Content: Although Moorthy is the main character in Kanthapura, the women in the story play roles just as important as the men. Since the narrator is Achakka, we hear the story of what happens in and around Kanthapura mostly from the women's perspective. The women actively participate in religious gatherings, prayer meetings, and political activities. They also manage their households, take care of the men, and look after the children. At the same time, they are very committed to maintaining rituals and traditions. Jayaramachar's storytelling about Mahatma Gandhi inspires them so much that they eagerly become volunteers in the Satyagraha Movement led by Moorthy.

Among the noble women of the village, Rangamma and Ratna stand out. Both of them fight alongside Moorthy, Range Gowda, and others against British oppression. When the Congress Committee is formed in the village, Moorthy insists on having a woman on the committee because the Congress represents the weak and the lowly. Everyone agrees that Rangamma is the best choice, and she reluctantly accepts the responsibility because of the popular demand.

Later, when Moorthy is arrested, Rangamma steps up and arranges for newspapers to be delivered from the city so the villagers can stay informed about the Congress activities across the country. When they hear that Moorthy will be released and is returning to the village, Rangamma organizes a proper welcome for him. She also forms a special group of women volunteers called the "Sevika Sangha," which is dedicated to serving the community.

The men of the village are not very supportive of the Sevika Sangha, fearing that the women will neglect their household duties because of their involvement in political and social activities. However, this doesn't discourage the women, led by Rangamma, from continuing on their chosen path. When Rangamma is eventually arrested, Ratna takes over the leadership from her.

Achakka, the narrator, is an elderly woman who provides the readers with a detailed account of the events in Kanthapura. Through her narration, she represents the collective voice and consciousness of the village women. While she does not take a direct role in the movement, her recounting of the story from a female perspective gives insight into the lives and struggles of the women in the village, highlighting their resilience and sense of community.

Ratna is a young widow who defies the traditional expectations placed upon her by society. Unlike other widows, who are expected to lead a life of seclusion and austerity, Ratna is bold, outspoken, and involved in the freedom movement. She represents the younger generation of women who are willing to challenge societal norms and take part in the fight for India's freedom. Ratna's involvement in the movement also reflects the broader theme of social change and the questioning of established traditions.

The women of Kanthapura, as a collective, play a vital role in supporting the Gandhian movement. They attend meetings, participate in protests, and spread Gandhi's message throughout the village. Their involvement is significant because it shows how the movement for independence permeated all levels of society, including those who were traditionally marginalized. The women's participation in picketing, non-cooperation, and other forms of civil disobedience underscores their crucial role in the larger struggle for freedom.

The novel also weaves in elements of Hindu mythology and tradition, where women are often seen as embodiments of Shakti (divine feminine power). This symbolic association is important as it underscores the latent strength and potential of the women in the village. Rangamma's leadership and the women's collective resistance can be seen as a manifestation of this Shakti, challenging both colonial oppression and traditional gender roles.

Conclusion: The role of women in "Kanthapura" reflects the changing dynamics of Indian society during the independence movement. While rooted in traditional roles, these women step beyond the confines of their expected behaviors to actively contribute to the national cause. Through characters like Rangamma, Achakka, and Ratna, Raja Rao emphasizes that the struggle for independence was not just a male endeavor but one that involved the entire community, including its women. Their courage, leadership, and participation in the movement highlight the essential role of women in shaping the course of India's history.

Q.2) What are the main features of Raja Rao's narrative technique in kanthapura ? Discuss.

Ans: Introduction: "for this section refer answer 1 of this chapter"

Main Content: Raja Rao's novel "Kanthapura" employs a unique and innovative narrative technique that blends traditional Indian storytelling methods with modern literary styles. This approach enriches the novel's texture and brings authenticity to its portrayal of rural Indian life during the struggle for independence.

Raja Rao tells the story of Kanthapura as a sthalapurana (a legendary tale about a place) in English, but it's influenced by the local language and culture of South India. The story feels like a visionary experience, as the narrator, Achakka, recalls the heroic and tragic events that the entire village went through. Since Kanthapura is a novel based on memories, Raja Rao uses techniques like reflection, dreams, flashbacks, and the recounting of connected episodes.

Instead of using the "stream of consciousness" style, he opts for a local way of narrating, which is a continuous, almost breathless storytelling style. The story begins with a description of the village and its surroundings, then quickly introduces the main characters, and dives into how the Gandhian Satyagraha Movement reached the village and its effects on the community. From start to finish, the narration is filled with emotion and is likely to deeply move the reader.

Narrator as a Storyteller: The story is narrated by Achakka, an elderly village woman who recounts the events in a conversational and anecdotal manner. This mirrors the oral storytelling traditions prevalent in Indian villages, where stories are passed down through generations by word of mouth.

Use of Puranic Style: Rao incorporates elements of Sthalapurana (legendary stories about places) into the narrative. This technique involves intertwining myth and reality, giving the village of Kanthapura a mythical and timeless quality. Achakka often references Hindu myths and legends, drawing parallels between the villagers' struggles and epic tales.

Communal Voice: Although Achakka is the primary narrator, she often uses the collective "we," representing the shared experiences and perspectives of the village community. This collective narration emphasizes the unity and solidarity among the villagers.

2. Language and Style

Indianized English: Raja Rao adapts the English language to capture the rhythms, idioms, and expressions of Indian speech. The language is rich with local phrases, proverbs, and colloquialisms, which lend authenticity and cultural depth to the narrative.

Long, Flowing Sentences: The novel features extended sentences that mimic the natural flow of spoken language. This creates a rhythmic and lyrical quality, drawing readers into the immersive and continuous flow of the story.

Repetition and Rhythm: Repetition is used effectively to emphasize certain ideas and to create a musical rhythm in the prose, echoing the patterns of traditional Indian chants and storytelling.

3. Stream of Consciousness

Interior Monologues: The narrative occasionally delves into the inner thoughts and feelings of characters, particularly through Achakka's reflections. This provides deeper insight into their emotions and motivations, and illustrates the psychological impact of the independence movement on ordinary people.

Non-linear Narrative: The story unfolds through a series of interconnected episodes, flashbacks, and memories. This non-linear approach reflects the way stories are told in oral traditions, where the past and present are woven together seamlessly.

4. Integration of Social and Political Themes

Blending Personal and Political: The narrative seamlessly integrates personal stories with broader social and political themes. The impact of Gandhi's philosophies and the independence movement are depicted through the everyday lives and struggles of the villagers.

Detailed Descriptions: Rao provides vivid and detailed descriptions of village life, rituals, and customs. These descriptions not only set the scene but also highlight the cultural and social milieu in which the story unfolds.

Conclusion

Raja Rao's narrative technique in "Kanthapura" is a masterful blend of traditional and modern storytelling methods. By employing an oral narrative style infused with cultural richness and linguistic innovation, Rao brings the story to life in a way that is both authentic and universally accessible. The technique effectively conveys the complexities of India's struggle for independence and the transformative impact it had on even the smallest and most remote communities.

Q.3) Mahatma Gandhi is the hidden protagonist in Raja Rao's Kanthapura. Discuss.

Or

Discuss Raja Rao's Kanthapura as a Gandhian novel.

Ans: Intoduction: "for this section refer answer 1 of this chapter"

Main Content: Mahatma Gandhi is indeed the hidden protagonist in Raja Rao's Kanthapura. Although Gandhi never physically appears in the novel, his influence is deeply felt throughout the story. Gandhi's ideas and principles shape the actions, thoughts, and motivations of the characters, particularly Moorthy, and drive the plot forward. Here's how Gandhi functions as the hidden protagonist:

1. Gandhi's Ideology as the Central Force

Gandhian Philosophy: Gandhi's principles of non-violence (Ahimsa) and civil disobedience (Satyagraha) are central to the novel. The entire narrative revolves around the villagers of Kanthapura adopting these ideas as they resist British colonial rule. Gandhi's teachings inspire the protagonist, Moorthy, who becomes a vehicle for spreading Gandhism in the village.

Moral and Spiritual Guidance: Gandhi represents not just a political leader but also a moral and spiritual guide for the villagers. His teachings provide a framework for how they live their lives and approach the struggle for independence. The villagers look up to Gandhi as a savior figure, and his ideas infuse their actions with purpose and direction.

2. Moorthy as Gandhi's Disciple and Representative

Moorthy's Transformation: Moorthy, the novel's main character, undergoes a transformation after being influenced by Gandhi's ideals. He becomes a devoted follower, spreading Gandhi's message among the villagers. Through Moorthy's journey, we see the impact of Gandhi's teachings on an individual and a community.

Symbol of Gandhism: Moorthy embodies Gandhism in the novel. He renounces his caste privileges, practices non-violence, and leads the village in protests against British oppression. His character is a direct reflection of Gandhi's influence, making Gandhi the driving force behind the events in the story, even though he never appears directly.

3. Gandhi as a Symbol of Resistance

National Struggle: Gandhi's presence in the novel symbolizes the larger Indian independence movement. The villagers' fight against the British in Kanthapura is a microcosm of the national struggle led by Gandhi. The novel portrays how Gandhi's movement reached even the remotest parts of India, inspiring ordinary people to join the fight for freedom.

Invisible Leader: Although Gandhi is not physically present in Kanthapura, his influence is pervasive. The villagers often talk about Gandhi, share stories of his actions, and draw inspiration from his example. Gandhi's absence makes his presence even more powerful, as he becomes an almost mythical figure who guides the villagers from afar.

4. Gandhi's Impact on the Community

Social Reforms: Gandhi's teachings lead to significant social changes in Kanthapura. Moorthy advocates for the inclusion of the lower castes, influenced by Gandhi's emphasis on equality and social justice. This challenges the traditional social order of the village, showing how Gandhi's ideas were not just about political independence but also about transforming society.

Collective Consciousness: Gandhi's influence unites the villagers in their resistance against the British. He becomes the shared symbol of their hopes, aspirations, and struggles. The villagers' collective actions are driven by their belief in Gandhi's vision for India, making him the hidden protagonist who shapes the narrative.

Conclusion

Mahatma Gandhi's presence in Kanthapura is felt in every aspect of the story, even though he never appears as a character. His ideas and principles drive the plot, influence the characters, and symbolize the larger struggle for Indian independence. As the hidden protagonist, Gandhi's influence permeates the novel, making him the central figure around whom the entire narrative revolves. Through this portrayal, Raja Rao highlights the profound impact Gandhi had on ordinary Indians and their fight for freedom.

Q.4) Discuss the role of Moorthy in Raja Rao's Kanthapura.

Ans: Introduction: "for this section refer answer 1"

Main Content: Moorthy, the main character in Raja Rao's Kanthapura, is introduced in a meaningful way. Early in the novel, the narrator compares Dore, the "University graduate," with Moorthy.

He was not like Corner-House Moorthy, who had gone
through life like a noble cow, quiet, generous, serene,
deferent and brahminic, a very prince, I tell you.
We loved him, of course, as you will see, and if only
I had not been a daughterless widow, I should have
offered him a grand-daughter, if I had one.

Achakka's simple statement about Moorthy gives us a clear idea of his character in the novel. In Hindu culture, the cow is honored and seen as a nurturing mother because of its milk. Calling someone a "noble cow" is a high compliment. This description hints that Moorthy is kind, non-violent, and caring. Unlike the harsh Waterfall Venkamma and the greedy Bhatta, Moorthy is gentle, generous, and respectful. He is seen as a prince among the ordinary people of Kanthapura. The villagers believe he possesses all the right qualities and are eager to follow him as their leader in the Satyagraha Movement.

Moorthy is a selfless young man with no personal ambitions. He cares deeply for others, especially the poor villagers, the outcastes (pariahs), and the workers at the Skeffington Coffee Estate. Moorthy is also good at organizing. When Rachanna's family is evicted from the Coffee Estate for speaking out against oppression, Moorthy quickly finds them a new place to stay. However, when he visits their new home, he struggles with the hospitality offered by Rachanna's wife. His upbringing as a Brahmin makes him question if he's doing the right thing. He hesitates to enter their home and feels uneasy about drinking the glass of milk she offers. When his mother refuses to let him into her kitchen, fearing he will pollute it, he quietly accepts her decision without arguing.

In his analysis of the role of Moorthy, the central character of Kanthapura, Paranjape writes:

Kanthapura is really a novel about a village rather than about a single individual; nevertheless, Moorthy, the Brahmin protagonist of the villagers' struggle against the government, is a prototypal hero. Moorthy is the leader of a political uprising, but for him as for Gandhi whom he follows, politics Characters provides a way of life indistinguishable from a spiritual quest, Action is the way to the Absolute. In Gandhi, he finds what is Right Action. Thus, for him, becoming a "Gandhi man" is a deep spiritual experience . . .

Conclusion:

Moorthy is a deeply principled character who embodies the ideals of Gandhi and serves as a catalyst for change in his village. His dedication to social justice, his leadership in the Satyagraha movement, and his moral struggles make him a complex and inspiring figure in Kanthapura. Through Moorthy, Raja Rao portrays the impact of the independence movement on ordinary people and the ways in which Gandhi's teachings influenced the social fabric of India.

Q.5) Write an essay on Raja Rao's art of characterisation as revealed through Kanthapura.

Ans: Intoduction: "for this section refer answer 1 of this chapter"

Main Content: The art of characterization is the representation of characters in dramatic and narrative works, such as films, plays, or books, in a way that makes them seem real and natural. It can also refer to the methods used by writers to represent characters through description and speech.

In Kanthapura, the entire story is told from the perspective of Achakka, the narrator. This includes both the daily life of the village and the political struggle the villagers become involved in. The characters are also presented through Achakka's eyes. As a respected grandmother in the village, she knows most of the main characters personally and treats them like her own children and grandchildren. She enjoys describing them in familiar terms and often shares their family and professional backgrounds when introducing them to the reader.

Since Kanthapura is a first-person narrative, Raja Rao doesn't directly comment on the characters himself. Instead, any opinions or descriptions he wants to convey are expressed through Achakka. Occasionally, the characters make remarks about each other or reveal their personalities through their actions as reported by Achakka.

The characters' beliefs, behaviors, and interactions are shaped by traditional customs, caste distinctions, and religious practices. For instance, Moorthy's struggle with his Brahmin upbringing when interacting with the lower castes is a reflection of the rigid caste system prevalent in the society. This cultural authenticity adds layers to the characters, making them relatable and realistic.

Raja Rao portrays his characters as sharing a common nature that reflects the spirit of India. This shared identity is something that British writer E.M. Forster couldn't fully grasp, but Raja Rao clearly understands it and shows it through the characters in Kanthapura. Instead of focusing on their individual traits, Rao presents them as a group united by common traditions and goals.

For example, Moorthy, despite his revolutionary enthusiasm, cannot completely separate himself from tradition and shared beliefs. He follows Mahatma Gandhi's teachings and fights for the rights of the untouchables, but he still has doubts about whether it's right to mix with them. Similarly, Bhatta isn't portrayed as entirely bad; some villagers even see him as a "fine fellow." Rao encourages us to view Bhatta and others within the broader context of human nature. Even when depicting the "Red-man," the British master of the Skeffington Coffee Estate, Rao invites us to see him with humor and irony rather than anger.

Most writers might portray Mahatma Gandhi as a superhuman figure, someone beyond criticism and out of reach. While Jayaramachar, the Harikatha man, does present Gandhi as an incarnation of Lord Vishnu, the villagers of Kanthapura don't see him that way. They respect Gandhi for his teachings, leadership, and compassion for the oppressed, but that doesn't stop some of them from criticizing him or speaking negatively about him.

Raja Rao's villagers are practical people. When the consequences of the satyagraha hurt them, they blame Gandhi for it. Moorthy's mother, for instance, doesn't hesitate to curse Gandhi for influencing her son to associate with the Pariahs. This reaction is part of human nature—specifically, a mother's protective instinct, wanting her son to succeed in society rather than be treated as an outcast.

Conclusion:

Raja Rao's art of characterization in Kanthapura is deeply intertwined with the novel's themes of social change, tradition, and the struggle for independence. By creating characters that are both culturally authentic and symbolically rich, Rao not only tells the story of a village but also explores the broader Indian experience during a crucial period in history. The characters in Kanthapura are memorable not just for their individuality but also for what they represent in the larger narrative of India's fight for freedom.

Q.6) Discuss the use of various Myths and Symbolism in Raja Rao's novel Kanthapura.

Ans: Intoduction: "for this section refer answer 1 of this chapter"

Main Content: Raja Rao's Kanthapura is a novel rich in myths and symbolism, which are integral to its narrative structure and thematic depth. These elements are not just decorative but serve to connect the local village life to the larger cultural and spiritual context of India. The use of myths and symbolism in Kanthapura reflects the blending of tradition and modernity, the sacred and the political, and the personal with the collective.

Myths in Kanthapura:

Sthalapurana (Legend of the Land):

The novel itself is structured like a sthalapurana, which is a traditional legend or mythological story about the origins and significance of a particular place. Achakka, the narrator, tells the story of Kanthapura as if it is a sacred history, intertwining the daily lives of the villagers with the spiritual significance of their land. This framing gives the novel a mythical dimension, elevating the village's struggles to the level of epic battles.

Goddess Kenchamma:

Kenchamma, the village goddess, is a powerful symbol in the novel. The villagers believe that Kenchamma is their protector who saved them from ancient demons, and they regularly offer prayers and sacrifices to her. She symbolizes the strength and resilience of the village community, and her presence in the story reinforces the connection between the villagers' spiritual beliefs and their everyday lives. Kenchamma also represents the idea of divine justice, which parallels the villagers' fight against colonial oppression.

Mythological References:

Throughout the novel, there are numerous references to Hindu mythology. For example, Moorthy is often compared to Lord Rama, who is a symbol of virtue and justice, while the colonial forces are likened to the demons (asuras) that Rama had to fight. These mythological parallels help to frame the independence movement as a cosmic struggle between good and evil, aligning the villagers' cause with the forces of righteousness.

Symbolism in Kanthapura:

Gandhi as a Symbol:

Mahatma Gandhi, although not a direct character in the novel, is a pervasive symbol. He is portrayed as a living incarnation of the divine, a figure who embodies the values of truth, non-violence, and justice. The villagers view Gandhi as a savior figure, much like a god or an avatar, sent to deliver them from the clutches of British rule. Gandhi's spinning wheel (charkha) also becomes a symbol of self-reliance and resistance against colonialism.

Moorthy as a Symbol of Change:

Moorthy, the protagonist, symbolizes the new India that Gandhi is trying to create. He represents the blending of tradition and modernity, as he tries to bring Gandhian ideals into the village while still respecting its customs. Moorthy's journey from being an ordinary villager to a leader in the Satyagraha movement symbolizes the awakening of the Indian masses and their readiness to fight for independence.

The Village as a Microcosm:

Kanthapura itself is symbolic of India. The village's struggles, divisions, and eventual unity mirror the larger national struggle for independence. The social hierarchy within the village, with its rigid caste divisions, symbolizes the entrenched social inequalities in India. The breaking down of these barriers through the influence of Gandhi's teachings reflects the broader social changes that were beginning to take place in Indian society.

Nature and the Landscape:

The natural landscape of Kanthapura, with its hills, rivers, and fields, is symbolically linked to the characters and their emotions. The River Himavathy, for instance, is not just a physical presence but also a symbol of purity and continuity, representing the flow of life in the village. The land itself is depicted as sacred, reinforcing the idea that the villagers' fight for independence is also a fight to protect their holy ground.

Kenchamma's Shrine:

The shrine of the goddess Kenchamma, where the villagers gather to pray and discuss important matters, symbolizes the unity and collective identity of the village. It serves as a focal point for both religious worship and political action, blending the sacred with the secular.

Conclusion:

The use of myths and symbolism in Kanthapura serves to deepen the reader's understanding of the novel's themes and characters. By integrating traditional myths with the contemporary political struggle, Raja Rao creates a narrative that is both timeless and relevant to the historical moment in which it is set. The symbols in the novel—whether they be characters, objects, or places—are all connected to the larger idea of India's fight for independence and the transformation of its society. Through these elements, Rao not only tells the story of a small village but also captures the spirit of an entire nation in the throes of change.

Q.7) What is the significance of the Skeffington Coffee Estate in the overall account of the village in Raja Rao's Kanthapura?

Ans: Intoduction: "for this section refer answer 1 of this chapter"

Main Content:

In Kanthapura, Raja Rao contrasts the village with the Skeffington Coffee Estate. The village represents Indian values, traditions, faith, and the influence of Mahatma Gandhi's teachings. In contrast, the coffee estate symbolizes British rule, colonial control, and the exploitation of the Indian people.

The Skeffington Coffee Estate is a massive area, stretching from Babbur Mound on one side to Kenchamma Hill on the other, and extending up to the jungles of Horse-head Hill. No one knew exactly how big it was or when it was established, but it was said to cover at least ten thousand acres. Some villagers in Kanthapura remembered hearing about the Hunter Sahib, who used his hunting skills to start the plantation. Over time, the estate grew larger and larger, eventually spreading to all the surrounding hills.

More and more coolies came from the area below the Ghats, speaking Tamil or Telugu, and they brought their families with them. These half-naked, starving workers marched past the Kenchamma Temple and headed to the Skeffington Estate. They carried their belongings bundled up in their arms or on their shoulders.

The Sahib's overseer, or maistri, had traveled to distant villages to let people know about job opportunities at the estate. He promised a quarter of a rupee per day for men and an eighth of a rupee for women. Despite the low pay, the coolies came eagerly because there had been a drought in their area. The maistri lured them with the promise of an advance of a rupee and plenty of food on the estate. He also told them that the British owner of the estate was kind and generous.

So, the coolies left their homes, took a tram part of the way, and walked the rest on foot. Once they arrived at the estate, the maistri closed the gates behind them. He introduced them to the estate owner, telling them they would be treated well if they worked hard but would be beaten if they didn't. The coolies soon realized they had become virtual prisoners and slaves of the British owner.

Or

In Raja Rao's Kanthapura, the Skeffington Coffee Estate is highly significant for several reasons:

Symbol of Colonial Oppression: The estate represents the harsh realities of British colonial rule in India. It stands as a powerful symbol of exploitation and the economic control exerted by the British over Indian laborers. The conditions at the estate highlight the stark contrast between the colonial rulers and the oppressed workers.

Contrast with Village Life: Kanthapura embodies traditional Indian values, spirituality, and the influence of Gandhi's non-violent resistance. The estate, in contrast, represents the harsh, impersonal nature of colonial exploitation. This contrast underscores the tension between the village's cultural and spiritual values and the brutal realities of colonialism.

Catalyst for Resistance: The estate's mistreatment of the coolies becomes a key trigger for the villagers' involvement in the Gandhian freedom struggle. The workers' harsh conditions and exploitation galvanize the villagers to support the Gandhian cause, illustrating how local injustices can spark broader political activism.

Representation of Social Injustice: The estate mirrors the broader socio-economic inequalities of colonial India. It reflects the systemic injustice and dehumanization faced by Indian workers under British rule, providing a microcosm of the larger social issues prevalent at the time.

Integration of Gandhian Principles: The estate's plight and the subsequent involvement of Kanthapura's villagers in protesting against it bring Gandhian principles into a new context. The struggle at the estate helps spread Gandhi's ideas of non-cooperation and civil disobedience beyond the village and into the realm of colonial exploitation.

Conclusion:

The Skeffington Coffee Estate is significant in Kanthapura as it contrasts sharply with the village's ideals, symbolizes colonial exploitation, and acts as a catalyst for the Gandhian resistance movement. Its presence in the narrative highlights.

Q.7) Discuss the importance of Harikatha in Raja Rao's Kanthapura.

Ans: Intoduction: "for this section refer answer 1 of this chapter"

Main Content:

In Raja Rao's Kanthapura, 'Harikatha' holds significant cultural and narrative importance. Harikatha is a religious practice that devout Hindus are expected to organize or attend from time to time. It can take place either at home or in a temple. The term "Harikatha" literally means "the story of

Hari," who is another name for the god Vishnu. During Harikatha, the story of Vishnu or another god is told, accompanied by singing and dancing.

Entire villages or communities, like those in Kanthapura, participate in Harikatha. It creates a strong sense of religious devotion and brings spiritual merit to those involved. Just as in other parts of India, Harikatha is very popular in Kanthapura. Whenever a Harikatha is organized, all the villagers eagerly gather at the temple to take part.

Here's a discussion of its significance:

Cultural Tradition: Harikatha is a traditional form of storytelling in South India, combining narration with music and drama to convey religious and moral tales. In Kanthapura, it reflects the rich cultural heritage of the village and serves as a means to communicate important social and political messages through a familiar and respected medium.

Narrative Style: The novel itself is narrated in a style reminiscent of Harikatha. Achakka, the narrator, recounts the story of Kanthapura in a way that mirrors the storytelling techniques of Harikatha, with a flowing, rhythmic narrative and a focus on oral tradition. This style helps to emphasize the oral and communal aspects of village life and aligns with the cultural practices of the characters.

Transmission of Values: Through the Harikatha tradition, Raja Rao is able to convey the values and teachings of Mahatma Gandhi in a manner that resonates with the villagers. The stories of Gandhi's principles, such as non-violence and civil disobedience, are presented in a way that is accessible and engaging to the rural audience, integrating these values into the cultural and religious framework of the village.

Community Engagement: Harikatha serves as a medium for community engagement and unity in the novel. The villagers gather for these storytelling sessions, which foster a sense of communal identity and collective action. The Harikatha sessions in Kanthapura are not only entertainment but also a platform for discussing social issues and rallying support for the Gandhian movement.

Symbolism: The use of Harikatha symbolizes the blending of traditional and modern values. It shows how ancient storytelling methods can be adapted to convey contemporary issues and ideas. The novel uses this symbolism to bridge the gap between traditional Indian life and the modern political struggle for independence.

Emotional Impact: The Harikatha sessions in the novel often evoke strong emotions and moral reflections. By integrating these traditional narratives into the story, Raja Rao enhances the emotional depth and moral resonance of the novel, making the political and social struggles of the characters more poignant and relatable.

Conclusion: Harikatha in Kanthapura is significant as it embodies the cultural and oral traditions of the village, serves as a narrative tool that reflects the storytelling style of the novel, and helps convey the teachings of Gandhi in a culturally relevant way. It also symbolizes the fusion of traditional values with modern political movements and strengthens community bonds.

Block 4 – Clear light of day

Scan the QR code to watch video

CHAPTER THIRTEEN

About Anita Desai: Career and Works

Anita Desai (born Anita Mazumdar on 24 June 1937) is an Indian author and a former professor of humanities at the Massachusetts Institute of Technology (MIT).

She has been nominated for the Booker Prize three times, and won the Sahitya Akademi Award in 1978 for her novel Fire on the Mountain. Desai also received the Guardian Prize for her book The Village by the Sea in 1983.

Some of her other well-known works include The Peacock, Voices in the City, and a collection of short stories titled Games at Twilight.

She is a member of the advisory board of Lalit Kala Akademi and a Fellow of the Royal Society of Literature in London. Since 2020, she has held the title of Companion of Literature.

CHAPTER FOURTEEN

Overview of the novel "Clear Light of Day"

Clear Light of Day by Anita Desai, first published in 1980, tells the story of the Das siblings—Bim, Raja, Tara, and Baba—whose lives are intertwined with the history of Old Delhi and the legacy of a post-partition India. Narrated by the elderly Achakka, the novel shifts between 1980 and the siblings' childhood in the 1930s and 1940s at their family home on Bela Road. The story centers on Moorthy-like transformation as the family confronts internal tensions, lost opportunities, and deep-seated resentments amid the backdrop of India's independence and partition. With themes of family bonds, forgiveness, and the impact of childhood, the narrative follows Bim, who remains unmarried and burdened with responsibility, as she struggles with bitterness over family sacrifices and unresolved conflicts. Ultimately, through an evolving process of self-reflection and reconciliation—highlighted by a long-suppressed letter from Raja and heartfelt apologies—the siblings begin to mend their fractured relationships, suggesting a renewed hope for familial unity in modern India.

CHAPTER FIFTEEN

Questions & Answers

Q.1) Critically comment on the structure of Clear Light of Day.

Ans: Introduction: Clear Light of Day is a novel written by Indian author Anita Desai, first published in 1980. Desai, a three-time Booker Prize finalist, sets the story in Old Delhi and explores the tensions within a post-partition Indian family. The novel begins with the characters as adults and gradually goes back into their earlier lives. While the main theme focuses on the importance of family, other key themes include the power of forgiveness, the influence of childhood, and the role of women, especially as mothers and caretakers, in modern India.

Main Content: The structure of Anita Desai's Clear Light of Day is both unconventional and intricate, contributing significantly to its thematic depth. The novel is divided into four parts, which reflect different time periods in the lives of the Das family. The narrative begins in the present (1980), then shifts back to the summer of 1947, moves further back to the siblings' childhood, and finally returns to the present with a more hopeful perspective. This non-linear structure is central to the novel's exploration of time, memory, and relationships, allowing Desai to weave together past and present seamlessly.

In an interview, Desai mentioned that Clear Light of Day was her attempt to write a "four-dimensional piece" that captures how a family's life moves back and forth through time. The fourth dimension, as Desai explained, is time itself. This approach mirrors the structure of T.S. Eliot's Four Quartets, which Desai admired. In both works, time plays a dual role, as both a force of destruction and preservation. The novel's central theme explores the paradox between change and continuity, illustrating how time shapes relationships and memories within the family.

The four-dimensional structure of Clear Light of Day allows Anita Desai to present reality from multiple perspectives. Events in the novel do not follow a linear order; instead, Desai uses the stream-of-consciousness technique to connect events through imagery rather than logic. She serves as an omniscient observer in the narrative, offering a third-person perspective that provides readers with a comprehensive view of the characters' inner worlds. This technique enables the story to flow fluidly between time periods and emotions, giving deeper insight into the characters' thoughts and feelings.

Asha Kanwar points out that in Clear Light of Day, there is a threefold portrayal of time: the passage of moments or hours, the transition from youth to old age, and the impact of historical events. Through Tara and Bim's memories, we are taken back to their childhood and watch their journey into adulthood and middle age. The novel also explores how time shapes nations. Rather than celebrating India's independence, Desai mourns the partition, not for its political significance, but because of the violence and irrational hatred that came in its aftermath.

Followings are the way in which Anita Desai has structured her novel The Clear Light of Day.

Non-linear Narrative: The novel avoids a straightforward, chronological progression. Instead, it moves back and forth in time, reflecting the characters' memories, especially those of Bim and Tara. This mirrors the fluid nature of memory, showing how the past continues to influence the present. By doing this, Desai blurs the boundaries between past and present, highlighting the continuity of emotions and experiences over time.

Stream of Consciousness: Desai employs a stream of consciousness technique, linking events through the characters' thoughts and reflections rather than in a rational, sequential manner. This technique allows for a deeper psychological exploration of the characters, particularly Bim and Tara, as they grapple with their shared past and the unresolved tensions in their relationship. The fragmented structure mirrors the fragmented memories and emotions that the characters experience.

Time as a Theme: Desai uses the novel's structure to emphasize time as both a destructive and preserving force. Echoing the influence of T.S. Eliot's Four Quartets, time is portrayed as cyclical, affecting both individuals and nations. The personal timelines of the Das family are intertwined with India's historical timeline, especially the partition of 1947. Desai uses this historical backdrop to reflect on the personal upheavals within the Das family, suggesting that time and history shape personal identities and family dynamics.

Paradox of Change and Continuity: The novel's structure underscores the paradox between change and continuity. Despite the passing years, certain aspects of the Das family's life remain unchanged. The family home in Old Delhi, for example, remains a constant symbol, anchoring the siblings to their past even as they grow older and their lives diverge. Desai's choice to return to the present in the final section allows for a reflection on how the past, no matter how distant, continues to exert influence on the present.

Multiple Perspectives: Through its four-part structure, the novel presents events from multiple perspectives. The readers are given insight into the inner thoughts of different characters, mainly Bim and Tara, which helps in understanding their psychological complexity. This structural choice emphasizes the subjective nature of memory and how the same events are perceived differently by different individuals.

Conclusion: The structure of Clear Light of Day is essential to its exploration of memory, time, and identity. By rejecting a linear narrative and employing a fragmented, cyclical structure, Desai creates a rich, multilayered narrative that reflects the complexity of family relationships and the enduring influence of the past.

Q.2) What role does music play in Clear Light Of Day?

Ans: Introduction: "for this section refer answer 1 of this chapter"

Main Content: In Clear Light of Day, music plays a significant and symbolic role, weaving through the narrative to underscore key themes such as memory, time, and the emotional states of the characters. Music serves as a link between past and present, as well as a means of communication, particularly for Baba, and it reflects the characters' inner emotions and their relationships with one another. Thus, Anita Desai's Clear Light of Day, is dominated by sound. The novel begins with the koels singing:

The koels began to call before daylight. Their voices rang out from the dark trees like an arrangement of bells, calling and echoing each other's calls, mocking and enticing each other into ever higher and shriller calls. More and more joined in as the sun rose. . . . . .

Interestingly, the novel ends with Mulk's teacher singing Iqbal's poetry. Desai uses music to highlight the main theme of the novel. Syed Amanuddin points out that, between the sweet songs of the koels (birds) and the musical performance of Iqbal's poetry, "we also hear the scratches and squeaks of old records." These "scratches and squeaks" represent the tensions and struggles of a nation falling apart and a family breaking up.

In Clear Light of Day, music acts as a remedy for the deeper emotional disturbances of the characters. Most of the people in the novel are connected to music in some way, and it reflects their inner struggles. Since the novel has a psychological focus, Desai often uses music to express the thoughts, emotions, and feelings of her characters, providing insight into their inner worlds.

Music is essential to the character of Baba, the youngest Das sibling, who has a developmental disability and communicates little through words. His obsession with his gramophone and old records symbolizes his way of connecting to the world. Baba listens repeatedly to the same songs, particularly from the 1940s and 1950s, indicating his desire for constancy and routine in a world that often seems overwhelming to him. His music becomes a comfort, insulating him from the changes happening around him and in the family.

Music in Clear Light of Day serves as a bridge to the past, evoking memories for the characters, particularly Bim and Tara. The songs that Baba plays evoke memories of their childhood, transporting Bim and Tara back to a time when their family life, though flawed, was still whole. This nostalgia reflects the novel's broader themes of time and memory—how the past, though inaccessible, continues to shape the present.

Music, particularly Baba's old records, becomes a symbol of the Das family's past, both its warmth and its dysfunction. The songs represent a time when the family was together, yet they also reflect the stagnation and the inability of the characters to move beyond their shared history. For Bim, the music serves as a constant reminder of the burden she bears in keeping the family together, while for Tara, it evokes a mixture of guilt and longing for a lost sense of belonging.

In Clear Light of Day, music symbolizes a deep, intuitive understanding of oneself and the reality hidden beneath appearances. Bim, through her "inner eyes," recognizes a sense of continuity in history—her own, her family's, and across time. This connection is not restrictive but provides a foundation, like soil nurturing roots that grow outward while drawing from the same source. Bim sees this hidden source as the essence of her being and that of her siblings.

The relationship between the old Guru and Mulk represents a meaningful link between past and present, as well as between generations. The song they share becomes a bridge, blending poetry and melody, rational and emotional expression. When the Guru sings a verse of Iqbal, both Bim and Baba respond to it, bringing them emotionally closer.

In the final scene, the music symbolizes Bim's reintegration with her family, society, and culture, as she recognizes unity within herself and the world around her. The song highlights the merging of different elements, both within Bim and in her relationships, bringing harmony to what was once divided.

Conclusion: Music in Clear Light of Day acts as a powerful motif, representing memory, emotional expression, and the complex dynamics within the Das family. It highlights both the comfort and the trap of living in the past, illustrating the characters' struggles to move forward while remaining tethered to their shared history.

Q.3) Enunciate Anita Desai's great contribution to the Indian - English novel.

Ans: Introduction: "for this section refer answer 1 of this chapter"

Main Content: Anita Desai is considered one of the major voices in modern Indian-English fiction. In his selection of women writers, K.R. Srinivasa Iyengar included an analysis of Desai's work and noted that her first two novels, Cry, the Peacock and Voices in the City, have added a new dimension to the achievements of Indian women writers. This new dimension takes on multiple forms, reflecting Desai's unique approach to themes and storytelling in Indian literature.

1. In Desai's novels, the focus shifts from society as a whole to individual people. Unlike authors like U.R. Anantha Murthy, who emphasize social issues more than characters, and Mulk Raj Anand, who focuses on economic and social backgrounds, Desai highlights individual characters and their inner thoughts and feelings. Her first two novels, Cry, the Peacock and Voices in the City, are credited with introducing psychological novels into Indian-English literature.

2. Desai's female characters show a "creative release of feminine sensibility" that emerged after World War II. Unlike ordinary women who struggle with daily survival, her characters come from affluent families and don't have to worry about basic needs. Instead, they focus on their emotional lives. Desai delves into the inner world of her heroines, revealing the deeper forces shaping their feminine sensibility.

3. Anita Desai's novels make significant contributions to Indian-English fiction by exploring the themes of self-discovery and freedom. Her works focus on the journey of self-exploration, a theme that runs

through all her novels. This focus on self-discovery, particularly for female characters, was quite innovative in the fiction of the 1960s.

4. Anita Desai focuses on her characters' inner lives rather than their actions. To portray their emotional depth, she uses the stream of consciousness technique. This approach helps capture the subtle details of their feelings through careful use of language and imagery.

5. Anita Desai's novels showcase a new type of female protagonist emerging in the 1970s. Unlike the traditional, self-sacrificing character like Rukmini from Kamala Markandaya's Nectar in a Sieve, Desai's heroines are intelligent and rebellious women who seek personal fulfillment and are ready to face life's challenges. Maya, the heroine of The Peacock (1963), stands out by rejecting traditional ideas of ideal womanhood. She is portrayed as neurotic, sensitive, and imaginative, offering a fresh perspective in the fiction of the late 1960s. This focus on the inner life of women was a significant departure from previous portrayals.

Conclusion: Desai's work has played a crucial role in shaping the Indian-English novel, influencing both contemporary and future writers. Her contributions have enriched the literary landscape, adding depth and diversity to the genre.

Q.4) What is the role of Baba in the novel 'Clear Light of Day' ?

Ans: Introduction: "for this section refer answer 1 of this chapter"

Main Content: In Anita Desai's novel Clear Light of Day, Baba plays a crucial role, symbolizing several key themes and dynamics within the story. Baba and Bim are the two'people who continue to live in their

childhood home in Old Delhi around which the novel unfolds itself. He is described by Desai in the novel as:

He looked like a delicate sculpture made of white marble or milk. Or maybe like a spider's web, barely visible, or just some moonlight scattered across the bed. His long, thin frame in white clothes seemed almost unreal, with no strong personality or noticeable traits.

Baba's role in the novel is significant despite his seeming lack of presence. His character is highlighted by the music from the forties, like "Smoke Gets in Your Eyes," "Don't Fence Me In," and "Donkey's Serenade," which reflect the confusion, lack of clarity, and feelings of entrapment experienced by the central characters.

Each character feels trapped in some way: Baba is limited by his autism, Bim is constrained by her life circumstances, Tara is burdened by guilt, and Raja feels trapped by the family home. Mira Masi is caught by poverty and later alcoholism, and the Ali family suffers because of the partition riots. The sense of directionlessness and the need for wisdom in the Das household mirrors the situation of independent India. Desai underscores this by describing Baba's face as "blanched, like a plant grown underground or in deepest shade." This imagery symbolizes both the Das children's struggle to handle life after their parents' departure and the nation's struggle to deal with its postcolonial reality.

Baba's music in Clear Light of Day plays a crucial role beyond just setting the mood. The novel's structure resembles a well-composed musical piece, with music being central to the story. It contrasts with the internal discord and struggles of the characters. The harmony of the music contrasts with the disarray and tension that the characters experience, highlighting their emotional conflicts and inner turmoil.

Baba plays a key role in Clear Light of Day because his existence leads to the introduction of Mira Masi, an important character. The narrator reveals that Baba was born when his parents were quite old. This detail suggests that Baba, conceived in their later years, lacked the vitality and energy of his older siblings. It's as though all their strength and will had already been given to the other children, leaving little for him.

Baba's most important role in Clear Light of Day is his relationship with Bim. He relies on her for care, and she needs him as well. Bim tells Tara that Baba was the one who stayed with her after everyone else left. Their mutual dependence is clearly shown when Jaya explains to Tara why Bim is so attached to Baba, even as Tara worries about Bim. Baba is also present with Bim during the musical evening at the Misras' house. There, as she listens to Mulk Misra and his guru, she gains new insights into her own life. A significant turning point for Bim occurs earlier when she vents her frustration with Raja onto Baba. She reviews her tight finances and suggests that Baba should move in with Raja.

Baba's presence is also tied to the family's tradition and cultural heritage. His connection to the past and to the family's history is underscored by his attachment to old music and memories, bridging the gap between past and present. Baba's condition and his interactions with other characters, especially with Bim, drive the narrative forward. His emotional needs and the care he requires are catalysts for the exploration of family relationships and individual identities.

Conclusion: Baba's role in Clear Light of Day is multifaceted, contributing to the exploration of themes such as familial duty, the weight of the past, and the impact of personal and historical changes on individual lives.

Q.5) Comment upon Anita Desai's use of 'Imagery' in 'Clear Light of Day'.

Ans: Introduction: "for this section refer answer 1 of this chapter"

Main Content: Powerful uses of imagery lend richness to Desai's novels.Nature which Includes animals, plants and birds, has a strong presence in almost all her works.

Anita Desai uses vivid and symbolic imagery in Clear Light of Day to enhance the emotional and thematic depth of the novel. The imagery Desai employs reflects the inner worlds of her characters and the complexities of their relationships, often serving as a bridge between the past and present, memory and reality.

Baba, the autistic son, in Clear Light of Day is described as a "harmless garden spider"

Desai's Clear Light of Day is full of different types of imagery. The novel starts with the sound of koels singing: "Their voices rang out from the dark trees like bells, calling and echoing each other. More and more joined in as the sun rose..." It ends with Mulk's guru singing Iqbal's poetry. Syed Amanuddin points out that between the koels' song and the guru's poetry, "we hear the scratches and squeaks of old records". These scratches and squeaks represent the tensions and problems of both a family and a nation falling apart. The sandstorm at the beginning of Part IV symbolizes the emotional turmoil that is about to take place between the Das sisters.

Nature and Decay: The imagery of the Das family garden, which is unkempt and overgrown, symbolizes the emotional neglect and decay in the relationships within the family. The garden reflects Bim's state of mind, her burden of responsibilities, and her struggle to keep things alive despite their deterioration. Similarly, the old house, which has remained unchanged over the years, represents the stagnation and emotional paralysis that the characters, particularly Bim, experience.

Music and Sound: Desai uses music as a recurring image throughout the novel. Baba's old gramophone, with its "scratches and squeaks," reflects the disharmony in the family. The nostalgic songs from the past evoke both a sense of continuity and a reminder of the tensions and unresolved conflicts. The imagery of sound, particularly in the form of music, becomes a metaphor for the characters' emotional lives and the fragmented nation of India post-Partition.

Water and Time: Water imagery is often used to symbolize the passage of time and the fluidity of memory. The River Jumna, which flows near the Das family home, is a constant reminder of the past, carrying with it memories of childhood and youth. Desai's imagery of flowing water serves as a metaphor for time, highlighting both its destructive and healing capacities.

Light and Darkness: Light and darkness are central images in the novel. The title itself, Clear Light of Day, suggests the possibility of clarity and understanding, but this light often reveals uncomfortable truths. Bim's perception of time and history is illuminated by this "clear light," but it also exposes the pain and scars of the past. Darkness, on the other hand, symbolizes the unknown and the suppressed emotions that the characters struggle to confront.

Conclusion:

Through this rich imagery, Desai creates a layered narrative that mirrors the emotional and psychological states of her characters, while also reflecting broader themes of memory, time, and history.

Q.6) Discuss the importance of Bim and Tara relationship in Anita Desai ˝s novel "Clear Light of Day."

Ans: Introduction: "for this section refer answer 1 of this chapter"

Main Content: The relationship between Bim and Tara, the two Das sisters, is central to Anita Desai's Clear Light of Day. Everything in the novel revolves around their bond. Although they are siblings, their distinct personalities create tension in their relationship. This complexity is highlighted in a comment made by Jaya, one of the Misra sisters, to Tara:

"Bim has her own mind," she said. "Bim always did. You were always so different, you two sisters."

Tara, however, disagrees: "We're not really," she said. "We may seem to be—but we have everything in common. That makes us one. No one else knows all we share, Bim and I."

This conversation captures the dual nature of their relationship—both connected by shared experiences but divided by their contrasting personalities.

Bim, short for Bimla, is the older of the two Das sisters. She is unmarried and works as a history teacher at a local college. Desai describes her as "grey and heavy now and not so unlike their mother in appearance" . After their Aunt Mira Masi falls ill, Bim takes on the role of a surrogate mother, caring for her siblings.

Tara, the younger sister, is depicted as "a languid little girl, listless, a dawdler" . She is married to an Indian Foreign Service officer and has two daughters. Desai skillfully highlights the differences between the sisters through subtle details, such as how they dress, reflecting their contrasting personalities. Desai uses this sibling relationship to explore themes of identity, responsibility, and emotional growth, all while reflecting the larger backdrop of post-Partition India.

The relationship between Bim and Tara forms the emotional core of Anita Desai's Clear Light of Day. Their bond, though deeply rooted in shared history and family, is fraught with tension and complexity. Desai uses this sibling relationship to explore themes of identity, responsibility, and emotional growth, all while reflecting the larger backdrop of post-Partition India.

Contrasting Personalities

Bim, the elder sister, is strong, independent, and practical. She shoulders the responsibilities of the family, caring for their autistic brother, Baba, and taking charge after the death of their parents. She remains unmarried, dedicating herself to her teaching career and her familial duties. On the other hand, Tara, the younger sister, is more submissive, emotional, and passive. She escapes the burdens of family life by marrying Bakul, an Indian Foreign Service officer, and moves away, distancing herself from the difficult realities at home.

The Emotional Distance

Though bound by their shared past, the sisters are emotionally distanced. Bim resents Tara for abandoning her to bear the weight of responsibility, while Tara feels guilty for leaving Bim alone with the burden of their family. This distance reflects their divergent life paths. Bim's bitterness and independence contrast with Tara's desire for escape and reconciliation. However, Tara constantly seeks Bim's approval, reflecting her emotional dependence on her older sister.

A Metaphor for Change and Continuity

Their relationship also mirrors the larger themes of change and continuity in the novel. While Tara represents change and the desire for escape and personal freedom, Bim embodies continuity and stability, remaining rooted in the family home. Their relationship symbolizes the conflict between the need to preserve family ties and the desire to break free from their limitations.

Mutual Dependency

Despite their differences, the bond between Bim and Tara is ultimately one of mutual dependency. Bim is outwardly strong, but as the novel progresses, we see that she is emotionally vulnerable and deeply affected by her family's fragmentation. Tara, despite her distance, feels a strong connection to Bim and seeks her forgiveness and understanding. Their shared childhood memories and experiences create a unique understanding between them that no one else can share.

Reconciliation and Healing

By the end of the novel, Bim begins to understand the importance of forgiveness and letting go of the past. She realizes that her anger towards Tara and Raja is only holding her back, and she begins to open herself up to the possibility of reconciling with her family. Tara, on her part, continues to reach out to Bim, demonstrating her desire to reconnect. Their relationship, while strained, ultimately embodies the potential for healing and the enduring nature of familial bonds.

Conclusion

The relationship between Bim and Tara in Clear Light of Day is central to the novel's exploration of family, memory, and personal identity. Through their contrasting personalities and emotional conflicts, Desai delves into the complexities of sibling relationships, capturing both the pain and the love that bind them together. Their bond, while fraught with tension, ultimately serves as a testament to the enduring power of family and the possibility of reconciliation.

Q.7) Comment upon the importance of the character of Raja in Desai's Clear Light of Day.

Ans: Introduction: "for this section refer answer 1 of this chapter"

Main Content: Raja is a key character in Clear Light of Day, and Anita Desai uses him for several important reasons. In the first part of the novel, set in the present, Raja is physically absent as he is already married to Benazir, the daughter of their neighbor and landlord, Hyder Ali, and lives in Hyderabad. The relationship between Raja and Hyder Ali plays a significant role in the novel. Through the kind way Hyder Ali supports Raja and the trust Raja has in him, Desai shows the peaceful and harmonious relationship between Hindus and Muslims in India before the partition.

Raja represents ambition and the desire to escape the confines of the family and the decaying Das household. He is portrayed as intelligent, charismatic, and dreamy, with a strong interest in Urdu poetry and culture. Raja's fascination with the Hyder Ali family, their wealth, and their sophisticated lifestyle becomes a defining aspect of his character. His admiration for Urdu poetry and the aristocratic Hyder Ali family reflects his yearning for a world beyond the limitations of his own middle-class upbringing.

Raja's decision to leave the family home and eventually marry Hyder Ali's daughter, Benazir, signifies his escape from the life of stagnation that Bim ultimately accepts. He distances himself from the responsibilities of family life and seeks a life of luxury and refinement, leaving Bim to shoulder the burdens of caring for Baba and maintaining the family home.

Raja's departure from the Das family creates a deep rift between him and Bim. She resents him for abandoning her and for his perceived betrayal of the family's unity. The strain on their relationship is exacerbated when Raja inherits the Hyder Ali family's properties and sends a formal letter regarding the rent for the Das family home. This letter, which Bim interprets as cold and indifferent, symbolizes the emotional distance between them and represents Raja's complete disconnection from the family.

For Bim, Raja's behavior serves as a reminder of the fragmentation within the family and the loss of the closeness they once shared. His actions deepen her feelings of bitterness and rejection, as she feels that Raja has not only abandoned the family but has also betrayed the values they were raised with. Tara, on the other hand, is less judgmental of Raja, though she too feels the effects of his absence.

Raja's character can also be interpreted as a metaphor for post-Partition India. His fascination with Urdu poetry and the Muslim culture of the Hyder Alis reflects the complexities of identity in a newly divided nation. Raja's departure to the Muslim household and his eventual inheritance of their property can be seen as a reflection of the cultural and religious tensions of the time, as well as the shifting loyalties and divisions caused by Partition.

In this sense, Raja's journey mirrors the disintegration of the Das family, much like the broader disintegration of India during Partition. Just as the country grapples with its newfound independence and the pain of division, the Das family struggles with the loss of unity and the emotional distance between its members.

Although Raja is physically absent for much of the novel, his influence on Bim is profound. Her anger and disappointment toward him act as significant obstacles to her emotional growth and healing. The turning point for Bim comes when she confronts her feelings toward Raja and realizes that holding on to her resentment is preventing her from moving forward. Through her eventual reconciliation with the past and with Raja, Bim learns to forgive and accept the imperfections of her family.

Conclusion

Raja's character in Clear Light of Day is essential to the novel's exploration of family, memory, and personal growth. His actions, though largely offstage, have a lasting impact on Bim and serve as a catalyst for her emotional journey. Raja represents both the ambition to escape and the emotional consequences of abandoning familial responsibilities. His role in the novel highlights the complexities of sibling relationships and the lasting effects of personal choices on family dynamics.

Q.8) The country's partition parallels the partition of the Das family in Clear Light of Day. Comment.

Ans: Introduction: "for this section refer answer 1 of this chapter"

In Anita Desai's Clear Light of Day, while the novel refers to the late 1930s and a few days in the 1970s, it mainly takes place during the summer of 1947. Unlike other writers who focus on the political events of 1947, Desai doesn't make them the central theme. Instead, she focuses on the history of the Das family, showing how their personal struggles mirror the national turmoil.

The partition of India symbolizes the breakup of the Das family. Just as post-independence India struggled to find its new identity, the Das children also face a crisis connected to their past. Each of them has grown in different ways, with separate goals and interests. Bim's struggle with her past reflects modern India's challenge of defining a new role while still being connected to history. Ironically, when Bim finally understands her importance within her family, she finds comfort not in recent events but in a time when there was harmony between Hindus and Muslims, a period that represented unity and wholeness.

In Midnight's Children, Salman Rushdie also blends family history with national politics, but he and Anita Desai take different approaches in how they explore these themes. Desai uses her characters' interactions, especially through dialogue and memories, to subtly build a sense of history.

Her portrayal is indirect, revealing the past through personal relationships and emotions. On the other hand, Rushdie's narrator, Saleem, is more explicit and self-aware. He reflects on the nature of memory and history, using direct statements like, "There is no escape from past acquaintance. What you were is forever who you are." Toward the end, he sums up his identity by saying, "I am the sum total of everything that went before me," capturing his belief that history and personal experience are inseparable.

In Clear Light of Day, the events of 1947 are seen through the eyes of the Das sisters, particularly Tara, who reflects on how life seems to move in sudden, dramatic shifts rather than a smooth flow. Tara observes that life often has long periods of calm, where nothing significant seems to happen, and then, without warning, major events or changes occur. She compares this to the summer of 1947, a time of great upheaval, referring to it as one of those pivotal moments in life. This reflects how personal and national histories intertwine, as the Partition of India shapes both the country's fate and the lives of the Das family.

Block 5 - Midnight's Children

Scan the QR code to watch video

About Salman Rushdie: Career and Works

Salman Rushdie is a prominent Indian-born British-American author known for his imaginative storytelling that often blends magical realism with historical and cultural themes. Born on June 19, 1947, in Mumbai, India, Rushdie has written several critically acclaimed novels that explore the intersections of Eastern and Western cultures.

One of his most famous works is Midnight's Children (1981), which won the Booker Prize and is considered one of the greatest novels of the 20th century. The book's success established Rushdie as a major literary figure.

However, his fourth novel, The Satanic Verses (1988), brought him significant controversy due to its portrayal of Islam, leading to widespread outrage in the Muslim world. The book was banned in several countries, and Iran's supreme leader, Ayatollah Khomeini, issued a fatwa calling for Rushdie's death. This forced him into hiding and sparked a global debate on freedom of speech and religious extremism.

In 2022, Rushdie survived a near-fatal stabbing during a New York lecture, losing an eye and sustaining severe injuries. Despite ongoing threats, he remains a vocal advocate for free speech, reflected in his memoir Joseph Anton (2012). Honored with knighthood (2007) and the U.S. Presidential Medal of Freedom (2023), Rushdie's legacy endures as a symbol of literary courage and resistance against censorship. His works, including Haroun and the Sea of Stories (1990) and Quichotte (2019), continue to shape postcolonial literature.

CHAPTER SEVENTEEN

Overview of the novel "Midnight's Children"

Midnight's Children by Salman Rushdie follows Saleem Sinai, who is born at the stroke of midnight on August 15, 1947—the moment India gains independence. Endowed with telepathic powers that connect him with other magically gifted children, Saleem's life becomes a microcosm of postcolonial India. His journey is marked by personal and political upheavals, from family tragedies and rivalries—especially with the fierce Shiva, his switched-at-birth adversary—to encounters with mystical figures like Parvati-the-Witch. As Saleem navigates the chaos of Partition, wars, and shifting national identities, his fragmented memories and lost abilities mirror the tumultuous evolution of the nation. Ultimately, his story intertwines the intimate with the epic, encapsulating the hopes, struggles, and ironies of a newly independent India.

CHAPTER EIGHTEEN

Questions & Answers

Q.1 Comment on Rushdies use of Magic Realism in Midnight's children.

Ans: Introduction: Midnight's Children is a novel by Salman Rushdie, first published in 1981. Salman Rushdie is a prominent Indian-born British-American author known for his imaginative storytelling that often blends magical realism with historical and cultural themes. Midnight's Children is one of the most acclaimed works in modern literature, blending elements of magic realism with historical fiction. The novel is set in the Indian subcontinent and explores the period before, during, and after India's independence from British rule in 1947.

Main Content: Magical realism has been a prominent literary device employed by numerous authors to create a unique blend of reality and fantasy in their works.

"Midnight's Children" is a type of fiction called magic realism. This style of writing began in Latin America and has gained followers around the world. When people think of magic realism, Salman Rushdie's name often comes to mind. Rushdie explains magic realism as a development from Surrealism that shows a unique 'Third World' perspective.

Rushdie's novels, including "Midnight's Children," share similarities with this style, which can also be found in other "half-made societies," as writer V.S. Naipaul described them. In such societies, impossible things happen openly and seem completely believable, as Rushdie notes about Gabriel Garcia Marquez's work, like "One Hundred Years of Solitude."

Many people have wondered if Rushdie was inspired by Marquez when writing "Midnight's Children." However, Rushdie claims he only discovered Marquez's work after finishing his own novel. Despite this, both authors use a similar style, creating worlds that are different from the real one we know. This genre of writing is a response to 19th-century realism, which focused on representing the real world as it is.

In different cultures and times, people have discussed the balance between the real and the unreal in art. For example, the ancient Greek philosopher Plato wanted to ban art from his ideal society because he thought it was too far from reality. On the other hand, in India, art often includes magical and fantastical elements. Here's how magical realism is significant in Midnight's Children:

Connection to India's History

The protagonist, Saleem Sinai, is born at the exact moment of India's independence on August 15, 1947. His life is inextricably linked with the nation's history, and this connection is portrayed through magical elements. For instance, Saleem and other children born at the same moment possess supernatural powers, symbolizing the potential and diversity of the new nation. Their powers are a metaphor for the cultural and political changes happening in India.

2. Exploration of Identity

Saleem's ability to hear the thoughts of others, as well as his discovery that he can communicate with the other "Midnight's Children," represents the fragmented and multifaceted nature of identity in post-colonial India. These magical abilities highlight the inner conflicts and the merging of different cultural identities within the country.

3. Reflection of Political Realities

The novel uses magical realism to reflect on the chaotic and often surreal political realities of India. For example, the character Shiva, another of the Midnight's Children, embodies violence and power, which ties into the turbulent political landscape of the time. The fantastical elements serve to underline the absurdity and unpredictability of political life in India during and after independence.

4. Commentary on Memory and History

Magical realism allows Rushdie to present history as subjective and malleable. Saleem's narrative is unreliable and filled with fantastical elements, suggesting that history is not just a series of factual events but is also shaped by personal memories and interpretations. The blending of the real and the magical emphasizes that history is a complex, layered story, rather than a straightforward account.

5. Themes of Fate and Destiny

The magical connection between Saleem and India's fate underscores themes of destiny and the inescapable links between individuals and their countries. The supernatural elements in the story serve as a reminder that larger forces—be they historical, political, or cultural—shape the lives of individuals in ways that can seem as strange and unpredictable as magic.

6. Cultural and Mythical References

Rushdie incorporates Indian myths, folklore, and cultural references into the magical realism of the novel. These elements add depth to the narrative, connecting contemporary events with ancient traditions, and highlighting the richness of Indian culture. The magical realism serves as a bridge between the modern world and traditional stories, showing how the past continues to influence the present.

Conclusion:

In Midnight's Children, magical realism is not just a stylistic choice; it's a powerful tool that allows Rushdie to explore the complexities of Indian history, identity, and culture. The magical elements in the novel create a rich, layered narrative that captures the essence of a nation in transition, blending the extraordinary with the ordinary to reveal deeper truths about the human experience.

Q.2) Discuss 'Midnight's Children' as an autobiography of Saleem Sina.

Ans: Introduction: "for this section refer answer 1 of this chapter"

Main Content: An autobiography is a well-known genre in writing and publishing. An autobiography is a self-written biography. The author writes about all or a portion of their own life to share their experience, frame it in a larger cultural or historical context, or inform and entertain the reader. This genre is also popular with ghostwriters, especially when the person writing the autobiography isn't a professional writer.

"Midnight's Children" by Salman Rushdie can be seen as an autobiographical novel, but not in the traditional sense of the term. Instead of directly recounting Rushdie's personal life, the novel uses the protagonist, Saleem Sinai, to explore themes and experiences that resonate with the author's life and the history of India.

It's important to compare Saleem, the narrator of Midnight's Children, with Salman Rushdie himself, despite the risks of doing so. Both Saleem and Rushdie were born in Bombay in 1947. Additionally, Rushdie's family has roots in Kashmir, a key location in the novel. Interestingly, just like Saleem, Rushdie moved to Pakistan at the age of 17. Another point of connection is their names: "Salman" and "Saleem" are closely related. Both names come from Arabic and share meanings like "safe," "whole," or "flawless," showing a deeper link between the author and his character.

Here are the aspects through which we can say that it is an autobiographical novel.

Parallel with Rushdie's Life:

Birth and Background: Saleem Sinai, the narrator, is born at the exact moment India gains independence from British rule. Similarly, Rushdie was born in 1947, the year India became independent. This connection draws a parallel between the life of the protagonist and the author, suggesting that Saleem's story reflects broader historical and cultural events that also influenced Rushdie's life.

Cultural Identity: Saleem's struggles with identity, heritage, and the sense of belonging mirror Rushdie's own experiences as an Indian-born British writer. The novel deals with the complexities of being torn between different cultures, much like Rushdie's own life, growing up in India and later moving to the UK.

2. Historical Autobiography:

India's History: The novel is deeply intertwined with the history of India, from independence to the partition and beyond. While it is not a direct autobiography of Rushdie, it is an autobiography of the Indian nation as seen through the eyes of Saleem. The events in the novel, including political and social upheavals, mirror real historical events that shaped the nation's identity, much as they would have shaped Rushdie's understanding of his own identity.

3. Personal and Family Dynamics:

Family Relationships: Saleem's complex relationships with his family members, particularly his feelings of alienation and confusion, can be seen as reflective of Rushdie's own experiences with family and society. Although not a direct recounting of his life, these dynamics provide insight into the emotional and psychological struggles that might have parallels in Rushdie's own experiences.

4. Narrative Voice:

Storytelling and Memory: The novel's structure, with Saleem recounting his life story in a fragmented, often non-linear way, can be seen as reflective of the nature of memory and storytelling. Rushdie uses this technique to explore how personal and collective histories are constructed, suggesting that autobiography is not just about recounting facts but also about interpreting and understanding them through the lens of memory and narrative.

5. Fictionalized Autobiography:

Blend of Fact and Fiction: "Midnight's Children" blurs the lines between autobiography and fiction, mixing real historical events with magical realism. This blending can be seen as a way for Rushdie to explore his own life and heritage in a more imaginative and expansive way, rather than being confined to the strictures of factual autobiography.

Conclusion:

While "Midnight's Children" is not a straightforward autobiography of Salman Rushdie, it can be interpreted as an autobiographical novel in a broader sense. It reflects the author's engagement with his cultural heritage, personal identity, and the historical context in which he grew up. Through the life of Saleem Sinai, Rushdie explores the intersection of personal and national histories, making the novel a deeply personal reflection on both his life and the life of a nation.

Q.3) Discuss the main features of Rushdie's characterization in Midnight's children.

Ans: Introduction: "for this section refer answer 1 of this chapter"

Whenever we discuss a novel, we focus mainly on its characters, obviously because they are the main players in the story. Characters are the people shown in stories or plays who are understood by readers to have specific moral, personality, and emotional traits. These traits are revealed through their dialogues (what they say), actions (what they do), or what other characters say about them. The reasons behind a character's behavior, desires, and values, which are shown in their speech and actions, are known as motivation.

1. **Saleem Sinai:** It's really interesting to explore the character of Saleem in Midnight's Children. Right from the start of the novel, Saleem identifies himself closely with India, its history, and its fate. He emphasizes that, as a child born at the exact moment of India's independence, he has a special responsibility. The bond between him and India is so strong that he even suggests that his face resembles the map of India. In Midnight's Children, he describes his features using words like "region," "eastern," and "western"—terms more commonly associated with maps than with human faces.

   In an interview, Salman Rushdie explained why he gave Saleem such a big nose in Midnight's Children. He mentioned that one day, while looking at a map of India, he suddenly noticed that it resembled a large nose hanging into the sea, with a drip at the end representing Sri Lanka. Rushdie thought that if Saleem was going to be a twin of the country, he might as well be an identical twin. So, Saleem ended up with this enormous nose. (1985)

Protagonist and Narrator: Saleem is the central character and narrator of the novel, telling his story in a blend of personal history and national history. He is deeply connected to the fate of India, as he is born at the exact moment of the country's independence. His character is marked by a sense of destiny and a burden of expectations.

Symbolic Representation: Saleem represents the fragmented identity of post-colonial India. His personal struggles mirror the political and social upheavals of the nation. His telepathic powers and the physical disintegration he experiences symbolize the challenges of maintaining unity in a diverse country.

Unreliable Narrator: Saleem's account is often unreliable, filled with exaggerations and fantastical elements, which adds a layer of complexity to his character. His narration blurs the lines between reality and fiction, highlighting the subjective nature of memory and history.

1. **Shiva**

Antagonist and Foil to Saleem: Shiva, born at the same time as Saleem but switched at birth, serves as his opposite. While Saleem is introspective and burdened by history, Shiva is aggressive, pragmatic, and focused on power. He represents the darker, more violent side of India's post-independence reality.

Symbol of Destruction: Named after the Hindu god of destruction, Shiva embodies chaos and conflict. His life, marked by physical strength and a talent for war, contrasts sharply with Saleem's introspective and intellectual nature.

3. **Padma**

Grounding Force: Padma, Saleem's companion and listener, serves as a grounding force in the narrative. She represents the practical, everyday reality that contrasts with Saleem's often fantastical and chaotic storytelling. Her skepticism and down-to-earth nature help to balance the narrative, providing a counterpoint to Saleem's more abstract musings.

Symbol of the Audience: Padma also represents the reader within the story, questioning and challenging Saleem's version of events, which adds depth to the narrative.

4. Amina Sinai (Mumtaz)

Saleem's Mother: Amina's character reflects the struggles of women in post-colonial India. She experiences significant personal and emotional turmoil, from her arranged marriage to her challenges as a mother. Her resilience and adaptability are central to her characterization.

Symbol of Change: Amina's name change from Mumtaz symbolizes the transformations individuals undergo in the face of societal pressures. Her life encapsulates the personal sacrifices and adjustments required in the rapidly changing social landscape of the time.

5. Mary Pereira

The Midwife: Mary Pereira is a key character in the novel, responsible for switching Saleem and Shiva at birth. Her guilt over this act haunts her throughout the story, making her a symbol of the unintended consequences of seemingly small actions.

Moral Complexity: Mary's character represents the moral ambiguities in the novel. Her actions, driven by love and political idealism, have far-reaching consequences, illustrating how personal decisions can shape history.

6. The Midnight's Children

Collective Characterization: The Midnight's Children, all born in the first hour of India's independence, each possess unique powers. Together, they represent the diverse and multifaceted nature of India. Their different abilities and backgrounds symbolize the potential and challenges of a new nation.

Symbol of India's Future: The children's abilities and eventual fate reflect the hopes, fears, and realities of post-independence India. Their eventual sterilization and loss of powers can be seen as a commentary on the suppression of potential in a newly independent nation.

7. Other Characters

Dr. Aadam Aziz: Saleem's grandfather, whose loss of faith and involvement in the independence movement reflect the complexities of colonial and post-colonial identity.

Ahmed Sinai: Saleem's father, representing the struggles of the business class in a rapidly changing India, as well as the personal toll of political instability.

Conclusion:

In Midnight's Children, characterization is not just about individual personalities but also about representing broader themes like identity, history, and the nation. Each character embodies different aspects of India's social, political, and cultural fabric, making them integral to the novel's exploration of post-colonial reality.

Q. 4) "Rushdie's Midnight's children is a trend setter of sorts". Discuss.

Ans: Introduction: "for this section refer answer 1 of this chapter"

Salman Rushdie's Midnight's Children is widely regarded as a trendsetter in modern literature for several reasons:

1. Introduction of Magical Realism to Indian Literature:

Midnight's Children popularized the use of magical realism in Indian English literature. While the genre had roots in Latin American literature, Rushdie's novel brought it to the forefront of Indian storytelling. The blending of the fantastical with the historical created a new narrative style that resonated deeply with readers and writers alike.

2. Reimagining Historical Narratives:

The novel reinterprets and reimagines the history of India, particularly the period around its independence in 1947. Rushdie's intertwining of personal and national histories was groundbreaking, showing how individual lives are deeply connected with broader historical events. This narrative approach influenced many subsequent works that explored the intersection of personal and political histories.

3. Postcolonial Identity Exploration:

Midnight's Children delves into themes of postcolonial identity, exploring the challenges and complexities of identity in a newly independent nation. Through the character of Saleem Sinai, Rushdie examines issues of hybridity, fragmentation, and cultural dislocation, which became key themes in postcolonial literature.

4. Innovative Narrative Structure:

The novel's structure, with its non-linear timeline and multiple layers of storytelling, was innovative and set a new standard for narrative complexity in modern literature. Rushdie's use of a first-person narrator who often addresses the reader directly, blurring the lines between fiction and reality, was a technique that influenced many later works.

5. Cultural Impact:

Midnight's Children had a significant cultural impact, not just in India but globally. It brought Indian literature in English to international attention and paved the way for a new generation of Indian writers who explored similar themes and narrative techniques.

6. Winning the Booker Prize:

The novel's success, particularly winning the Booker Prize in 1981 and later being declared the "Booker of Bookers," solidified its status as a trendsetter. It set a precedent for Indian English novels to be recognized on the global literary stage.

Conclusion:

Midnight's Children is a trendsetter because it introduced new narrative techniques, explored complex postcolonial identities, and had a lasting influence on both Indian and global literature. Its innovative approach to storytelling and its blending of the magical with the real have made it a landmark work in modern fiction.

Q.5 Discuss the use of history in Salman Rushdie's novel Midnight's Children.

Ans: Introduction: "for this section refer answer 1 of this chapter"

Main Content: The use of history in Salman Rushdie's Midnight's Children is central to the novel's narrative and thematic structure. Rushdie employs history not just as a backdrop but as a living, breathing entity that interacts with and shapes the lives of the characters, particularly the protagonist, Saleem Sinai. In Midnight's Children, Rushdie establishes a strong connection between the history of India and the life of Saleem, his protagonist as if the two were Siamese twins. . The novel's treatment of history is complex, blending factual events with fictional elements, and offering a commentary on the nature of history itself.

In Salman Rushdie's novel, he carefully links personal events in Saleem's life and his family's life with the political and historical events in independent India. This connection is kept throughout the book, although sometimes it can feel a bit forced, especially in the later parts.

Intertwining of Personal and National History:

In Midnight's Children, the personal history of Saleem Sinai is inextricably linked with the history of India. Born at the exact moment of India's independence on August 15, 1947, Saleem's life is presented as a metaphor for the nation. His experiences, triumphs, and tragedies mirror the broader events of Indian history. This intertwining suggests that the fate of individuals is deeply connected to the historical and political context in which they live.

2. Reimagining Historical Events:

Rushdie reimagines and fictionalizes significant events in Indian history, such as the Partition, the Emergency, and various wars, through the lens of magical realism. By doing so, he challenges the conventional, linear understanding of history. The novel portrays history as a subjective and fragmented narrative, where personal memories and myths play as important a role as documented facts.

3. Critique of Historical Narratives:

The novel questions the idea of a singular, authoritative historical narrative. Through Saleem's unreliable narration, Rushdie suggests that history is often a construct, shaped by those in power and subject to interpretation. The fluidity with which the novel moves between different versions of events highlights the idea that history is not objective but is instead composed of multiple, often conflicting, perspectives.

4. Magic Realism as a Tool for Historical Commentary:

The use of magical realism allows Rushdie to explore the surreal and absurd aspects of historical events. The magical elements in the novel, such as the midnight's children and their supernatural abilities, serve as metaphors for the political and social realities of postcolonial India. This blending of the real and the fantastic enables Rushdie to comment on the strangeness and unpredictability of history.

5. The Role of Memory in Shaping History:

Memory plays a crucial role in Midnight's Children. Saleem's recollections are often unreliable, fragmented, and influenced by his emotions and experiences. This portrayal of memory emphasizes the idea that history is not just a series of objective facts but is also shaped by personal recollections, which can be selective and biased.

6. Symbolism of Saleem's Body as a Historical Archive:

Saleem's body becomes a symbol of the nation's history. His physical and mental disintegration mirrors the political and social turmoil in India. The cracks and fissures in his body symbolize the divisions and conflicts within the country. This metaphor underscores the intimate connection between the individual and the collective history.

7. Satire of Historical Figures and Events:

Rushdie uses satire to critique historical figures and events. Characters like Prime Minister Indira Gandhi and events like the Emergency are depicted with a blend of humor and criticism. By exaggerating certain traits or actions, Rushdie exposes the absurdities and contradictions of political power and historical narratives.

8. Postcolonial Perspective on History:

Midnight's Children offers a postcolonial perspective on history, challenging colonial narratives and highlighting the complexities of independence and nation-building. The novel reflects on the legacy of colonialism and the struggles of newly independent nations to forge their identities. It suggests that the postcolonial experience is marked by fragmentation, hybridity, and a constant negotiation with the past.

Conclusion: History in Midnight's Children is not a static backdrop but an active force that shapes and is shaped by the characters. Through the novel, Rushdie offers a rich, layered exploration of history, memory, and identity, questioning the nature of historical truth and emphasizing the multiplicity of perspectives that contribute to our understanding of the past.

Q.6) Write a critical note on Rushdie's use of English in Midnight's children.

Ans: Introduction: "for this section refer answer 1 of this chapter"

Main Content:

Rushdie is one of the most important Indian English writers, like Raja Rao. He talks a lot about his writing style, which makes people compare him to Rao. Even though Rushdie says he doesn't follow Rao's style, both have been groundbreaking in how they use English and their writing techniques.

In 1984, in his lecture "Describing Reality as a Political Act," Rushdie shared his thoughts on using English that are similar to what Rao had said, though Rushdie might have developed these ideas on his own. He explained that: One change is how we see using English for Indian stories. We shouldn't use it the same way the British did; instead, we need to adapt it to fit our needs.

Salman Rushdie's Midnight's Children showcases a unique approach to the English language, which is pivotal to the novel's style and thematic depth. His use of English is not merely a tool for storytelling but a medium through which he explores and challenges colonial legacies, cultural identities, and historical narratives.

1. Hybrid Language: Rushdie employs a hybrid form of English that blends traditional British structures with elements of Indian languages and dialects. This amalgamation reflects the cultural and historical confluence of the Indian subcontinent. Terms and phrases from Hindi, Urdu, and other local languages are woven into the narrative, giving it a distinctly Indian flavor. This linguistic blend helps to create a sense of authenticity and roots the story in its Indian setting.

2. Subverting Colonial English: Rushdie's approach to English is a form of linguistic resistance. By incorporating Indian idioms, expressions, and vernacular, he subverts the colonial dominance of the English language. This subversion is not just a stylistic choice but a political act that challenges the traditional hierarchies of language and cultural expression. It highlights the post-colonial struggle to reclaim and redefine cultural identity.

3. Magical Realism: The use of English in Midnight's Children also plays a crucial role in conveying the novel's magical realism. The blend of the mundane with the fantastical is seamlessly integrated into the narrative through Rushdie's distinctive language. His ability to shift between the ordinary and the extraordinary through linguistic innovation enhances the novel's surreal quality and enriches its storytelling.

4. Characterization and Voice: Rushdie's use of English helps in the development of his characters, particularly Saleem Sinai. The language reflects his personal and cultural identity, as well as his role as a representative of India's tumultuous history. Saleem's voice, filled with a mix of formal English and colloquial expressions, captures his complex character and the novel's thematic concerns.

5. Criticisms and Challenges: While Rushdie's use of English is widely celebrated, it is not without its critics. Some argue that the hybrid language can be challenging for readers unfamiliar with Indian languages and cultural references. Additionally, the blending of languages and the use of non-standard English can sometimes appear forced or overly stylized, potentially detracting from the narrative flow for some readers.

Conclusion: Salman Rushdie's use of English in Midnight's Children is a deliberate and effective choice that serves multiple functions: it asserts post-colonial identity, enhances magical realism, and deepens characterization. While it may present challenges for some readers, it remains a powerful aspect of Rushdie's innovative storytelling and a testament to his role in reshaping the literary landscape.

Q.7) Comment upon the use of language and techniques used in Rushdie's 'Midnight's Children'.

Ans: Introduction: "for this section refer answer 1 of this chapter"

Main Content: Salman Rushdie's Midnight's Children is not only notable for its rich narrative but also for the innovative use of language and literary techniques. Published in 1981, the novel combines elements of magical realism with historical fiction, creating a unique storytelling experience that has earned it critical acclaim. The use of language in Midnight's Children is distinctively marked by its blending of Indian and English idioms, while its narrative techniques, such as non-linear storytelling and the use of multiple perspectives, further enrich the text.

Language:

Rushdie's use of language in Midnight's Children is a significant departure from traditional English prose. He incorporates a variety of linguistic influences, including Indian vernacular, British English, and elements of Hindi and Urdu. This fusion creates a distinctive voice that reflects the cultural diversity of India. The narrative is peppered with Indian idioms, phrases, and colloquialisms, which not only add authenticity to the setting but also challenge the reader to engage with the text on a deeper level.

Rushdie's language is also marked by its playfulness and inventiveness. He often bends the rules of grammar and syntax to create a rhythm and flow that mirrors the chaotic and vibrant life of his characters. The use of puns, wordplay, and metaphor is frequent, adding layers of meaning and humor to the narrative.

Techniques: Midnight's Children is classified under a type of fiction known as magical realism. This style, called El realismo mágico in Spanish, originated in Latin America and has fans all over the world. Nowadays, when people think of magical realism, Salman Rushdie's name often comes to mind. In his essay on Gabriel Garcia Marquez, Rushdie defines this genre as something that evolved from Surrealism and reflects a truly "Third World" perspective. Rushdie's novels, including Midnight's Children, can also be linked to a kind of magical realism that has roots in his own culture.

There are similarities between societies that author V.S. Naipaul refers to as "half-made societies," which develop their own unique type of realism. What Rushdie says about Marquez's work applies to Midnight's Children and Rushdie's other novels as well: "In the world Marquez describes, impossible things happen all the time, and they seem completely believable, even in broad daylight."

Magical Realism: Rushdie masterfully employs magical realism in Midnight's Children to blur the lines between reality and fantasy. Characters possess supernatural abilities, and extraordinary events are treated as everyday occurrences. This technique allows Rushdie to explore complex themes, such as identity and history, in a way that transcends the limitations of conventional realism.

Non-Linear Narrative: The narrative structure of Midnight's Children is non-linear, frequently shifting between different time periods and perspectives. This technique reflects the fragmented and tumultuous history of India itself, as well as the personal turmoil of the protagonist, Saleem Sinai. The non-linear structure also serves to emphasize the interconnectedness of personal and national histories.

Multiple Perspectives: Rushdie employs a narrative style that often shifts perspectives, providing the reader with a multi-faceted view of events. This technique enriches the narrative by offering different interpretations of the same event, highlighting the subjective nature of memory and history.

Metafiction: The novel frequently draws attention to its own storytelling process, with Saleem often commenting on the act of narrating his story. This self-referential technique, known as metafiction, adds another layer of complexity to the text, prompting readers to question the reliability of the narrator and the nature of storytelling itself.'

Symbolism and Allegory: Midnight's Children is rich in symbolism and allegory, with characters and events often representing larger historical and political themes. Saleem, for example, is born at the exact moment of India's independence, making him a symbol of the nation itself. The personal struggles of the characters often mirror the broader social and political challenges faced by India during this period.

Conclusion:

The use of language and literary techniques in Midnight's Children is central to its success as a novel. Rushdie's inventive use of language, combined with his mastery of narrative techniques such as magical realism, non-linear storytelling, and multiple perspectives, creates a rich and multifaceted text. These elements not only enhance the reader's engagement with the novel but also deepen the exploration of its themes, making Midnight's Children a landmark work in modern literature.

Q.8) Discuss Salman Rushdie's 'Midnight's Children' as a post-colonial novel.

Ans: Introduction: "for this section refer answer 1 of this chapter"

Main Content:

"Midnight's Children" is a story narrated by the main character, Saleem, who tells his tale from the perspective of being 31 years old. The story begins with the "midnight hour" when India gains its independence, which is also when Saleem Sinai and a thousand other children, whom Rushdie calls "midnight's children," are born. Saleem, who has blue eyes, is actually born to Vanita, an Indian Hindu woman, and Methwold, a departing Englishman. However, he is raised by a Muslim couple, making him a perfect example of post-colonial hybridity, as discussed by Homi K. Bhabha in his book "The Location of Culture.

" Bhabha talks about the importance of thinking beyond traditional narratives and focusing on the "in-between" spaces where cultural differences come together. These spaces create opportunities for new identities and ways for people to work together or challenge each other, ultimately helping to define the idea of society itself.

Salman Rushdie's Midnight's Children is often seen as a classic example of a post-colonial novel. This is because it deals with India's history after gaining independence from British rule and looks at the cultural, social, and political struggles of a country trying to find its identity after colonialism.

Exploration of National Identity:

Midnight's Children intertwines the personal life of its protagonist, Saleem Sinai, with the larger narrative of India's emergence as an independent nation. Saleem, who is born at the exact moment of India's independence, symbolizes the birth of the nation itself. Through his story, Rushdie explores the challenges India faces as it seeks to carve out a new identity, free from colonial influence but still grappling with the legacy of its colonial past.

2. Critique of Colonial Legacy:

Rushdie critiques the lingering effects of colonialism on India's political, social, and cultural structures. The novel presents the post-colonial nation as one burdened by the partition, communal tensions, and political instability, all of which can be traced back to the colonial period. This critique is evident in the chaotic and often tragic lives of the characters, who are trying to navigate a world still deeply affected by colonial power dynamics.

3. Use of Magical Realism:

Rushdie employs magical realism to reflect the surreal and complex nature of post-colonial India. The blending of the real with the fantastical serves to highlight the contradictions and absurdities that exist in a country trying to reconcile its rich cultural heritage with the impositions of colonial modernity. The magical elements in the novel, such as the supernatural abilities of the midnight's children, serve as metaphors for the diverse and multifaceted experiences of post-colonial India.

4. Language and Narrative Style:

The novel's narrative style is reflective of post-colonial literature's tendency to challenge traditional Western narrative forms. Rushdie's use of English, infused with Indian vernacular, and his non-linear, fragmented storytelling reflect the hybrid nature of post-colonial identity. By remaking the English language to suit Indian themes and experiences, Rushdie subverts the colonial power structure that once imposed English as a tool of control.

5. Critique of Nationalism:

While the novel celebrates India's independence, it also offers a critical perspective on nationalism. The idea of the nation, as portrayed in Midnight's Children, is fraught with contradictions, where the promise of independence is often undercut by the harsh realities of political corruption, religious strife, and the marginalization of various communities. Saleem's life story becomes a vehicle for exploring how the ideal of a unified nation is often compromised by these forces.

6. Multiplicity of Voices:

Post-colonial literature often seeks to give voice to those marginalized by colonial and nationalist narratives. Midnight's Children is populated by a diverse cast of characters, each representing different facets of Indian society. Through these characters, Rushdie explores the complexities of identity, power, and resistance in a post-colonial context. The multiplicity of voices in the novel mirrors the plurality of post-colonial India itself.

Conclusion:

Midnight's Children is a post-colonial novel that delves deep into the challenges of forging a new identity in the wake of colonial rule. Through its exploration of national identity, critique of colonial legacies, innovative use of language, and its rich, multifaceted narrative, the novel captures the tumultuous experience of post-colonial India.

Q.9) Discuss the narrative technique or Salman Rushdie's novel Midnight's Children.

Ans: Introduction: "for this section refer answer 1 of this chapter"

Main Content :

Salman Rushdie's Midnight's Children introduces a completely new narrative style, different from the traditional techniques of storytelling. Rushdie's approach set a trend for experimenting with narrative techniques and the use of the English language, giving a fresh direction to Indian writing in English. William Walsh rightly praised this innovative technique, noting that by combining elements of magic and fantasy with stark realism, extravagant imagination, multi-layered analogies, and a powerful symbolic structure, Rushdie has captured an extraordinary energy in his novel. This achievement is unprecedented in the 150-year-old tradition of the Indian novel in English.

1. The Technique of first Person Narration: In Midnight's Children, Salman Rushdie uses the first-person narrative technique. The narrator, Saleem Sinai, tells his story, introducing characters long before they actually appear in the novel. This approach creates suspense and keeps readers engaged. The novel spans 75 years of Indian subcontinent history, with Saleem recounting both his birth and the birth of India. The narrative often blurs the lines of time, jumping between different periods. Just like Sanjay in the Mahabharata, who could see and narrate the events of the Kurukshetra war from a distance, Saleem is also given a magical ability to see from afar and even read the minds of others.

2. Non-Linear Timeline:

The narrative in Midnight's Children is non-linear, frequently jumping back and forth in time. Saleem often digresses from the main storyline to provide background information or reflect on events, creating a layered and complex narrative structure. This technique allows the novel to cover a vast span of history, from before India's independence to the years following it.

3. Blending of History and Fiction:

Rushdie merges historical events with fictional elements, blurring the lines between reality and imagination. Saleem's life is intertwined with the history of India, and he often claims to have a direct influence on major historical events. This blending of history and fiction is a hallmark of Rushdie's style and adds depth to the narrative.

4. Magical Realism:

The novel incorporates elements of magical realism, where extraordinary and fantastical events are presented as part of everyday life. Saleem and the other "midnight's children" possess special powers, and these supernatural elements are seamlessly woven into the narrative. This technique adds a layer of wonder and symbolism to the story.

5. Unreliable Narrator:

Saleem, as the narrator, is not always reliable. He admits to forgetting or misremembering events and sometimes questions his own version of the story. This creates ambiguity and challenges the reader to question the truth of the narrative, adding complexity and depth to the storytelling.

6. Self-Reflective Commentary:

Throughout the novel, Saleem often breaks the fourth wall by addressing the reader directly and commenting on the process of writing and storytelling. This self-reflective commentary adds a metafictional element to the novel, making readers aware of the narrative's construction.

7. Symbolism and Allegory:

The narrative is rich in symbolism and allegory. Saleem himself represents the new nation of India, and his life parallels the country's post-independence journey. Rushdie uses symbolic language and imagery to convey deeper meanings and explore themes like identity, nationalism, and cultural hybridity.

8. Intertextuality and Allusions:

Rushdie's narrative is filled with references to various literary, historical, and cultural texts. The novel alludes to epic tales like the Mahabharata and draws parallels with other literary works, enriching the text with multiple layers of meaning.

9. Fragmented Structure:

The narrative is deliberately fragmented, mirroring the chaotic and fragmented nature of India's history and identity. This structure reflects the complexity of post-colonial realities and the challenges of constructing a cohesive national narrative.

10. Experimental Language:

Rushdie's use of language in Midnight's Children is experimental and playful. He blends English with Indian vernaculars, creating a unique linguistic style that reflects the multicultural and multilingual reality of India. This innovative use of language challenges traditional notions of English literature and contributes to the novel's distinct voice.

Conclusion:

Overall, the narrative technique in Midnight's Children is a blend of innovative storytelling methods that reflect the complexity of post-colonial identity, history, and culture. Rushdie's approach to narration not only captivates readers but also pushes the boundaries of literary form, making the novel a landmark work in modern literature.

Q.10) What are the various themes that Rushdie deals with in Midnight's Children?

Ans: Introduction: "for this section refer answer 1 of this chapter"

Main Content: The theme of the novel joins reality with the imagination of the novelist. Indeed, the actual and the fancy move side by side. The events move around the exact time of independence of India and the protagonist also born at the same time. The theme of the novel is to exhibit the Indian society after independence and to focus on its various aspects. It is the story of the pain of the people. After independence there is a bloody partition of the country which makes people to kill each other mercilessly in the name of the religion. The protagonist of the novel, who is born along with India, considers himself to be the main centre of events. This novel is based on the memory of the protagonist who tries to remember some of the most important events of his life and then records them.

Thus Salman Rushdie's Midnight's Children is a rich and complex novel that explores numerous themes, reflecting the multifaceted nature of Indian society, history, and identity. Here are some of the key themes in the novel:

1. **Identity:** In Midnight's Children, the idea that names create identity is very important. Many characters in the novel have names that connect to the roles they play. For example, Saleem's grandfather, Aadam, is named after the Biblical Adam, the first man. Saleem's grandmother becomes known as Reverend Mother, showing how she is deeply connected to her religious identity. The women in the story change their names after marriage, which symbolizes leaving their old selves behind and becoming someone new in their marriage. At one point, Saleem even forgets his own name because he feels ashamed of his actions. This shows how he has lost his sense of self and the name that gave him purpose.

2. **Post-Colonial Identity:** The novel deeply examines the struggles of post-colonial identity, both at the individual and national levels. Saleem Sinai's life parallels the story of India's independence and its subsequent challenges. The theme of hybridity, where Saleem embodies multiple

cultural and religious identities, underscores the complexities of identity in a post-colonial world.

3. **Post-Colonialism:** Before India became an independent nation, it was ruled by the British Empire. The British tried to erase Indian customs and replace them with their own culture and values. As a result, many Indians struggled to remember and hold onto their traditions. Some people abandoned the "old ways" of polytheistic religion and elaborate ceremonies, attempting to steer the country toward Western culture. Others tried to return to their traditional customs but found themselves caught in an identity crisis. The influence of the British Empire still lingered, making it hard for India to move forward with its own identity. Characters like William Methwold and Evie Lilith Burns serve as reminders of how white characters made Indians feel inferior and out of place in their own country.

4. **The Unreliability of Oral Storytelling:** Midnight's Children is told entirely by Saleem Sinai, who recounts the magical events of his life from his deathbed. He expects Padma, who represents the readers, to believe his story, which blends supernatural elements with a realistic setting. However, there are moments when Saleem admits he might have forgotten dates or mixed up events due to his failing memory. This creates a dilemma for the reader: they can either accept Saleem's fantastical story and overlook his memory lapses, or they can be skeptical and question his account. Either way, Saleem's reliability as a narrator is challenged by the mix of magical realism and his own admissions of confusion.

5. **History and Memory:** Midnight's Children is a narrative where personal and national histories are intertwined. The theme of history is central, as the novel explores how history is remembered, recorded, and interpreted. Saleem's unreliable narration raises questions about the nature of historical truth and how personal memories can shape and distort the past.

6. **Magical Realism:** Magical realism is a key theme in the novel, blending the fantastical with the real. This technique reflects the chaotic and unpredictable nature of Indian history and culture. The supernatural abilities of the "midnight's children" serve as a metaphor for the potential and challenges of a newly independent nation.

7. **Nationalism and Politics:** The novel critically examines the rise of nationalism and the political turmoil that follows India's independence.

Through the lens of Saleem's life, Rushdie explores the impact of political events like the Partition of India, the Emergency, and the rise of authoritarianism. The theme of nationalism is depicted as both a source of pride and a cause of division and violence.

8. **Fate and Free Will**: The theme of fate versus free will is explored through Saleem's belief that his life is destined to mirror the fate of the nation. The novel questions whether individuals have control over their lives or whether they are bound by historical and political forces beyond their control.

9. **Cultural Hybridity**: Cultural hybridity is a recurring theme, reflecting the diverse and pluralistic nature of Indian society. Saleem's mixed heritage symbolizes the blending of different cultures, religions, and languages in India. The novel celebrates this hybridity while also acknowledging the tensions and conflicts it can create.

10. **Family and Inheritance**: Family relationships and the idea of inheritance, both genetic and cultural, are central to the novel. Saleem's family history is closely linked to the broader history of India, and the novel explores how personal and national legacies are passed down through generations.

11. **Storytelling and Narration**: The act of storytelling itself is a major theme in Midnight's Children. Saleem's narrative is a meditation on the power of stories to shape reality and history. Rushdie plays with narrative techniques, questioning the reliability of the narrator and the nature of truth in storytelling.

12. **Colonialism and Its Aftermath**: The legacy of British colonialism is a critical theme in the novel. The effects of colonialism are explored through the characters' lives, the partition of India, and the ongoing struggles for power and identity in the post-colonial state. Rushdie critiques both the colonial powers and the new ruling class in independent India.

13. **Religious and Cultural Conflicts**: The novel addresses the religious and cultural tensions that have shaped Indian history. Saleem's life is marked by the conflicts between Hindus, Muslims, and other religious communities, reflecting the broader religious and cultural diversity of India. The theme of religious identity is explored in the context of both personal relationships and national politics.

14. **Power and Corruption**: Power, its acquisition, and its corrupting influence are significant themes in the novel. The novel portrays how

political leaders manipulate history, culture, and religion to gain and maintain power, often at the expense of the common people. The Emergency declared by Indira Gandhi is depicted as a time of significant abuse of power.

15. **Sexuality and Gender**: Gender roles and sexuality are explored in various ways throughout the novel. The characters' experiences often reflect the societal norms and expectations of the time, and the novel critiques the limitations imposed by traditional gender roles. Female characters in the novel, such as Saleem's mother and grandmother, navigate complex personal and societal challenges, highlighting issues of gender inequality.

Conclusion:

In Midnight's Children, Rushdie weaves these themes together to create a narrative that is both a reflection on India's past and a commentary on its present, offering a profound exploration of the complexities of identity, history, and culture in a post-colonial world.

Block 6 - Short Stories

CHAPTER NINETEEN

About short story

WHAT IS A SHORT STORY?

Ans:Introduction: A short story is a brief work of fiction that usually focuses on a single plot, a few characters, and one main idea. It is shorter than a novel and often aims to convey a message or evoke an emotional response in just a few pages or words. Short stories typically have a clear beginning, middle, and end, and are meant to be read in one sitting.

Main Content : To define a short story some might quickly say that it's simply a short piece of writing, using fewer words. But a short story is more than just something brief – it needs a special way of being written. Edgar Allen Poe believes it should be easy to read in one sitting to keep the story's impact strong. However, it's not just a rushed story or a short version of a novel. In his review of Hawthorne's "Twice-Told Tales," Poe explains what makes a good short story.

A skilled writer creates a story with a clear purpose. Instead of forcing the plot to fit random ideas, the writer carefully thinks about the effect they want to create. Then, they come up with events and details that help achieve that effect. If the opening sentences don't work toward this goal, the writer has already made a mistake. Every word in the story should contribute, directly or indirectly, to the overall purpose. When done with care and skill, the story leaves the reader with a strong sense of satisfaction because the main idea has been clearly and effectively presented without distractions.

A broad analysis of a short story highlights three key elements:

Familiarity: The story uses vivid details to make it feel real and relatable, suggesting deeper meanings. Even though the situation may seem familiar, the writer must avoid making it boring, predictable, or clichéd. A short story is not just a copy of real life but a dramatization of it.

Empathy: We should connect closely with the characters and their situations, making us feel like we're part of their world. This makes even well-known themes feel fresh and unique.

Readability: A good short story should be engaging enough that we can't stop reading until we know what happens. Beyond just being an interesting tale, there's often deeper meaning to uncover.

Traditional ideas about short stories, like structure, continuity, and effect, are being challenged by modern writers and critics. Some believe that readability isn't always necessary, especially in contemporary stories. A story can be exciting and meaningful even without a clear plot or traditional structure. The modern short story explores new themes and forms, reflecting changes in personal, social, and global dynamics. It becomes a journey of discovery—both for the characters and, more importantly, for the reader.

BASIC ELEMENTS OF A SHORT STORY.

The basic elements of a short story are key building blocks that give the story its structure, meaning, and emotional impact. Let's explore each of these elements in detail:

1. Plot

The plot refers to the sequence of events that make up the story. It generally follows a structure that includes:

Introduction (Exposition): Introduces the characters, setting, and basic situation.

Rising Action: Builds tension as the story progresses, with conflicts or challenges introduced.

Climax: The turning point or moment of highest emotional intensity, where the main conflict reaches its peak.

Falling Action: The events that occur after the climax, leading towards resolution.

Resolution (Denouement): The conclusion where the story's conflicts are resolved, leaving the reader with a sense of closure.

Example: In a story about a detective solving a crime, the plot would follow the detective's journey from learning about the crime (introduction), gathering clues (rising action), confronting the criminal (climax), and solving the case (resolution).

2. Characters

Characters are the people, animals, or beings that drive the story's action. They can be:

Protagonist: The main character, often facing challenges or conflicts.

Antagonist: The character or force opposing the protagonist, creating conflict.

Supporting Characters: Characters that help move the plot forward but aren't the central focus.

Character Development: In a short story, characters are usually less developed than in novels due to space limitations, but the protagonist's personality, goals, and motivations should still beclear.Short stories often focus on a small number of characters to keep the story focused.

3. Setting

The setting refers to the time and place in which the story occurs. It includes details such as:

Time: When the story is set (e.g., past, present, future, specific season, or historical period).

Place: Where the story takes place (e.g., a city, countryside, outer space).

Environment: The physical and social environment (e.g., weather, mood, political or social conditions).

In a short story, the setting is often simple but crucial to creating the mood and atmosphere. It provides context for the characters' actions and helps to immerse the reader in the **story.**

4. Conflict

Conflict is the central struggle or problem that drives the story. Without conflict, there's no story. Conflicts can be:

Internal Conflict (Man vs. Self): A character struggles with inner thoughts, emotions, or decisions.

External Conflict (Man vs. Man, Man vs. Nature, Man vs. Society, etc.): The character faces external challenges, such as other characters, nature, or societal norms.

Conflict creates tension and motivates the protagonist to take action, which moves the plot forward.

Example: A character may struggle internally with guilt (internal conflict) while also facing a lawsuit (external conflict).

5. Theme

The theme is the underlying message or central idea that the story explores. It's the "big idea" or lesson the reader is meant to take away from the story. Common themes in short stories include:

Love

Death

Survival

Human nature

Justice and injustice

The theme may not always be directly stated but is often revealed through the characters' actions, conflicts, and resolutions.

Example: A short story about a war veteran's return home might explore themes of trauma, loss, and healing.

6. Point of View

The point of view (POV) determines through whose perspective the story is told. The most common types are:

First-Person POV: The narrator is a character in the story, using "I" or "we" to describe events.

Third-Person Limited POV: The narrator is outside the story, focusing on the thoughts and experiences of one character.

Third-Person Omniscient POV: The narrator is all-knowing and can describe the thoughts and experiences of multiple characters.

The choice of POV influences how much information the reader has and how they relate to the characters.

Example: In first-person POV, the reader experiences the story through the narrator's eyes, gaining insight into their personal feelings and thoughts.

7. Tone and Mood

Tone: The author's attitude toward the subject or characters, which can be formal, informal, serious, playful, sarcastic, etc.

Mood: The emotional atmosphere of the story, which affects how the reader feels while reading it.

Tone and mood work together to create the overall feeling of the story, whether it's suspenseful, lighthearted, dark, or hopeful.

Example: A ghost story might have a dark, eerie mood with a serious, suspenseful tone.

8. Style

The style of the short story refers to the author's unique way of writing. It includes:

Language: Word choice, sentence structure, and use of literary devices like metaphors, similes, and imagery.

Pacing: How quickly or slowly the events of the story unfold.

Dialogue: How characters speak, revealing their personality, background, and emotions.

Style can vary widely from author to author, shaping how readers experience the story.

9. Symbolism

Symbolism is when objects, characters, or events represent something larger than themselves, adding layers of meaning to the story.

Example: In a story about growing up, a withered flower might symbolize lost innocence.

Conclusion

These basic elements work together to create a short story that is engaging, meaningful, and satisfying. While a short story is brief, it often contains depth through its characters, conflicts, and themes, making it a powerful and concise form of storytelling. The effectiveness of a short story lies in how well these elements are woven together to create an impactful narrative.

R.K. Narayan: An Astrologer's Day & Engine Trouble

Scan the QR code to watch video

About R.K. NarayanR. K. Narayan (1906–2001) was a renowned Indian writer best known for his stories set in the fictional South Indian town of Malgudi. Among the early Indian authors writing in English alongside Mulk Raj Anand and Raja Rao, his work was greatly supported by his friend and mentor, Graham Greene, who helped publish his first books, including the semi-autobiographical trilogy Swami and Friends, The Bachelor of Arts, and The English Teacher. Narayan's compassionate and humorous portrayals of everyday life have drawn comparisons to William Faulkner and Guy de Maupassant. Over his 60-year career, he received numerous awards, such as the AC Benson Medal, Padma Vibhushan, Padma Bhushan, and the Sahitya

Akademi Fellowship, and he was also nominated to India's Rajya Sabha.

An Astrologer's Day

Summary

"The Astrologer's Day" tells the story of a fake astrologer in Malgudi, South India, who sets up his modest business under a tamarind tree near Town Hall Park. Dressed in sacred ash, vermilion, and a saffron turban, he captivates his customers with a mix of guesswork and keen psychological insight, despite knowing nothing of real astrology. One evening, a man named Guru Nayak challenges him to a wager: if the astrologer can reveal a hidden truth, he will earn eight annas, but failure would cost him sixteen annas.

Under pressure, the astrologer prophesies that Guru Nayak, who was once left for dead in a knife attack and now seeks vengeance, will find his assailant dead, crushed under a lorry. Satisfied with the prediction and paying him only twelve and a half annas, Guru Nayak departs. Later, the astrologer confesses to his wife that the man he predicted had died was not another person but himself—he had nearly killed Guru Nayak in his youth. This unexpected twist lifts the weight of guilt he had carried, knowing that Guru Nayak was still alive.

Question and Answer

Q.1) There are no good or bad characters in Narayan's work. Apply this statement to the short story An Astrologer's Day.

Ans: Introduction: An Astrologer's Day is a short story written by R.K Narayana. R. K. Narayan, was an Indian writer famous for his stories set in the imaginary South Indian town of Malgudi. Along with Mulk Raj Anand and Raja Rao, he was one of the early Indian authors writing in English. Narayan focused on the daily lives and social situations of his characters .Narayan focused on the daily lives and social situations of his characters.

An Astrologer's Day is a thriller, suspense short story. While it had been published earlier, it was the titular story of Narayan's fourth collection of short stories published in 1947 by Indian Thought Publications. It was the first chapter of the world famous collection of stories Malgudi Days which was later telecasted on television in 2006.

Main Content: In R.K. Narayan's An Astrologer's Day, the statement that "there are no good or bad characters" is intricately woven into the fabric of the story. Narayan's world is often filled with characters who, while flawed and imperfect, are shaped by their circumstances and past experiences. This complexity makes them neither entirely good nor entirely bad, but rather human—multidimensional and morally ambiguous. This theme is central to understanding the story's characters, particularly the astrologer and Guru Nayak.

The Astrologer: More than a Fraud

The astrologer, who is the protagonist of the story, appears at first glance to be a charlatan. He sets up shop every day, pretending to possess mystical powers of foresight and prediction, while in reality, he is simply skilled at reading people's faces and manipulating their emotions. This deceit could easily mark him as a "bad" character, one who makes a living by fooling others. However, Narayan reveals that the astrologer is not driven by malice but by necessity. He left his village, abandoned his family's farming occupation, and fled to the city, fearing he had committed murder in his youth. His choice to become an astrologer is not a path of deliberate deceit but one born out of desperation and survival. He is simply trying to make ends meet in a world where he has no other options.

This complexity in the astrologer's character becomes clearer when we realize that his false predictions often leave people satisfied. His understanding of human psychology and his ability to perceive what his clients want to hear mean that he actually provides a kind of comfort and reassurance to them, even if through deception. In this sense, the astrologer cannot be seen as entirely bad. He plays the role of a healer or counselor for his clients, giving them peace of mind, albeit through guesswork and manipulation. Thus, he operates in a moral gray area—his actions are deceptive, but they are not done out of cruelty or selfish gain, but out of the need to survive and, in some way, to help others.

Guru Nayak: Neither Villain Nor Victim

Guru Nayak, the astrologer's former victim, also defies simple categorization as a "bad" or "good" character. He enters the story with a sense of menace, challenging the astrologer to prove his abilities with a test, which creates a sense of tension and suspense. Nayak is depicted as someone filled with anger and revenge, seeking the person who had once attacked him and left him for dead. At first, his quest for vengeance might make him seem like a vengeful, morally dubious character. However, when we learn of his traumatic past, having nearly been killed and left to die in a well, his motivations become more understandable.

Nayak's search for his attacker is not born purely from malice but from the desire for closure. He has spent years trying to track down the person responsible for his suffering. In this context, his actions are not entirely wrong. He has been deeply wronged, and his search for justice—or at least revenge—is a way for him to find peace. When the astrologer tells him that his attacker is dead, Guru Nayak accepts this truth and leaves without further confrontation. He could have reacted violently or continued his search, but instead, he allows the astrologer's words to put an end to his pursuit. This response shows that Nayak, despite his initial portrayal as a threatening figure, is not purely driven by hatred. He is simply a man shaped by his pain and loss.

The Astrologer's Guilt and Redemption

The astrologer's moral ambiguity deepens when we learn that he is the very man Guru Nayak has been searching for. Years ago, in a fit of drunken rage, the astrologer attacked Nayak and left him for dead, thinking he had killed him. This act of violence forced the astrologer to flee his village and start a new life in Malgudi. For years, he has lived with the guilt of believing himself to be a murderer, constantly haunted by the past. This burden has shaped his entire life, leading him to adopt a new identity as an astrologer and live in fear of being discovered.

However, when Guru Nayak comes to him unknowingly, the astrologer's guilt and fear resurface. At first, he tries to escape the situation, but ultimately, he faces his past by answering Nayak's questions. In doing so, he not only saves himself from physical harm but also finds a kind of redemption. The astrologer tells Guru Nayak that his attacker is dead, which is not entirely untrue—symbolically, the "old" version of the astrologer, the violent and reckless man he once was, has died. He has transformed into someone else, even if that someone is not entirely honest. By telling Nayak that his attacker has been crushed by a lorry, the astrologer puts an end to both Nayak's search and his own guilt. This moment frees both characters from their pasts, allowing them to move forward.

A World Without Absolute Morality

Narayan's portrayal of both the astrologer and Guru Nayak emphasizes that human beings cannot be reduced to simple categories of good and evil. Both characters are shaped by the circumstances of their lives and their past mistakes. The astrologer, though a liar, is not without a sense of morality and guilt. He seeks redemption and ultimately provides peace to both Guru Nayak and himself. Guru Nayak, though initially threatening, is driven by a desire for justice rather than pure malice, and he accepts the astrologer's words with surprising grace.

Conclusion:

In An Astrologer's Day, Narayan shows that morality is often complex and fluid. The astrologer's past actions do not define him as wholly evil, just as Guru Nayak's desire for revenge does not make him a villain. Both characters inhabit a moral gray area, shaped by the unpredictable twists and turns of life. Narayan's work suggests that people are products of their environments and experiences, and that labeling them as purely good or bad fails to capture the complexity of their humanity.

Ultimately, Narayan's story reflects his broader worldview: that human nature is too complex to be reduced to moral extremes. His characters live in a world where the lines between right and wrong blur, and where people are defined by their choices, regrets, and redemptions. This nuanced portrayal of human nature is what makes An Astrologer's Day such a compelling and enduring tale.

Q.2 Attempt a character sketch of the astrologer. Does this story evoke sympathy or anger for him in you?

Ans: Introduction: An Astrologer's Day is a short story written by R.K Narayana. R. K. Narayan, was an Indian writer famous for his stories set in the imaginary South Indian town of Malgudi. Along with Mulk Raj Anand and Raja Rao, he was one of the early Indian authors writing in English. Narayan focused on the daily lives and social situations of his characters .Narayan focused on the daily lives and social situations of his characters. An Astrologer's Day is a thriller, suspense short story. While it had been published earlier, it was the titular story of Narayan's fourth collection of short stories published in 1947 by Indian Thought Publications. It was the first chapter of the world famous collection of stories Malgudi Days which was later telecasted on television in 2006.

Main Content: The astrologer in R.K. Narayan's An Astrologer's Day is a complex character, shaped by circumstances and driven by necessity. At first glance, he appears to be a typical, perhaps even fraudulent, astrologer sitting in a marketplace, dressed in the garb of someone with deep spiritual knowledge. However, as the story unfolds, we realize there is much more to him than meets the eye, making him a fascinating character worthy of a deeper examination.

Physical Appearance and Role in Society

The astrologer's outward appearance is designed to invoke awe and trust. He sits under a banyan tree, illuminated by artificial lights in a bustling marketplace. His forehead is smeared with sacred ash and vermilion, his eyes shine with a seemingly divine glow, and his attire is that of a holy man. This calculated look gives him an air of mystery and credibility, making people believe in his supposed powers of divination. Yet, this image is carefully constructed. His appearance is a facade that allows him to survive in a world where knowledge of the stars, or the pretence of it, is a marketable skill.

He is a man on the fringes of society, operating in a space between genuine knowledge and cunning trickery. The people who come to him are desperate for answers, and he uses his keen sense of observation and understanding of human nature to provide them with what they need. His real skill is not astrology, but his ability to read people and situations, and this is what sustains his livelihood.

Cunning and Observant

One of the astrologer's most striking traits is his cunning. He may not have any real knowledge of astrology, but he compensates with his keen powers of observation and an understanding of human psychology. When people come to him seeking guidance, he reads their faces, listens carefully to their words, and uses subtle cues to construct a believable narrative. This requires a certain level of intelligence and quick thinking, and he does it remarkably well. His customers are satisfied because they feel seen and understood, even if the astrologer is simply telling them what they want to hear.

For instance, when a stranger (later revealed to be Guru Nayak, his enemy from the past) approaches him, the astrologer expertly reads his demeanor and guesses that he has traveled far and is searching for answers related to a personal issue. Without revealing his lack of real astrological knowledge, the astrologer manipulates the conversation to steer it in a direction that benefits him, ultimately allowing him to escape a potentially dangerous situation.

Haunted by the Past

The astrologer's calm exterior and deceptive profession hide a dark and turbulent past. The story reveals that he once fled his village after thinking he had killed a man during a drunken brawl. This revelation adds layers of complexity to his character, showing that his life as an astrologer is not just a simple case of trickery but is instead shaped by the need to escape a crime he believes he committed.

The guilt of his past haunts him, though he has managed to bury it deep within. His role as an astrologer, ironically, seems to mirror his own internal state—just as he tries to guide others by fabricating stories about their futures, he is constantly trying to rewrite his own past, distancing himself from the crime he thinks he committed. His entire existence, therefore, is a form of survival. He isn't just surviving in a material sense by earning a living in the market, but also emotionally and psychologically, by suppressing the guilt and fear that follow him.

A Survivor

Survival is a central theme in the astrologer's life. He has had to adapt quickly to a world where opportunities for men like him are limited. His decision to become an astrologer was likely driven by necessity rather than any particular desire for power or manipulation. In many ways, his entire life has been about survival—first, running from the crime he thought he committed, and later, making a living through whatever means possible.

This makes him a deeply human character. While some might view his profession as dishonest, the story encourages us to see it from his perspective. He is not a man driven by greed or evil intentions; rather, he is doing what he must to survive in a harsh and unforgiving world. His deception is not a sign of malicious intent but of resourcefulness in the face of limited options.

The Encounter with Guru Nayak

The turning point in the story—and in the astrologer's life—comes when he is confronted by Guru Nayak, the man he thought he had killed years ago. This encounter reveals much about the astrologer's character. Initially, he is filled with fear, thinking his past has finally caught up with him. However, he quickly regains his composure and uses his cunning to control the situation. He doesn't recognize Guru Nayak immediately, but through clever manipulation of the conversation, he uncovers the truth and realizes that this man is his supposed victim.

The astrologer could have fled or refused to engage with Guru Nayak, but instead, he chooses to confront his past, albeit in a roundabout way. He tells Guru Nayak that the man he is looking for is dead, a lie that ultimately sets both of them free. For Guru Nayak, this lie brings closure, allowing him to move on from his quest for revenge. For the astrologer, it brings a sense of relief, as he learns that the man he thought he had killed is still alive. This moment also gives the astrologer an opportunity for redemption. While he doesn't admit to his crime, his relief at knowing he is not a murderer suggests that he has been carrying the weight of that guilt for years.

Sympathy or Anger?

When considering the character of the astrologer, it's easy to feel sympathy rather than anger. While he is, on the surface, a deceiver, his actions are not driven by malice but by desperation. He is a man who has been shaped by his circumstances—his guilt over a crime he believes he committed, his need to survive in a world where opportunities are scarce, and his ability to use his wits to navigate difficult situations.

His confrontation with Guru Nayak humanizes him even more. He is not an evil man, but a flawed one, grappling with his past and trying to make a life for himself. The fact that he finds a way to bring closure to both himself and Guru Nayak without resorting to violence or further deceit shows that he has some moral compass, even if his methods are questionable.

In the end, the astrologer is a man doing his best in a difficult situation. His deception is not meant to harm but to survive. This evokes a sense of empathy for him. The story presents him as a deeply human character, filled with flaws, guilt, and a desire for redemption. His journey is one of survival, and while his methods might be questionable, the reasons behind them are understandable and relatable, making him a sympathetic figure.

Conclusion

In An Astrologer's Day, the astrologer emerges as a deeply layered and human character. His life is marked by both deception and survival, driven by the need to escape a dark past and make a living in a tough world. Through his skillful manipulation of human emotions, he constructs an identity that not only sustains him but also keeps his inner demons at bay. Despite his profession's dishonesty, the astrologer is not portrayed as a malicious figure, but rather as a resourceful, tormented soul trying to survive.

The encounter with Guru Nayak, his supposed victim, brings the astrologer's past crashing into his present, offering him a chance at redemption. In telling Guru Nayak that the man he seeks is dead, the astrologer creates a closure that both frees him from guilt and provides his former enemy with peace. His story is ultimately one of human frailty, where survival is not just about material gain but also about emotional and psychological redemption.

Far from evoking anger, the astrologer's journey invites sympathy. His life of deception is framed as a necessary evil in a world where opportunities are limited. The astrologer is not a villain, but a survivor—resourceful, flawed, and ultimately human. His story reflects the moral complexity of life, where people often navigate between right and wrong, trying to find some balance in the pursuit of survival and inner peace.

Q.3) Discuss R.K Narayana as a short story writer.

Ans: Introduction: An Astrologer's Day is a short story written by R.K Narayana. R. K. Narayan, was an Indian writer famous for his stories set in the imaginary South Indian town of Malgudi. Along with Mulk Raj Anand and Raja Rao, he was one of the early Indian authors writing in English. Narayan focused on the daily lives and social situations of his characters .Narayan focused on the daily lives and social situations of his characters. An Astrologer's Day is a thriller, suspense short story. While it had been published earlier, it was the titular story of Narayan's fourth collection of short stories published in 1947 by Indian Thought Publications. It was the first chapter of the world famous collection of stories Malgudi Days which was later telecasted on television in 2006.

Main Content: R. K. Narayan is recognized as one of the most important pioneers of Indian literature written in English, alongside other literary giants like Mulk Raj Anand and Raja Rao. He is widely credited for introducing Indian English literature to a global audience, making him one of the most celebrated novelists in Indian literary history. What makes Narayan stand out is his ability to bring the essence of India—its culture, its people, and its daily life—to readers around the world, through the medium of English. His unique storytelling style and relatable characters have left a lasting impact on Indian literature.

The majority of Narayan's stories take place in the fictional town of Malgudi, first introduced in his novel Swami and Friends. Malgudi, though imaginary, feels incredibly real because of the rich detail Narayan uses to describe it. It represents a typical small town in India, with its own blend of tradition, superstition, and a mix of characters who mirror ordinary Indians. Narayan's stories capture the everyday struggles, joys, and simple pleasures of life in Malgudi, and through this, he invites readers to experience the life of common people in India. His ability to make this fictional place feel like a genuine town filled with real people is one of his most admired qualities as a writer.

Narayan's writing style has often been compared to that of the American writer William Faulkner. Like Faulkner, who created the fictional town of Yoknapatawpha to represent real-life southern America, Narayan's Malgudi stands as a symbol for the everyday reality of India. Both authors were masters at bringing out the humour, warmth, and energy in ordinary life while displaying deep empathy and compassion for their characters. Narayan, like Faulkner, was able to capture the spirit of small-town life in a way that made it both familiar and engaging for readers.

However, when it comes to short stories, Narayan's style has been more frequently compared to the French writer Guy de Maupassant. Both authors had the ability to compress a narrative into just a few pages without losing any of the essential elements of the story. Narayan could tell a full, satisfying tale within a short span, managing to capture the complexity of his characters' lives in just a few words. His short stories, much like Maupassant's, leave a strong impression, making the reader feel as though they've lived through the experiences of the characters, despite the brevity of the narratives.

Narayan's most famous collection of short stories is Malgudi Days, which was published in 1982. This book contains stories that provide a vivid portrait of life in Malgudi, showcasing the variety of characters, situations, and emotions that make the town feel so alive. Another famous collection, Under the Banyan Tree and Other Stories, offers further insight into his storytelling skills. Through these collections, Narayan gives readers a peek into the social and political changes happening in India during both the British colonial period and the post-independence era, all the while maintaining a focus on the ordinary lives of his characters.

One of the standout features of Narayan's writing is his simplicity and natural humour. His prose is unpretentious and easy to read, yet filled with deep meaning. Narayan had the remarkable ability to focus on the small, everyday experiences of people, making his characters and their lives relatable to readers. His stories often evoke the feeling of sitting down with a neighbor or a cousin, listening to their tales, which makes his work accessible and emotionally engaging.

Unlike many other Indian writers of his time, Narayan did not feel the need to follow the trends or stylistic fashions of contemporary fiction writing. He remained true to his voice, writing about Indian society in a straightforward, yet meaningful way. His use of dialogue often carried subtle Tamil overtones, reflecting the natural speech patterns of his characters. This made his work authentic and true to the cultural context he was writing about, without needing to alter his style to fit Western literary expectations.

Critics have often compared Narayan's works to the short stories of Russian author Anton Chekhov. Both writers shared a gentle, compassionate approach to storytelling, focusing on the beauty and humor present in even tragic situations. British author Graham Greene, a close friend and admirer of Narayan, once remarked that Narayan was more similar to Chekhov than any other Indian writer of his time. Both authors shared a talent for presenting simple but profound insights into human nature through seemingly ordinary events.

Pulitzer Prize-winning author Jhumpa Lahiri has also praised Narayan's short stories, noting how they manage to offer readers a full glimpse into the lives of his characters in just a few pages. Most of his short stories are less than ten pages long, yet they convey emotions and situations that many novelists struggle to achieve over hundreds of pages. Lahiri placed Narayan in the company of short-story greats like O. Henry, Frank O'Connor, and Flannery O'Connor, all of whom could evoke powerful emotions and meaningful insights within a short narrative span.

Lahiri also compared Narayan to Guy de Maupassant for their shared ability to compress complex stories into brief narratives without losing the depth of the characters or the story itself. Both authors often explored themes of middle-class life, offering an unflinching and realistic look at human behavior without succumbing to pity or sentimentality. Narayan's ability to portray the struggles, hopes, and dreams of ordinary people with such clarity and honesty is one of his most celebrated strengths.

Narayan's stories are often described as being more descriptive than analytical. He focused on providing readers with a clear, authentic depiction of life in small-town India rather than delving into deep philosophical or psychological analysis. This objective approach allowed him to create characters and situations that felt real and relatable to readers, whether they were familiar with Indian culture or not. His stories also highlight the unique norms and traditions that shaped the lives of people in Malgudi, giving readers a glimpse into the superstitions and customs that were part of everyday life in India.

Narayan's writing style, with its focus on humor, compassion, and the small details of life, has often been compared to William Faulkner's. Both authors managed to juxtapose the demands of society with the confusion of individuality, showing how ordinary people navigate the complexities of their social roles while also grappling with their personal struggles. However, while Faulkner used complex, rhetorical prose to make his points, Narayan's approach was much simpler and more realistic, yet equally effective in capturing the essence of life.

Some critics have pointed out that Narayan's stories often end with sudden twists or unexpected reversals, similar to the style of O. Henry. While these endings can sometimes feel unconvincing, they add a layer of surprise and reflection that leaves a lasting impact on the reader.

Narayan's greatest achievement lies in his ability to make India accessible to readers worldwide through his literature. He brought to life the charm, struggles, and beauty of small-town India, allowing readers to connect with his characters and their lives. Along with Raja Rao and Mulk Raj Anand, Narayan is regarded as one of the three most influential Indian English-language fiction writers. Through his creation of Malgudi and its rich cast of characters, Narayan gave readers a new way to experience India—a place full of unique individuals with their own quirks, dreams, and challenges, all presented in a way that felt both authentic and relatable.

Conclusion: R. K. Narayan's contributions to Indian literature, particularly through his fictional town of Malgudi, have made him a literary icon. His simple yet powerful storytelling, which focuses on the lives of ordinary people, has given readers both in India and around the world a deep insight into the nuances of Indian society. His ability to create relatable, authentic characters and settings—without succumbing to trends or complexity—has cemented his place as one of the most significant Indian English writers. Through Malgudi, Narayan has allowed readers to experience small-town India, blending humor, humanity, and an exploration of social dynamics in a way that remains timeless. His works continue to resonate with readers, reminding us of the beauty and complexity of everyday life, and his impact on Indian English literature remains unparalleled.

Q.4 Write on structure and theme of R.K Narayan's An Astrologer's Day.

Ans: Introduction: An Astrologer's Day is a short story written by R.K Narayana. R. K. Narayan, was an Indian writer famous for his stories set in the imaginary South Indian town of Malgudi. Along with Mulk Raj Anand and Raja Rao, he was one of the early Indian authors writing in English. Narayan focused on the daily lives and social situations of his characters

.Narayan focused on the daily lives and social situations of his characters. An Astrologer's Day is a thriller, suspense short story. While it had been published earlier, it was the titular story of Narayan's fourth collection of short stories published in 1947 by Indian Thought Publications. It was the first chapter of the world famous collection of stories Malgudi Days which was later telecasted on television in 2006.

Main Content: R.K. Narayan's short story An Astrologer's Day follows a simple yet structured narrative, which allows the theme of fate, irony, and human deception to unfold gradually. The story is set in a bustling Indian marketplace, where the astrologer, the central character, conducts his business. The narrative is divided into distinct sections that collectively build suspense, leading to a surprising climax that reveals the astrologer's hidden past. The theme of the story focuses on a single day in the life of an ordinary astrologer who suddenly faces past life in the present drastic situation. The story has a twist in the tale. The otherwise adventure less life of the astrologer suddenly poses a grave problem from his past life and demands alertness to tackle the situation. The story describes of a single day in the lives of the sleepy town of Malgudi. The story also deals with the darker side of human nature with its hypocrisies, shrewdness, revengeful nature and selfishness. The characters in the story are no exception to these qualities of human nature. Finally all is well that ends well with the astrologer coming out with flying colors in his examination of befooling his opponent, saving his life and also saw to it that he does not face the man again in future.

The story begins by describing the astrologer's environment and daily routine. He sits under a tamarind tree, relying on his colorful appearance and convincing manner to attract customers. The exposition introduces us to his method of work, where he does not possess real astrological knowledge but uses keen observation and generic statements to read his clients' minds. This sets the foundation for the theme of deception and human gullibility. The astrologer's livelihood is based on creating an illusion, and his ability to read people's emotions becomes a crucial element later in the story.

As the plot progresses, the astrologer encounters a man named Guru Nayak, who demands a genuine reading. The tension rises as the astrologer struggles to provide a prediction. Through this meeting, the reader is slowly introduced to the theme of fate and karma. Unbeknownst to Guru Nayak, the astrologer has a hidden connection to him—he is the man whom Guru

Nayak has been searching for, believing that he had been killed years ago. The astrologer's past is revealed: he had once attacked Guru Nayak in a brawl and left him for dead, fleeing his village to avoid punishment.

The story reaches its climax when the astrologer, realizing that his life is in danger, manipulates the situation. Using his astute observational skills, he tells Guru Nayak what he wants to hear—that the man he is searching for is dead. This revelation not only saves the astrologer's life but also frees him from the burden of guilt. The irony here lies in the fact that both men walk away satisfied: Guru Nayak believes his quest for revenge is over, and the astrologer feels absolved of his past sin.

The theme of fate runs throughout the story, suggesting that no one can escape the consequences of their actions. The astrologer, despite his deception, is a victim of fate himself. Narayan's use of irony, deception, and the unpredictability of life makes An Astrologer's Day a powerful story about human nature and the inescapable force of destiny.

Conclusion: R.K. Narayan's An Astrologer's Day is a masterfully structured story that uses irony, deception, and the theme of fate to explore the complexities of human nature. Through the astrologer's encounter with his past, the story reveals how people often manipulate truth and illusion to survive and navigate life's unpredictability. The themes of karma and destiny are intricately woven into the plot, highlighting that no one can truly escape the consequences of their actions. The astrologer's life, built on deception, ultimately comes full circle, showing that while fate can be delayed or disguised, it remains unavoidable. Narayan's simple yet profound storytelling brings out these universal themes, leaving readers with a thought-provoking reflection on the nature of life, guilt, and redemption.

Q.5) Discuss the prose style of R.K.Narayan with reference to his short stories prescribed in your syllabus.

Ans: Introduction: An Astrologer's Day is a short story written by R.K Narayana. R. K. Narayan, was an Indian writer famous for his stories set in the imaginary South Indian town of Malgudi. Along with Mulk Raj Anand and Raja Rao, he was one of the early Indian authors writing in English. Narayan focused on the daily lives and social situations of his characters .Narayan focused on the daily lives and social situations of his characters. An Astrologer's Day is a thriller, suspense short story. While it had been published earlier, it was the titular story of Narayan's fourth collection of short stories published in 1947 by Indian Thought Publications. It was the first chapter of the world famous collection of stories Malgudi Days which was later telecasted on television in 2006.

Main Content: R.K. Narayan's prose style is distinctive and influential in Indian literature, characterized by its simplicity, clarity, and the ability to convey profound themes through relatable characters and everyday situations. In his works An Astrologer's Day and Engine Trouble, Narayan demonstrates these qualities, employing a narrative style that is both engaging and thought-provoking.

1. Simplicity and Clarity

Narayan's language is simple, clear, and direct, making his stories accessible to readers of all ages. He avoids elaborate or ornamental descriptions, opting instead for straightforward narration. This allows readers to focus on the characters and their situations without being distracted by complex language or metaphor.

In "An Astrologer's Day", the opening paragraph is a good example of this clarity:

"Punctually at midday he opened his bag and spread out his professional equipment, which consisted of a dozen cowrie shells, a square piece of cloth with obscure mystic charts on it, a notebook, and a bundle of palmyra writing."

The reader is immediately introduced to the protagonist and his profession in a few succinct sentences. The economy of words gives an almost journalistic tone to the setting.

2. Realism and Everyday Life

Narayan's stories are firmly grounded in the realities of Indian society, particularly the small-town and village life of southern India. His characters are often ordinary people with ordinary problems, but he imbues their lives with universality and depth.

In "Engine Trouble", the narrator wins a road engine in a lottery and the rest of the story revolves around the absurd consequences of this event. The protagonist's attempts to get rid of the engine are depicted with an understated humor that reflects the challenges of rural life in India.

Narayan doesn't romanticize the characters' lives; instead, he portrays them with subtle irony. The simplicity of the problems (an astrologer deceiving his clients, a man struggling with an unwanted prize) draws the reader into their everyday predicaments.

3. Humor and Irony

Narayan's sense of humor is gentle, often situational, and emerges from the characters' interactions with their circumstances. His humor tends to highlight the absurdity of life and human behavior.

In "Engine Trouble", the protagonist's plight is hilariously portrayed as he struggles to manage the engine, which is both a blessing and a curse. The story is filled with moments where the absurdity of the situation is played for comic effect, but it is always a soft humor, never cruel.

Likewise, in "An Astrologer's Day", there is an irony in the astrologer's life. He, who has no real powers, survives by pretending to predict people's futures, and fate itself turns up at his doorstep in the form of a former victim. This ironic twist at the end showcases Narayan's skill at blending humor with dramatic tension.

4. Characterization

Narayan's characters are often ordinary individuals, yet they are drawn with such depth that they resonate with readers on a personal level. He brings out their inner conflicts and motivations in a few deft strokes.

In "An Astrologer's Day", the astrologer is not a powerful, mystical figure but a common man making a living through deceit. Despite this, the reader can empathize with his need to survive. Similarly, in "Engine Trouble", the protagonist is a relatable figure, an everyman caught in circumstances beyond his control. His frustrations and struggles are humorously depicted, yet we also feel sympathy for him.

5. Moral Subtlety

Narayan's stories often explore moral dilemmas but do so in a way that avoids heavy-handedness. The morality of his characters' actions is not always clear-cut, and he leaves room for the reader's interpretation.

In "An Astrologer's Day", for instance, the astrologer's deception of his clients might be seen as unethical, yet his encounter with a former victim adds layers to this moral question. The astrologer is revealed to have his own past to contend with, and his survival depends on a lie, making the moral conclusion ambiguous.

6. Effective Use of Short Story Form

Both stories are tight and well-constructed, utilizing the short story form effectively. Narayan wastes no words, each sentence serving to move the plot forward or deepen the reader's understanding of the characters. The twists in both "An Astrologer's Day" and "Engine Trouble" come as a surprise but feel earned, adding a final layer of meaning to the stories.

Conclusion

R.K. Narayan's prose style is marked by simplicity, realism, gentle humor, and an insightful portrayal of human nature. In both "An

Astrologer's Day" and "Engine Trouble", these elements are woven together to create engaging, thought-provoking, and relatable stories. His ability to make the ordinary extraordinary through his language and storytelling makes him a master of the short story form.

Engine Trouble

Scan the QR code to watch video

About story:

"Engine Trouble" tells the story of an unlucky narrator who wins a road engine at a local fair, only to find it becomes a heavy burden. Unable to use or sell the unwanted prize, he incurs mounting expenses for its storage and attempts to move it. His efforts involve hiring laborers, trying to enlist help from bus drivers, and even borrowing a temple elephant—all of which lead to chaos, the destruction of a compound wall, and ultimately, his arrest.

Overwhelmed by debt and public ridicule, the narrator's misadventures force him to leave town, leaving behind a trail of legal and financial troubles. In an ironic twist, an earthquake later displaces the engine, which is eventually discovered lodged in an abandoned well, much to the bemusement of its owner. The story uses humor and irony to highlight the absurdity of fate and the often fruitless struggle against everyday misfortune.

Question and Answer

Q.1 In what way does R.K Narayan's story Engine trouble appeal to you? Discuss.

Ans: Introduction: Engine Trouble is a short story written by R.K. Narayan in his book Malgudi Days, published in 1943 by Indian Thought Publications. RK Narayan was a famous Indian writer globally known for his fictional writings of Malgudi. R.K. Narayan's short story "Engine Trouble" is a humorous tale about a man's misfortune after winning an unwanted prize. Themes of realism, optimism, good fortune, accountability, authority, resolve, and resourcefulness are present throughout Engine Trouble. An everyday, regular resident tells the tale in the first person. There is a little irony in depicting people, events, and locations.

Main Content:

R.K. Narayan's short story "Engine Trouble" offers a humorous yet insightful take on the unpredictable nature of life and how situations that initially seem favorable can turn into burdens. The story's protagonist, a humble, ordinary man, wins a road engine in a raffle, but what appears to be a stroke of luck soon turns into an unexpected and frustrating ordeal. The engine becomes an enormous burden, symbolizing how life's gifts sometimes come with hidden costs and responsibilities.

The theme of "Engine Trouble" resonates deeply with my personal and professional experiences. As someone with over ten years of experience in IT project handling and currently managing trading applications like XTS, I have often faced situations where opportunities that seemed golden at first later turned into complex challenges. In the story, the protagonist's initial joy at winning the engine mirrors the excitement I've felt when taking on ambitious projects or responsibilities in my career. These opportunities promised growth and success, but they also came with their own set of hurdles—much like how the protagonist quickly realizes that the engine, instead of being a prize, is a cumbersome responsibility.

The story speaks to the broader experience of life's unpredictability. Much like the protagonist who suddenly finds himself burdened with a massive engine that he can neither use nor easily get rid of, I have encountered situations where projects or tasks that seemed manageable initially required far more effort and resources than anticipated. For example, in IT projects, unexpected technical issues, client demands, or resource shortages often arise, much like the unforeseen difficulties the protagonist faces when trying to move or dispose of the engine. These challenges can lead to frustration, as I've experienced when striving to exceed my salary in a difficult financial situation or when navigating complex professional tasks.

Narayan's story also reflects the struggle to deal with circumstances beyond one's control. The protagonist's efforts to resolve his problem—by seeking help from local authorities, appealing to a circus troupe, and trying various other methods—often fail due to reasons outside his influence. This is reminiscent of my own experiences in seeking career advancement or exploring remote job fields. Despite my best efforts to learn new skills, manage projects, or seek high-paying roles, external factors like market trends, competition, or organizational dynamics sometimes dictate the outcome. Just as the protagonist could not control the obstacles in his path, I've realized that certain challenges in life, especially in the professional sphere, are influenced by factors beyond individual control.

The story, however, does not end in despair but rather teaches a valuable lesson in perseverance and resilience. The protagonist finally gets rid of the engine, not through his own efforts but by a stroke of luck when an earthquake causes the engine to be moved. This conclusion resonates with my belief that while hard work and planning are crucial, life sometimes requires a bit of patience and luck. When I've been frustrated with professional setbacks—whether it's trying to break into a new field for remote jobs with a package of 40 lacs or striving to earn more than 50 lacs through API development and management—I've learned that persistence often pays off. Sometimes, solutions come unexpectedly, just like how the engine problem is solved in the story.

Furthermore, "Engine Trouble" highlights the importance of humor and perspective in dealing with life's trials. Despite the protagonist's frustration, the tone of the story is light-hearted, reminding us that even in difficult situations, a sense of humor can provide relief and clarity. In my own life, I've found that maintaining a positive outlook, even when facing career-related challenges or personal struggles, helps me to keep things in perspective. Whether it's managing complex projects or balancing personal responsibilities, like caring for a child with autism and ADHD, as in my case, laughter and optimism can often provide the strength needed to move forward.

Conclusion:

R.K. Narayan's "Engine Trouble" serves as a reflection of the challenges we face in life and work. It teaches us that while opportunities can sometimes come with hidden difficulties, perseverance, adaptability, and a positive outlook can help us navigate even the most burdensome situations. Whether it's dealing with a troublesome engine or a demanding career, the story reminds us that life's challenges are temporary, and with the right mindset, they can be overcome, often in unexpected ways.

Q.2) Discuss the narrative technique used in the story.

Ans: Introduction: Engine Trouble is a short story written by R K Narayan .He (1906–2001) was one of India's most celebrated English-language writers, renowned for creating the fictional town of Malgudi that mirrored Indian society with warmth and humor.R.K. Narayan's "Engine Trouble" from Malgudi Days presents a richly textured narrative that begins with a seemingly fortunate event at a bustling local fair in the fictional town of Malgudi. The protagonist, an ordinary man caught up in the excitement of the fair's lottery, finds himself the unexpected winner of a massive road engine. His initial reaction is one of uncontainable joy, imagining the prestige and financial security this impressive machine will bring him. Friends and neighbors share in his excitement, reinforcing his belief that fate has finally smiled upon him. This early section of the story effectively establishes the protagonist's naive optimism while subtly hinting at the impractical nature of his prize through carefully placed descriptions of the engine's enormous size and mechanical complexity.

As the story progresses, the narrative takes a sharp turn into the realm of comic misfortune. The protagonist quickly discovers that his prized possession is essentially a white elephant - impossible to operate, expensive to maintain, and stubbornly immobile. Narayan masterfully depicts the growing burden through a series of escalating frustrations, from the engine's physical obstruction of public space to the mounting costs of its upkeep. The protagonist's desperate attempts to solve his predicament form the heart of the story, with each proposed solution more absurd than the last. His hiring of fifty laborers to move the engine, followed by the employment of a temple elephant in a spectacularly failed relocation attempt, showcase Narayan's gift for blending humor with social commentary. These scenes not only provide comic relief but also reveal the protagonist's increasing desperation and the community's growing amusement at his plight.

The story reaches its climax as the protagonist, now thoroughly defeated by his mechanical burden, contemplates abandoning his life in Malgudi. Just when his situation appears most hopeless, Narayan introduces a deus ex machina in the form of an earthquake that neatly resolves all conflicts. The seismic event sends the troublesome engine tumbling into an abandoned well, where it fits with perfect precision. This resolution, while seemingly miraculous, maintains the story's internal logic and reinforces its central themes. The conclusion sees the protagonist liberated from his burden, the creditors satisfied with their newly plugged well, and the community moving on to the next spectacle. Through this circular narrative structure, Narayan completes his meditation on the unpredictable nature of fortune and the human capacity to find relief in unexpected places.

What makes "Engine Trouble" particularly compelling is Narayan's ability to weave multiple layers of meaning into a deceptively simple narrative. The road engine serves as a powerful metaphor for life's unexpected burdens - those gifts that turn out to be curses in disguise. Narayan's portrayal of the protagonist's psychological journey from elation to despair and eventual relief captures universal human experiences with remarkable economy. The story's setting in the vibrant world of Malgudi, with its colorful secondary characters and rich social dynamics, adds depth and authenticity to what might otherwise be a straightforward cautionary tale. Narayan's characteristic gentle irony and understated humor prevent the story from becoming heavy-handed, allowing the moral to emerge organically from the events rather than being imposed upon them. This delicate balance between entertainment and insight is what makes "Engine Trouble" a standout piece in Narayan's celebrated Malgudi Days collection.

Q.3) Discuss the themes of the story Engine Trouble.

Ans: Introduction: Engine Trouble is a short story written by R K Narayan .He (1906–2001) was one of India's most celebrated English-language writers, renowned for creating the fictional town of Malgudi that mirrored Indian society with warmth and humor.One of the central themes in "Engine Trouble" is the irony of fortune and misfortune. The story begins with the protagonist winning what appears to be a valuable prize—a road engine—only to realize it brings more problems than benefits. Narayan highlights how life's unexpected windfalls can sometimes turn into burdens. The protagonist's initial excitement quickly fades as he struggles with the engine's impracticality, showing that what seems like good luck may not always be so. The story suggests that happiness cannot be measured by material possessions, as the engine, despite its impressive appearance, becomes a source of stress rather than prosperity.

Another important theme is human helplessness against larger forces. The protagonist tries everything to rid himself of the engine—selling it, moving it with laborers, even using an elephant—but nothing works. His struggles reflect how people often find themselves powerless in the face of uncontrollable circumstances. Narayan, known for his subtle humor, portrays these attempts with comedy, but beneath the laughter lies a deeper message: no matter how hard we try, some problems are beyond our control. The resolution, where an earthquake solves the problem, reinforces this idea—sometimes, fate intervenes where human effort fails.

The story also explores society's influence on individual happiness. At first, the protagonist is proud of his prize because others admire it. His neighbors congratulate him, reinforcing his belief that the engine is valuable. However, as the engine becomes a nuisance, society's opinion shifts, and he feels embarrassed. This shows how much our sense of worth depends on others' perceptions. Narayan critiques how people often chase status symbols to gain approval, only to realize too late that these possessions bring no real joy. The protagonist's journey from pride to frustration mirrors the emptiness of societal validation.

Fate and chance play a significant role in the story. The protagonist wins the engine purely by luck, and in the end, it is another random event—the earthquake—that saves him. Narayan suggests that life is unpredictable, and humans have little control over their circumstances. The story's circular structure, where the protagonist ends up where he started, emphasizes how life's ups and downs are often governed by chance. This theme is common in Narayan's works, where characters frequently face situations beyond their understanding or control.

Finally, humor as a coping mechanism is a subtle but important theme. Despite the protagonist's troubles, the story is filled with funny moments—like the elephant dragging the engine or the chaotic attempts to move it. Narayan uses humor to soften the story's darker undertones, showing how people laugh at life's absurdities even in difficult times. The comedy makes the protagonist's struggles relatable, reminding readers that sometimes, the best way to deal with problems is to see the lighter side.

Conclusion:

In "Engine Trouble," Narayan weaves these themes together to create a story that is both entertaining and thought-provoking. Through simple yet powerful storytelling, he explores human nature, society's expectations, and the role of luck in our lives. The tale remains relevant because these themes are universal—everyone has faced unexpected challenges, struggled with societal pressures, or laughed in the face of misfortune. Narayan's genius lies in presenting these deep ideas in a way that feels lighthearted yet meaningful, making "Engine Trouble" a timeless piece of literature.

Q.4) Discuss the Characterisation in Engine Trouble.

Ans: Introduction: Engine Trouble is a short story written by R K Narayan .He (1906–2001) was one of India's most celebrated English-language writers, renowned for creating the fictional town of Malgudi that mirrored Indian society with warmth and humor.R.K. Narayan's "Engine Trouble" features a cast of memorable characters who bring the story to life through their distinct personalities and roles in the narrative. The protagonist, an unnamed everyman, serves as the central figure whose experiences drive the plot. He is portrayed as an ordinary person with simple dreams and aspirations, making him relatable to readers. His initial excitement over winning the road engine reveals his hopeful and somewhat naive nature. However, as the story progresses, we see his transformation from an optimistic winner to a frustrated and helpless victim of circumstance. This character arc effectively captures the human tendency to equate material gains with happiness, only to realize that appearances can be deceiving. Narayan skillfully uses the protagonist's journey to highlight universal human experiences of hope, disappointment, and eventual relief.

The protagonist's wife provides an interesting contrast to his character. While she initially shares his enthusiasm about the engine, she quickly becomes the voice of practicality when problems arise. Her growing frustration with her husband's inability to solve the engine dilemma reflects the typical dynamics of marital relationships, where one partner often serves as the realist balancing the other's optimism. Though she appears only briefly, her threat to leave and return to her father's house adds tension to the story while reinforcing the domestic consequences of the protagonist's predicament. Narayan uses her character to show how personal troubles can strain relationships and how family members often bear the brunt of poor decisions.

Secondary characters in the story, though not deeply developed, play crucial roles in advancing the plot and enriching the narrative. The showman who organizes the lottery represents the cunning side of human nature, willing to exploit people's desires for quick fortune. His decision to include the impractical road engine as a prize demonstrates how people in positions of power often manipulate others for profit. The dismissed bus driver Joseph, who attempts to operate the engine, adds comic relief while also symbolizing the common man's struggle with technology and modernization. The various townspeople who gather to watch the spectacle of moving the engine represent society's fascination with others' misfortunes, highlighting how communities often treat personal tragedies as public entertainment.

Narayan's characterization technique is notable for its simplicity and effectiveness. He doesn't provide detailed physical descriptions or complex backstories for his characters, yet they feel authentic and recognizable. This minimalist approach allows readers to project their own experiences onto the characters, making them more relatable. The absence of proper names for most characters (they are referred to by their roles or relationships) gives the story a universal quality, suggesting that these could be people from any small town. The characters' dialogues and actions reveal their personalities naturally, without need for lengthy explanations. For instance, the protagonist's talkative nature emerges through his detailed recounting of his troubles, while the showman's shrewdness is evident in his business decisions.

What makes Narayan's characterization particularly effective is how he uses ordinary people to explore deeper themes. The protagonist isn't a hero with special qualities but an average person reacting to unusual circumstances. This makes his struggles more meaningful because they reflect challenges anyone might face. The supporting characters, while not deeply developed, represent various facets of society - from opportunistic businessmen to curious onlookers - creating a rich tapestry of human behavior. Through these characters, Narayan comments on human nature, societal norms, and the ironies of life without being preachy or judgmental.

The characterization in "Engine Trouble" ultimately serves the story's larger themes of fate, human folly, and the unpredictability of life. By creating characters who are flawed, relatable, and often humorous in their shortcomings, Narayan crafts a narrative that is both entertaining and thought-provoking. The protagonist's journey resonates because it mirrors our own experiences with unexpected challenges, while the secondary characters add color and depth to the world of Malgudi. Narayan's genius lies in his ability to make ordinary characters extraordinary through their very normalcy, proving that you don't need heroic figures to tell a compelling story - sometimes, the most memorable characters are the ones who remind us of ourselves.

CHAPTER TWENTY-ONE

Arun Joshi: The Only American From our Village

Scan to watch the video

About Arun Joshi

Arun Joshi (1939–1993) was a prominent Indian existentialist novelist and short-story writer whose works explored themes of alienation, cultural displacement, and moral decay in postcolonial India. Educated in India and the U.S., Joshi blended Western existentialist influences (Camus, Kafka) with Indian socio-cultural dilemmas, as seen in novels like The Foreigner (1968) and The Strange Case of Billy Biswas (1971). His protagonists—often rootless, disillusioned men—grappled with identity crises, filial neglect (e.g., Dr. Khanna in The Only American from Our Village), and the hollowness of material success. With sparse, introspective prose and open-ended narratives, Joshi critiqued modernity's dehumanizing effects while underscoring the enduring need for spiritual and emotional authenticity. His works remain a significant contribution to Indian English literature for their psychological depth and philosophical rigor.

The Only American From our Village

About Novel:

Dr. Khanna, a celebrated Indian-American physicist, returns to India with his American family after fifteen years abroad. His homecoming is marked by pomp and celebration—meetings with high-ranking officials and prestigious lectures—but the superficiality of these long-distance relationships is evident in the trivial gifts he receives from relatives.

During his final lecture in his hometown, a poor ashramp seller named Radhey Mohan disrupts the event to recount the tragic tale of Dr. Khanna's late father, Kundan Lal, who had sacrificed everything for his son's success. This heartbreaking revelation leaves Dr. Khanna overwhelmed with guilt, paralyzing him both emotionally and professionally. The story critiques the cost of material success and cultural displacement, challenging the values of Western individualism and the immigrant experience.

Question and Answer

Q.1 How Arun Joshi has portrayed his characters in the short story The Only American From our Village.

Ans: Introduction: The Only American From our Village is a short story written by Arun Joshi. He was a prominent Indian existentialist novelist and short-story writer whose works explored themes of alienation, cultural displacement, and moral decay in postcolonial India. Arun Joshi masterfully crafts his characters to reveal profound truths about human nature and modern society. Each character serves as a mirror reflecting different aspects of our contemporary dilemmas.

Dr. Khanna is the epitome of the successful immigrant—a renowned physicist settled in America with a foreign wife and children. On the surface, he embodies the Indian dream of global achievement, but Joshi peels back these layers to expose his moral and emotional shortcomings. His interactions during his India visit are marked by formality and detachment. He delivers lectures, meets dignitaries, and distributes trivial gifts to relatives, all while remaining emotionally distant. His indifference to his father's plight underscores his complete assimilation into Western individualism. The climax, where he is reduced to staring at his feet, consumed by guilt, reveals the fragility of his success. Joshi uses Dr. Khanna to critique the modern pursuit of ambition at the cost of human connections.

Kundan Lal, Dr. Khanna's father, is the story's tragic heart. Once a brilliant student whose name adorned his school's honor board, he sacrifices everything for his son's future. His gradual decline—from a proud father boasting about his son to a broken man waiting in vain for a ticket or a letter—is portrayed with poignant simplicity. Small details, like his daily shaving in hopeful anticipation or his final act of standing barefoot on scorching sand, symbolize his unacknowledged suffering. Kundan Lal's character is a powerful indictment of filial neglect, showing how societal progress often comes at the expense of familial bonds.

Radhey Mohan, the humble ashramp farosh (court paper seller), serves as the story's moral anchor. Despite his low social status, he possesses the clarity and courage to confront Dr. Khanna with uncomfortable truths. His monologue about Kundan Lal's despair is the story's emotional core, delivered with raw honesty that shatters Dr. Khanna's complacency. Radhey Mohan embodies wisdom that transcends formal education, highlighting Joshi's belief that true understanding comes from empathy, not academic accolades.

Joanne and the children represent Dr. Khanna's detached, Westernized life. Their tourist-like behavior during the India visit—distributing cheap gifts, treating relatives as strangers—mirrors Dr. Khanna's own emotional disconnect. They symbolize the cultural gap that widens when traditions are abandoned for assimilation.

Conclusion: Joshi's characterization thrives on contrasts:

Success vs. Failure: Dr. Khanna's professional achievements pale against his moral failure as a son.

Wealth vs. Poverty: Radhey Mohan, though poor, holds the moral wealth Dr. Khanna lacks.

Modernity vs. Tradition: The clash between Dr. Khanna's Western lifestyle and Kundan Lal's traditional expectations.

Through these characters, Joshi delivers a timeless message: success devoid of humanity is meaningless. The story lingers in the reader's mind, urging reflection on the true cost of ambition and the irreplaceable value of familial bonds.

Q.2) Discuss the narrative technique used in the story The Only American From our Village.

Ans: Introduction: The he Only American From our Village is a short story written by Arun Joshi. He was a prominent Indian existentialist novelist and short-story writer whose works explored themes of alienation, cultural displacement, and moral decay in postcolonial India.Arun Joshi uses simple but powerful storytelling methods to make this story emotionally impactful. The way he tells the story helps readers feel the characters' pain and understand the deeper messages.

The story follows a linear structure, moving from Dr. Khanna's arrival in India to his final breakdown. This straightforward timeline makes it easy for readers to follow the events. However, Joshi cleverly uses flashbacks through Radhey Mohan's speech to reveal Kundan Lal's past. These flashbacks are the most emotional parts, showing how Dr. Khanna's success came at the cost of his father's happiness.

Joshi writes in a third-person limited perspective, focusing mostly on Dr. Khanna's experiences. This helps readers see the world through Dr. Khanna's eyes while also noticing his flaws. We see his pride during his lectures and meetings, but we also see his growing discomfort when faced with his father's story. This technique makes Dr. Khanna's final guilt feel more real and personal. The story uses symbolism to deepen its meaning. Dr. Khanna's "burning feet" at the end symbolize his guilt and his father's suffering (since Kundan Lal stood barefoot on hot sand). The small gifts Dr. Khanna's family brings to India represent shallow relationships—expensive items that mean nothing emotionally. These symbols make the story's message stronger without needing long explanations.

Dialogue is used sparingly but effectively. Most of the story is description, but when Radhey Mohan speaks, his words carry great weight. His long monologue about Kundan Lal is the emotional peak of the story. The contrast between Radhey Mohan's simple, honest speech and Dr. Khanna's silent reactions shows the power of truth over success.

Joshi also uses contrasts to highlight his themes. Dr. Khanna's rich, busy life in America is contrasted with his father's poor, lonely life in India. Radhey Mohan's wisdom is contrasted with Dr. Khanna's educated but empty mind. These contrasts make the story's message clear: success without love and responsibility is meaningless.

The ending is open, leaving readers to think about what happens next. Does Dr. Khanna recover? Does he change his ways? This technique makes the story linger in our minds, forcing us to reflect on its themes long after reading.

Conclusion : Joshi's narrative technique is simple but powerful. He uses clear storytelling, strong symbols, and emotional contrasts to make readers feel the pain of neglected relationships. The story feels real and stays with us because of how honestly it is told. It doesn't need fancy words or complicated plots—just truthful writing about human mistakes and their consequences.

Q.3) Attempt the critical appreciation of The Only American From Our Village.

Ans: Introduction: The Only American From our Village is a short story written by Arun Joshi. He was a prominent Indian existentialist novelist and short-story writer whose works explored themes of alienation, cultural displacement, and moral decay in postcolonial India Arun Joshi's The Only American From Our Village is a poignant exploration of cultural displacement, filial neglect, and the hollowness of material success. Through its deceptively simple narrative, the story delivers a powerful critique of modern values while offering profound insights into human relationships and identity.

1. Themes and Social Commentary

The story's central theme revolves around the conflict between traditional familial duty and Western individualism. Joshi presents Dr. Khanna as the archetypal successful immigrant—educated, wealthy, and settled abroad—but exposes the moral bankruptcy beneath this glittering facade. The father Kundan Lal's tragic decline serves as a metaphor for how traditional Indian family structures are crumbling under the weight of Western aspirations. Joshi doesn't merely tell a story about a neglectful son; he holds up a mirror to India's growing middle-class obsession with foreign validation at the cost of indigenous values.

2. Characterization and Symbolism

Joshi's characters are masterfully crafted to represent broader societal forces. Dr. Khanna embodies the educated elite who measure success solely in professional achievements while becoming emotionally illiterate. His physical journey to India contrasts sharply with his inability to make an emotional homecoming. Kundan Lal symbolizes the forgotten generation that sacrificed everything for their children's future, only to be discarded.

The burning feet imagery brilliantly encapsulates the inescapable nature of guilt—what begins as Kundan Lal's physical penance becomes his son's psychological torment.

3. Narrative Technique

Joshi employs a restrained, economical prose style that makes the emotional impact more devastating. The third-person limited perspective allows readers to gradually perceive Dr. Khanna's moral blindness. The story's structure—moving from the superficial celebrations of Dr. Khanna's visit to the raw emotional climax with Radhey Mohan—creates a powerful dramatic arc. The open ending is particularly effective, transforming what could be a simple morality tale into a lingering existential question about redemption and responsibility.

4. Cultural Critique

The story offers a subtle but sharp critique of both Indian and Western cultures. It exposes the hypocrisy of Indian society that worships NRI success stories while ignoring their human cost. Simultaneously, it questions Western individualism that prioritizes career over kinship. The token gifts from America symbolize how globalization has reduced meaningful human connections to transactional exchanges.

5. Universal Relevance

While rooted in specific Indian immigrant experiences, the story's themes have universal resonance. In an increasingly globalized world where professional success often demands geographical and emotional displacement, Joshi's story asks fundamental questions: What constitutes true success? Can achievement compensate for lost relationships? The psychological realism with which Dr. Khanna's breakdown is portrayed makes these questions deeply personal for readers across cultures.

Conclusion

The Only American From Our Village transcends its specific context to become a timeless meditation on human values. Joshi combines the precision of a short story writer with the depth of a philosopher, creating a narrative that is both emotionally devastating and intellectually stimulating. The story's enduring power lies in its ability to make readers examine their own priorities and relationships, long after the final sentence. Through its austere prose and

unflinching honesty, it achieves what all great literature should—it disturbs the comfortable and comforts the disturbed.

Q.5) Discuss the themes of the story The Only American From our Village

Ans: Introduction: The Only American From our Village is a short story written by Arun Joshi. He was a prominent Indian existentialist novelist and short-story writer whose works explored themes of alienation, cultural displacement, and moral decay in postcolonial India. Arun Joshi's The Only American From Our Village explores profound themes that resonate deeply in today's globalized world. Through the story of Dr. Khanna and his neglected father, Joshi examines the human cost of ambition, the fragility of relationships, and the clash between tradition and modernity.

1. Filial Neglect and Family Bonds

The central theme revolves around the breakdown of familial duty. Dr. Khanna's abandonment of his father, Kundan Lal, symbolizes how modern aspirations can erode traditional values. Kundan Lal's tragic loneliness—waiting endlessly for a letter or visit that never comes—highlights the emotional consequences of neglect. Joshi critiques a society that celebrates professional success while ignoring basic human responsibilities, asking whether achievement means anything without meaningful relationships.

2. Cultural Displacement and Identity Crisis

Dr. Khanna represents the immigrant dilemma—caught between two worlds but belonging to neither. Though physically Indian, he has emotionally assimilated into Western individualism, losing touch with his roots. His hollow gifts to relatives (razors, neckties) symbolize superficial connections, contrasting with Radhey Mohan's deep, albeit poor, ties to community and tradition. The story questions what happens when people sacrifice cultural identity for material success.

3. The Illusion of Success

On the surface, Dr. Khanna embodies the "American Dream"—prestige, wealth, and global recognition. Yet, his guilt-ridden breakdown reveals the emptiness beneath. Joshi contrasts Dr. Khanna's professional accolades with his moral failure, suggesting that success devoid of humanity is meaningless. The burning sensation in his feet mirrors his father's suffering, symbolizing how unresolved guilt can torment even the most accomplished individuals.

4. Generational Sacrifice and Betrayal

Kundan Lal's life mirrors the sacrifices many parents make for their children's futures. Once a brilliant student, he spends his later years in poverty, clinging to the hope that his son will reciprocate his love. His tragic end underscores the betrayal felt by generations who give everything but receive nothing in return. Joshi forces readers to confront an uncomfortable truth: progress often comes at the expense of those who enable it.

5. Truth and Moral Awakening

Radhey Mohan, the humble ashramp farosh, serves as the story's moral compass. His unflinching honesty shatters Dr. Khanna's complacency, revealing the power of truth to provoke change. Though poor, Radhey Mohan possesses a wisdom Dr. Khanna lacks, emphasizing that integrity and empathy outweigh material wealth. The open-ended conclusion leaves Dr. Khanna's redemption uncertain, questioning whether moral awakening can undo years of neglect.

6. Alienation and Loneliness

Both Dr. Khanna and Kundan Lal suffer profound isolation—one from choice, the other from abandonment. Dr. Khanna's alienation is self-imposed; his detachment from family and culture leaves him emotionally barren. Kundan Lal's loneliness, however, is a consequence of love rejected. Joshi portrays loneliness not just as physical solitude but as the psychological toll of broken connections.

Conclusion

Through these themes, Joshi crafts a timeless critique of modernity's dehumanizing effects. The story challenges readers to weigh the true cost of ambition and reconsider what it means to live a meaningful life. Its enduring relevance lies in its universal questions: How do we balance personal aspirations with familial duty? Can success compensate for lost relationships? By leaving these questions unanswered, Joshi invites introspection, making The Only American From Our Village a powerful commentary on the human condition.

Q.6) **"Comment upon the prose style used by Arun Joshi in 'The Only American from our Village'.**

Ans: Introduction: The Only American From our Village is a short story written by Arun Joshi. He was a prominent Indian existentialist novelist and short-story writer whose works explored themes of alienation, cultural displacement, and moral decay in postcolonial India. Arun Joshi's prose in The Only American from our Village exemplifies a masterful blend of economy and emotional depth, characterized by its understated yet powerful narrative voice. His writing style serves as the perfect vehicle for the story's profound themes of cultural displacement and filial neglect, achieving remarkable impact through carefully chosen simplicity rather than ornate flourishes.

Joshi employs a lean, restrained prose that mirrors the emotional detachment of his protagonist, Dr. Khanna. The sentences are typically short and declarative, reflecting the clinical precision of the successful physicist's worldview. When describing Dr. Khanna's professional achievements and social interactions, the language remains deliberately flat and unadorned: "He was received by an official of the Council of Scientific Research, addressed a conference on Inter-planetary Radiation." This stylistic choice subtly underscores the hollowness beneath the character's accomplished exterior.

The author's use of contrast in his prose style becomes particularly striking during the story's emotional climax. The matter-of-fact tone used to describe Radhey Mohan's devastating revelations about Kundan Lal's suffering creates a powerful dissonance. Joshi relates the father's tragic decline in simple, almost reportorial language: "When informed telegraphically about his father's illness, he sent an ordinary letter saying that he had to attend a conference." This unembellished narration makes the emotional impact more profound, allowing the painful facts to speak for themselves without sentimental manipulation.

Joshi demonstrates exceptional control of narrative perspective, maintaining a third-person limited viewpoint that aligns closely with Dr. Khanna's consciousness while permitting subtle authorial commentary. The prose subtly shifts during Radhey Mohan's monologue, adopting a more rhythmic quality that echoes oral storytelling traditions: "Crossing half a mile of boiling sand in May without shoes every morning and evening must have been harrowing." This temporary modulation in style highlights the cultural divide between the Westernized protagonist and his indigenous roots.

The writer's symbolic use of concrete details exemplifies his prose mastery. Small, carefully selected elements - the cheap razors gifted to relatives, Kundan Lal's new suit bought in hopeful anticipation, the recurring image of burning feet - accumulate profound significance through Joshi's restrained treatment. These images resonate beyond their literal meaning without ever becoming heavy-handed allegories, demonstrating the author's faith in the reader's interpretive ability.

Joshi's dialogue is spare but devastatingly effective. Radhey Mohan's speech patterns reflect his humble background while conveying immense emotional weight: "He used to say the son would be a big government man when he came back." The economy of words in these exchanges creates an almost theatrical intensity, where every line carries significant subtext about cultural values and personal failure.

The structural pacing of the prose contributes significantly to the story's impact. Joshi builds the narrative with patient accumulation of detail before delivering the emotional payload in Radhey Mohan's revelatory monologue. The concluding paragraphs, describing Dr. Khanna's psychological breakdown, are rendered with the same clinical precision used earlier to describe his successes, creating a powerful circularity that underscores the story's themes.

Conclusion:

Ultimately, Joshi's prose style in this story represents a perfect marriage of form and content. The unadorned language mirrors the protagonist's emotional sterility while simultaneously revealing the profound human drama beneath the surface. This paradoxical combination of restraint and depth makes the story's conclusion all the more devastating, as the carefully controlled prose finally cracks open to reveal the protagonist's unbearable guilt. Joshi demonstrates how simplicity in style can achieve extraordinary emotional and philosophical complexity, marking this work as a masterpiece of Indian short fiction in English.

Q.7) Discuss Arun Joshi as a short story writer.

Ans: Introduction : Arun Joshi (1939–1993), best known for his existential novels like The Foreigner and The Strange Case of Billy Biswas, also made significant contributions to Indian short fiction in English. Though his short stories are fewer in number, they exhibit the same philosophical depth, psychological insight, and crisp prose that define his novels. His collection Survivor (1975) and standalone stories like The Only American from Our Village reveal a writer deeply engaged with the human condition, particularly the tensions between tradition and modernity, East and West, and individual ambition and moral responsibility.

1. Existential Themes and Psychological Depth

Joshi's short stories, much like his novels, grapple with existential questions—alienation, identity crises, and the search for meaning in a fragmented world. In The Only American from Our Village, for instance, he explores the guilt of a successful NRI who neglects his roots, while in A Trip for Mr. Lele, he examines middle-class disillusionment. His protagonists are often introspective, flawed individuals caught in moral dilemmas, reflecting Joshi's belief that modern life, despite its material comforts, leaves people spiritually empty.

2. Minimalist yet Evocative Prose

Joshi's writing style is marked by restraint and precision. He avoids elaborate descriptions, relying instead on sparse, impactful prose to convey deep emotions. In The Only American from Our Village, the understated narration of Kundan Lal's suffering—waiting for a ticket that never arrives, standing barefoot on hot sand—makes the tragedy more piercing. This economy of language allows readers to project their own interpretations, making his stories resonate long after reading.

3. Cultural Critique and Social Realism

While Joshi's themes are universal, his settings are distinctly Indian. He critiques the postcolonial Indian middle class's obsession with Western validation, as seen in Dr. Khanna's hollow success or the bureaucratic absurdities in The Apprentice. His stories often highlight the cost of urbanization and industrialization, where characters lose their moral compass in pursuit of progress. Yet, Joshi avoids outright pessimism; his work suggests that redemption, though difficult, is possible through self-awareness and reconnection with one's roots.

4. Symbolism and Open-Ended Narratives

Joshi's stories are rich in symbolism. The "burning feet" in The Only American... symbolize inescapable guilt, while the jungle in A Trip into the Jungle (by Manoj Das, but thematically similar to Joshi's work) represents primal human savagery beneath civilized facades. His endings are often ambiguous, refusing neat resolutions. Dr. Khanna's breakdown, for example, leaves readers questioning whether he can ever atone for his neglect, mirroring life's unresolved complexities.

5. Influence and Legacy

Though Joshi wrote fewer short stories compared to contemporaries like R.K. Narayan or Mulk Raj Anand, his impact lies in their intensity. His works anticipate later writers like Jhumpa Lahiri and Aravind Adiga, who similarly explore immigrant angst and moral ambiguity. Joshi's stories remain relevant today, as globalization continues to strain cultural identities and familial bonds.

Conclusion

Arun Joshi's short fiction, though limited in volume, is monumental in its exploration of existential and societal conflicts. His ability to distill complex emotions into concise narratives, combined with his unflinching gaze at human frailty, cements his place as a master of the form. For readers seeking literature that interrogates modernity's costs while offering no easy answers, Joshi's stories are indispensable.

CHAPTER TWENTY-TWO

Manoj Das: A Trip into the Jungle

Scan the QR code to watch video

About Writer :

Manoj Das (1934–2021) was a celebrated Indian author, professor, and columnist, renowned for his contributions to both English and Odia literature. Born in Balasore, Odisha, he displayed a deep passion for writing from an early age, publishing his first book, Satabdira Artanada, in Odia at just 14.

A master storyteller, Das blended realism, fantasy, and satire to explore human nature, social hypocrisy, and moral dilemmas. His works—ranging from short stories and novels to children's tales—often critiqued modern society while retaining a touch of irony and philosophical depth. Some of his notable works include A Trip into the Jungle, The Submerged Valley and Other Stories, and The Man Who Lifted the Mountain and Other Fantasies.

A recipient of prestigious awards like the Saraswati Samman and Sahitya Akademi Award, Das also taught English at Sri Aurobindo International Centre of Education in Pondicherry and edited The Heritage magazine. His writing, marked by simplicity and profound insight, continues to resonate with readers for its timeless exploration of human follies and virtues.

A Trip into the Jungle

Summary

Five wealthy city people - Raja Sahib, Mr. and Mrs. Mity, and Mr. and Mrs. Chakodi - decide to experience "primitive freedom" by spending a wild night in the jungle. They want to escape civilized rules by eating, drinking and behaving like savages. Their jeep is driven by Shyamal, Raja Sahib's poor half-brother whom they treat badly because of his lower status. After heavy drinking, they go hunting but Shyamal refuses to join. Mrs. Mity stays behind too and secretly seduces Shyamal, then later lies that he attacked her. Without checking the truth, the drunken group beats Shyamal unconscious and locks him in a room with a half-dead boar they had caught.

That night, in their wild drunken state, they roast and eat pieces of the still-living boar while dancing around the fire. The next morning, as they wake up with terrible hangovers, Mrs. Mity suddenly realizes something horrifying - in their confusion, they might have actually cooked and eaten Shyamal instead of the boar. Too scared to check the room where they left Shyamal, they quickly leave the jungle, pretending nothing happened. But they can't escape the terrible thought that they may have become cannibals during their night of "freedom." The story ends without telling us what really happened, making us think about how easily people can become cruel and lose their humanity when they abandon rules and morals. It shows the dark side of human nature that hides beneath polite society.

Question and Answer

Q.1 Discuss the narrative technique used in the story A Trip into the Jungle.

Ans: , Introduction: A Trip into the Jungle is short story written by Manoj Das.He was a celebrated Indian author, professor, and columnist, renowned for his contributions to both English and Odia literature.Manoj Das uses simple but powerful storytelling techniques in A Trip into the Jungle to create a disturbing and thought-provoking tale. The way he tells the story makes readers feel the growing tension and horror while leaving important questions unanswered. Here are the main narrative techniques he uses:

1. Third-Person Objective Narration

The story is told by an outside narrator who does not explain the characters' thoughts or feelings. Instead, the narrator only describes what happens, like a camera recording events without commentary. This makes readers form their own opinions about the characters' cruel actions. For example, when Mrs. Mity lies about Shyamal attacking her, the narrator does not say she is evil—we understand her cruelty from her actions alone.

2. Suspense and Gradual Horror

Das slowly builds tension to make the ending more shocking. At first, the trip seems like just a wild adventure. But as the characters drink more and act violently, the mood turns darker. The real horror comes at the end when Mrs. Mity suggests they may have eaten Shyamal. The narrator does not confirm whether this is true, leaving readers in suspense.

3. Contrast Between Civilized and Savage Behavior

The story starts with rich, educated people who seem respectable. But as they enter the jungle, they shed their civilized manners and become brutal. The narrator shows this change without judging them, making readers see how easily people can turn savage when free from society's rules.

4. Irony

The story is full of irony—situations where the opposite of what we expect happens. For example:

- Mrs. Mity cries over a crushed butterfly but has no pity for Shyamal.
- The group wants to "be free like primitive humans," but their freedom turns into cruelty.
- They think they are roasting a boar but may have killed a man instead.
- This irony makes the story more disturbing and memorable.

5. Open Ending

The narrator does not tell us what really happened to Shyamal. Did they eat him? Is he still locked in the room? By not giving answers, Das forces readers to think about the story's deeper meaning. This technique makes the horror last even after finishing the story.

6. Simple but Strong Language

Das uses easy words, but they create strong images. For example:

"They cut slices from the boar while it was still half-alive." (This shows their cruelty in simple but shocking words.)

"They didn't look into the room. After all, Shyamal was just a chauffeur." (This simple line exposes their heartless attitude.)

Why These Techniques Work

By using these methods, Das makes readers:

Feel the growing horror without graphic descriptions.

Question human nature and society's thin layer of civilization.

Remember the story because of its unanswered mystery.

The power of the story comes not from complicated words but from the way it is told. The neutral narration, suspense, irony, and open ending work together to create a tale that is both simple and deeply disturbing. It shows how easily people can become monsters when they lose their morals, making readers think long after they finish reading.

Q.2 Discuss the characterisation of Manoj Das's short story A Trip into the Jungle.

Ans: Introduction: A Trip into the Jungle is short story written by Manoj Das.He was a celebrated Indian author, professor, and columnist, renowned for his contributions to both English and Odia literature.Manoj Das creates powerful characters in this story to show how people can hide cruelty behind polite faces. Each character represents different flaws in human nature. Let's examine them one by one.

Raja Sahib is the leader of the group but also the most disgusting. He comes from a rich family but has no real values. The story describes him as "ugly, drained of all life from reckless indulgences." He treats his half-brother Shyamal like a servant because of his lower status. His only interests seem to be drinking and bothering women. Even his friends see him as dirty - Mrs. Mity calls him "a pile of filth" with flies around his mouth. He represents how power and money can make people heartless.

Mrs. Mity is the most complex and hypocritical character. At first, she seems sensitive - she screams when a butterfly gets crushed. But this is just pretend kindness. When Shyamal refuses to shoot a pregnant deer, she gets furious because he disobeyed orders. Her real nature shows when she seduces Shyamal, then lies about him attacking her. She starts the violence but steps back to watch, showing she's both cruel and cowardly. Her false goodness makes her the most dangerous character.

Mr. Mity follows whatever the group does without thinking. He joins in beating Shyamal without asking questions. His wife calls him "a wolf," suggesting he has animal-like instincts under his civilized appearance. He represents people who do evil things just because others are doing them.

Mr. and Mrs. Chakodi complete this horrible group. Mrs. Chakodi makes rude comments that make others uncomfortable, while Mr. Chakodi pretends to be wise but is just as bad as the rest. He gives a speech about the "philosophy" of acting wild, showing how people use big words to excuse bad behavior. Together, they show how couples can encourage each other's worst qualities.

Shyamal is the only good character, which makes his suffering more painful. As Raja Sahib's half-brother, he represents how society treats poor relatives. Despite being family, he works as their driver and faces their cruelty. His refusal to shoot the pregnant deer shows he has more morals than the others. Even when Mrs. Mity seduces him, he smiles ironically, as if he understands how fake these rich people are. His silent suffering makes readers sympathize with him.

The characters work together to show different types of evil:

Raja Sahib shows cruelty from power

Mrs. Mity shows hypocrisy

Mr. Mity shows mindless following

The Chakodis show false intelligence

Together, they show how groups can become more brutal than individuals

What makes the characterization special is how normal these people seem at first. They aren't monsters - they're educated, rich city people. This makes their transformation more shocking. Das shows that cruelty isn't about being a monster - it's about ordinary people choosing to do terrible things when they think no one is watching.

The characters also represent different social problems:

Class difference (how they treat Shyamal)

Gender issues (how the women are treated)

Alcohol abuse

Violence in groups

Conclusion:

By making each character represent a different flaw, Das creates a complete picture of society's dark side. The story makes us ask: Are we really better than these characters? Could we become like them in the right (or wrong) situation? This is why the characters stay in our minds long after reading - they show the evil that exists in all humans, waiting for the chance to come out.

Q.3) 'Degeneration of the worst kind is common to all the characters in the story A Trip into the Jungle.' Do you agree? Discuss.

Ans: Introduction: A Trip into the Jungle is short story written by Manoj Das.He was a celebrated Indian author, professor, and columnist, renowned for his contributions to both English and Odia literature.Manoj Das's short story "A Trip into the Jungle" presents a disturbing examination of human nature through its portrayal of five seemingly civilized individuals who descend into complete moral degradation. The narrative powerfully demonstrates how the veneer of civilization is frighteningly thin, and how easily educated, privileged people can abandon all ethical constraints when removed from societal oversight. Each character, despite their superficial differences, contributes to this collective moral collapse in ways that reveal the darkest aspects of human psychology.

The Facade of Civilization

At the beginning of the story, the group appears as typical representatives of urban elite society - wealthy, cultured, and sophisticated. Raja Sahib is a landowner, the Mitys and Chakodis are presumably professionals, and they all engage in intellectual discussions about human nature. However, this cultivated exterior quickly crumbles when they decide to experiment with "primitive freedom." Their very plan to deliberately shed civilized behavior reveals an underlying moral vacuum, suggesting that their refinement was merely performative rather than rooted in genuine values.

The Descent into Barbarity

The transformation from civilized beings to savage creatures happens gradually but unmistakably. Their initial drinking seems harmless, but soon escalates into unrestrained drunkenness. The hunting expedition, meant to be a playful return to primal instincts, turns genuinely violent when they capture and torture a boar. Most shockingly, their treatment of Shyamal exposes their complete moral bankruptcy. When Mrs. Mity falsely accuses him of assault, none of the others pause to consider the truth of her claim or show any mercy. Their immediate, brutal response demonstrates how quickly human empathy can evaporate in group settings, especially when fueled by alcohol and mob mentality.

Individual Paths to Corruption

While all characters share in this collective moral collapse, each represents a different facet of human depravity:

Raja Sahib embodies the corruption of inherited privilege. His treatment of Shyamal, his own half-brother, as a disposable servant shows how class prejudice can override basic familial bonds. His physical repulsiveness (described as "a pile of filth") mirrors his moral decay.

Mrs. Mity represents the danger of performative morality. Her exaggerated distress over a crushed butterfly contrasts starkly with her cruelty toward Shyamal, revealing how superficial displays of sensitivity can mask profound selfishness and malice.

Mr. Mity demonstrates passive complicity in evil. He participates in the violence without protest, showing how ordinary people become accomplices to atrocity through silent obedience to group norms.

The Chakodis illustrate the intellectual justification of barbarism. Mr. Chakodi's philosophical rationalizations for their "deliberate relapse" into savagery show how educated people can use sophisticated reasoning to excuse base behavior.

The Final Moral Abyss

The story's climax presents their ultimate moral failure. When confronted with the possibility that they may have cannibalized Shyamal, they choose willful ignorance over truth. This decision is perhaps more damning than their previous violent acts - it shows a conscious rejection of moral responsibility. Their silent agreement to never speak of the incident again demonstrates how people conspire to hide their worst actions even from themselves.

Psychological and Social Implications:

Das's portrayal goes beyond individual failings to comment on broader human tendencies. The story suggests that: Civilization is a fragile construct that requires constant maintenance, Social hierarchies enable dehumanization (as seen in their treatment of Shyamal), Group dynamics can rapidly erode individual morality, Privilege often correlates with moral blindness.

Contemporary Relevance

The story remains profoundly relevant today, mirroring how Corporate executives commit fraud while maintaining respectable facades, Political leaders justify unethical actions through sophisticated rhetoric, Ordinary people participate in systemic discrimination while considering themselves good.

Conclusion

The complete moral degeneration of all characters in "A Trip into the Jungle" serves as a powerful cautionary tale. Das shows that evil is not the domain of monsters, but a potential within all humans that emerges when societal restraints are removed. The characters' shared descent into barbarity, despite their different personalities and roles, proves that no one is immune to moral collapse under certain conditions. This unsettling realization forces readers to confront uncomfortable questions about their own capacity for cruelty, making the story both timeless and universally disturbing. The narrative ultimately suggests that true civilization must be more than superficial manners - it requires constant ethical vigilance against the savage impulses that lurk beneath our polished exteriors.

Q.4) Attempt critical appreciation of the story A Trip into the Jungle.

Ans: Introduction: A Trip into the Jungle is short story written by Manoj Das.He was a celebrated Indian author, professor, and columnist, renowned for his contributions to both English and Odia literature.Manoj Das's "A Trip into the Jungle" is a powerful story that shows how civilized people can quickly turn into savages. The story makes us think deeply about human nature and society. Through simple but effective storytelling, Das exposes the dark side of people who appear normal and respectable.

Theme of Civilization vs. Savagery

The main theme of the story is the conflict between civilized behavior and primitive instincts. The five city people believe they are superior because of their wealth and education. However, when they go to the jungle, they willingly abandon all civilized manners. They drink heavily, act violently, and enjoy cruelty. This shows that civilization is just a thin layer that can easily break under pressure. The story suggests that all humans have a savage side that can come out when there are no rules to control them.

Symbolism of the Jungle

The jungle in the story is not just a place—it is a symbol. It represents the wild, untamed side of human nature. When the characters enter the jungle, they also enter a state of moral darkness. The jungle becomes a testing ground where their true selves are revealed. The fact that they behave worse than animals in the jungle is ironic because they claim to be superior to nature.

Critique of Class Inequality

The story strongly criticizes how rich people treat the poor. Shyamal, who is Raja Sahib's half-brother, is treated like a servant just because his mother was not officially married. The rich characters show no respect or kindness towards him. They beat him without hesitation when Mrs. Mity lies about him. This shows how power and wealth can make people heartless. The story makes us question whether society is fair or just.

Use of Irony

Irony is used effectively in the story. Mrs. Mity cries for a crushed butterfly but has no pity for Shyamal. The group talks about freedom but becomes cruel and violent. They want to experience primitive life but end up committing acts worse than animals. These ironies make the story more impactful and force readers to think about human hypocrisy.

Open-Ended Conclusion

The story ends without telling us what really happened to Shyamal. This open ending is very effective because it makes readers uncomfortable. We are left wondering: Did they really eat a human being? Why didn't they check? This uncertainty stays with the reader long after finishing the story. It makes us question how far ordinary people can go when they lose their morals.

Simple but Powerful Language

Das uses very simple language, but it creates strong images in our minds. Sentences like "They cut slices from the boar while it was still half-alive" are short but shocking. The simple style makes the horror feel more real because it is not exaggerated. The story feels like it could happen in real life, which makes it even more disturbing.

Relevance to Modern Society

The story remains relevant today because it shows how people in power often misuse their position. We see examples in real life where rich and powerful people escape punishment for their crimes. The story also warns us about mob mentality—how people in groups can do terrible things that they would never do alone.

Conclusion

"A Trip into the Jungle" is a masterpiece of psychological and social commentary. Through simple storytelling, Das exposes the hypocrisy and cruelty hidden in civilized society. The story stays with readers because it forces us to face uncomfortable truths about human nature. It reminds us that without strong morals and self-control, any of us could become like those jungle travelers—civilized on the outside but savage within. The story's lasting power comes from its ability to make readers examine their own hearts and ask: "Am I really better than these characters?" This self-reflection is the mark of truly great literature.

CHAPTER TWENTY-THREE

Subhadra Sen Gupta: The Fourth Daughter

Scan to watch the video

About Subhadra Sen Gupta

Subhadra Sen Gupta (June 1952 – 3 May 2021) was a celebrated Indian writer renowned for her contributions to children's literature. Born in Delhi with a master's degree in history, she began writing in college and later worked as a copywriter. Over her prolific career, she authored more than 30 books and was honored with the Sahitya Akademi's Bal Sahitya Puraskar in 2015.

Her versatile works ranged from historical fiction and non-fiction to travelogues, comic strips, detective stories, and ghost tales. Among her popular titles, Mystery of the House of Pigeons was adapted into the

Doordarshan series Khoj Khazana Khojher. Other notable works include Goodbye, Pasha Begum!, Bishnu - The Dhobi Singer, A Mauryan Adventure, The Secret Diary of the World's Worst Cook, A Flag, A Song And a Pinch of Salt, A Children's History of India, The Constitution of India for Children, and Mahal: Power and Pageantry in the Mughal Harem.

o3-mini

The Fourth Daughter

About Story:

The Fourth Daughter offers a searing critique of gender discrimination in affluent Indian families through the story of Mini, an unwanted girl rejected by her mother Radha simply because she is the fourth daughter. Abandoned at birth, Mini is rescued and nurtured by the compassionate family maid, Parvati. Growing up in a household that favors a son—who is groomed for wealth and status—Mini faces neglect and isolation, even as she excels academically despite her mother's resistance to her education.

Eventually, Mini becomes a successful doctor, in stark contrast to her indulgent yet wayward brother. In a poignant turn of events, she returns to care for her aging parents, symbolizing both reconciliation and the enduring value of a daughter. The story powerfully highlights the cruelty of gender bias while celebrating the resilience and transformative power of education.

Questions & Answers

Q.1) How are the characters portrayed in The Fourth Daughter?

Ans: Introduction: The story The Fourth Daughter is written by Subhadra Sen Gupta. Subhadra Sen Gupta (June 1952 – 3 May 2021) was a renowned Indian writer known for her contributions to children's literature. She won the Sahitya Akademi's Bal Sahitya Puraskar in 2015 and authored over 30 books.

The short story The Fourth Daughter presents a powerful critique of gender discrimination in Indian society, particularly among affluent families. It tells the story of Mini, a girl born into a wealthy family but abandoned by her own mother simply because she is the fourth daughter.

In The Fourth Daughter, Subhadra Sen Gupta uses exaggerated characterization to highlight the deep-rooted gender discrimination in society. The parents and grandparents are portrayed as entirely traditional and obsessed with having a male heir, to the extent that they nearly abandon Mini at birth. While in reality, disappointed parents might curse their fate or scold their daughters, the author magnifies their cruelty to emphasize the injustice. On the other hand, Parvati and her family are depicted as Mini's true caregivers, providing her with love and support in contrast to her biological family's rejection. Though Parvati is shown as kind, she is also practical, initially questioning how she can afford to raise Mini, making her character slightly more realistic than the others. Mini's sisters, however, appear unnaturally indifferent; despite knowing Mini is their sibling, they never attempt to comfort or support her, reinforcing the idea that gender bias is deeply ingrained from a young age. The most striking irony is seen in the much-pampered son, who ultimately wastes his family's wealth on gambling and abandons his parents, proving that their obsession with a male heir was misplaced. However, his downfall is not explored in detail; it is simply reported in the story. Most characters remain static throughout, serving as symbols of societal attitudes rather than evolving individuals. This stark contrast between extreme cruelty and extreme kindness makes the story impactful but also slightly unrealistic, as the characters function more as representations of social issues than fully developed personalities.

Conclusion: The characterization in The Fourth Daughter serves as a powerful tool to highlight deep-rooted gender bias and societal discrimination. The characters are largely stereotypical, representing the rigid attitudes that the author critiques. Radha and her husband embody the conventional mindset that favors sons over daughters, while Parvati and her family represent kindness, love, and a sense of justice. Mini, as the protagonist, symbolizes resilience and transformation, proving that one's worth is not determined by societal biases. The son's downfall and Mini's eventual success serve as poetic justice, reinforcing the story's central message. Although the characters remain mostly static, their roles effectively drive home the contrast between cruelty and compassion, ultimately encouraging reflection on the need for change in societal attitudes.

Q.2) Discuss the Narrative Technique used in The Fourth Daughter.

Ans: Introduction: The story The Fourth Daughter is written by Subhadra Sen Gupta. Subhadra Sen Gupta (June 1952 – 3 May 2021) was a renowned Indian writer known for her contributions to children's literature. She won the Sahitya Akademi's Bal Sahitya Puraskar in 2015 and authored over 30 books. The short story The Fourth Daughter presents a powerful critique of gender discrimination in Indian society, particularly among affluent families. It tells thestory of Mini, a girl born into a wealthy family but abandoned by her own mother simply because she is the fourth daughter.

The story The Fourth Daughter is narrated in a third-person omniscient style, allowing the reader to see and understand the thoughts, emotions, and actions of multiple characters. This perspective is particularly effective in highlighting the stark contrast between Mini's rejection by her biological parents and the love and care she receives from Parvati and her family. The narration is straightforward and follows a chronological pattern, beginning with Mini's birth and ending with the eventual change of heart in her biological parents, who once abandoned her but later come to depend on her. This structure helps maintain clarity while emphasizing the emotional and social issues at the heart of the story.

Despite its apparent simplicity, the narration is layered with irony and social critique. The author frequently contrasts Mini's struggles with the privileges of her much-pampered brother, exposing the deep-rooted gender bias in society. By portraying Mini's suffering in detail, the narrative challenges the conventional mindset that favors sons over daughters. The tone of the narration is critical, emotional, and thought-provoking, making the reader sympathize with Mini while also questioning societal norms. Through subtle yet impactful descriptions, the author compels the reader to reflect on the unfair treatment of the girl child in many families.

The pacing of the story is well-balanced, with Mini's childhood and adolescence described in detail, especially the instances where her biological parents could have accepted her but chose to ignore her instead. These moments serve to highlight the cruel indifference of Radha and her family in contrast to Parvati's warmth and care. However, towards the end of the story, the pace accelerates dramatically. The deaths of Mini's grandparents and sister occur abruptly, with minimal detail, making their impact feel sudden and somewhat rushed. Similarly, the son's departure is presented in a brief but decisive manner, almost as if his actions are poetic justice for the way Mini was once treated.

The ending, though expected, is left open to interpretation. The narrative suggests that Mini's return to her parental home symbolizes a shift in her parents' attitudes, yet it raises an important question—are they welcoming Mini back out of love, or is it because they now see her as a successful doctor and the mother of a son? The striking similarity between

Mini's homecoming and the celebrations that once accompanied her brother's birth reinforces the irony of the situation. The story thus comes full circle, subtly questioning whether true change has occurred or if society's preference for sons continues, even in a different form. Through this nuanced narrative style, the author not only tells Mini's story but also invites the reader to think critically about gender bias and social expectations.

Conclusion: The narrative technique in *The Fourth Daughter* is deceptively simple yet deeply impactful. Following a chronological structure, the story moves from Mini's birth and rejection to her eventual success and reluctant acceptance by her biological parents. The contrast between Radha's cruelty and Parvati's highlighting missed opportunities for reconciliation. The abrupt events towards the end—such as the sudden deaths and the son's betrayal—serve to heighten the emotional impact and reinforce the theme of poetic justice. The repetition of the celebration scene, mirroring the one for Mini's brother years ago, subtly questions whether the parents' change of heart is genuine or merely a result of circumstances. Through this structured yet thought-provoking storytelling, the author effectively critiques societal biases and leaves the reader reflecting on the lingering inequalities faced by girls.

Q.3) Attempt a critical appreciation of The Fourth Daughter?

Ans: Introduction: The story The Fourth Daughter is written by Subhadra Sen Gupta. Subhadra Sen Gupta (June 1952 – 3 May 2021) was a renowned Indian writer known for her contributions to children's literature. She won the Sahitya Akademi's Bal Sahitya Puraskar in 2015 and authored over 30 books. The short story The Fourth Daughter presents a powerful critique of gender discrimination in Indian society, particularly among affluent families. It tells thestory of Mini, a girl born into a wealthy family but abandoned by her own mother simply because she is the fourth daughter.

The Fourth Daughter is a poignant short story that sheds light on the deep-rooted gender bias prevalent in society. Through a simple yet compelling narrative, the story critiques the preference for sons over daughters and explores themes of rejection, resilience, and poetic justice.

Theme and Social Commentary

The central theme of the story revolves around gender discrimination, particularly the neglect and rejection faced by girl children in traditional families. Mini, the protagonist, is abandoned by her own mother because she is not a boy. This highlights the stark reality of societal norms that devalue daughters. However, the story also explores themes of unconditional love and support through the character of Parvati, the maid who raises Mini as her own. The contrast between Radha's indifference and Parvati's compassion emphasizes how societal hierarchies do not always define human kindness.

Characterization

The characters in The Fourth Daughter are largely symbolic, representing the rigid attitudes of society. Radha and her husband embody the patriarchal mindset that prioritizes sons over daughters. Their cruelty toward Mini is exaggerated to stress the inhumanity of gender discrimination. In contrast, Parvati and her family symbolize empathy and selflessness. Parvati's husband and son treat Mini with kindness, reinforcing the idea that love is not bound by biological ties. Mini's sisters, despite sharing her fate as neglected daughters, remain indifferent, showcasing how deeply ingrained such biases are. The son, once the favored child, ultimately abandons his parents, serving as poetic justice for their past actions.

Narrative Technique

The story follows a chronological pattern, beginning with Mini's birth and ending with her parents' eventual acceptance of her. The seemingly simple narration is deceptive, as it raises thought-provoking questions about societal values. The use of contrast—between Radha's rejection and Parvati's care, between Mini's mistreatment and her eventual success—enhances the emotional depth of the story. The fast-paced conclusion, where multiple events unfold quickly, reinforces the unpredictability of life and fate's ironic twists.

Symbolism and Irony

The story effectively uses symbolism and irony to drive its message. The most striking instance of irony is the fate of Radha's son, who, despite being given all the privileges, turns out to be a failure and abandons his parents. This is contrasted with Mini, who, despite being unwanted, becomes their only source of support in old age. The ending, where Mini is welcomed home with garlands and celebration—just like her brother was years ago—questions whether her parents truly value her or merely rejoice in the birth of a male heir through her son.

Conclusion:

The Fourth Daughter is a powerful critique of gender bias, wrapped in a deeply emotional narrative. The exaggerated portrayal of cruelty and kindness serves to emphasize the extremes of societal attitudes toward girls. Through poetic justice and irony, the story makes a strong statement about the consequences of discrimination and the unpredictable nature of fate. By the end, the reader is left questioning not only the actions of Mini's parents but also the larger societal norms that continue to perpetuate such biases. This makes the story both a compelling read and an important social commentary.

Q.4) Discuss Subhadra Sen Gupta's The Fourth Daughter as a feminist text.

Ans: Introduction: The story The Fourth Daughter is written by Subhadra Sen Gupta. Subhadra Sen Gupta (June 1952 – 3 May 2021) was a renowned Indian writer known for her contributions to children's literature. She won the Sahitya Akademi's Bal Sahitya Puraskar in 2015 and authored over 30 books. The short story The Fourth Daughter presents a powerful critique of gender discrimination in Indian society, particularly among affluent families. It tells thestory of Mini, a girl born into a wealthy family but abandoned by her own mother simply because she is the fourth daughter.

Subhadra Sen Gupta's The Fourth Daughter is a powerful feminist text that critiques the deeply entrenched gender bias in society and highlights the struggles of women who challenge patriarchal norms. Through its narrative, the story brings attention to the discrimination faced by the girl child in traditional families, where sons are prioritized and daughters are often neglected or seen as burdens. Feminism as a movement aims to dismantle these oppressive structures and advocate for gender equality. The story strongly aligns with these ideals by questioning traditional gender roles, emphasizing the agency of women, and critiquing societal norms that reinforce male dominance.

At the heart of The Fourth Daughter is the theme of gender discrimination. From the very beginning, Mini, the protagonist, faces rejection simply because she is a girl. Her mother, Radha, refuses to feed her as a newborn, an act that symbolizes the extreme devaluation of daughters in a society that worships sons. This preference for male children is further reinforced by the family's actions—Mini's brother is given all the privileges, including a prestigious education and material comforts, while Mini and her sisters are sent to a government school and treated as secondary members of the family. This stark contrast highlights the deeply ingrained biases that deny girls equal opportunities and force them into roles of subservience.

Feminist literature often critiques such social structures that perpetuate inequality, and The Fourth Daughter effectively exposes how these biases operate within the domestic sphere.

A key feminist element in the story is the character of Parvati, the family's maid, who plays the role of Mini's true mother figure. While Radha, Mini's biological mother, completely rejects her, Parvati steps in to care for the child, ensuring her survival and well-being. Parvati's actions challenge the traditional notion of motherhood, showing that maternal love is not solely defined by biology but by care and responsibility. Furthermore, Parvati's defiance of Radha's authority—insisting that Mini deserves an education despite Radha's belief that girls belong in the kitchen—is a strong feminist statement. She represents the women who resist oppression, even when they are in a vulnerable social position. Despite being a maid, she displays greater moral strength and compassion than Mini's privileged family, highlighting the irony that the person with the least power in the household is the one who fights for Mini's rights.

Mini's own journey in the story is a testament to female resilience and self-determination. Unlike her sisters, who have accepted their subordinate status, Mini refuses to be defined by societal expectations. She excels in school, aspires to become a doctor, and resists her parents' attempts to confine her to traditional domestic roles. Her determination to pursue education is a direct challenge to the patriarchal belief that a woman's place is in the home. Education is a crucial tool in feminist empowerment, and Mini's success represents the power of knowledge in breaking the cycle of gender oppression. Her achievements contrast sharply with her brother's fate—despite receiving all the privileges, he squanders his wealth, falls into bad habits, and ultimately abandons his parents. This reversal serves as a critique of the blind preference for sons and reinforces the idea that gender should not determine a person's worth or capabilities.

The ending of the story raises an important feminist question about recognition and acceptance. Mini, once unwanted and neglected, returns to her parental home not as a helpless daughter but as a successful doctor and mother. Her parents, who once discarded her, now stand at the door, ready to welcome her. While this may seem like a moment of redemption, a deeper feminist reading questions whether this acceptance is truly genuine. Do Radha and her husband regret their past actions, or are they merely seeking comfort now that their beloved son has abandoned them? The repetition of the celebratory scene that once surrounded Mini's brother's birth suggests that society continues to value women primarily when they achieve success in traditionally male-dominated fields. This subtle critique underscores the need for a deeper transformation in attitudes toward women, beyond just recognizing their worth when they become successful.

Conclusion: The Fourth Daughter is a compelling feminist text that exposes the deep-rooted gender inequalities within traditional families, celebrates female agency, and challenges patriarchal values that privilege men over women. Through Mini's struggles and triumphs, the story highlights the importance of education, the power of resilience, and the need for societal change. The contrast between Radha and Parvati further reinforces the central feminist message—that women are not inherently weak or submissive, but rather, their roles and status are shaped by societal conditioning. While the story ends with a sense of justice, it also leaves the reader questioning whether true change has occurred or if Mini's acceptance is still tied to traditional expectations. In doing so, The Fourth Daughter encourages reflection on the persistent gender biases in society and the ongoing struggle for genuine equality.

Q.5) Discuss Subhadra Sen Gupta as a short story writer.

Ans: Introduction: The story The Fourth Daughter is written by Subhadra Sen Gupta. Subhadra Sen Gupta (June 1952 – 3 May 2021) was a renowned Indian writer known for her contributions to children's literature. She won the Sahitya Akademi's Bal Sahitya Puraskar in 2015 and authored over 30 books.

The short story The Fourth Daughter presents a powerful critique of gender discrimination in Indian society, particularly among affluent families. It tells the story of Mini, a girl born into a wealthy family but abandoned by her own mother simply because she is the fourth daughter.

Subhadra Sen Gupta as a Short Story Writer

Subhadra Sen Gupta was a distinguished Indian writer, particularly known for her short stories, historical fiction, and children's literature. She had a unique ability to weave compelling narratives that were both informative and thought-provoking. Her stories often dealt with themes of social inequality, gender discrimination, history, and cultural heritage. Through her simple yet powerful storytelling, she brought to life complex issues, making them accessible to readers of all ages. Her works, especially short stories, stand out for their strong characterization, engaging narratives, and deep social commentary, making her one of the most respected voices in Indian literature.

One of the most remarkable aspects of Sen Gupta's short stories was her ability to address pressing social issues, particularly gender discrimination. Her short story The Fourth Daughter is a poignant example of how she used fiction to highlight the plight of women in Indian society. The story revolves around a girl named Mini, who is neglected and almost abandoned by her biological parents simply because she is not a boy. This theme of preference for male children over female children is deeply ingrained in Indian society, and through Mini's journey, Sen Gupta sheds light on the injustices faced by many girls. By focusing on the life of one girl, she manages to tell a much larger story about societal biases and the struggles of women in patriarchal setups. This ability to discuss larger issues through personal, relatable narratives is what made her short stories so impactful.

Another striking feature of her short stories was her ability to create well-rounded, memorable characters. In The Fourth Daughter, the contrast between Radha, the indifferent mother, and Parvati, the kind-hearted maid, is sharply drawn. Radha represents the rigid and traditional mindset that values sons over daughters, while Parvati embodies warmth, love, and a sense of justice. Despite being a maid, Parvati emerges as the true mother figure for Mini, showing that maternal love is not defined by blood but by care and affection. Sen Gupta's characters often represent different perspectives within society, offering readers a nuanced view of complex social issues. Her protagonists, especially young girls like Mini, often go through a journey of struggle and self-discovery, ultimately emerging as strong and independent individuals. This emphasis on resilience and empowerment is a recurring theme in her stories.

Sen Gupta's storytelling was also deeply rooted in history and cultural heritage. Many of her short stories and books, such as *Bishnu – The Dhobi Singer* and *A Mauryan Adventure*, reflect her deep interest in history and her ability to bring historical events and figures to life. She did not just recount historical facts; she wove them into compelling narratives that made history engaging and relatable. Her historical short stories often featured young protagonists who navigated historical settings, allowing readers to experience history through their eyes. This approach made her works especially appealing to young readers, as they could connect with the characters while learning about different time periods and cultures.

Another notable characteristic of her short stories was her strong narrative technique. She often used a linear, chronological style that made the stories easy to follow. However, beneath this simplicity lay deeper themes and social critiques. For instance, in The Fourth Daughter, the story begins with Mini's birth and traces her life through different stages, showing how each event shapes her personality. Despite this conventional storytelling structure, the story raises important questions about gender bias, societal expectations, and justice. Sen Gupta's ability to balance a simple, engaging narrative with profound social commentary is what made her stories both accessible and meaningful.

Her use of irony was another effective tool in her storytelling. In *The Fourth Daughter*, the very son who was favored by his parents ends up abandoning them, while the daughter they rejected returns to take care of them. This twist serves as poetic justice, forcing the parents to confront their past mistakes. Such ironic reversals were common in her stories, highlighting the consequences of social injustices in a way that was both satisfying and thought-provoking for readers.

Sen Gupta also had a remarkable ability to blend different genres within her short stories. While many of her works focused on social issues and history, she also wrote mystery, adventure, and ghost stories. Her horror story *Goodbye, Pasha Begum!* takes readers on a thrilling journey where the protagonist finds herself transported to the Mughal era. Similarly, her book *The Secret Diary of the World's Worst Cook* combines humor with a relatable coming-of-age theme. This versatility allowed her to reach a wide audience, from young children to adults, and her stories often carried subtle lessons even when they were entertaining.

A significant aspect of her storytelling was her feminist perspective. Throughout her works, she portrayed strong female characters who challenged societal norms and refused to accept discrimination. Her stories often questioned traditional gender roles and highlighted the importance of education and self-reliance for women. Mini's determination to become a doctor despite her parents' opposition in *The Fourth Daughter* is a powerful example of this. Through such narratives, Sen Gupta not only entertained her readers but also inspired them to think critically about social norms and injustices.

Sen Gupta's language and style were another reason for the success of her short stories. She wrote in a simple yet evocative manner, ensuring that her stories could be understood by young readers while still engaging older audiences. Her dialogues were natural and realistic, making her characters feel authentic. She often used humor, irony, and vivid descriptions to enhance her storytelling, making her narratives lively and immersive.

Conclusion: Subhadra Sen Gupta was a masterful short story writer who combined engaging storytelling with deep social and historical insights. Her ability to create memorable characters, highlight important social issues, and use compelling narrative techniques made her stories impactful and relevant. Whether addressing gender discrimination, historical events, or personal struggles, she brought a unique perspective that resonated with readers across generations. Her legacy as a writer continues to inspire, educate, and provoke thought, making her one of the most significant voices in Indian literature.

CHAPTER TWENTY-FOUR

Shashi despande: Miracle

Scan the QR code to watch video

About Writer:

Shashi Deshpande was born in Dharwad, Karnataka, into a family with strong literary and artistic traditions. Influenced by her father, a renowned dramatist and Sanskrit scholar, she moved to Bombay at fifteen, earning a degree in Economics from Elphinstone College before studying Law in Bangalore—where she won two gold medals. Though her early married life centered on raising her two sons, her passion for writing led her to study Journalism, garnering several awards, including the Times of India Gold Medal.

Her literary career began in 1970 with short stories and later expanded into novels and children's literature. Deshpande's works, including notable titles like The Dark Holds No Terrors, That Long Silence (which won the Sahitya Akademi Award), and The Binding Vine, explore themes of loneliness, identity, and the inner lives of women in a patriarchal society. Now residing in Bangalore with her husband, a pathologist, Deshpande remains one of India's most respected feminist writers, renowned for her insightful storytelling and nuanced portrayal of human relationships.

Miracle

Shashi Deshpande's short story Miracle is about the clash between science and faith. It is set in a medical lab where doctors experiment on monkeys to find a cure for a deadly disease caused by a poisonous plant. The story focuses on one monkey, Raaja, who strangely survives the poison, leading to a debate between logic and belief in miracles.

About Story:

In Shashi Deshpande's short story Miracle, a research lab becomes the battleground for a clash between science and faith when a poisonous plant experiment on monkeys leads to the unexpected survival of one monkey, Raaja. While the doctors dismiss the event as mere chance, a lab worker named Narayan believes Raaja's survival is a divine miracle, even hinting at a connection to the god Hanuman. The lab typist supports Narayan's view, arguing that everyday moments—like a baby's first cry—are miracles that defy scientific explanation.

The debate intensifies until Raaja mysteriously disappears and then reappears, reinforcing the idea that miracles exist when one is open to them. In the end, even the skeptical male doctor softens his stance, accepting that faith and science can coexist. The story concludes on a light note with the doctor and typist marrying, symbolizing the harmonious blending of reason and belief in everyday life.

Question and Answer

Q.1) Discuss Characterization in Shashi Deshpande's "Miracle"

Ans: Introduction:he Miracle is a short story written by Shashi Deshpande. Shashi Deshpande (1938) is an acclaimed Indian authoTr known for her nuanced portrayals of women's struggles in middle-class India. Her Sahitya Akademi-winning novel That Long Silence (1988) and other works like The Dark Holds No Terrors blend feminist perspectives with subtle storytelling.Her short story Miracle features a small but impactful cast of characters, each representing distinct perspectives on science, faith, and humanity. The characters are carefully crafted to highlight the tension between rationality and belief, as well as the complexities of human relationships.

1. The Female Doctor

The female doctor embodies strict scientific rationality. She views living beings—whether humans or monkeys—as mere subjects for experimentation, with no room for emotions or faith. Her commitment to logic is so absolute that she dismisses Narayan's beliefs as irrational and even ignores the presence of the typist in the room. She is portrayed as competent and dedicated to her work, but her cold, unyielding demeanor makes her unsympathetic. Her frustration when Raaja's survival disrupts her research underscores her inability to accept anything beyond empirical evidence.

2. The Male Doctor

In contrast to his female counterpart, the male doctor is more open-minded and humane. While initially aligned with scientific reasoning, he gradually begins to acknowledge other perspectives. He listens to Narayan's concerns and, after the typist's passionate argument about the limits of science, starts to see value in faith and the intangible aspects of life. His character arc is significant—he evolves from a rigid scientist to someone who accepts that "there are miracles everywhere if you only open your eyes." His eventual marriage to the typist symbolizes his acceptance of emotional and spiritual dimensions beyond pure logic.

3. The Typist

The typist is a strong, independent woman who defies societal expectations. Though she holds a subordinate position in the lab, she is unafraid to voice her opinions, even at the risk of losing her job. Her love for the male doctor is silent yet steadfast, and her decision to free Raaja demonstrates her moral courage. She challenges the doctors' rigid views, arguing that life cannot be reduced to mere scientific analysis—a baby's first cry or a monkey's will to live are miracles in themselves. Her character represents the new, educated Indian woman who asserts her identity and stands by her convictions.

4. Narayan

Narayan, the only named human character, symbolizes traditional faith and devotion. He sees Raaja's survival as divine intervention, believing the monkey to be Hanuman's reincarnation. His unwavering belief contrasts sharply with the doctors' skepticism, highlighting the story's central conflict between science and spirituality. Though initially dismissed as superstitious, his perspective gains validity as the narrative progresses.

5. Raaja (The Monkey)

Raaja is more than just an animal—he becomes a catalyst for the story's philosophical debate. His mysterious survival and disappearance challenge the doctors' understanding of life and death. To Narayan and the typist, Raaja represents something sacred, while the female doctor sees him only as a failed experiment. His presence (and absence) forces the characters to confront their beliefs, making him a silent yet powerful figure in the narrative.

Conclusion I

Deshpande's characterization in Miracle effectively contrasts different worldviews—science versus faith, logic versus emotion, authority versus individuality. Through these characters, she explores deeper questions about the nature of life, the limits of human understanding, and the possibility of coexistence between opposing beliefs. The male doctor's transformation, the typist's defiance, and even Raaja's symbolic role all contribute to a rich, thought-provoking narrative.

Q.2) Discuss the narrative technique used in short story Miracle.

Ans: Introduction: The Miracle is a short story written by Shashi Deshpande. Shashi Deshpande (1938) is an acclaimed Indian authoTr known for her nuanced portrayals of women's struggles in middle-class India. Her Sahitya Akademi-winning novel That Long Silence (1988) and other works like The Dark Holds No Terrors blend feminist perspectives with subtle storytelling.Deshpande employs several subtle yet powerful narrative techniques .

Miracle employs a mastul blend of narrative techniques to explore its central themes of science versus faith and the complexity of human perception. Through carefully crafted storytelling methods, Deshpande creates a thought-provoking narrative that challenges readers to reconsider the boundaries between rationality and spirituality.

One of the most striking aspects of Deshpande's narrative technique is her use of perspective and characterization. While the story maintains an objective third-person narration, it cleverly adopts the clinical viewpoint of the laboratory setting to mirror the doctors' detached scientific mindset. The two doctors remain unnamed throughout the story, a deliberate choice that transforms them into symbols of rigid scientific rationalism rather than fully fleshed individuals. In contrast, characters like Narayan and Raaja the monkey are given names and distinct personalities, representing the human elements of faith and individuality that the doctors overlook. This contrast between named and unnamed characters serves as a powerful narrative device to highlight the story's central conflict.

Dialogue plays a crucial role in developing the story's themes and character dynamics. Deshpande uses stark contrasts in language to emphasize the differing worldviews of her characters. The doctors speak in cold, clinical terms, referring to patients as "cases" and "bronchogenic carcinoma," reducing human beings to mere medical conditions. On the other hand, the typist uses emotionally charged language, calling them "poor child" and "that poor man with three children," restoring their humanity. This linguistic juxtaposition creates a compelling tension between scientific detachment and human compassion, inviting readers to question which perspective holds more truth.

Symbolism and imagery are employed with remarkable subtlety throughout the narrative. Raaja the monkey serves as the story's central symbol, representing the inexplicable mysteries of life that science cannot fully account for. Deshpande portrays Raaja with deliberate naturalism - he eats bananas, hesitates, and behaves like any ordinary monkey, making his miraculous survival more believable. The use of color symbolism further enriches the narrative, with the typist's bright yellow sari and the vibrant gulmohar tree standing in stark contrast to the female doctor's sterile white coat. These visual elements reinforce the story's exploration of life's vibrancy versus clinical detachment.

Deshpande's narrative style appears deceptively simple, yet it conceals profound thematic depth. The laboratory setting, with its mundane routines and matter-of-fact tone, serves as the perfect backdrop for the story's philosophical questions to emerge organically. The male doctor's gradual transformation, culminating in his quotation of Walt Whitman's line about miracles, feels earned rather than forced, demonstrating Deshpande's skill in character development. Similarly, the typist's quiet rebellion against the doctors' worldview is portrayed with nuance, avoiding didacticism while making a powerful statement about individual agency.

The story's resolution, with the male doctor acknowledging life's miracles and the typist freeing Raaja, achieves a perfect balance between its competing worldviews. Deshpande doesn't dismiss science entirely but suggests that it must make room for the inexplicable wonders of existence. Through her sophisticated narrative techniques - objective narration, symbolic characterization, contrasting dialogue, and subtle imagery - Deshpande crafts a story that lingers in the reader's mind, inviting contemplation long after the final page. Miracle stands as a testament to her ability to explore profound philosophical questions through seemingly simple storytelling, making it a masterpiece of the short story form.

Q.3) Discuss the themes of the story Miracle.

Ans Introduction:The Miracle is a short story written by Shashi Deshpande. Shashi Deshpande (1938) is an acclaimed Indian authoTr known for her nuanced portrayals of women's struggles in middle-class India. Her Sahitya Akademi-winning novel That Long Silence (1988) and other works like The Dark Holds No Terrors blend feminist perspectives with subtle storytelling.

Shashi Deshpande's short story Miracle explores profound philosophical questions through its deceptively simple narrative. At its core, the story presents a compelling examination of the clash between scientific rationalism and spiritual faith. The laboratory setting, with its sterile environment and methodical doctors, represents the world of empirical evidence and clinical detachment. In contrast, characters like Narayan and the typist embody more humanistic perspectives that acknowledge life's mysteries. This central tension plays out through Raaja the monkey's inexplicable survival, which scientists dismiss as an anomaly but others interpret as divine intervention. Deshpande doesn't resolve this conflict but suggests both viewpoints have validity in understanding human existence.

A closely related theme is the dehumanizing potential of scientific objectivity. The doctors' clinical language - referring to living belngs as "cases" and "specimens" - reveals how excessive reliance on data can strip away compassion. Their namelessness in the story reinforces their role as symbols of impersonal science rather than fully realized individuals. Meanwhile, the typist's insistence on seeing patients as "that poor man with three children" represents the essential human connection that gets lost in pure analysis. Deshpande seems to caution against allowing methodology to completely override empathy, showing how the typist's emotional intelligence ultimately influences the male doctor's perspective.

The story also develops the theme of personal transformation through openness. The male doctor's gradual shift from rigid skepticism to acknowledging life's mysteries demonstrates intellectual growth. His Walt Whitman quotation marks a turning point where he begins valuing emotional truth alongside scientific truth. This character arc suggests that wisdom comes from balancing reason with wonder, and that intellectual humility - recognizing the limits of human understanding - is a virtue. His relationship with the typist, who maintains her convictions despite her subordinate position, further illustrates how genuine connection can bridge ideological divides.

Perhaps the most subtle yet powerful theme is the sacred in the ordinary. Raaja performs no supernatural feats - he simply eats bananas and hesitates like any monkey. Yet his normal behavior becomes extraordinary when seen through eyes open to wonder. Deshpande suggests that miracles aren't necessarily supernatural events but rather moments that transcend our usual ways of understanding. The typist's bright clothing against the lab's sterile white environment visually reinforces this message - that vibrancy and meaning exist in everyday life if we choose to perceive them.

Conclusion

Ultimately, Miracle presents these themes not as abstract ideas but as lived experiences of its characters. Through their interactions around a seemingly insignificant monkey, Deshpande explores how we find meaning, how we relate to knowledge, and how different worldviews can coexist. The story's quiet power lies in its refusal to preach, instead inviting readers to reflect on where they position themselves between clinical detachment and spiritual awe in interpreting life's mysteries.

Q.4) Attempt critical appreciation of the story The Miracles.

Ans: Introduction:The Miracle is a short story written by Shashi Deshpande. Shashi Deshpande (1938) is an acclaimed Indian authoTr known for her nuanced portrayals of women's struggles in middle-class India. Her Sahitya Akademi-winning novel That Long Silence (1988) and other works like The Dark Holds No Terrors blend feminist perspectives with subtle storytelling."The Miracle" is a beautiful story that makes us think deeply about life in a simple way. The story shows us how different people see the world differently - some believe only in science, while others believe in miracles and faith.

The story is set in a medical lab where doctors are testing medicines on monkeys. What makes the story special is how Deshpande shows us the characters. The doctors don't even have names - this makes them seem like machines that only care about science. But other characters like Narayan and the typist have names and feelings, making them seem more human. The monkey Raaja becomes very important - though he's just doing normal monkey things like eating bananas, his survival makes everyone think differently.

The way the story is written is simple but clever. The conversations show us the difference between people who only believe in facts (like the doctors) and people who care about feelings (like the typist). When the doctors say "interesting case," the typist says "poor child" - this small difference in words shows a big difference in how they see the world.

The story uses simple things to show big ideas. The bright colors of the typist's clothes show she's full of life, while the doctors' white coats make them seem cold. The lab is clean and organized like science, while outside there's a colorful tree representing life's beauty. These small details help us understand the story's message without using difficult words.

What's really great about this story is how it doesn't tell us what to think. It shows us both sides - the scientists who want to understand everything and the believers who accept mysteries. The male doctor slowly changes his mind when he starts seeing that some things can't be explained by science alone. This change happens naturally, not suddenly, making it feel real.

The story makes us ask important questions: Can science explain everything? Is there room for miracles in our modern world? But it doesn't give easy answers. Instead, it shows that life is complicated and both science and faith have value. The most ordinary things - like a monkey eating or a baby crying - can seem like miracles if we look at them differently.

What makes "The Miracle" so good is that it talks about big ideas in a simple way. The language is easy to understand, but the ideas stay with you long after reading. It shows that great stories don't need fancy words or dramatic events - they can use everyday situations to make us think about life's big questions. The story stays balanced, never saying science is bad or faith is silly, but showing that both ways of thinking have value.

In today's world where people often fight about science versus religion, this story reminds us to stay open-minded. It teaches us that sometimes the most amazing things are right in front of us - we just need to look properly. That's why this simple story about a monkey in a lab becomes something much bigger - a story about how we understand life itself.

Conclusion: Shashi Deshpande's "The Miracle" is a simple yet profound story that explores the balance between science and faith. Through ordinary characters and everyday moments, it shows how life's mysteries can't always be explained by logic alone. The story teaches us to stay open-minded—valuing both reason and wonder—and reminds us that sometimes, the real miracles are found in the small, unexpected moments of life. Its quiet wisdom leaves a lasting impression, making us rethink how we see the world around us.

CHAPTER TWENTY-FIVE

Raji Narasimha: A Toast to Herself

Scan the QR code to watch video

About Writer:

Raji Narasimhan, born in 1930 in Madras, Tamil Nadu , is an Indian writer, journalist, and literary critic. She worked as a reporter and feature writer for The Indian Express before leaving journalism in the 1970s to focus on creative writing. Her notable works include four novels—The Heart of Standing is You Cannot Fly (1973), Forever Free(1979), Drifting to a Dawn (1983), and The Sky Changes (1991)—along with a short story collection, The Marriage of Bela and Other Stories (1978). She has also contributed to literary criticism with .Sensibility Under Stress: Aspects of Indo-English Fiction (1976), which is recomended reading in some Indian universities. Her first short story, The Poor Folk Around Town , was published in Quest in 1969, and A Toast to Herself appeared in Indian Literature in 1986. Apart from writing, she has been a dance and theatre critic for *The Patriot and continues to live in Delhi.

About Story:

A Toast to Herself tells the story of Priya, a middle-aged writer struggling with financial insecurity and societal expectations in contemporary India. Despite publishing her fifth book and eagerly awaiting a critical review from The Herald, Priya grapples with the harsh reality that writing rarely pays well. For her, books are as precious as children, yet her mother—firm in traditional beliefs—insists that writing is merely a hobby and that marriage, particularly to Dr. Kesavan, would offer the security she lacks. This generational clash reflects the broader tension between personal passion and conventional expectations.

Throughout the story, Priya's inner conflict emerges: she fiercely values her independence and creative expression, yet she also experiences moments of vulnerability, longing for the companionship and financial stability that marriage promises. In a symbolic celebration of her work, she toasts her latest achievement with lemonade under the open sky, a small act of defiance against societal pressures. Ultimately, the narrative highlights the sacrifices and challenges faced by women who choose unconventional paths, questioning the notion that financial security and marital conformity are the only remedies for a woman's struggles.

Questions and answers

1) How does Raji Narasimhan portray the characters in A Toast to Herself? Discuss.

Ans: Introduction: Raji Narasimhan, an Indian writer and critic, is known for her insightful exploration of women's struggles, societal expectations, and personal conflicts. Her works often depict strong yet vulnerable female protagonists who navigate the challenges of independence, relationships, and financial instability. In *A Toast to Herself*, she presents a deeply introspective portrayal of her characters, focusing on their inner conflicts and societal pressures. The story revolves around Priya, a middle-aged writer, her mother, and Dr. Kesavan. Through these characters, Narasimhan explores themes of independence, traditional expectations, financial hardship, and emotional longing. Each character represents a different perspective—Priya embodies resilience and artistic passion, her mother reflects conventional beliefs and concerns for security, while Dr. Kesavan symbolizes societal hesitation towards independent women. The characterization in the story highlights the tension between personal ambition and societal norms, making it a compelling study of human emotions and relationships.

The story focuses on three key characters—Priya, her mother, and Dr. Kesavan—each representing different viewpoints on life, ambition, and societal norms. Priya, the central character, is a 50-year-old divorced writer who challenges traditional expectations. She is fiercely independent and dedicated to her craft, despite the financial struggles that come with it. Even though her writing earns her very little, she refuses financial help from her mother and values her books more than material wealth. However, despite her strong exterior, she experiences moments of vulnerability. At times, she longs for companionship and emotional comfort, especially from Dr. Kesavan, revealing an inner conflict between her independence and natural human desires. Priya represents the modern, self-reliant woman, determined to live life on her own terms, even if it means facing hardships.

Priya's mother, in contrast, embodies traditional Indian values. She worries constantly about her daughter's future, believing that marriage is the only path to stability for a woman. She fails to understand Priya's dedication to writing, as she sees it as an unprofitable pursuit that cannot provide financial security. Her dependence on her widow's pension is a reflection of her own financial struggles, and she anxiously waits for the postman each month, fearing an uncertain future. Her insistence on remarriage stems from her deep concern for Priya's well-being, as she cannot imagine a life without the security of a husband.

Dr. Kesavan is portrayed as a typical Indian man with conflicting emotions. He is drawn to Priya but hesitates to act on his feelings, possibly due to societal views on divorced women. In Indian society, divorced women are often seen as independent and unconventional, which may make him uncertain about whether she would be a suitable wife. Though he is likely older than Priya and remains unmarried, the story does not explain why he has never settled down. His presence in the narrative highlights the societal reluctance to fully embrace independent women , especially those who do not conform to traditional roles.

Through these three characters, A Toast to Herself explores the clash between tradition and modernity, financial security and personal ambition, and independence versus emotional needs. Priya's journey reflects the struggles faced by many women who pursue their passions instead of following societal expectations, showing both the rewards and sacrifices that come with such a choice.

Q.2) Discuss the themes of the short story A Toast to herself.

Ans: Introduction: The short story A Toast to Herself by Raji Narasimhan explores several themes that are central to the narrative and reflect the struggles and conflicts faced by the protagonist, Priya, as well as the broader societal context in which she lives. Below is a detailed discussion of the key themes in the story:

1. Independence and Identity

Priya's Independence: The story revolves around Priya's determination to live life on her own terms, despite societal pressures and financial hardships. She is a middle-aged, divorced woman who has chosen writing as her profession, even though it does not provide her with financial stability. Her independence is a central theme, as she refuses to conform to traditional expectations, such as remarrying for security. Instead, she values her creative freedom and the fulfillment she derives from her writing.

Identity as a Writer: Priya's identity is deeply tied to her work as a writer. She sees her books as her "children," reflecting how much of herself she invests in her writing. This theme highlights the importance of personal passion and creative expression in shaping one's identity, even when it comes at the cost of financial security or societal approval.

2. Financial Insecurity and the Struggles of an Artist

Financial Hardships: The story vividly portrays the financial struggles faced by writers, especially those who do not write commercially popular books. Priya earns very little from her writing, sometimes just a few hundred rupees for a story or article. This theme reflects the harsh reality of many artists who pursue their passion despite the lack of financial rewards.

Art vs. Commerce: The tension between artistic integrity and financial stability is a recurring theme. Priya's mother represents the conventional view that writing should be a hobby, not a profession, especially for someone without financial security. This conflict underscores the challenges faced by artists who must choose between their passion and the need to earn a living.

3. Societal Expectations and Traditional Values

Marriage as a Solution: Priya's mother embodies traditional Indian values, believing that marriage is the only path to stability for a woman. She constantly urges Priya to remarry, suggesting that marriage to Dr. Kesavan would provide financial security and solve all her problems. This theme reflects the societal expectation that women should prioritize marriage and family over personal ambitions.

Generational Conflict: The story highlights the generational gap between Priya and her mother. While Priya represents modernity and independence, her mother clings to traditional beliefs, unable to understand or support her daughter's choices. This conflict is a microcosm of the broader societal tension between traditional and modern values.

4. Emotional Longing and Vulnerability

Human Desires: Despite her strong exterior and commitment to independence, Priya experiences moments of vulnerability and longing for companionship. Her interactions with Dr. Kesavan reveal her suppressed desire for emotional comfort and security. This theme adds depth to her character, showing that even the most independent individuals have emotional needs.

Conflict Between Independence and Emotional Needs: Priya's inner conflict between her desire for independence and her natural human longing for love and companionship is a key theme. It highlights the complexity of human emotions and the difficulty of balancing personal ambition with emotional fulfillment.

5. Gender Roles and Societal Hesitation

Societal Views on Divorced Women: Dr. Kesavan's hesitation to act on his feelings for Priya reflects societal attitudes toward divorced women. In Indian society, divorced women are often seen as independent and unconventional, which can make them less desirable in the traditional marriage market. This theme explores the societal reluctance to fully accept women who do not conform to traditional roles.

The Role of Women in Society: The story critiques the traditional view that a woman's primary role is to be a wife and mother. Priya's decision to prioritize her writing over marriage challenges these norms, but it also comes with sacrifices, as she faces financial insecurity and societal judgment.

6. Sacrifice and Passion

Sacrifices for Passion: Priya's story is one of sacrifice. She has chosen a path that brings her personal fulfillment but comes with significant challenges, including financial instability and societal disapproval. This theme emphasizes the sacrifices that individuals, especially women, must make when they choose passion over societal expectations.

The Rewards of Passion: Despite the hardships, Priya finds deep satisfaction in her writing. The act of raising a toast to herself symbolizes her celebration of her achievements and her commitment to her chosen path. This theme highlights the intrinsic rewards of pursuing one's passion, even in the face of adversity.

7. Self-Acceptance and Celebration of Individuality

A Toast to Herself: The title of the story is symbolic of Priya's self-acceptance and celebration of her individuality. Despite the lack of external recognition and financial success, she takes pride in her work and her choices. This theme underscores the importance of self-validation and the courage to live authentically, even when it means going against societal norms.

Conclusion:

In A Toast to Herself, Raji Narasimhan explores themes of independence, financial insecurity, societal expectations, emotional longing, and the sacrifices that come with pursuing one's passion. Through the character of Priya, the story highlights the challenges faced by women who choose unconventional paths, as well as the tension between personal ambition and societal norms. The narrative ultimately celebrates the strength and resilience of women who dare to live life on their own terms, even in the face of adversity.

Q.3) Discuss the narrative technique.

Ans. Introduction: In A Toast to Herself, Raji Narasimhan employs a simple yet powerful narrative technique that effectively conveys the protagonist's inner struggles, societal pressures, and emotional conflicts. The narrative style is introspective and reflective, allowing readers to delve deeply into Priya's thoughts and feelings. Below is an analysis of the narrative techniques used in the story:

1. Third-Person Limited Point of View

The story is narrated in the third-person limited point of view, focusing primarily on Priya's perspective. This allows readers to closely follow her thoughts, emotions, and experiences, while also providing some insight into the other characters' actions and motivations.

By limiting the narrative to Priya's viewpoint, the author creates a sense of intimacy and empathy, enabling readers to connect with her struggles and aspirations. This technique also highlights the internal conflict between Priya's independence and her moments of vulnerability.

2. Introspective and Reflective Tone

The narrative is deeply introspective, with frequent reflections on Priya's past, her choices, and her current situation. This reflective tone allows readers to understand the complexity of her character and the reasons behind her decisions.

For example, Priya's thoughts about her divorce, her relationship with Dr. Kesavan, and her financial struggles are all explored through her internal monologues. This technique helps to reveal her inner conflicts and the emotional weight of her choices.

3. Symbolism

The story uses symbolism to convey deeper meanings and themes. For instance, the act of Priya raising a toast to herself with lemonade (instead of alcohol) symbolizes her self-celebration and acceptance of her life choices, despite the lack of external validation.

The open sky under which Priya, her mother, and Dr. Kesavan share the toast can be seen as a symbol of freedom and possibility, contrasting with the constraints of societal expectations and financial struggles.

4. Contrast and Juxtaposition

The narrative frequently employs contrast and juxtaposition to highlight the differences between Priya's values and those of the people around her, particularly her mother. For example:

Priya vs. Her Mother: Priya's dedication to her writing and her rejection of traditional marital security are contrasted with her mother's insistence on marriage as the only solution to financial instability. Art vs. Commerce: The story juxtaposes Priya's passion for writing with the harsh reality of financial insecurity, emphasizing the tension between artistic integrity and the need to earn a living.These contrasts serve to underscore the central themes of the story, such as the clash between tradition and modernity, and the sacrifices required to pursue one's passion.

5. Minimalist Dialogue

The story uses minimalist dialogue, with much of the narrative driven by Priya's thoughts and reflections rather than conversations. This technique emphasizes the internal nature of her struggles and the isolation she feels as a result of her unconventional choices.

When dialogue is used, it is often brief and loaded with meaning. For example, the conversations between Priya and her mother reveal the generational gap and the mother's inability to understand her daughter's choices.

6. Flashbacks and Memories

The narrative incorporates flashbacks and memories to provide context for Priya's current situation. These glimpses into her past help readers understand her motivations and the events that have shaped her character.

For instance, Priya's reflections on her divorce and her interactions with Dr. Kesavan in the past add depth to her character and explain her current emotional state.

7. Realism and Relatability

The narrative style is realistic, portraying the everyday struggles of a middle-aged woman writer in a way that feels authentic and relatable. The detailed descriptions of Priya's financial struggles, her interactions with her mother, and her moments of self-doubt create a vivid and believable portrayal of her life.

This realism makes the story accessible and allows readers to empathize with Priya's challenges, even if they do not share her specific circumstances.

8. Subtle Social Commentary

Through the narrative, the author provides subtle social commentary on issues such as gender roles, societal expectations, and the challenges faced by women who choose unconventional paths. The story critiques the traditional view that marriage is the only solution to a woman's problems, while also highlighting the financial and emotional struggles of pursuing a creative career. The narrative does not overtly criticize society but instead allows readers to draw their own conclusions based on Priya's experiences and the reactions of the other characters.

Conclusion:

Raji Narasimhan's narrative technique in A Toast to Herself is characterized by its introspective tone, use of symbolism, contrast, and minimalist dialogue. The third-person limited point of view allows readers to closely follow Priya's thoughts and emotions, while the realistic portrayal of her struggles makes the story relatable and impactful. Through these techniques, the author effectively explores themes of independence, financial insecurity, societal expectations, and the sacrifices required to pursue one's passion. The narrative style is both simple and powerful, making the story a poignant reflection on the challenges faced by women who dare to live life on their own terms.

Q.3) Attempt a Critical Appreciation of A Toast to Herself.

Ans: Introduction: Raji Narasimhan's A Toast to Herself is a poignant and introspective short story that delves into the life of a middle-aged woman writer, Priya, who grapples with financial insecurity, societal expectations, and her passion for writing. The story is a powerful exploration of themes such as independence, identity, and the sacrifices required to pursue one's passion in a society that often prioritizes traditional roles for women. Narasimhan's narrative technique, characterized by its simplicity and depth, allows readers to connect intimately with Priya's struggles, making the story both relatable and thought-provoking.

One of the most striking aspects of the story is its realistic portrayal of the challenges faced by women who choose unconventional paths. Priya, as a divorced woman and a writer, represents a departure from traditional Indian societal norms, which often prioritize marriage and financial stability over personal ambition. Her financial struggles, earning meager sums from her writing, reflect the harsh reality of many artists who pursue their passion despite the lack of monetary rewards. Narasimhan does not romanticize Priya's life; instead, she presents it with honesty, showing the sacrifices and hardships that come with choosing a creative career. This realism makes Priya's character deeply relatable, especially for readers who understand the tension between following one's passion and meeting societal expectations.

The story also excels in its exploration of generational conflict and societal expectations. Priya's mother, who represents traditional Indian values, constantly reminds her daughter of the importance of marriage as a means of security. Her inability to understand Priya's dedication to writing highlights the generational gap between the two women. This conflict is a microcosm of the broader societal tension between tradition and modernity, where women like Priya are often caught between their personal aspirations and the expectations placed upon them by family and society. Narasimhan skillfully uses this dynamic to critique the traditional view that marriage is the ultimate solution to a woman's problems, while also showing the emotional toll this pressure takes on Priya.

Narasimhan's use of symbolism adds depth to the narrative. The act of Priya raising a toast to herself with lemonade, rather than alcohol, is a powerful symbol of self-celebration and acceptance. It signifies her acknowledgment of her achievements, despite the lack of external validation. Similarly, the open sky under which the toast takes place symbolizes freedom and possibility, contrasting with the constraints of societal expectations and financial struggles. These symbols enrich the story, allowing readers to engage with its themes on a deeper level.

The characterization in the story is another strength. Priya is a complex and multi-dimensional character, embodying both strength and vulnerability. Her fierce independence and dedication to her craft are admirable, but her moments of doubt and longing for companionship make her human and relatable. Dr. Kesavan, on the other hand, represents societal hesitation towards independent women. His attraction to Priya, coupled with his reluctance to act on it, reflects the broader societal discomfort with women who do not conform to traditional roles. Through these characters, Narasimhan explores the tension between personal ambition and societal norms, making the story a compelling study of human emotions and relationships.

Conclusion: A Toast to Herself is a deeply moving and thought-provoking story that offers a nuanced exploration of the challenges faced by women who choose to live life on their own terms. Raji Narasimhan's simple yet powerful narrative technique, combined with her realistic portrayal of Priya's struggles, makes the story both relatable and impactful. The themes of independence, financial insecurity, societal expectations, and the sacrifices required to pursue one's passion are explored with sensitivity and depth, making the story a timeless reflection on the complexities of modern womanhood. Through Priya's journey, Narasimhan celebrates the strength and resilience of women who dare to defy societal norms, offering a poignant reminder of the importance of self-acceptance and the courage to live authentically.

Q4.) In ways does Raji Narasimha's story A Toast to herself appeal to you.

Ans: Introduction: Raji Narasimhan's A Toast to Herself is a deeply compelling story that appeals to me on multiple levels—emotionally, intellectually, and socially. The story's exploration of independence, identity, and the struggles of pursuing one's passion resonates strongly, especially in a world where societal expectations often clash with personal aspirations. Below are the ways in which the story appeals to me:

1. Relatable Protagonist and Emotional Depth

Priya, the protagonist, is a character I find deeply relatable. Her struggles as a middle-aged woman writer, balancing her passion for writing with financial insecurity and societal pressures, mirror the challenges many individuals face when pursuing non-traditional or creative careers. Her moments of vulnerability—such as her longing for companionship and her occasional doubts about her choices—make her a multi-dimensional and human character. This emotional depth allows me to empathize with her journey and reflect on my own experiences of balancing passion with practicality.

The story's portrayal of Priya's inner conflict—her desire for independence versus her natural human need for emotional comfort—is particularly moving. It highlights the complexity of human emotions and the difficulty of making choices that go against societal norms. This duality in her character makes her story both inspiring and heartbreaking, as it shows the sacrifices she must make to stay true to herself.

2. Exploration of Societal Expectations

The story's critique of societal expectations, particularly those placed on women, is one of its most appealing aspects. Priya's mother represents the traditional view that marriage is the ultimate solution to a woman's problems, while Priya herself embodies the modern, independent woman who prioritizes her passion and individuality over societal norms. This generational conflict is something many readers, including myself, can relate to, as it reflects the ongoing tension between tradition and modernity in many societies.

The story also sheds light on the stigma surrounding divorced women in traditional societies. Priya's independence and refusal to conform to societal expectations make her a target of judgment, and Dr. Kesavan's hesitation to act on his feelings for her further underscores the societal reluctance to accept women who do not fit into conventional roles. This aspect of the story resonates with me as it highlights the need for greater acceptance and understanding of women who choose to live life on their own terms.

3. Themes of Sacrifice and Passion

One of the most inspiring aspects of the story is its exploration of sacrifice and passion. Priya's decision to pursue writing, despite the financial hardships it brings, is a testament to her dedication and love for her craft. Her willingness to prioritize her passion over financial stability is both admirable and thought-provoking. It makes me reflect on the sacrifices I am willing to make for my own passions and the value of staying true to oneself, even in the face of adversity.

The act of Priya raising a toast to herself with lemonade is a powerful symbol of self-acceptance and celebration. It appeals to me because it represents the importance of recognizing and valuing one's own achievements, even when they are not acknowledged by others. This moment of self-validation is a reminder that true fulfillment comes from within, rather than from external validation.

4. Realistic Portrayal of Financial Struggles

The story's realistic portrayal of financial struggles is another aspect that appeals to me. Priya's meager earnings from her writing reflect the harsh reality faced by many artists and writers who pursue their passion without commercial success. This aspect of the story is both sobering and inspiring, as it highlights the resilience and determination required to continue pursuing one's passion despite financial instability.

The contrast between Priya's financial struggles and her mother's dependence on a widow's pension adds another layer of realism to the story. It underscores the generational differences in attitudes toward financial security and the challenges faced by women who lack traditional sources of support. This realism makes the story relatable and impactful, as it reflects the struggles many people face in balancing passion with practicality.

5. Symbolism and Narrative Technique

The symbolism in the story, such as the open sky under which Priya raises her toast, appeals to me because it represents freedom and possibility. This imagery contrasts with the constraints of societal expectations and financial struggles, offering a sense of hope and optimism. The narrative technique, with its introspective tone and minimalist dialogue, allows readers to connect deeply with Priya's thoughts and emotions, making her journey feel personal and intimate.

The use of flashbacks and memories to provide context for Priya's current situation adds depth to the story and helps readers understand her motivations and choices. This narrative technique makes the story more engaging and allows for a deeper exploration of its themes.

Conclusion:

Raji Narasimhan's A Toast to Herself appeals to me because of its relatable protagonist, exploration of societal expectations, themes of sacrifice and passion, and realistic portrayal of financial struggles. The story's emotional depth, combined with its powerful symbolism and narrative technique, makes it a thought-provoking and inspiring read. It encourages readers to reflect on their own choices, the sacrifices they are willing to make for their passions, and the importance of self-acceptance in a world that often prioritizes conformity over individuality. Through Priya's journey, the story celebrates the strength and resilience of women who dare to live life on their own terms, making it a timeless and impactful piece of literature.

Q 5) Discuss the stereotypical mentality of Indian society with reference to Raji Narasimhan's short story A Toast to Herself. How does the story reflect and critique traditional beliefs and societal expectations, particularly regarding gender roles, marriage, and the pursuit of personal ambition?

Ans: Introduction: Raji Narasimhan's A Toast to Herself provides a nuanced critique of the stereotypical mentality of Indian society, particularly regarding gender roles, marriage, and the expectations placed on women. Through the characters and their interactions, the story highlights the deep-rooted traditional beliefs that often clash with modern, individualistic aspirations. Below is a detailed discussion of how the story reflects and critiques these societal stereotypes:

1. Marriage as the Ultimate Goal for Women

One of the most prominent stereotypes in Indian society, as depicted in the story, is the belief that marriage is the ultimate goal and solution for a woman's problems. Priya's mother embodies this traditional mindset, constantly urging her daughter to remarry, even at the age of 50. She believes that marriage to Dr. Kesavan would provide Priya with financial security and stability, which she sees as more important than her daughter's passion for writing.

This stereotype reflects the societal expectation that a woman's primary role is to be a wife and mother, rather than pursuing her own ambitions or career. Priya's mother cannot understand or accept her daughter's dedication to writing, viewing it as an unprofitable and frivolous pursuit. This attitude underscores the societal devaluation of women's creative and intellectual contributions, reducing their worth to their marital status.

2. Financial Dependence and the Role of Men

The story also critiques the stereotype that women are financially dependent on men. Priya's mother, who relies on her widow's pension, represents the traditional view that women need male support to survive. She anxiously waits for the postman to deliver her pension, fearing an uncertain future without a husband. This dependence on a man's income is a reflection of the broader societal belief that women cannot achieve financial independence on their own.

In contrast, Priya challenges this stereotype by choosing to live independently, despite her financial struggles. She refuses to rely on her mother's pension or seek financial security through remarriage. Her determination to support herself through her writing, even though it brings little monetary reward, is a powerful rejection of the traditional belief that women need men to provide for them.

3. Stigma Surrounding Divorced Women

The story highlights the stigma surrounding divorced women in Indian society. Priya's divorce marks her as unconventional and independent, which makes her a target of judgment and hesitation, particularly from Dr. Kesavan. His reluctance to act on his feelings for her reflects the societal discomfort with women who do not conform to traditional roles.

In Indian society, divorced women are often seen as "damaged" or "unmarriageable," and their independence is viewed with suspicion. This stereotype is evident in the way Priya's mother and Dr. Kesavan perceive her. While her mother sees her divorce as a problem that can only be solved through remarriage, Dr. Kesavan's hesitation suggests that he is unsure whether a divorced woman like Priya would make a suitable wife. This societal stigma adds to Priya's struggles, as she must navigate not only financial insecurity but also the judgment of those around her.

4. Generational Conflict and Resistance to Change

The generational conflict between Priya and her mother is a reflection of the broader societal resistance to change. Priya represents the modern, independent woman who prioritizes her passion and individuality over traditional expectations. Her mother, on the other hand, embodies the older generation's adherence to conventional values and beliefs.

This conflict highlights the difficulty of challenging deeply ingrained societal stereotypes. Even though Priya has chosen a path that brings her personal fulfillment, she faces constant pressure from her mother to conform to traditional norms. This pressure reflects the broader societal resistance to accepting women who choose unconventional paths, particularly those that prioritize personal ambition over marriage and family.

5. The Devaluation of Creative Pursuits

Another stereotype critiqued in the story is the devaluation of creative pursuits, particularly when they do not bring financial success. Priya's mother sees writing as a hobby, not a profession, and cannot understand why her daughter would prioritize it over financial stability. This attitude reflects the broader societal belief that creative careers are less valuable or respectable than traditional, financially secure professions.

Priya's financial struggles as a writer highlight the challenges faced by artists and writers in a society that often prioritizes material success over creative expression. Despite her passion and dedication, she earns very little from her writing, which underscores the societal lack of support for creative professions. This devaluation of creative pursuits is a barrier for many women (and men) who wish to pursue their passions but face societal pressure to choose more "practical" careers.

6. The Ideal of the "Suitable" Woman

The story also touches on the stereotype of the "suitable" woman in Indian society, who is expected to be submissive, dependent, and conforming to traditional roles. Priya, as a divorced, independent woman who prioritizes her writing, does not fit this ideal. Her mother's insistence that she remarry and give up writing reflects the societal expectation that women should conform to this ideal, rather than pursuing their own ambitions.

Dr. Kesavan's hesitation to pursue a relationship with Priya further underscores this stereotype. His uncertainty about whether a divorced, independent woman like Priya would make a suitable wife reflects the societal discomfort with women who do not fit the traditional mold. This stereotype limits women's choices and reinforces the idea that their value lies in their ability to conform to societal expectations, rather than in their individuality or achievements.

Conclusion:

Through A Toast to Herself, Raji Narasimhan critiques the stereotypical mentality of Indian society, particularly regarding gender roles, marriage, and the expectations placed on women. The story highlights the societal pressure on women to conform to traditional norms, such as prioritizing marriage over personal ambition, relying on men for financial security, and adhering to the ideal of the "suitable" woman. At the same time, it celebrates the strength and resilience of women like Priya, who dare to challenge these stereotypes and live life on their own terms. By exposing the limitations and injustices of these societal beliefs, the story encourages readers to reflect on the need for greater acceptance and support for women who choose unconventional paths.

CHAPTER TWENTY-SIX

Githa Hariharan: Gajar Halwa

Scan the QR code to watch video

About Author:

Githa Hariharan (born 1954) is a prominent Indian writer and editor based in New Delhi, acclaimed for her novels, short stories, essays, and children's literature. Her notable works include The Thousand Faces of Night—which won the Commonwealth Writers Prize for Best First Book in 1993—The Art of Dying, The Ghosts of Vasu Master, When Dreams Travel, In Times of Siege, Fugitive Histories, and Almost Home: Cities and Other Places. Her writings, available in several Indian languages, delve into contemporary issues like the misuse of religion, tradition, and the status of women, often blending myth and storytelling to expand the narrative of people's lives.

Born in Coimbatore into a Tamil Brahmin family, Hariharan studied in Mumbai, Manila, and the United States, earning a Master's degree in Communication from Fairfield University, Connecticut. After a stint as a television scriptwriter in New York, she worked as an editor for Orient Longman before turning to freelance writing. In addition to her literary achievements, she writes a regular column for The Telegraph and has edited various anthologies. Today, she is widely recognized as one of India's most significant contemporary writers, celebrated both nationally and internationally.

About Story:

"Gajar Halwa" is a short story from Githa Hariharan's 1993 collection The Art of..., in which she reflects on her place in the world through the simple act of peeling and grating carrots.

Perumayee, a young girl from a small Salem village, faces hardship after her father abandons the family, leaving her mother to struggle with poverty. With no work available at home, her mother sends her to Delhi with Chellamma to find work as a domestic helper. In the overwhelming chaos of the city, Perumayee adjusts to life in a cramped, converted garage, earning a meager income while dreaming of supporting her family back home. One day, when tasked with preparing the unfamiliar dessert Gajar Halwa, she perseveres through the laborious process. The sweet aroma and her small triumph mark the beginning of her slow adaptation to urban life, symbolizing resilience amidst the harsh realities of poverty, illiteracy, and child labor.

Question and Answer

Q.1) Discuss the narrative technique used by Githa Hariharan in her story "Gajar Halwa".

Introduction: Gajar Halwa" was first published in Githa Hariharan's 1993 collection of short stories, The Art of Dying.Through Perumayee's experiences, Hariharan addresses the challenges marginalized people face when adjusting to new environments and navigating complex social structures. In Githa Hariharan's story "Gajar Halwa," the narrative techniques play a crucial role in bringing out the themes of migration, exploitation, and the loss of innocence. The story revolves around Perumayee, a young girl from rural Salem, who moves to Delhi in search of a better life, only to find herself entangled in the harsh realities of urban existence. Hariharan employs a variety of narrative techniques to vividly portray Perumayee's journey and the socio-economic disparities she encounters. These techniques not only enhance the emotional depth of the story but also provide a critical commentary on the societal structures that perpetuate inequality and exploitation.

The narrative techniques employed in this story contribute to its depth and impact, enhancing the reader's engagement and understanding of the themes explored. One of the prominent narrative techniques in "Gajar Halwa" is the use of multiple perspectives. The story is narrated through the alternating viewpoints of different characters, providing diverse insights into the events and emotions. This technique allows readers to gain a comprehensive understanding of the complex relationships and dynamics within the story. Each perspective adds a layer of depth and complexity, enriching the narrative and inviting readers to contemplate the subjective nature of truth and perception.

Githa also employs a non-linear narrative structure in "Gajar Halwa." The story unfolds through a series of fragmented memories, thoughts, and reflections, ratherthan following a linear chronological sequence. This fragmented structure mirrors the fragmented nature of memory itself, capturing the protagonist's internal struggles, conflicts, and introspections. It adds a sense of mystery and intrigue to the story, compelling readers to piece together the fragments and construct their own interpretation.

Symbolism is another narrative technique utilized in "Gajar Halwa." Githa employs various symbols to convey deeper meanings and evoke emotions. For example, the gajar halwa (carrot pudding) itself becomes a symbol of desire, longing,and nostalgia. It represents the protagonist's yearning for a sense of belonging and fulfillment. The symbolism adds layers of richness to the narrative, allowing readers to delve into the subconscious dimensions of the story and explore universal themes of human experience.

Hariharan uses stark contrasts to highlight the differences between rural and urban life. The scarcity and simplicity of Perumayee's life in Salem are juxtaposed with the abundance and complexity of her new life in Delhi. This contrast underscores the socio-economic disparities and the cultural shock experienced by rural migrants.

The characters are portrayed in a way that reflects broader social issues. Perumayee's transformation from an innocent village girl to a pragmatic city dweller illustrates the impact of urban migration on individuals. The mistress's indifference and Chellamma's opportunistic behavior highlight the lack of empathy and exploitation prevalent in society.

Conclusion: Overall, these narrative techniques work together to create a poignant and vivid portrayal of Perumayee's journey, highlighting the broader themes of migration, exploitation, and the loss of innocence. Through these techniques, Hariharan not only tells a compelling story but also invites readers to reflect on the societal structures that shape the lives of individuals like Perumayee.

Q.2) Do you agree that Gita Hariharan's 'Gajar Halwa' offers a scathing comment on our social inequalities ? Give reasons.

Ans: Introduction: Yes, Githa Hariharan's "Gajar Halwa" offers a scathing comment on social inequalities, particularly those rooted in class, gender, and rural-urban divides. Through the story of Perumayee, a young girl from rural Salem who migrates to Delhi in search of a better life, Hariharan exposes the harsh realities of exploitation, systemic oppression, and the loss of innocence that many marginalized individuals face. Here are several reasons why the story serves as a powerful critique of social inequalities:

1. Rural-Urban Divide and Exploitation

The story starkly contrasts Perumayee's life in rural Salem with her experiences in urban Delhi. In Salem, she lives in poverty, with her family struggling to survive due to failed rains and lack of work. Her mother works tirelessly on a highway construction site, carrying gravel on her head, while Perumayee takes on the role of a caregiver for her siblings, sacrificing her childhood. This portrayal highlights the economic disparities between rural and urban areas, where rural communities often lack basic resources and opportunities.

When Perumayee moves to Delhi, she is thrust into a world of abundance, but it comes at a cost. She becomes a domestic worker, subjected to long hours of labor, low wages, and a lack of empathy from her employer. The story critiques how urban centers exploit rural migrants, offering them menial jobs while denying them dignity and fair treatment. The city, symbolized by the gajar halwa, is alluring but ultimately consumes and dehumanizes individuals like Perumayee.

2. Class Inequality and Power Dynamics

The relationship between Perumayee and her mistress exemplifies the deep class divide in Indian society. The mistress, though educated and affluent, shows no compassion or understanding toward Perumayee. She treats her as a mere servant, not bothering to learn her name or inquire about her personal life. This indifference reflects the dehumanization of domestic workers, who are often seen as disposable labor rather than individuals with their own struggles and aspirations.

Chellamma, the intermediary who brings Perumayee to Delhi, further underscores the exploitation within the system. She charges Perumayee a portion of her earnings, highlighting how even those from similar backgrounds can perpetuate inequality for personal gain. The story critiques how systemic oppression forces individuals to exploit one another, creating a cycle of inequality.

3. Gender Inequality

Perumayee's story is also a commentary on gender inequality. As a young girl, she is burdened with responsibilities far beyond her age, caring for her siblings and performing household chores while her father abandons the family. Her migration to Delhi is driven by economic necessity, but it also reflects the limited opportunities available to women in rural areas. In the city, she is confined to domestic work, a role traditionally assigned to women, further reinforcing gender stereotypes.

The mistress, despite her privilege, is also constrained by societal expectations. She relies on Perumayee to manage her household and care for her child, reflecting the pressures placed on women to balance work and family. However, her lack of empathy toward Perumayee highlights how privilege can blind individuals to the struggles of those less fortunate.

4. Loss of Innocence and Human Bonds

The story poignantly depicts how social inequalities strip individuals of their innocence and humanity. Perumayee, once a caring and hardworking girl, learns to cut corners and prioritize her survival over honesty. The city, with its material allure, saps her emotional ties to her family, as she dreams of buying a sweater for herself before sending money home. This transformation reflects how systemic inequalities force individuals to adapt in ways that erode their moral and emotional foundations.

5. Symbolism of Gajar Halwa

The preparation of gajar halwa serves as a metaphor for the exploitation and absorption of rural migrants into urban life. The labor-intensive process mirrors Perumayee's struggles, while the dish's sweetness symbolizes the false promise of a better life in the city. The story critiques how the city consumes individuals, offering them little in return for their labor.

Conclusion

In "Gajar Halwa," Githa Hariharan masterfully critiques social inequalities through the lens of Perumayee's journey. The story exposes the exploitation of rural migrants, the dehumanization of domestic workers, and the systemic oppression rooted in class and gender. By highlighting these issues, Hariharan calls for greater empathy and systemic change, urging readers to recognize and address the inequalities that perpetuate suffering and injustice.

Q.3) How Githa hariharan has portrayed the characters in Gajar halwa.

Ans: Introduction: In "Gajar Halwa," Githa Hariharan portrays her characters with depth and nuance, using them to reflect broader social issues such as class inequality, gender roles, and rural-urban migration. Each character is carefully crafted to highlight the complexities of their circumstances and the societal structures that shape their lives. Here's an analysis of how Hariharan portrays the main characters:

1. Perumayee:Perumayee is the protagonist, a young girl from rural Salem who migrates to Delhi in search of a better life. Hariharan portrays her as a symbol of innocence and resilience. In Salem, Perumayee is burdened with responsibilities beyond her years, caring for her siblings and performing household chores. Her migration to Delhi marks a significant transformation as she adapts to the harsh realities of urban life.

Innocence and Adaptation: Initially, Perumayee is naive and honest, but she quickly learns to navigate the complexities of city life. She learns to cut corners in her work and prioritize her survival, reflecting the loss of innocence and the harsh realities of her new environment.

Symbol of Rural Migration: Perumayee represents the countless rural migrants who move to cities in search of better opportunities, only to face exploitation and hardship. Her journey underscores the socio-economic disparities between rural and urban areas.

2. Perumayee's Mother

Perumayee's mother is portrayed as a hardworking and resilient woman who struggles to provide for her family in the face of extreme poverty and her husband's abandonment.

Strength and Sacrifice: She works tirelessly on a highway construction site, carrying gravel on her head, even when she is sick or hungry. Her sacrifices highlight the extreme measures that marginalized individuals must take to survive.

Representation of Rural Women: Her character reflects the struggles of rural women who bear the brunt of economic hardships and societal expectations. Despite her hardships, she makes the difficult decision to send Perumayee to Delhi, hoping for a better future for her daughter.

3. Chellamma

Chellamma is a pragmatic and opportunistic character who serves as an intermediary between rural migrants and urban employers.

Exploitation and Pragmatism: Chellamma charges Perumayee a portion of her earnings, highlighting how systemic oppression forces individuals to exploit one another. Her character critiques the cycle of inequality and the lack of solidarity among the marginalized.

Adaptation to Urban Life: Chellamma's ability to navigate the urban landscape and negotiate with employers reflects her adaptation to city life. She represents those who have learned to survive and even thrive within the exploitative system.

4. The Mistress

The mistress is an affluent urban woman who employs Perumayee. Her character is portrayed with a lack of empathy and understanding toward her domestic worker.

Class Privilege and Indifference: The mistress treats Perumayee as a mere servant, not bothering to learn her name or inquire about her personal life. Her indifference reflects the dehumanization of domestic workers and the deep class divide in Indian society.

Constraints of Gender Roles: Despite her privilege, the mistress is also constrained by societal expectations. She relies on Perumayee to manage her household and care for her child, highlighting the pressures placed on women to balance work and family.

5. Perumayee's Father

Perumayee's father is a minor but significant character whose abandonment of the family underscores the themes of gender inequality and economic hardship.

Irresponsibility and Abandonment: His laziness and alcoholism lead to his abandonment of the family, leaving Perumayee's mother to fend for the children alone. His character critiques the societal norms that often absolve men of their responsibilities while burdening women with the consequences.

Conclusion

Through these characters, Githa Hariharan paints a vivid picture of the social inequalities and systemic oppression that shape their lives. Each character, from the resilient Perumayee to the indifferent mistress, serves as a lens through which the reader can examine the broader issues of class, gender, and rural-urban divides. Hariharan's portrayal of these characters is both empathetic and critical, urging readers to recognize and address the societal structures that perpetuate inequality and injustice.

Q.4) How do you view Chellamma 's role in the story? Does she to take advantage of the situation in her own way?

Ans: Introduction: Chellamma's role in "Gajar Halwa" is complex and multifaceted. She serves as a bridge between rural migrants like Perumayee and urban employers, but her actions also reveal the exploitative dynamics within the system. Here's an analysis of Chellamma's role and whether she takes advantage of the situation:

Chellamma's Role in the Story

Intermediary and Facilitator: Chellamma acts as a facilitator for rural girls seeking employment in Delhi. She brings Perumayee and other girls from the village to the city, helping them find jobs as domestic workers. In this capacity, she provides a crucial service, offering these girls a chance to earn a livelihood and support their families.

Pragmatic Survivor:

Having been in Delhi for years, Chellamma has learned to navigate the urban landscape. She understands the needs and expectations of employers and knows how to present the girls in a way that secures them jobs. Her pragmatism and street-smart nature are essential for survival in a competitive and often exploitative environment.

Does Chellamma Take Advantage of the Situation?

Exploitation for Personal Gain:

Chellamma charges Perumayee fifty rupees from her monthly salary for her services. This fee, while seemingly small, represents a significant portion of Perumayee's earnings. By taking a cut from the girls' salaries, Chellamma benefits financially from their labor, highlighting a form of exploitation within the marginalized community itself.

Manipulation and Deception:

Chellamma lies to the mistress about Perumayee's skills, claiming she can cook, clean, and care for children, even though she knows Perumayee has limited experience. This deception is driven by the necessity to secure a job for Perumayee, but it also places the girl in a difficult position, forcing her to learn quickly and often cut corners to meet expectations.

Cycle of Exploitation:

Chellamma's actions reflect the broader cycle of exploitation that pervades the system. Having once been in Perumayee's position, she has adapted to the urban environment by exploiting others in similar circumstances. This cycle underscores the systemic nature of inequality, where individuals are forced to exploit one another to survive.

Conclusion

Chellamma's role in the story is both supportive and exploitative. While she provides essential assistance to rural girls like Perumayee, helping them find employment and navigate the challenges of city life, she also takes advantage of their vulnerability for personal gain. Her actions highlight the complexities of survival in an unequal society, where even those from marginalized backgrounds may perpetuate exploitation. Chellamma's character serves as a critique of the systemic inequalities that force individuals into such roles, urging readers to reflect on the broader social structures that enable and sustain exploitation.

Q.5) Discuss the themes of the story Gajar Halwa

Ans: Introduction: Githa Hariharan's Gajar Halwa is a poignant exploration of social inequalities, migration, and the loss of innocence in a rapidly urbanizing India. Through the story of Perumayee, a young girl from rural Tamil Nadu who migrates to Delhi for work, Hariharan critiques systemic oppression, class hierarchies, and the dehumanizing effects of urban labor. Below are the key themes in the story:

1. Rural-Urban Divide and Migration

The story highlights the stark contrast between Perumayee's impoverished village life and the deceptive allure of Delhi. In Salem, she faces drought, unemployment, and hunger, while Delhi promises opportunity but delivers exploitation. The city symbolizes false hope—while it offers material comforts (gas stoves, refrigerators, meat), it also consumes and discards migrant laborers.

2. Exploitation of Domestic Labor

Perumayee's work as a maid exposes the harsh realities of domestic labor—long hours, low wages, and emotional neglect. The mistress treats her as disposable labor, never learning her real name (calling her "Prema" instead of Perumayee) or acknowledging her humanity. Chellamma, the middlewoman, profits from Perumayee's labor, reinforcing how systemic oppression forces the poor to exploit each other.

3. Loss of Innocence and Moral Compromise

Perumayee starts as an honest, hardworking girl but soon learns to cut corners (skipping chores, hiding mistakes) to survive. Her desire for a sweater before sending money home shows how city life erodes her familial bonds and moral values. The story suggests that survival in an unjust system often requires compromising one's integrity.

4. Class and Caste Hierarchies

The mistress's indifference reflects the entrenched class divide—Perumayee is seen as a servant, not a person.The story critiques how education and wealth do not necessarily foster empathy; the educated mistress remains oblivious to Perumayee's suffering. The lack of names for some characters (Perumayee's mother, the mistress) symbolizes how the poor are often invisible in society.

5. Symbolism of "Gajar Halwa"

The labor-intensive process of making gajar halwa mirrors Perumayee's struggles—peeling, grating, and stirring represent her grueling work. The dish's sweetness contrasts with its bitter preparation, symbolizing the false promises of city life—attractive on the surface but built on exploitation.

Just as the carrots absorb sugar and milk, the city "absorbs" migrants, stripping them of their identity and innocence.

6. Gender and Power Dynamics

Perumayee's mother embodies the struggles of rural women—abandoned by her husband, she works backbreaking jobs to feed her children.The mistress, though privileged, is also trapped in gendered expectations, relying on Perumayee to manage her household. The story critiques how patriarchy and capitalism intersect, forcing women into cycles of labor and dependence.

Conclusion

Gajar Halwa is a powerful critique of India's socio-economic disparities, exposing how urbanization exploits the rural poor. Through vivid symbolism and unflinching realism, Hariharan portrays the dehumanizing effects of migration, labor exploitation, and systemic inequality. The story urges readers to question societal structures that perpetuate such injustices, making it a timeless commentary on class, gender, and survival in modern India.

Q.6) Attempt Critical Appreciation of Githa Hariharan's "Gajar Halwa"

Ans: Introduction: Githa Hariharan's Gajar Halwa is a masterful short story that blends stark realism with poignant symbolism to critique socio-economic inequalities in contemporary India. Through the lens of a young migrant worker's journey, Hariharan exposes the harsh realities of rural-urban migration, labor exploitation, and the erosion of innocence. The story's strength lies in its layered narrative, vivid imagery, and unflinching portrayal of systemic oppression.

Githa Hariharan's "Gajar Halwa" is a profound literary work that deftly captures the harsh realities of rural-urban migration and systemic exploitation in contemporary India. Through the poignant journey of Perumayee, a young girl from rural Tamil Nadu who becomes a domestic worker in Delhi, Hariharan weaves a narrative that is both intimate and universally resonant. The story's brilliance lies in its ability to balance stark realism with rich symbolism, creating a narrative that lingers long after the final lines. Hariharan's prose is economical yet deeply evocative, immersing readers in Perumayee's world through sensory details—the biting cold of Delhi's water, the pungent smell of Chellamma's cramped room, and the rhythmic monotony of grating carrots. These elements coalesce to form a vivid tapestry of struggle and survival.

At the heart of the story is the titular gajar halwa, a dish that serves as a powerful metaphor for the deceptive allure of urban life. The laborious process of making the halwa—peeling, grating, and stirring for hours—mirrors Perumayee's own grueling journey. The sweetness of the dish belies the bitterness of its creation, much like the city's false promises of prosperity that mask the exploitation of migrant labor. Hariharan's use of color imagery, particularly the "red-gold warmth" of the halwa, contrasts sharply with the drabness of Perumayee's village life, underscoring the stark disparities between rural scarcity and urban abundance. This symbolism extends to the endless flow of water from the city tap, a luxury unimaginable in her drought-stricken village, highlighting the systemic inequalities that define her existence.

The characters in "Gajar Halwa" are meticulously crafted to reflect broader societal critiques. Perumayee's transformation from an innocent, hardworking girl to a pragmatic survivor is both heartbreaking and illuminating. Her gradual acceptance of cutting corners—skipping chores, hiding mistakes—reveals the moral compromises forced upon the marginalized. Chellamma, the intermediary who facilitates Perumayee's employment, embodies the paradox of survival within an oppressive system. While she provides a lifeline to rural migrants, she also exploits them, taking a cut of their meager earnings. This duality underscores the story's central theme: how systemic oppression perpetuates cycles of exploitation, even among its victims. The mistress, though a secondary character, is a potent symbol of class privilege and indifference. Her failure to learn Perumayee's real name or show any genuine concern for her well-being lays bare the dehumanization inherent in employer-servant relationships.

Hariharan's narrative technique further elevates the story's impact. The third-person omniscient perspective allows readers to inhabit Perumayee's inner world while also understanding the broader social forces at play. The story's circular structure, beginning and ending with the imagery of gajar halwa, reinforces the cyclical nature of exploitation and migration. Repetitive phrases like "peel, peel, grate, grate" not only mirror the monotony of Perumayee's labor but also evoke a sense of inescapable drudgery. Hariharan's tone shifts subtly from hopeful to resigned, mirroring Perumayee's own disillusionment as she navigates the harsh realities of city life.

"Gajar Halwa" transcends its specific setting to offer a universal commentary on migration, labor, and inequality. While rooted in the Indian context, its themes resonate globally, making it a timeless exploration of the human cost of economic disparity. The story's enduring power lies in its ability to compel readers to confront uncomfortable truths about privilege, exploitation, and the often invisible labor that sustains daily life. Hariharan's masterful storytelling and incisive social critique cement "Gajar Halwa" as a significant work in postcolonial literature, one that challenges us to see the world through the eyes of those who are too often overlooked.

Conclusion: Githa Hariharan's "Gajar Halwa" is a poignant exploration of India's social inequalities through the lens of rural-urban migration. The story follows Perumayee, a young village girl whose journey to Delhi exposes the harsh realities of domestic labor and systemic exploitation. Hariharan skillfully uses the metaphor of making gajar halwa - with its laborious preparation contrasting with its sweet taste - to symbolize how cities consume migrant workers while offering false promises of prosperity. The narrative reveals how class and gender hierarchies perpetuate cycles of oppression, as seen in Perumayee's transformation from an innocent girl to a pragmatic survivor and in characters like Chellamma who both aid and exploit fellow migrants. With its rich symbolism and unflinching realism, the story offers a powerful critique of social injustice while humanizing those caught in its grip. Hariharan's economical yet evocative prose makes "Gajar Halwa" a memorable commentary on the human cost of economic disparity in modern India.

CHAPTER TWENTY-SEVEN

Ruskin Bond: No Room for Leopard & Copperfeild in Jungle

Scan the QR code to watch video

About Writer: Ruskin Bond is a renowned Indian author known for his evocative stories that celebrate nature, adventure, and the simple joys of life. Born in 1934 in Kasauli and now a resident of Mussoorie, his works often reflect the landscapes of hills, forests, and small towns, capturing the warmth and beauty of India. Bond began writing at a young age, with his debut novel The Room on the Roof published when he was just 17. Over his long career, he has authored more than a hundred books spanning novels, short stories, and essays, appealing to both children and adults with his clear, engaging style and subtle life lessons.

No Room for Leopard

About Story:

The story begins with a young boy who forms a deep, respectful bond with the forest near his Himalayan home. Daily, he wanders among oaks, maples, and rhododendrons, quietly observing and earning the trust of its inhabitants—from kaleej pheasants and langurs to a majestic golden leopard. The forest, in turn, responds to his gentle presence; the langurs even warn him of approaching danger, a testament to the extraordinary connection he shares with nature.

This fragile harmony shatters when a band of shikaris (hunters) invades the forest, driven by greed and a desire for trophies. Their callous traps and guns lead to a devastating loss when the trusting leopard, a symbol of the forest's spirit, is caught and killed. As the hunters celebrate their grim prize, the boy is left to mourn the death of innocence and the collapse of a delicate interspecies trust. Through his silent grief, the story powerfully critiques humanity's destructive impact on nature, urging readers to reflect on whether true harmony between humans and the wild is still possible.

Question & Answer

Q.1) Discuss Ruskin Bond as a short story writer.

Ans: Introduction: Ruskin Bond is one of India's most beloved writers, especially known for his simple yet powerful short stories. His works often focus on nature, childhood, and the relationship between humans and the environment. Two of his famous stories, No Room for a Leopard and Copperfield in the Jungle, perfectly showcase his storytelling style—simple language, deep emotions, and strong messages about life and nature.

In No Room for a Leopard, Bond tells a heartbreaking story about a young boy who shares a special bond with the animals in a forest. The boy walks through the forest every day, and the creatures, including a beautiful leopard, grow to trust him. However, their peace is destroyed when greedy hunters arrive and kill the leopard for its skin. The story shows the cruelty of humans and how nature suffers because of their selfishness. Bond's writing makes us feel the boy's sadness and anger, making us think about how we treat animals and forests. The story is not just about a leopard; it is about trust, innocence, and the damage caused by human greed.

Copperfield in the Jungle is another wonderful story that reflects Bond's love for books and nature. It is based on his own childhood experience when he went on a hunting trip with his uncle but found more joy in reading books than in hunting. While the adults were busy trying to shoot animals, young Ruskin discovered a hidden shelf of books in an old bungalow. Among them was David Copperfield by Charles Dickens, which captured his imagination. This story shows how Bond, even as a child, preferred the world of stories over violence against animals. It also tells us how books can be our best friends, especially when we feel out of place in the real world.

What makes Ruskin Bond a great short story writer is his ability to connect with readers of all ages. His language is simple, but his stories carry deep meanings. He does not use complicated words, yet his writing makes us feel strong emotions—joy, sadness, anger, and hope. In No Room for a Leopard, we feel the pain of the boy and the leopard, and in Copperfield in the Jungle, we share Bond's excitement when he finds his favorite books. His stories are short, but they stay in our hearts for a long time.

Another special quality of Bond's writing is his love for nature. Most of his stories are set in the hills, forests, and small towns of India. He describes trees, animals, and mountains with such detail that we can almost see them in front of our eyes. In No Room for a Leopard, the forest feels alive, and the leopard is not just an animal but a character with feelings. In Copperfield in the Jungle, the jungle is not just a background; it is a place of adventure and discovery. Bond teaches us to respect nature and understand that animals and trees are as important as humans.

Bond's stories also often have a moral lesson, but he never preaches. Instead, he lets the story teach us in a natural way. No Room for a Leopard makes us think about wildlife conservation without directly saying, "Do not hunt animals." Copperfield in the Jungle shows us the joy of reading without forcing us to pick up a book. His stories are like gentle reminders of what is right and wrong in life.

Conclusion:, Ruskin Bond is a master of the short story. His tales are simple, emotional, and meaningful. Through stories like No Room for a Leopard and Copperfield in the Jungle, he shares his love for nature, books, and childhood. His writing style is easy to understand, yet it touches the heart. Whether he is writing about a boy and a leopard or a child lost in the world of books, Bond always leaves us with something to think about. That is why readers of all ages continue to love his stories even today.

Q.2) Discuss the themes of the short story No Room for Leopard.

Ans : Introduction: No Room for Leopard is a short story written by Ruskin Bond. Bond is one of India's most beloved writers, especially known for his simple yet powerful short stories. His works often focus on nature, childhood, and the relationship between humans and the environment.Bond's No Room for a Leopard is a touching story that explores several important themes through simple yet powerful storytelling. The tale follows a young boy who shares a special bond with the animals in a forest, particularly a leopard, until hunters destroy this relationship. Through this narrative, Bond highlights key ideas about nature, human behavior, and innocence.

One of the main themes of the story is the harmony between humans and nature. The boy in the story walks through the forest every day, respecting the animals and their space. Over time, the creatures, including the leopard, grow to trust him. They no longer see him as a threat, and some, like the langurs, even warn him of danger. This shows how peaceful coexistence is possible when humans treat nature with kindness and respect. Bond suggests that if people approach the natural world with care, animals can learn to live alongside them without fear.

Another important theme is the destructive nature of human greed. The hunters in the story do not kill the leopard for food or survival but for profit. They value the leopard's skin more than its life, showing how greed can lead to cruelty. The boy, who represents innocence and compassion, is heartbroken when he sees the dead leopard. His sadness reflects the damage caused by human selfishness. Bond uses this contrast to criticize those who exploit nature for personal gain, reminding readers that such actions have painful consequences.

The story also explores the loss of innocence and trust. The boy's relationship with the animals is built on trust, but the hunters destroy this bond in a single act of violence. After the leopard is killed, the animals will likely become fearful of humans again. This loss of trust is not just a tragedy for the boy but for the entire forest. Bond shows how one cruel act can undo years of peaceful coexistence, leaving behind fear and distrust. The theme suggests that once innocence is lost, it is hard to regain, whether in nature or in human relationships.

Deforestation and habitat destruction are also key themes in the story. The hunters easily find and kill the leopard because the forest has been shrinking, forcing animals into smaller areas. Bond hints that human activities like logging and hunting are making it harder for wildlife to survive. The title itself, No Room for a Leopard, suggests that the natural world is being taken over by humans, leaving animals with nowhere safe to live. This theme serves as a warning about the consequences of destroying forests and ignoring the needs of wildlife.

Finally, the story touches on the contrast between childhood innocence and adult indifference. The boy sees the forest and its animals with wonder and respect, while the hunters view them only as targets or sources of profit. Bond often writes about how children have a pure connection with nature that many adults lose as they grow older. The boy's sadness at the end of the story shows how painful it is when this innocence is confronted with the harsh realities of the world.

Conclusion: No Room for a Leopard is a story rich with themes about nature, greed, trust, and innocence. Ruskin Bond uses simple language and a heartfelt narrative to make readers think about their relationship with the natural world. The story teaches us that harmony with nature is possible but can easily be broken by human cruelty. It also reminds us to protect wildlife and cherish the innocence that allows us to see the beauty in the world around us. Through this tale, Bond encourages readers to be more compassionate and responsible toward the environment and its creatures.

Q. 3) "Write an essay on Ruskin Bond's treatment of nature in the short stories in your course."

Ans: Introduction: Ruskin Bond, one of India's most beloved writers, has a unique way of portraying nature in his short stories. His works, especially those in our course like No Room for a Leopard and Copperfield in the Jungle, show nature not just as a background but as a living, breathing character. Bond's treatment of nature is filled with love, respect, and a deep understanding of its beauty and fragility. Through simple yet powerful storytelling, he makes readers see the natural world in a new light.

In No Room for a Leopard, nature is presented as a peaceful and harmonious place where humans and animals can coexist. The young boy in the story walks through the forest every day, and the animals, including a majestic leopard, grow to trust him. Bond describes the forest with such detail that readers can almost hear the rustling leaves and the calls of birds. The langurs, the pheasants, and even the leopard are given personalities, making them feel like important characters in the story. This shows Bond's skill in bringing nature to life, making it as vivid and real as the human characters. However, the story also highlights how fragile this harmony is. When hunters kill the leopard for its skin, the trust between humans and animals is broken. Bond uses this moment to show how human greed can destroy the delicate balance of nature. The boy's sadness reflects the author's own sorrow over such destruction, making readers feel the loss deeply.

Similarly, in Copperfield in the Jungle, nature plays a central role in the story. The jungle is not just a setting but a place of adventure and discovery for the young protagonist. While the adults are busy hunting, the boy finds joy in exploring the jungle and reading books about nature. Bond's descriptions of the jungle are so vivid that readers can almost smell the damp earth and feel the cool shade of the trees. The story contrasts the beauty and wonder of nature with the violence of hunting, showing Bond's belief that nature should be appreciated, not exploited. The boy's love for books about nature, like A Naturalist on the Prowl, reflects Bond's own passion for the natural world. Through this character, the author encourages readers to see nature as a source of knowledge and inspiration, not something to be conquered or destroyed.

One of the most striking aspects of Bond's treatment of nature is his ability to make it relatable. He does not describe nature in a distant or scientific way but through the eyes of his characters, especially children. In his stories, children often have a special connection with nature, seeing its magic and wonder in ways that adults overlook. This is evident in both No Room for a Leopard and Copperfield in the Jungle, where the young protagonists understand and respect nature more than the grown-ups around them. Bond seems to suggest that this childlike wonder is the key to truly appreciating the natural world.

Another important theme in Bond's stories is the idea of conservation. Through his narratives, he subtly teaches readers about the importance of protecting nature. In No Room for a Leopard, the death of the leopard is a powerful reminder of what happens when humans prioritize greed over conservation. In Copperfield in the Jungle, the boy's fascination with nature books hints at the value of learning about and preserving the environment. Bond does not preach but lets the stories themselves convey these messages, making them more impactful.

Conclusion: Ruskin Bond's treatment of nature in his short stories is both beautiful and thought-provoking. He portrays nature as a living, breathing entity that deserves respect and protection. Through vivid descriptions and relatable characters, he makes readers see the world around them with fresh eyes. His stories remind us of the magic of nature, the importance of conservation, and the need to live in harmony with the environment. Bond's love for nature shines through every word, inspiring readers to appreciate and protect the natural world just as he does.

Copperfeild in Jungle

Scan the QR code to watch video

About Story:

"Copperfield in the Jungle" is a heartwarming autobiographical story by Ruskin Bond that recounts his early love for books and nature. During a hunting trip to the Terai forests near the Siwalik hills with his Uncle Henry and friends, young Ruskin feels out of place among the excited hunters. Instead of joining in, he finds solace in a forgotten shelf of dusty books in a jungle rest house, discovering treasures like Wodehouse's "Love Among the Chickens," ghost stories, and most importantly, Dickens's "David Copperfield," which captivates him with its vivid characters.

When the hunting party returns with little success, dismissing his imaginative account of a leopard, Ruskin clings to his half-finished "David Copperfield." This simple act marks the beginning of his lifelong passion for literature, highlighting how the quiet joy of reading can transport us far beyond the harsh realities of the world.

Q.1) Discuss the themes of the story Copperfeild in Jungle.

Ans: Introduction: Copperfeild in Jungle is a short story written by Ruskin Bond.Bond is one of India's most beloved writers, especially known for his simple yet powerful short stories. His works often focus on nature, childhood, and the relationship between humans and the environment. "Copperfield in the Jungle" is a charming autobiographical story that explores several important themes through the eyes of a young boy. The story beautifully captures the contrast between different worlds and values, while highlighting the power of literature and the importance of staying true to oneself.

One of the main themes is the conflict between violence and peace. The story shows two very different ways of interacting with nature - the adults enjoy hunting and killing animals for sport, while young Ruskin finds no pleasure in it. He inherits his grandfather's dislike for hunting, believing it is wrong to kill animals just for fun. This theme makes us think about how humans should treat nature - with violence or with respect. The hunting trip becomes boring for Ruskin because he doesn't share the excitement of killing, showing how people can have completely different views about the same experience.

Another important theme is the magic of books and reading. While the adults are out hunting, Ruskin discovers a shelf of old books that become his escape. The moment he finds Charles Dickens' "David Copperfield", he gets lost in its world. Books become his real adventure, much more exciting than hunting. This theme shows how literature can transport us to different places and teach us important lessons about life. For Ruskin, reading isn't just passing time - it's discovering a lifelong passion that will eventually make him a famous writer.

The story also explores the theme of imagination versus reality. When Ruskin tells the hunters about seeing a leopard, they don't believe him, thinking his imagination has been influenced by reading too much. This shows how adults often dismiss children's experiences and perceptions. The hunters represent practical, unimaginative people, while Ruskin represents the creative, observant mind. This theme makes us question - what is more valuable? The "real" experience of hunting that the adults have, or the imaginative journey Ruskin has through books?

Nature as a teacher is another significant theme. While the hunters see nature as something to conquer, Ruskin learns from it. The jungle becomes his classroom where he discovers not just animals and plants, but also himself. His quiet observations in the jungle contrast with the noisy, destructive hunting of the adults. This theme shows that nature has different lessons to teach - for some it's about domination, for others it's about understanding and appreciation.

Lastly, the story touches on the theme of finding one's path. Young Ruskin doesn't follow what everyone else is doing. He stays true to what he loves - reading and observing nature. This early decision to follow his own interests eventually leads him to become a writer. The theme teaches us that it's okay to be different, and that our true passions can guide us to our destiny.

Conclusion: "Copperfield in the Jungle" is about a boy who discovers that books can be more exciting than hunting, that nature should be appreciated not destroyed, and that it's fine to be different. Through these themes, Ruskin Bond gives us a beautiful story that celebrates reading, respects nature, and encourages us to follow our true interests. The story remains special because it's not just about what happens in the jungle, but about how those experiences shape the person we become.

Block 7 - Poetry

Scan the QR code to watch video

CHAPTER TWENTY-EIGHT

Background to Indian English Poetry

Introduction

This unit provides an overview of the birth, growth, and development of Indian English poetry, exploring its historical, social, and cultural contexts. It discusses the origin of Indian English poetry, the impact of British colonization, the identity of Indian English poetry, its periodization, and future possibilities.

Questioning how Indians started writing poetry in English, a foreign language. It highlights the foreignness of English in India, especially in rural areas, and explores how English became a medium for Indian poets even before it was institutionalized.

The Origin of Indian English Poetry

The first Indian English poet is Henry Derozio, who published his collection in 1827. However, Indians had been learning and writing in English for at least 25 years before that. The essay by Cavelley Venkata Boriah (1809) and Raja Rammohun Roy's work (1817) are early examples of Indian writing in English. The unit emphasizes that Indian English poetry emerged gradually, requiring the Indianization of English and the Anglicization of Indians.

The Impact of British Colonization

British colonization had a profound impact on Indian society, leading to the rise of Indian English literature. The Battle of Plassey (1757) marked a turning point, as the British gained control of Bengal. British Orientalists like Sir William Jones played a significant role in studying Indian culture and languages. The Anglicization of Indians increased as British power grew, leading to the establishment of English education in India, formalized by Macaulay's Minute of 1835.

The Identity of Indian English Poetry

Indian English poetry has faced identity issues, often being seen as an appendage to Anglo-Indian literature. Terms like "Anglo-Indian," "Indo-Anglian," and "Indian Writing in English" have been used to describe it. The unit argues that Indian English poetry is a hybrid form, reflecting both Indian and English influences, and that its identity is shaped by its colonial origins.

The Growth and Periodization of Indian English Poetry

Indian English poetry can be periodized into different phases, reflecting both literary and political changes. The unit suggests three broad phases: proto-nationalist (1825-1900), nationalist (1900-1950), and post-nationalist (1950-present). Modernist poets like Nissim Ezekiel mark a significant shift in Indian English poetry, moving away from traditional themes to more individual and private concerns.

The Future Possibilities

The unit expresses concern about the future of Indian English poetry, noting a decline in its popularity and publication. It calls for renewed interest and innovation in the study of Indian English poetry to ensure its continued growth and relevance.

CHAPTER TWENTY-NINE

Henry Derozio

Henry Louis Vivian Derozio

Henry Vivian Derozio (1809–1831) was a poet, teacher, and social reformer who played a key role in Bengal's intellectual awakening during British rule. His progressive ideas challenged traditions and inspired young minds toward change. As a poet, he was influenced by European Romanticism and is considered the first national poet of modern India.

His famous works, like To India – My Native Land and The Fakeer of Jungheera, reflect his patriotic spirit. Through his teachings and writings, he laid the foundation for future social reform and nationalist movements in India.

<u>The Harp of India</u>

Why hang'st thou lonely on yon withered bough?
Unstrung for ever, must thou there remain;
Thy music once was sweet ? who hears it now?
Why doth the breeze sigh over thee in vain?
Silence hath bound thee with her fatal chain;
Neglected, mute, and desolate art thou,
Like a ruined monument on a desert plain:
O! Many a hand more worthy far than mine
Once thy harmonious chords to sweetness gave,
And many a wreath for them did Fame entwine
Of flowers still blooming on the minstrel's grave:
Those hands are cold ? but if thy notes divine
Maybe by mortal wakened once again,
Harp of my country, let me strike the strain!

Explanation:

Written during the early 19th century under British colonial rule in India, "The Harp of India" reflects Derozio's anguish over the cultural and spiritual decay of his homeland. As a Eurasian poet and leader of the Young Bengal Movement, Derozio sought to rekindle national pride and resistance against colonial oppression. The poem uses the harp as a central metaphor for India's suppressed cultural identity, lamenting its silenced voice while expressing hope for revival. Rooted in Romanticism, the poem blends emotional intensity with patriotic fervor, making it a cornerstone of India's nationalist literature.

Stanza 1 (Lines 1–4)

"Why hang'st thou lonely on yon withered bough?
Unstrung for ever, must thou there remain;
Thy music once was sweet — who hears it now?
Why doth the breeze sigh over thee in vain?"

The poem opens with a poignant image of a neglected harp hanging on a "withered bough," symbolizing India's forsaken cultural heritage. The harp's "unstrung" state signifies the silencing of India's artistic and spiritual traditions under colonial rule. The rhetorical questions ("Who hears it now?") emphasize the poet's despair over the loss of India's former glory. Even the breeze, personified as a mourner, sighs futilely over the harp, underscoring nature's helplessness against cultural decay. This stanza sets the tone of lamentation, mourning a once-vibrant civilization reduced to silence.

Stanza 2 (Lines 5–8)

"Silence hath bound thee with her fatal chain;
Neglected, mute, and desolate art thou,
Like ruined monument on desert plain:"

He suffocating grip of colonialism on India's voice. The harp's desolation is compared to a "ruined monument on desert plain," evoking imagery of abandonment and forgotten grandeur. This simile highlights the erasure of India's historical and cultural achievements, reduced to relics in a barren landscape. The stanza amplifies the poem's central theme: the tragic neglect of a once-proud civilization.ere, Silence is personified as a captor who binds the harp with a "fatal chain," symbolizing th

Stanza 3 (Lines 9–11)

"O! many a hand more worthy far than mine
Once thy harmonious chords to sweetness gave,
And many a wreath for them did Fame entwine
Of flowers still blooming on the minstrel's grave:"

Derozio shifts to honoring India's past poets and artists ("minstrels") who once brought the harp to life. The "hands more worthy" refer to India's cultural heroes, whose artistry earned them fame and reverence. The "flowers still blooming on the minstrel's grave" symbolize the enduring legacy of these figures, even in death. This stanza serves as a tribute to India's rich pre-colonial heritage, contrasting sharply with its current state of neglect. It underscores the poet's humility, positioning himself as an heir to this legacy rather than its equal.

Stanza 4 (Lines 12–14)
"Those hands are cold — but if thy notes divine
May be by mortal wakened once again,
Harp of my country, let me strike the strain!"

The final stanza transitions from mourning to resolve. The "cold hands" signify the death of India's past artists, but Derozio vows to revive the harp's "notes divine" (India's cultural spirit). The exclamation "Harp of my country, let me strike the strain!" is a passionate call to action, declaring the poet's determination to reignite India's voice. Though acknowledging the difficulty of this task ("long in woeful silence nursed"), the poem ends on a note of hope, envisioning a resurgence of India's cultural and national pride.

Conclusion

"The Harp of India" is a masterful blend of Romantic lyricism and nationalist fervor. Derozio mourns the loss of India's cultural vibrancy but transforms grief into a rallying cry, urging his compatriots to revive their heritage. The poem's enduring power lies in its ability to balance despair with hope, making it a timeless anthem of resistance and renewal.

<u>**To India – My Native Land**</u>

My country! In thy days of glory past
A beauteous halo circled round thy brow
and worshipped as a deity thou wast—
Where is thy glory, where the reverence now?
Thy eagle pinion is chained down at last,
And grovelling in the lowly dust art thou,
Thy minstrel hath no wreath to weave for thee
Save the sad story of thy misery!
Well—let me dive into the depths of time
And bring from out the ages, that have rolled
A few small fragments of these wrecks sublime
Which human eye may never more behold

And let the guerdon of my labour be,
My fallen country! One kind wish for thee!

Explanation:

Written in the early 19th century during British colonial rule in India, this poem reflects Derozio's anguish over India's cultural and political subjugation. As a leader of the Young Bengal Movement, Derozio sought to awaken national pride by contrasting India's glorious past with its colonized present. The poem is a patriotic lament and a call to remember India's heritage, blending Romantic melancholy with fiery nationalism.

My country! In thy days of glory past
A beauteous halo circled round thy brow
and worshipped as a deity thou wast—
Where is thy glory, where the reverence now?
Thy eagle pinion is chained down at last,
And grovelling in the lowly dust art thou,
Thy minstrel hath no wreath to weave for thee
Save the sad story of thy misery!

Explanation:

Derozio begins by addressing India as a fallen deity, once revered and radiant ("beauteous halo") but now reduced to a state of humiliation. The "eagle pinion" (a symbol of strength and freedom) is chained, signifying colonial oppression that has forced India to "grovell[e] in the dust." The poet laments that he, as a "minstrel" (bard), can no longer sing of India's greatness but only chronicle its suffering. The rhetorical questions ("Where is thy glory...?") underscore the contrast between India's past splendor and present degradation.

Well—let me dive into the depths of time
And bring from out the ages, that have rolled
A few small fragments of these wrecks sublime
Which human eye may never more behold
And let the guerdon of my labour be,
My fallen country! One kind wish for thee!

Explanation:

Shifting from despair to determination, Derozio vows to excavate India's forgotten history ("depths of time") to recover fragments of its "sublime" past. These "wrecks" (relics of ancient glory) are buried under colonial erasure, invisible to the modern eye. The poet's "labour" (effort) is not for personal reward but to earn a "kind wish" for his country—a hope that remembering its heritage might inspire renewal. The stanza ends on a note of quiet resolve, balancing sorrow with a call to preserve cultural memory.

CHAPTER THIRTY

Toru Dutt

Toru Dutt, whose full name was Tarulatta Datta, was a famous Indian poet and translator from Bengal during British rule. She wrote in both English and French. Born on March 4, 1856, she became one of the pioneers of Indo-Anglian literature, alongside other notable figures like Henry Louis Vivian Derozio, Manmohan Ghose, and Sarojini Naidu. Toru Dutt is best known for her English poetry collections, Sita, A Sheaf Gleaned in French Fields (1876), and Ancient Ballads and Legends of Hindustan (1882), as well as a French novel, Le Journal de Mademoiselle d'Arvers (1879). Her works often explore themes of loneliness, longing, love for her country, and nostalgia. Sadly, she passed away at the young age of 21 due to tuberculosis on August 30, 1877.

<u>Sita</u>

The three happy children in a darkened room!
What do they gaze on with wide-open eyes?
A dense, dense forest, where no sunbeam pries,
And in its centre a cleared spot. —There bloom
Gigantic flowers on creepers that embrace
Tall trees: there, in a quiet lucid lake
The while swans glide; there, "whirring from the brake,"
The peacock springs; there, herds of wild deer race;
There, patches gleam with yellow waving grain;
There, blue smoke from strange altars rises light.
There, dwells in peace, the poet-anchorite.
But who is this fair lady? Not in vain
She weeps,—for lo! at every tear she sheds
Tears from three pairs of young eyes fall amain,
And bowed in sorrow are the three young heads.
It is an old, old story, and the lay

Which has evoked sad Sîta from the past
Is by a mother sung.... 'Tis hushed at last
And melts the picture from their sight away,
Yet shall they dream of it until the day!
When shall those children by their mother's side
Gather, ah me! as erst at eventide?

Context:

"Sita" by Toru Dutt is a poem that tells a story within a story. It describes a scene where three children are sitting in a dark room, listening to their mother sing an old tale. The poem is rich with imagery and emotion, and it connects the past with the present through the power of storytelling. Let's break it down stanza by stanza in simple English.

Explanation:

Stanza 1 (Lines 1–10):

"Three happy children in a darkened room! / What do they gaze on with wide-open eyes? / A dense, dense forest, where no sunbeam pries, / And in its centre a cleared spot.—There bloom / Gigantic flowers on creepers that embrace / Tall trees: there, in a quiet lucid lake / The while swans glide; there, 'whirring from the brake,' / The peacock springs; there, herds of wild deer race; / There, patches gleam with yellow waving grain; / There, blue smoke from strange altars rises light."

This stanza describes three children sitting in a dark room, completely engrossed in a story. Their mother is telling them about a dense forest, and the children imagine it vividly. The forest is so thick that sunlight cannot enter. In the middle of the forest, there is a peaceful clearing filled with beauty. Giant flowers grow on vines that wrap around tall trees. A calm, clear lake is home to graceful swans. Peacocks flutter, wild deer run freely, and fields of golden grain sway in the breeze. Blue smoke rises from altars, suggesting a sacred or spiritual place. The children are transported to this magical world through their mother's storytelling.

Stanza 2 (Lines 11–14):

"There, dwells in peace, the poet-anchorite. / But who is this fair lady? Not in vain / She weeps,—for lo! at every tear she sheds / Tears from three pairs of young eyes fall amain,"

In this stanza, the focus shifts to a wise poet or hermit who lives peacefully in the forest. Then, the children notice a beautiful lady who is crying. Her tears are not in vain because the children are so moved by her sorrow that they also begin to cry. Their young hearts feel her pain deeply.

This lady is Sita, a character from the ancient Indian epic, the Ramayana. Sita is known for her suffering and devotion, and her story touches the children deeply. The stanza shows how stories can evoke strong emotions and create a connection between the listener and the characters.

Stanza 3 (Lines 15–18):

"And bowed in sorrow are the three young heads. / It is an old, old story, and the lay / Which has evoked sad Sîta from the past / Is by a mother sung.... 'Tis hushed at last"

Here, the children are so overcome with emotion that they bow their heads in sadness. The story of Sita is an ancient one, but it feels alive and real as the mother sings it. The mother's song brings Sita's sorrow and strength to life, and the children are deeply affected. However, the song eventually ends, and the story fades away. The stanza highlights the power of storytelling to bring the past into the present and make it meaningful for the listeners.

Stanza 4 (Lines 19–22):

"And melts the picture from their sight away, / Yet shall they dream of it until the day! / When shall those children by their mother's side / Gather, ah me! as erst at eventide?"

In the final stanza, the vivid picture of the forest and Sita disappears as the story ends. However, the children will continue to dream about it and remember it for a long time. The poem ends with a sense of longing. The speaker wonders when the children will gather by their mother's side again, just as they did in the evening when she sang to them. This longing adds a touch of sadness, as it suggests that such precious moments may not last forever. The stanza reflects on the fleeting nature of time and the importance of cherishing moments spent with loved ones.

Conclusion:

The poem "Sita" by Toru Dutt is about the power of storytelling and how it connects the past with the present. The children in the poem are deeply moved by their mother's song about Sita, a character from the Ramayana. The vivid imagery of the forest and Sita's sorrow brings the story to life, and the children feel her pain as if it were their own. The poem also reflects on the fleeting nature of time andthe preciousness of moments spent with family. Through simple yet powerful language, Toru Dutt shows how stories can inspire, teach, and create lasting memories.

<u>**Lotus**</u>

Love came to Flora asking for a flower

That would of flowers be undisputed queen,
The lily and the rose, long, long had been
Rivals for that high honour. Bards of power
Had sung their claims. "The rose can never tower
Like the pale lily with her Juno mien"--
"But is the lily lovelier?" Thus between
Flower-factions rang the strife in Psyche's bower.
"Give me a flower delicious as the rose
And stately as the lily in her pride"--
"But of what colour?"--"Rose-red," Love first chose,
Then prayed,--"No, lily-white,--or, both provide;"
And Flora gave the lotus, "rose-red" dyed,
And "lily-white,"--the queenliest flower that blows.

Context

Toru Dutt (1856–1877), an Indian poet writing during British colonial rule, blends Western and Indian symbols in this sonnet. The poem pits the Western lily (majesty) and rose (beauty) against the Indian lotus, which Flora crowns queen for uniting their virtues (rose-red, lily-white).

Stanza 1 (Lines 1–4):

"Love came to Flora asking for a flower / That would of flowers be undisputed queen, / The lily and the rose, long, long had been / Rivals for that high honour. Bards of power"

In this stanza, Love approaches Flora, the goddess of flowers, and asks for a flower that can be the undisputed queen of all flowers. For a long time, the lily and the rose have been rivals for this title. Poets (referred to as "bards of power") have sung about the beauty and merits of both flowers, but neither has been able to claim the title of queen definitively. The stanza sets up the central conflict: which flower is truly the most beautiful and deserving of the crown?

Stanza 2 (Lines 5–8):

"Had sung their claims. 'The rose can never tower / Like the pale lily with her Juno mien'-- / 'But is the lily lovelier?' Thus between / Flower-factions rang the strife in Psyche's bower."

Here, the poem describes the arguments made by supporters of the lily and the rose. Supporters of the lily say that the rose can never match the lily's tall, majestic beauty, which is compared to the dignified appearance of Juno, the Roman queen of the gods. On the other hand, supporters of the rose question whether the lily is truly lovelier than the rose. This debate between the two "flower-factions" (groups supporting each flower) creates a conflict, and the argument echoes in Psyche's bower, a place associated with beauty and the soul. The stanza highlights the ongoing rivalry between the two flowers and the difficulty in choosing a winner.

Stanza 3 (Lines 9–12):

"'Give me a flower delicious as the rose / And stately as the lily in her pride'-- / 'But of what colour?'--'Rose-red,' Love first chose, / Then prayed,-- 'No, lily-white,--or, both provide;'"

In this stanza, Love makes a request to Flora. Love wants a flower that combines the best qualities of both the rose and the lily. The flower should be as sweet and delightful as the rose and as stately and majestic as the lily. When asked about the color, Love first chooses rose-red, then changes their mind and asks for lily-white. Finally, Love suggests combining both colors. This shows Love's desire for perfection and balance, as well as the difficulty in choosing between the two flowers.

Stanza 4 (Lines 13–14):

"And Flora gave the lotus, 'rose-red' dyed, / And 'lily-white,'--the queenliest flower that blows."

In the final stanza, Flora solves the problem by creating the lotus. The lotus combines the best of both worlds: it is rose-red and lily-white, embodying the sweetness of the rose and the stateliness of the lily. The lotus is declared the "queenliest flower that blows" (the most queenly flower that blooms), resolving the rivalry and satisfying Love's request. The poem ends with the idea that true beauty lies in balance and harmony, rather than in choosing one extreme over the other.

Conclusion:

The poem "Love came to Flora asking for a flower" is about the search for the perfect flower that can be the undisputed queen of all flowers. The lily and the rose, both beautiful in their own ways, have long been rivals for this title. Love asks Flora for a flower that combines the best qualities of both: the sweetness of the rose and the majesty of the lily. After some deliberation, Flora creates the lotus, which is both rose-red and lily-white. The lotus becomes the queen of flowers, symbolizing the idea that true beauty lies in balance and harmony. The poem uses the rivalry between the lily and the rose to explore themes of perfection, compromise, and the blending of different qualities to create something truly magnificent.

<u>Our Casuarina Tree</u>

Like a huge Python, winding round and round

The rugged trunk, indented deep with scars,
Up to its very summit near the stars,
A creeper climbs, in whose embraces bound
No other tree could live. But gallantly
The giant wears the scarf, and flowers are hung
In crimson clusters all the boughs among,
Whereon all day are gathered bird and bee;
And oft at nights the garden overflows
With one sweet song that seems to have no close,
Sung darkling from our tree, while men repose.
When first my casement is wide open thrown
At dawn, my eyes delighted on it rest;
Sometimes, and most in winter,—on its crest
A gray baboon sits statue-like alone
Watching the sunrise; while on lower boughs
His puny offspring leap about and play;
And far and near kokilas hail the day;
And to their pastures wend our sleepy cows;
And in the shadow, on the broad tank cast
By that hoar tree, so beautiful and vast,
The water-lilies spring, like snow enmassed.
But not because of its magnificence
Dear is the Casuarina to my soul:
Beneath it we have played; though years may roll,
O sweet companions, loved with love intense,
For your sakes, shall the tree be ever dear.
Blent with your images, it shall arise
In memory, till the hot tears blind mine eyes!
What is that dirge-like murmur that I hear
Like the sea breaking on a shingle-beach?
It is the tree's lament, an eerie speech,
That haply to the unknown land may reach.
Unknown, yet well-known to the eye of faith!
Ah, I have heard that wail far, far away
In distant lands, by many a sheltered bay,
When slumbered in his cave the water-wraith
And the waves gently kissed the classic shore
Of France or Italy, beneath the moon,

When earth lay trancèd in a dreamless swoon:
And every time the music rose,—before
Mine inner vision rose a form sublime,
Thy form, O Tree, as in my happy prime
I saw thee, in my own loved native clime.
Therefore I fain would consecrate a lay
Unto thy honor, Tree, beloved of those
Who now in blessed sleep, for aye, repose,
Dearer than life to me, alas! were they!
Mayst thou be numbered when my days are done
With deathless trees—like those in Borrowdale,
Under whose awful branches lingered pale
"Fear, trembling Hope, and Death, the skeleton,
And Time the shadow;" and though weak the verse
That would thy beauty fain, oh fain rehearse,
May Love defend thee from Oblivion's curse.

Context

Toru Dutt (1856–1877) wrote Our Casuarina Tree as an elegy for her deceased siblings, Abju and Aru, and a tribute to her childhood in Calcutta. The casuarina tree in her family garden symbolizes her connection to her "native clime" (India) and her longing to preserve memories of lost loved ones. Written during British colonial rule, the poem blends Indian themes with Western literary influences (like Wordsworth's nature poetry), reflecting Dutt's bicultural identity and her struggle to immortalize grief through art.

Stanza 1

Like a huge Python, winding round and round
The rugged trunk, indented deep with scars,
Up to its very summit near the stars,
A creeper climbs, in whose embraces bound
No other tree could live. But gallantly
The giant wears the scarf, and flowers are hung
In crimson clusters all the boughs among,
Whereon all day are gathered bird and bee;
And oft at nights the garden overflows
With one sweet song that seems to have no close,
Sung darkling from our tree, while men repose.

The first stanza of 'Our Casuarina Tree' starts by describing the tree. The poet remembers a creeper wrapping around the tree like a snake. The creeper's grip was so tight that it left marks on the tree's trunk. The poet says that no other tree could have handled this grip, but her tree did. The tree, being strong, wore those marks like a scarf, showing its strength. The poet also describes the tree as having red flowers on every branch, like a crown, which attracted birds and bees. Sometimes, when the poet couldn't sleep at night, she would listen to the sounds in her garden, which seemed endless.

Stanza 2

When first my casement is wide open thrown
At dawn, my eyes delighted on it rest;
Sometimes, and most in winter,—on its crest
A gray baboon sits statue-like alone
Watching the sunrise; while on lower boughs
His puny offspring leap about and play;
And far and near kokilas hail the day;
And to their pastures wend our sleepy cows;
And in the shadow, on the broad tank cast
By that hoar tree, so beautiful and vast,
The water-lilies spring, like snow enmassed.

In the second stanza of Our Casuarina Tree, the poet describes how the dawn fills her with joy. Every morning, when she opens her window, her eyes fall on the tree, and she feels happy. She paints a picture of the changing scenes through the seasons. In winter, she often sees a baboon sitting on the top branch of the tree, still like a statue, waiting for the first sunlight. Meanwhile, its small child plays on the lower branches. Along with this beautiful scene, the poet also hears the welcoming call of the kokilas (cuckoos). She notices cows being led to the pastures and water lilies blooming under the tree's shadow, looking like snow.

Stanza 3

But not because of its magnificence
Dear is the Casuarina to my soul:
Beneath it we have played; though years may roll,
O sweet companions, loved with love intense,
For your sakes, shall the tree be ever dear.
Blent with your images, it shall arise
In memory, till the hot tears blind mine eyes!

What is that dirge-like murmur that I hear
Like the sea breaking on a shingle-beach?
It is the tree's lament, an eerie speech,
That haply to the unknown land may reach.

In the third stanza, the poet becomes more personal in her memories of the tree. She explains why the tree will always be special to her. Besides enjoying its beauty in the morning, the tree also reminds her of the times she played with her siblings. The tree, along with those memories, brings back the deep love they shared, making her emotional. She mourns for her loved ones who have passed away as she looks back on those moments. She also feels that the tree understands her sorrow, as its sound seems like a sad song, similar to waves crashing on a pebble beach.

Stanza 4

Unknown, yet well-known to the eye of faith!
Ah, I have heard that wail far, far away
In distant lands, by many a sheltered bay,
When slumbered in his cave the water-wraith
And the waves gently kissed the classic shore
Of France or Italy, beneath the moon,
When earth lay trancèd in a dreamless swoon:
And every time the music rose,—before
Mine inner vision rose a form sublime,
Thy form, O Tree, as in my happy prime
I saw thee, in my own loved native clime.

In the fourth stanza, the poet deepens her connection with the tree. Using the image of waves, she takes us to a distant land that feels both unfamiliar and familiar at the same time. She describes how the waves gently touch the shore, creating a soothing sound. Whenever she hears this sound, it brings back the memory of the tree, just as she saw it in her youth.

Stanza 5

Therefore I fain would consecrate a lay
Unto thy honor, Tree, beloved of those
Who now in blessed sleep, for aye, repose,
Dearer than life to me, alas! were they!
Mayst thou be numbered when my days are done
With deathless trees—like those in Borrowdale,
Under whose awful branches lingered pale
"Fear, trembling Hope, and Death, the skeleton,

And Time the shadow;" and though weak the verse
That would thy beauty fain, oh fain rehearse,
May Love defend thee from Oblivion's curse.

In the final stanza, the poet wishes to honor the casuarina tree, as it was loved by those who are now gone. She hopes it will live on, like the ancient yew trees in Wordsworth's Borrowdale. By comparing the casuarina tree to the trees of England, she highlights her mixed emotions—while the casuarina tree represents nostalgia, love, and cherished memories, the trees of England symbolize her sense of loneliness and separation. In the closing lines, she expresses a deep desire for "Love" to preserve both the tree and her poem, protecting them from the effects of time and forgetting.

CHAPTER THIRTY-ONE

Sri Aurobindo

Sri Aurobindo, born in Calcutta on August 15, 1872, received his education in England at St. Paul's School and King's College, Cambridge. After returning to India in 1893, he worked in Baroda for thirteen years, secretly engaging in revolutionary activities against British rule. In 1906, following the Partition of Bengal, he became a prominent nationalist in Calcutta, openly demanding complete independence through his newspaper, Bande Mataram. While involved in politics, he also began practicing Yoga, experiencing a profound spiritual awakening in 1908. In 1910, he withdrew from political life to devote himself to spirituality, eventually developing Integral Yoga—a practice aimed at transforming human nature—and establishing the Sri Aurobindo Ashram in Pondicherry in 1926 with his spiritual partner, the Mother. His influential writings include The Life Divine, The Synthesis of Yoga, and Savitri. Sri Aurobindo passed away on December 5, 1950.

<u>A Tree</u>

A tree beside the sandy river-beach
Holds up its topmost boughs
Like fingers towards the skies they cannot reach,
Earth-bound, heaven amorous.
This is the soul of man. Body and brain
Hungry for earth our heavenly flight detain.

Context:

In this poem, Sri Aurobindo presents a tree standing by a sandy riverbank, stretching its branches toward the sky but unable to reach it. This symbolizes the human soul, which aspires for spiritual enlightenment but remains tied to the material world. The poet highlights the contrast between worldly attachments and the soul's deep yearning for the divine.

Explanation:

The poet describes the tree's branches as fingers reaching toward the sky, much like how the human soul longs for something beyond its earthly existence. However, just as the tree is rooted in the ground, humans are held back by their physical and mental attachments. The phrase "earth-bound, heaven amorous" captures this duality—while the soul desires spiritual liberation, the body and mind remain tied to worldly concerns. The poem reflects Sri Aurobindo's philosophical ideas about the struggle between material existence and spiritual aspiration.

<u>Bride of the Fire</u>

Bride of the Fire, clasp me now close, -
Bride of the Fire!
I have shed the bloom of the earthly rose,
I have slain desire.
Beauty of the Light, surround my life, -
Beauty of the Light!
I have sacrificed longing and parted from grief,
I can bear thy delight.
Image of Ecstasy, thrill and enlace, -
Image of Bliss!
I would see only thy marvellous face,
Feel only thy kiss.
Voice of Infinity, sound in my heart, -
Call of the One!
Stamp there thy radiance, never to part,
O living sun

Context:

Sri Aurobindo's poetry often explores the themes of spiritual transformation and divine realization. In this poem, the speaker addresses the Bride of the Fire, a symbolic representation of the divine force or spiritual energy that purifies and elevates the soul. The poet expresses his willingness to give up worldly desires and embrace the divine light. Through metaphors of light, ecstasy, and infinity, he seeks complete immersion in the divine presence.

Stanza 1:

"Bride of the Fire, clasp me now close, -
Bride of the Fire!
I have shed the bloom of the earthly rose,
I have slain desire."

In this stanza, the poet addresses the Bride of the Fire, a symbolic representation of divine energy or spiritual power. The phrase "clasp me now close" suggests a deep longing to be embraced by this divine presence.

He declares that he has "shed the bloom of the earthly rose", meaning he has given up worldly pleasures and attachments. The rose represents material desires and fleeting beauty, which he has now abandoned.

The final line, "I have slain desire", emphasizes his complete renunciation of earthly cravings, which often distract the soul from spiritual awakening. By doing so, he prepares himself for divine union.

Stanza 2:

"Beauty of the Light, surround my life, -
Beauty of the Light!
I have sacrificed longing and parted from grief,
I can bear thy delight."

Here, the poet refers to the divine as the "Beauty of the Light", which symbolizes spiritual illumination, truth, and divine grace. He asks for this radiant presence to completely surround and fill his life.

He expresses that he has let go of all longings and has detached himself from grief and suffering. This indicates a state of spiritual surrender, where personal desires and sorrows no longer control him.

By freeing himself from worldly emotions, he feels prepared to experience the divine's delight, which suggests a state of blissful enlightenment.

Stanza 3:

"Image of Ecstasy, thrill and enlace, -
Image of Bliss!
I would see only thy marvellous face,
Feel only thy kiss."

In this stanza, the divine is addressed as the "Image of Ecstasy" and "Image of Bliss", highlighting the supreme joy and fulfillment that comes from spiritual realization. The poet desires to be thrilled and enlaced, meaning he wants to be completely immersed in this divine presence.

He expresses a wish to perceive nothing but the divine ("I would see only thy marvellous face"), showing that he has turned away from the distractions of the material world.

The phrase "Feel only thy kiss" suggests a deep, intimate union with the divine, much like the soul's merging with the eternal truth in mystical experiences.

Stanza 4:
"Voice of Infinity, sound in my heart, -
Call of the One!
Stamp there thy radiance, never to part,
O living sun."

In the final stanza, the divine is addressed as the "Voice of Infinity", representing an eternal, all-encompassing truth. The poet prays that this divine voice may resonate within his heart, guiding him toward spiritual awakening.

The "Call of the One" refers to the supreme divine calling that leads the soul toward ultimate realization. By answering this call, the poet seeks to transcend human limitations.

He asks the divine to stamp its radiance on his heart forever, ensuring that this divine presence never leaves him. The phrase "O living sun" reinforces the image of divine light as a source of enlightenment, truth, and eternal energy.

Conclusion:

Sri Aurobindo's Bride of the Fire describes the spiritual transformation of the soul as it renounces worldly attachments and longs for divine union. Each stanza represents a stage of spiritual awakening—from renouncing desires, seeking divine light, immersing in divine bliss, and finally becoming one with the infinite. The poem beautifully captures the idea of surrendering to the divine and experiencing the ultimate joy of spiritual realization.

The Golden Light

Thy golden Light came down into my brain
And the grey rooms of mind sun-touched became
A bright reply to Wisdom's occult plane,
A calm illumination and a flame.
Thy golden Light came down into my throat,
And all my speech is now a tune divine,
A paean-song of Thee my single note;
My words are drunk with the Immortal's wine.
Thy golden Light came down into my heart
Smiting my life with Thy eternity;
Now has it grown a temple where Thou art
And all its passions point towards only Thee.
Thy golden Light came down into my feet,

My earth is now Thy playfield and Thy seat.

Explanation:

Sri Aurobindo's poetry often explores spiritual transformation and divine consciousness. In this poem, he describes how divine light enters his body, bringing wisdom, inspiration, love, and ultimate surrender to the divine. Each stanza represents a different aspect of the human being—mind, speech, heart, and body—being transformed by this divine force.

Stanza 1:

"Thy golden Light came down into my brain
And the grey rooms of mind sun-touched became
A bright reply to Wisdom's occult plane,
A calm illumination and a flame."

The poet describes how divine light (Golden Light) enters his brain, transforming his "grey rooms of mind"—a symbol for ordinary, limited human intellect. The divine light brightens his thoughts and connects him to higher wisdom.

The phrase "Wisdom's occult plane" refers to a hidden, deeper source of divine knowledge. The poet's mind is no longer restless but experiences "a calm illumination and a flame", meaning that it gains both peace and a burning aspiration for higher truth.

Stanza 2:

"Thy golden Light came down into my throat,
And all my speech is now a tune divine,
A paean-song of Thee my single note;
My words are drunk with the Immortal's wine."

Here, the divine light enters the poet's throat, which symbolizes communication and expression. As a result, his speech is no longer ordinary but becomes "a tune divine", meaning it is filled with spiritual truth.

The phrase "paean-song of Thee" suggests that everything he speaks is now a hymn of praise to the divine. His words are "drunk with the Immortal's wine", meaning that they carry the essence of divine truth and bliss, much like a poet or prophet inspired by spiritual ecstasy.

Stanza 3:

"Thy golden Light came down into my heart
Smiting my life with Thy eternity;
Now has it grown a temple where Thou art
And all its passions point towards only Thee."

In this stanza, the divine light enters the heart, which symbolizes emotions, desires, and love. The phrase "Smiting my life with Thy eternity" means that his temporary, human emotions are now replaced by an eternal, divine love.

His heart is no longer filled with worldly desires but has become a "temple", meaning a sacred space where only the divine resides. The last line suggests that all his passions, which once might have been scattered towards worldly things, are now focused solely on the divine presence.

Stanza 4:
"Thy golden Light came down into my feet,
My earth is now Thy playfield and Thy seat."

In the final stanza, the divine light enters the poet's feet, which represent action and connection to the physical world. This suggests that his entire existence, including his earthly life, is now surrendered to the divine will.

The phrase "My earth is now Thy playfield and Thy seat" means that his worldly life is no longer separate from spiritual life. The divine is both the ruler ("seat") and the creative force ("playfield") of his existence. It suggests that he sees everything—life, movement, and action—as an expression of the divine.

Conclusion:
The Golden Light is a poem about the complete transformation of the human being through divine grace. The golden light represents divine wisdom, love, and power. As it descends into different parts of the poet's being—mind, speech, heart, and body—it elevates him spiritually. His thoughts become enlightened, his words become divine hymns, his emotions become pure devotion, and his entire life becomes an offering to the divine. This poem reflects Sri Aurobindo's vision of spiritual evolution, where human consciousness is not just liberated but also transformed into a vessel for divine presence.

CHAPTER THIRTY-TWO

Sarojini Naidu

Sarojini Naidu (born Sarojini Chattopadhyay) was an Indian poet and political leader. She was born on 13 February 1879 and passed away on 2 March 1949. After India gained independence, she became the first woman to serve as the Governor of the United Provinces. She was an important leader in India's fight for freedom from British rule. She was also the first Indian woman to become the President of the Indian National Congress and the first woman to be appointed as a state governor in India.

Indian Dancer

Eyes ravished with rapture, celestially panting, what passionate bosoms aflaming with fire

Drink deep of the hush of the hyacinth heavens that glimmer around them in fountains of light;

O wild and entrancing the strain of keen music that cleaveth the stars like a wail of desire,

And beautiful dancers with houri-like faces bewitch the voluptuous watches of night.

The scents of red roses and sandalwood flutter and die in the maze of their gem-tangled hair,

And smiles are entwining like magical serpents the poppies of lips that are opiate-sweet;

Their glittering garments of purple are burning like tremulous dawns in the quivering air,

And exquisite, subtle and slow are the tinkle and tread of their rhythmical, slumber-soft feet.

Now silent, now singing and swaying and swinging, like blossoms that bend to the breezes or showers,

Now wantonly winding, they flash, now they falter, and, lingering, languish in radiant choir;

Their jewel-girt arms and warm, wavering, lily-long fingers enchant through melodious hours,

Eyes ravished with rapture, celestially panting, what passionate bosoms aflaming with fire!

Reference to Context:

These lines are taken from the poem Indian Dancer by Sarojini Naidu. She was a prominent Indian poet known as the "Nightingale of India" for her lyrical and evocative poetry. This poem vividly describes the beauty, grace, and passion of an Indian dancer performing under the night sky. Through rich sensory imagery and musical rhythm, Naidu captures the dancer's movements, emotions, and the enchanting atmosphere surrounding her performance.

1st Stanza:

"Eyes ravished with rapture, celestially panting, what passionate bosoms aflaming with fire

Drink deep of the hush of the hyacinth heavens that glimmer around them in fountains of light;"

Explanation:

The poem opens with a striking image of the dancer's rapturous eyes and passionate heart, portraying her as consumed by the ecstasy of her performance. The phrase "celestially panting" suggests both divine inspiration and deep physical exertion, emphasizing that her dance is both spiritual and sensual.

The "hyacinth heavens" (blue-purple sky) create a dreamlike setting, while the "fountains of light" evoke the imagery of stars or stage lights, illuminating the dancer as if she is the center of the universe.

This suggests that the dance is not merely entertainment but an artistic and almost divine act.

2nd Stanza:

"O wild and entrancing the strain of keen music that cleaveth the stars like a wail of desire,

And beautiful dancers with houri-like faces bewitch the voluptuous watches of night."

Explanation:

The music that accompanies the dancer is described as "wild and entrancing," implying that it has a mystical, almost hypnotic power.

The phrase "cleaveth the stars like a wail of desire" suggests that the music is so intense and passionate that it seems to pierce through the sky, much like a cry of longing or devotion.

The dancers are compared to houris (beautiful maidens from Islamic mythology), highlighting their otherworldly beauty and charm.

The phrase "bewitch the voluptuous watches of night" conveys the idea that their dance captivates the night itself, as if time is enchanted by their movements.

3rd Stanza:

"The scents of red roses and sandalwood flutter and die in the maze of their gem-tangled hair,

And smiles are entwining like magical serpents the poppies of lips that are opiate-sweet;"

Explanation:

Here, Naidu uses olfactory (smell) and visual imagery to intensify the richness of the scene.

The scents of red roses and sandalwood symbolize passion and spirituality, suggesting that the dancer's presence is intoxicating.

The phrase "maze of their gem-tangled hair" presents the dancers as dazzling and adorned, their beauty further enhanced by precious jewels.

"Smiles are entwining like magical serpents"—this simile suggests an enchanting, hypnotic effect, where their expressions are as mesmerizing as serpents moving in a spellbinding dance.

The "poppies of lips that are opiate-sweet" refers to the intoxicating and almost drug-like allure of the dancer, reinforcing the theme of seduction and mysticism.

4th Stanza:

"Their glittering garments of purple are burning like tremulous dawns in the quivering air,

And exquisite, subtle and slow are the tinkle and tread of their rhythmical, slumber-soft feet."

Explanation:

The dancer's garments are compared to the colors of dawn, suggesting vibrancy and movement. The word "burning" gives a sense of passion and energy, while "tremulous dawns" emphasizes their delicate and ever-changing beauty.

The gentle sound of their feet—marked by rhythmic, musical movement—adds to the dreamlike and almost hypnotic nature of their dance.

The phrase "slumber-soft feet" suggests a delicate grace, as if their dance is both powerful and soothing, like a lullaby.

5th Stanza:

"Now silent, now singing and swaying and swinging, like blossoms that bend to the breezes or showers,

Now wantonly winding, they flash, now they falter, and, lingering, languish in radiant choir;"

Explanation:

The repetition of movement-related words (silent, singing, swaying, swinging) mimics the fluidity of the dancer's performance.

The simile comparing them to blossoms suggests grace and responsiveness to nature, emphasizing that their dance is organic and spontaneous.

The contrast between "flash" (quick, intense movements) and "falter" (gentle pauses) mirrors the rhythm of an actual dance, where moments of stillness enhance the impact of motion.

The phrase "radiant choir" suggests harmony, implying that the dance is not just an individual performance but a collective, almost spiritual experience.

Final Lines (Refrain):

"Eyes ravished with rapture, celestially panting, what passionate bosoms aflaming with fire!"

Explanation:

The poem concludes by returning to its opening line, reinforcing the image of the dancer's intense passion and divine inspiration.

The repetition suggests the cyclical nature of the dance, as if it is an eternal, timeless art form.

Conclusion:

Through Indian Dancer, Sarojini Naidu celebrates Indian art, beauty, and spirituality by portraying the dancer as a mesmerizing figure who embodies both sensuality and divinity. The rich imagery, musical rhythm, and passionate descriptions make this poem a tribute to the power of dance as an art form that transcends the physical and touches the divine.

The Old Woman

A lonely old woman sits out in the street
'Neath the boughs of a banyan tree,
And hears the bright echo of hurrying feet,
The pageant of life going blithely and fleet

To the feast of eternity.
Her tremulous hand holds a battered white bowl,
If perchance in your pity you fling her a dole;
She is poor, she is bent, she is blind,
But she lifts a brave heart to the jest of the days,
And her withered, brave voice croons its pæan of praise,
Be the gay world kind or unkind:
"La ilaha illa-l-Allah,
La ilaha illa-l-Allah,
Muhammad-ar-Rasul-Allah."
In hope of your succour, how often in vain,
So patient she sits at my gates,
In the face of the sun and the wind and the rain,
Holding converse with poverty, hunger and pain,
And the ultimate sleep that awaits ...
In her youth she hath comforted lover and son,
In her weary old age, O dear God, is there none
To bless her tired eyelids to rest? ...
Tho' the world may not tarry to help her or heed.
More clear than the cry of her sorrow and need
Is the faith that doth solace her breast:
"La ilaha illa-l-Allah,
La ilaha illa-l-Allah,
Muhammad-ar-Rasul-Allah."

Reference to Context:

These lines are taken from the poem The Old Woman by Sarojini Naidu, a poet known for her lyrical and evocative portrayal of Indian life, culture, and struggles. This poem presents a poignant image of an old woman sitting beneath a banyan tree, enduring poverty and neglect in her final years. Despite her suffering, she finds solace in faith and remains resilient against life's hardships. Naidu uses this individual figure to symbolize the universal suffering of the elderly, the neglect of the vulnerable, and the unwavering strength of faith.

1st Stanza:

"A lonely old woman sits out in the street
'Neath the boughs of a banyan tree,
And hears the bright echo of hurrying feet,
The pageant of life going blithely and fleet

To the feast of eternity."

Explanation:

The poem opens with a striking image of a lonely old woman, sitting under a banyan tree, a symbol of endurance and wisdom in Indian culture.

She is surrounded by hurrying feet—a metaphor for the bustling life around her, which contrasts with her own stillness and isolation.

The "pageant of life" suggests that the world moves on joyfully and quickly, while she remains forgotten.

The phrase "feast of eternity" could symbolize death as the ultimate destination, indicating that while the world enjoys life, she waits for her final rest.

2ⁿᵈ Stanza:

"Her tremulous hand holds a battered white bowl,

If perchance in your pity you fling her a dole;

She is poor, she is bent, she is blind,

But she lifts a brave heart to the jest of the days,

And her withered, brave voice croons its pæan of praise,

Be the gay world kind or unkind:"

Explanation:

The "tremulous hand" and "battered white bowl" symbolize her frailty and dependence on charity.

The poet directly addresses the reader, suggesting that people may or may not offer her alms out of pity.

Despite being poor, bent, and blind, she is courageous—she does not allow her misery to defeat her.

The phrase "jest of the days" suggests that life is cruel and indifferent, yet she remains resilient.

Her "withered, brave voice" sings a hymn of praise, showing her unshaken faith in God, despite the world's neglect.

Chorus (Refrain):

"La ilaha illa-l-Allah,

La ilaha illa-l-Allah,

Muhammad-ar-Rasul-Allah."

Explanation:

This is the Islamic declaration of faith, meaning "There is no god but Allah, and Muhammad is His Prophet."

The old woman recites this prayer, showing that her faith sustains her despite her suffering.

The repetition of this refrain emphasizes that faith is her only true solace, regardless of worldly hardships.

3rd Stanza:

"In hope of your succour, how often in vain,

So patient she sits at my gates,

In the face of the sun and the wind and the rain,

Holding converse with poverty, hunger and pain,

And the ultimate sleep that awaits ..."

Explanation:

The old woman waits for help, but her hope is often in vain, meaning people frequently ignore her.

Despite this, she remains patient, enduring extreme conditions ("sun, wind, and rain"), symbolizing life's hardships.

The phrase "holding converse with poverty, hunger, and pain" suggests that she has accepted suffering as her only companions.

The "ultimate sleep" refers to death, implying that she knows her end is near but continues to wait with dignity.

4th Stanza:

"In her youth she hath comforted lover and son,

In her weary old age, O dear God, is there none

To bless her tired eyelids to rest? ..."

Explanation:

The poet contrasts the woman's past and present:

In her youth, she loved and cared for others, possibly as a mother and wife.

Now, in her old age, she is abandoned and uncared for.

The rhetorical question "Is there none to bless her tired eyelids to rest?" conveys deep sorrow and injustice, highlighting how the aged are often neglected despite their past sacrifices.

Final Lines (Refrain Repeated):

"Tho' the world may not tarry to help her or heed,

More clear than the cry of her sorrow and need

Is the faith that doth solace her breast:

'La ilaha illa-l-Allah,

La ilaha illa-l-Allah,

Muhammad-ar-Rasul-Allah.'"

Explanation:

The world does not stop to help or acknowledge her suffering.

However, her faith remains stronger than her sorrow, giving her inner peace even in neglect.

The repetition of the Islamic prayer reinforces that faith is her only true companion, giving her the strength to endure loneliness, pain, and the approach of death.

Conclusion:

In The Old Woman, Sarojini Naidu presents a heartbreaking yet dignified portrait of an elderly woman abandoned by society. Despite her poverty, blindness, and suffering, she remains strong in faith. The poem critiques the neglect of the elderly, showing how those who once nurtured others are often forgotten in their final years. However, through her unshaken belief in God, the old woman finds resilience and solace, making the poem a powerful reflection on faith, suffering, and the indifference of the world.

Love and Death

I dreamed my love had set thy spirit free,

Enfranchised thee from Fate's o'ermastering power,

And girt thy being with a scatheless dower

Of rich and joyous immortality;

Of Love, I dreamed my soul had ransomed thee,

In thy lone, dread, incalculable hour

From those pale hands at which all mortals cower,

And conquered Death by Love, like Savitri.

When I awoke, alas, my love was vain

E'en to annul one throe of destined pain,Or by one heart-beat to prolong thy breath;

O Love, alas, that love could not assuage

The burden of thy human heritage,

Or save thee from the swift decrees of Death

Reference to Context:

The poem Love and Death by Sarojini Naidu is a deeply emotional and philosophical meditation on the power of love and its limitations in the face of fate and mortality. Known for her evocative and lyrical style, Naidu explores the theme of human helplessness against the inevitable force of death.

The poem reflects the speaker's dream that love has the power to save the beloved from death, just as Savitri in Hindu mythology saved her husband. However, upon waking, she realizes that love is powerless against destiny, and death remains an unavoidable reality.

1ˢᵗ Quatrain (Lines 1-4):

"I dreamed my love had set thy spirit free,
Enfranchised thee from Fate's o'ermastering power,
And girt thy being with a scatheless dower
Of rich and joyous immortality;"

Explanation:

The speaker dreams that her love has freed the beloved's soul from the grip of fate.

The word "enfranchised" (meaning liberated) suggests that love could release the beloved from suffering.

The "scatheless dower" (an untouched gift) refers to a promise of eternal joy and immortality, implying that the speaker wishes to protect the beloved from death and pain.

This idealistic vision of love portrays it as a divine force capable of overcoming mortality.

2ⁿᵈ Quatrain (Lines 5-8):

"Of Love, I dreamed my soul had ransomed thee,
In thy lone, dread, incalculable hour
From those pale hands at which all mortals cower,
And conquered Death by Love, like Savitri."

Explanation:

The speaker dreams that her love could "ransom" the beloved, meaning save them from death, as if love were a price paid to protect them.

The "lone, dread, incalculable hour" symbolizes the mystery and terror of death, which all humans must face alone.

The "pale hands" represent Death itself, which frightens all mortals.

The reference to Savitri is crucial:

According to Hindu mythology, Savitri's unwavering devotion and intelligence helped her defeat Yama (the god of death) and bring her husband Satyavan back to life.

The speaker hopes that her love can achieve the same miraculous victory, highlighting love's ultimate power over death.

3ʳᵈ Quatrain (Lines 9-11):

"When I awoke, alas, my love was vain
E'en to annul one throe of destined pain,
Or by one heart-beat to prolong thy breath;"

Explanation:

The dream ends, and the speaker wakes up to harsh reality:

Love is powerless against fate and death.

The word "vain" emphasizes the futility of love in the face of destiny.

The speaker realizes that she could not even reduce a single moment of suffering ("one throe of destined pain") or prolong life by even a single heartbeat.

This marks a transition from hope to sorrow, showing human helplessness against death.

Final Couplet (Lines 12-14):

"O Love, alas, that love could not assuage

The burden of thy human heritage,

Or save thee from the swift decrees of Death."

Explanation:

The speaker mourns the limitations of love.

"The burden of thy human heritage" refers to the unavoidable suffering, aging, and death that all humans must endure.

The final line acknowledges the absolute power of death—despite the depth of love, it cannot overturn the decrees of fate.

Conclusion:

In Love and Death, Sarojini Naidu contrasts the idealistic power of love with the cruel reality of fate and mortality. The dream sequence symbolizes hope and faith in love's ability to overcome death, while the waking reality underscores the inevitability of human suffering. The reference to Savitri reflects a mythological ideal, but the poem ultimately shows that such miracles are rare, and death remains an unavoidable part of life.

Through lyrical beauty and emotional intensity, Naidu expresses the deep sorrow of losing a loved one and the universal truth that even the strongest love cannot defy destiny.

CHAPTER THIRTY-THREE

Kamla Das

Kamala Surayya (born Kamala; 31 March 1934 – 31 May 2009), also known as Madhavikutty and Kamala Das, was a famous Indian writer and poet. She wrote in both English and Malayalam. In Kerala, she was well known for her short stories and her autobiography My Story. Her English writings, especially her poems, made her famous under the name Kamala Das.

Her works were original, diverse, and deeply connected to Indian culture. She was also a popular columnist, writing about topics like women's rights, child care, and politics. She openly discussed female sexuality, which made her a bold and unconventional figure in her time. She passed away on 31 May 2009 at Jehangir Hospital in Pune at the age of 75.

An Introduction

I don't know politics but I know the names
Of those in power, and can repeat them like
Days of week, or names of months, beginning with Nehru.
I amIndian, very brown, born inMalabar,
I speak three languages, write in
Two, dream in one.
Don't write in English, they said, English is
Not your mother-tongue. Why not leave
Me alone, critics, friends, visiting cousins,
Every one of you? Why not let me speak in
Any language I like? The language I speak,
Becomes mine, its distortions, its queernesses
All mine, mine alone.
It is half English, halfIndian, funny perhaps, but it is honest,
It is as human as I am human, don't
You see? It voices my joys, my longings, my
Hopes, and it is useful to me as cawing

Is to crows or roaring to the lions, it
Is human speech, the speech of the mind that is
Here and not there, a mind that sees and hears and
Is aware. Not the deaf, blind speech
Of trees in storm or of monsoon clouds or of rain or the
Incoherent mutterings of the blazing
Funeral pyre. I was child, and later they
Told me I grew, for I became tall, my limbs
Swelled and one or two places sprouted hair.
WhenI asked for love, not knowing what else to ask
For, he drew a youth of sixteen into the
Bedroom and closed the door, He did not beat me
But my sad woman-body felt so beaten.
The weight of my breasts and womb crushed me.
I shrank Pitifully.
Then ... I wore a shirt and my
Brother's trousers, cut my hair short and ignored
My womanliness. Dress in sarees, be girl
Be wife, they said. Be embroiderer, be cook,
Be a quarreller with servants. Fit in. Oh,
Belong, cried the categorizers. Don't sit
On walls or peep in through our lace-draped windows.
Be Amy, or be Kamala. Or, better
Still, be Madhavikutty. It is time to
Choose a name, a role. Don't play pretending games.
Don't play at schizophrenia or be a
Nympho. Don't cry embarrassingly loud when
Jilted in love ... I met a man, loved him. Call
Him not by any name, he is every man
Who wants. a woman, just as I am every
Woman who seeks love. In him... the hungry haste
Of rivers, in me... the oceans' tireless
Waiting. Who are you, I ask each and everyone,
The answer is, it is I. Anywhere and,
Everywhere, I see the one who calls himself I
In this world, he is tightly packed like the
Sword in its sheath. It is I who drink lonely
Drinks at twelve, midnight, in hotels of strange towns,

It is I who laugh, it is I who make love
And then, feel shame, it is I who lie dying
With a rattle in my throat. I am sinner,
I am saint. I am the beloved and the
Betrayed. I have no joys that are not yours, no
Aches which are not yours. I too call myself I.

Kamala Das' poem An Introduction is a deeply personal and confessional piece that reflects on themes of identity, gender roles, language, and personal freedom. She challenges societal norms and expresses her struggles as a woman and a poet. The poem is a powerful assertion of her individuality and rejection of imposed identities.

Explanation:

Stanza 1:

"I don't know politics but I know the names
Of those in power, and can repeat them like
Days of the week, or names of months, beginning with Nehru."

Explanation:

The poet begins by stating that although she does not understand politics, she is familiar with the names of political leaders, just like she knows the names of the days and months. This reflects how political figures dominate public life, even for those who do not actively engage with politics. By mentioning Nehru, she sets the poem in post-independence India, subtly suggesting that political power is distant yet omnipresent in her life.

Stanza 2:

"I am Indian, very brown, born in Malabar,
I speak three languages, write in
Two, dream in one."

Explanation:

Here, the poet asserts her Indian identity and her connection to Malabar (Kerala). She highlights her multilingualism, indicating her cultural diversity and her struggle between different languages. The phrase "dream in one" suggests that despite speaking and writing in multiple languages, she feels most connected to one language at an emotional or subconscious level.

Stanza 3:

"Don't write in English, they said, English is
Not your mother tongue. Why not leave
Me alone, critics, friends, visiting cousins,

Every one of you? Why not let me speak in
Any language I like?"
Explanation:
The poet addresses criticism she has received for writing in English rather than her native Malayalam. She expresses frustration at societal expectations and argues for her right to choose the language she wants to express herself in. The repetition of "Why not leave me alone?" emphasizes her plea for freedom and individuality.

Stanza 4:
"The language I speak,
Becomes mine, its distortions, its queernesses
All mine, mine alone.
It is half English, half Indian, funny perhaps, but it is honest,"
Explanation:
Kamala Das asserts that the way she speaks English is unique to her and does not have to conform to strict grammatical norms. Her language may be "half English, half Indian" and may sound odd, but it is honest—it truly reflects her identity. She challenges the rigid rules imposed on language and claims ownership over her way of speaking.

Stanza 5:
"It is as human as I am human, don't
You see? It voices my joys, my longings, my
Hopes, and it is useful to me as cawing
Is to crows or roaring to the lions,"
Explanation:
The poet compares her language to natural expressions, like a crow's cawing or a lion's roar. Just as animals use sounds to express themselves, she uses her language instinctively. She argues that language is not just about correctness—it is about expressing emotions and being human.

Stanza 6:
"I was child, and later they
Told me I grew, for I became tall, my limbs
Swelled and one or two places sprouted hair."
Explanation:
This stanza marks the transition from childhood to puberty. Society imposes the idea of growth on her, as if her physical changes define her maturity. The detached tone suggests how she feels like an outsider to her own body, highlighting the discomfort of societal expectations.

Stanza 7:

"When I asked for love, not knowing what else to ask
For, he drew a youth of sixteen into the
Bedroom and closed the door. He did not beat me
But my sad woman-body felt so beaten.
The weight of my breasts and womb crushed me.
I shrank pitifully."

Explanation:

This stanza reflects on her early experiences with love and relationships. Seeking love, she finds herself in a physical relationship that leaves her emotionally wounded. The "sad woman-body" and "weight of my breasts and womb" suggest the burden of womanhood and societal expectations of marriage and sexuality. She feels trapped rather than empowered by her femininity.

Stanza 8:

"Then ... I wore a shirt and my
Brother's trousers, cut **my hair short and ignored**
My womanliness."

Explanation:

After feeling crushed by the expectations of being a woman, she attempts to escape gender roles by dressing in men's clothing and rejecting traditional femininity. This act symbolizes her rebellion against society's rigid definitions of what a woman should be.

Stanza 9:

"Dress in sarees, be girl
Be wife, they said. Be embroiderer, be cook,
Be a quarreller with servants. Fit in."

Explanation:

Society pressures her to conform to traditional female roles—wearing sarees, becoming a wife, doing household work, and managing domestic life. The phrase "Fit in" captures how women are expected to mold themselves to fit societal expectations.

Stanza 10:

"Be Amy, or be Kamala. Or, better
Still, be Madhavikutty. It is time to
Choose a name, a role. Don't play pretending games."

Explanation:

She is given different identities (Amy, Kamala, Madhavikutty), showing how society forces her to conform to predefined roles. The idea of "choosing a name, a role" suggests that a woman's identity is shaped by others rather than by herself.

Stanza 11:

"Don't play at schizophrenia or be a

Nympho. Don't cry embarrassingly loud when

Jilted in love ..."

Explanation:

Society labels women who express emotions as mentally unstable (schizophrenic) or sexually deviant (nympho). Women are expected to remain silent in pain and heartbreak.

Stanza 12:

"I met a man, loved him. Call

Him not by any name, he is every man

Who wants a woman, just as I am every

Woman who seeks love."

Explanation:

She describes a universal love experience—her lover represents "every man", and she represents "every woman" who desires love. This removes individuality, showing how love and longing are common human experiences.

Stanza 13:

"Who are you, I ask each and everyone,

The answer is, it is I."

Explanation:

The poet questions the identity of others, and the universal response is "I". This suggests that every person is a reflection of the self and that identity is fluid and ever-changing.

Stanza 14:

"It is I who drink lonely

Drinks at twelve, midnight, in hotels of strange towns,

It is I who laugh, it is I who make love

And then, feel shame, it is I who lie dying

With a rattle in my throat."

Explanation:

Here, she takes on multiple identities—someone who drinks alone, someone who loves and regrets, someone who dies. This emphasizes her complex, multifaceted nature.

Stanza 15:

"I am sinner,
I am saint. I am the beloved and the
Betrayed. I have no joys that are not yours, no
Aches which are not yours. I too call myself I."

Explanation:

The poem ends with a powerful statement—she embodies all human experiences, both good and bad. By saying "I too call myself I", she asserts her individuality while also connecting with universal human emotions.

Conclusion:

An Introduction is a bold declaration of identity, personal freedom, and resistance against societal norms. Kamala Das challenges gender roles, language restrictions, and societal expectations, making the poem a powerful feminist and autobiographical piece.

CHAPTER THIRTY-FOUR

Nissim Ezekiel

Nissim Ezekiel (16 December 1924 – 9 January 2004) was an Indian poet, actor, playwright, editor, and art critic. He played an important role in shaping Indian English poetry after India's independence. In 1983, he received the Sahitya Akademi Award for his poetry collection Latter-Day Psalms.

Ezekiel was known for his simple yet deep writing style. He wrote about everyday life in a thoughtful and realistic way, without unnecessary emotions. His work influenced many Indian poets who came after him. He helped develop Indian English poetry by introducing modern ideas and techniques. Instead of only focusing on spiritual or traditional themes, he wrote about personal experiences, family issues, and questioned society with a critical eye.

Enterprise

It started as a pilgrimage, Exalting minds and making all The burdens light. The second stage Explored but did not test the call. The Sun beat down to match our rage.

We stood it very well, I thought, Observed and put down copious notes On things the peasants sold and bought, The way of serpents and of goats, Three cities where a sage had taught.

But when the differences arose On how to cross a desert patch, We lost a friend whose stylish prose Was quite the best of all our batch. A shadow falls on us and grows.

Another phase was reached when we Were twice attacked, and lost our way. A section claimed its liberty To leave the group. I tried to pray. Our leader said he smelt the sea.

We noticed nothing as we went, A straggling crowd of little hope, Ignoring what the thunder meant, Deprived of common needs like soap. Some were broken, some merely bent.

When, finally, we reached the place, We hardly knew why we were there. The trip had darkened every face, Our deeds were neither great nor rare. Home is where we have to gather grace.

Explanation:

Enterprise by Nissim Ezekiel is a symbolic poem that explores the struggles of a group on a pilgrimage, which can be interpreted as a metaphor for life's journey.

"It started as a pilgrimage,
Exalting minds and making all
The burdens light. The second stage
Explored but did not test the call.
The Sun beat down to match our rage."

Explanation:

The poem begins with a sense of enthusiasm as the journey is described as a "pilgrimage," symbolizing an idealistic venture. The travelers feel mentally uplifted and enthusiastic, making their burdens feel lighter. The second stage involves exploration, but they do not truly "test the call," meaning they have not yet faced real hardships. However, the phrase "The Sun beat down to match our rage" introduces a shift—while they are still passionate, external challenges (symbolized by the sun) begin to intensify, hinting at the difficulties ahead.

"We stood it very well, I thought,
Observed and put down copious notes
On things the peasants sold and bought,
The way of serpents and of goats,
Three cities where a sage had taught."

Explanation:

The speaker initially believes that the group is enduring the journey well. They remain focused on their purpose, taking detailed notes about their surroundings, including the economic activities of the peasants. The mention of "serpents and of goats" introduces a symbolic contrast—serpents often represent danger or deception, while goats symbolize endurance and resilience. This suggests that their journey is not without challenges. The reference to "three cities where a sage had taught" highlights the group's search for wisdom and knowledge, reinforcing the idea that their journey is more than just physical—it has intellectual and spiritual dimensions.

"But when the differences arose

On how to cross a desert patch,
We lost a friend whose stylish prose
Was quite the best of all our batch.
A shadow falls on us and grows."

Explanation:

Disagreements break out over how to navigate a difficult stretch of the journey—the "desert patch" symbolizes adversity. Amidst the discord, they lose a talented companion whose "stylish prose" suggests intellectual brilliance. This loss represents the breakdown of unity and the cost of internal conflicts. The growing "shadow" is a metaphor for increasing despair and challenges, hinting at the journey's deteriorating spirit.

"Another phase was reached when we
Were twice attacked, and lost our way.
A section claimed its liberty
To leave the group. I tried to pray.
Our leader said he smelt the sea."

Explanation:

The travelers are attacked twice, which could symbolize external threats or personal struggles. They become lost, both physically and metaphorically, as their original sense of purpose fades. Some members abandon the group, asserting their independence. The speaker, in desperation, turns to prayer, suggesting a search for divine guidance. Meanwhile, the leader remains optimistic, claiming to "smell the sea," which could represent hope or an anticipated end to their troubles. However, this hope appears uncertain, as the group remains in turmoil.

"We noticed nothing as we went,
A straggling crowd of little hope,
Ignoring what the thunder meant,
Deprived of common needs like soap.
Some were broken, some merely bent."

Explanation:

The group has lost its sense of awareness and purpose, moving forward mechanically. The phrase "a straggling crowd of little hope" suggests they are no longer a united team but a disorganized group, drained of energy. They ignore signs of danger, such as "thunder," which could symbolize an impending disaster or realization. Even basic necessities like "soap" are neglected, showing their physical decline. Some members are completely broken in spirit, while others are only partially affected. This highlights the varying degrees of suffering experienced by individuals on life's journey.

"When, finally, we reached the place,
We hardly knew why we were there.
The trip had darkened every face,
Our deeds were neither great nor rare.
Home is where we have to gather grace."

Explanation:

After enduring numerous hardships, the travelers finally reach their goal, but instead of joy or fulfillment, they feel lost. The phrase "We hardly knew why we were there" emphasizes the hollowness of their achievement. Their struggles have "darkened every face," both literally and figuratively, showing the emotional and physical toll of the journey. They realize that their accomplishments are neither significant nor unique—what they endured was not extraordinary. The final line, "Home is where we have to gather grace," suggests that true fulfillment and wisdom are not found in external quests but within oneself and in everyday life.

Nissim Ezekiel's Enterprise is a powerful allegory about human ambition, struggle, and ultimate disillusionment. The poem suggests that great journeys often lead to exhaustion rather than enlightenment, and that true meaning is found in ordinary life rather than grand pursuits.

Background Casually

A poet-rascal-clown was born,
The frightened child who would not eat
Or sleep, a boy of meager bone.
He never learned to fly a kite,
His borrowed top refused to spin.

I went to Roman Catholic school,
A mugging Jew among the wolves.
They told me I had killed the Christ,
That year I won the scripture prize.
A Muslim sportsman boxed my ears.

I grew in terror of the strong
But undernourished Hindu lads,
Their prepositions always wrong,
Repelled me by passivity.
One noisy day I used a knife.

At home on Friday nights the prayers
Were said. My morals had declined.

I heard of Yoga and of Zen.
Could 1, perhaps, be rabbi saint?
The more I searched, the less I found.
Twenty two: time to go abroad.
First, the decision, then a friend
To pay the fare. Philosophy,
Poverty and Poetry, three
Companions shared my basement room.
The London seasons passed me by.
I lay in bed two years alone,
And then a Woman came to tell
My willing ears I was the Son
Of Man. I knew that I had failed
In everything, a bitter thought.
So, in an English cargo ship
Taking French guns and mortar shells
To Indo China, scrubbed the decks,
And learned to laugh again at home.
How to feel it home, was the point.
Some reading had been done, but what
Had I observed, except my own
Exasperation? All Hindus are
Like that, my father used to say,
When someone talked too loudly, or
Knocked at the door like the Devil.
They hawked and spat. They sprawled around.
I prepared for the worst. Married,
Changed jobs, and saw myself a fool.
The song of my experience sung,
I knew that all was yet to sing.
My ancestors, among the castes,
Were aliens crushing seed for bread
(The hooded bullock made his rounds).
One among them fought and taught,
A Major bearing British arms.
He told my father sad stories
Of the Boer War. I dreamed that
Fierce men had bound my feet and hands.

The later dreams were all of words.
I did not know that words betray
But let the poems come, and lost
That grip on things the worldly prize.
I would not suffer that again.
I look about me now, and try
To formulate a plainer view:
The wise survive and serve–to play
The fool, to cash in on
The inner and the outer storms.
The Indian landscape sears my eyes.
I have become a part of it
To be observed by foreigners.
They say that I am singular,
Their letters overstate the case.
I have made my commitments now.
This is one: to stay where I am,
As others choose to give themselves
In some remote and backward place.
My backward place is where I am.

Stanza 1

"A poet-rascal-clown was born,
The frightened child who would not eat
Or sleep, a boy of meager bone.
He never learned to fly a kite,
His borrowed top refused to spin."

Explanation:

Ezekiel introduces himself as a complex individual—both a poet, a mischievous "rascal," and a "clown" who doesn't fit in. The phrase "frightened child" highlights his insecurity and physical frailty. His inability to "fly a kite" or spin a borrowed top symbolizes his struggle to engage with childhood joys, hinting at his outsider status. The use of "borrowed" suggests he lacked a sense of belonging, foreshadowing his lifelong quest for identity.

Stanza 2

Lines for Explanation:
"I went to Roman Catholic school,
A mugging Jew among the wolves.

They told me I had killed the Christ,
That year I won the scripture prize.
A Muslim sportsman boxed my ears."

Explanation:

The phrase "mugging Jew among the wolves" reflects his struggle to fit in, as he faced both religious discrimination and bullying. The irony of winning a "scripture prize" despite being accused of killing Christ highlights religious hypocrisy. The mention of a "Muslim sportsman" boxing his ears suggests that he faced casual violence, reinforcing his sense of alienation and vulnerability.

Stanza 3

Lines for Explanation:

"I grew in terror of the strong
But undernourished Hindu lads,
Their prepositions always wrong,
Repelled me by passivity.
One noisy day I used a knife."

Explanation:

He contrasts his fear of strong yet "undernourished" Hindu boys with his intellectual superiority, noting their grammatical mistakes. The phrase "repelled me by passivity" suggests he found their lack of ambition frustrating. However, his own frustration culminates in an act of violence—"One noisy day I used a knife"—possibly a metaphor for a moment of rebellion or real conflict.

Stanza 4

Lines for Explanation:

"At home on Friday nights the prayers
Were said. My morals had declined.
I heard of Yoga and of Zen.
Could I, perhaps, be rabbi saint?
The more I searched, the less I found."

Explanation:

Despite coming from a religious Jewish family, with prayers recited every Friday night, he acknowledges his declining morals. His exposure to different spiritual traditions like Yoga and Zen sparks a philosophical curiosity. The rhetorical question about becoming a "rabbi saint" suggests a desire for spiritual guidance, but ultimately, he finds no clear answers, deepening his existential crisis.

Stanza 5
Lines for Explanation:
"Twenty-two: time to go abroad.
First, the decision, then a friend
To pay the fare. Philosophy,
Poverty and Poetry, three
Companions shared my basement room."
Explanation:

At 22, he decides to leave, symbolizing a quest for self-discovery. His financial struggles are evident as a friend funds his journey. The alliteration in "Philosophy, Poverty, and Poetry" reflects his experiences in London—intellectual exploration, financial hardship, and literary passion. His "basement room" reinforces the idea of a struggling writer living on the margins.

Stanza 6 & 7
"The London seasons passed me by.
I lay in bed two years alone,
And then a Woman came to tell
My willing ears I was the Son
Of Man."
"I knew that I had failed
In everything, a bitter thought.
So, in an English cargo ship
Taking French guns and mortar shells
To Indo-China, scrubbed the decks,
And learned to laugh again at home."
Explanation:

The loneliness of London is expressed through the passage of "seasons," showing his alienation. The mysterious "Woman" who calls him the "Son of Man" (a biblical reference) possibly symbolizes an attempt to find meaning. However, he ultimately feels like a failure and takes up menial work on a cargo ship, transporting weapons. Ironically, through physical labor, he finds humor and reconnects with home.

Final Stanzas
"The Indian landscape sears my eyes.
I have become a part of it
To be observed by foreigners.
They say that I am singular,

Their letters overstate the case."
"I have made my commitments now.
This is one: to stay where I am,
As others choose to give themselves
In some remote and backward place.
My backward place is where I am."

Explanation:

The "Indian landscape sears my eyes" suggests both pain and deep connection. While he once felt alienated, he now sees himself as part of India. However, foreigners exoticize him, exaggerating his uniqueness. The final lines affirm his decision to stay in India, paralleling missionaries who dedicate themselves to "backward" places. But for him, home itself was once a "backward place"—now embraced fully.

Conclusion:

Background, Casually is an autobiographical reflection on Ezekiel's struggles with identity, religion, and belonging. From childhood alienation to finding acceptance in India, the poem highlights the complex journey of self-discovery.

CHAPTER THIRTY-FIVE

A.K Ramanujan

Attipate Krishnaswami Ramanujan (16 March 1929 – 13 July 1993) was an Indian poet and scholar who studied Indian literature and languages. He was also a professor of Linguistics at the University of Chicago. Ramanujan was a poet, translator, playwright, and expert in different languages.He worked with five languages: English, Tamil, Kannada, Telugu, and Sanskrit. He wrote about both old and modern literature and believed that local dialects should be respected. His poems are known for being unique, deep, and artistic. In 1999, he was posthumously awarded the Sahitya Akademi Award for The Collected Poems.

A Self Portrait

I resemble everyone
But myself, and sometimes see.
in shop- windows
despite the well-knownlaws
of optics,
the portrait of a stranger,
date unknown,
often signed in a corner
by my father.

Explanation

The poem Self Portrait by A.K. Ramanujan is a simple poem about identity. The poet feels that he is like everyone else in the world. He sees others in himself, but he cannot see or understand his own true identity. This shows that he is facing an identity crisis—he feels lost and does not know who he really is.

Sometimes, he sees his reflection in shop windows. But even when he looks at himself, he does not recognize his own face. Instead, he sees a stranger. He describes himself as "a portrait of a stranger" because his reflection feels unfamiliar to him.

The poet also mentions the laws of optics, which explain how light reflects and refracts. Even though he understands these scientific laws, he still sees a stranger in the mirror. This suggests that his identity is not something he has created on his own. Instead, it has been passed down to him by his father.

A River

In Madurai,
city of temples and poets,
who sang of cities and temples,
every summer
a river dries to a trickle
in the sand,
baring the sand ribs,
straw and women's hair
clogging the watergates
at the rusty bars
under the bridges with patches
of repair all over them
the wet stones glistening like sleepy
crocodiles, the dry ones
shaven water-buffaloes lounging in the sun
The poets only sang of the floods.
He was there for a day
when they had the floods.
People everywhere talked
of the inches rising,
of the precise number of cobbled steps
run over by the water, rising
on the bathing places,
and the way it carried off three village houses,
one pregnant woman
and a couple of cows
named Gopi and Brinda as usual.
The new poets still quoted
the old poets, but no one spoke
in verse
of the pregnant woman

drowned, with perhaps twins in her,
kicking at blank walls
even before birth.
He said:
the river has water enough
to be poetic
about only once a year
and then
it carries away
in the first half-hour
three village houses,
a couple of cows
named Gopi and Brinda
and one pregnant woman
expecting identical twins
with no moles on their bodies,
with different coloured diapers
to tell them apart.

Explanation:

The poem A River by A.K. Ramanujan critiques traditional poets for their selective and romanticized portrayal of nature, particularly the river in Madurai. The poem contrasts the poetic descriptions of the river with its harsh reality, showing how old poets ignored human suffering in favor of grand imagery.In this poem. In this poem the poet describes how the river in Madurai dries up in summer, exposing an unpleasant scene, yet traditional poets only focus on its floods. He then shifts to a time when the river floods and people discuss it in technical terms while ignoring the real tragedy it brings.

Stanza 1:
"In Madurai,
city of temples and poets,
who sang of cities and temples,
every summer
a river dries to a trickle
in the sand,
baring the sand ribs,
straw and women's hair
clogging the watergates

at the rusty bars
under the bridges with patches
of repair all over them
the wet stones glistening like sleepy
crocodiles, the dry ones
shaven water-buffaloes lounging in the sun."

Explanation:

The poem begins with a description of Madurai, a famous city known for its temples and poets. The poet criticizes these poets for only singing about cities and temples while ignoring the harsh realities of life. He describes how, during summer, the river in Madurai dries up, leaving behind a barren landscape. The imagery of "sand ribs," "straw and women's hair clogging the watergates", and "rusty bars" highlights decay and neglect. The stones are compared to sleepy crocodiles (wet ones) and shaven buffaloes (dry ones), creating an unromantic picture of the river.

Stanza 2:

"The poets only sang of the floods.
He was there for a day
when they had the floods.
People everywhere talked
of the inches rising,
of the precise number of cobbled steps
run over by the water, rising
on the bathing places,
and the way it carried off three village houses,
one pregnant woman
and a couple of cows
named Gopi and Brinda as usual."

Explanation:

The poet points out that traditional poets only wrote about the floods, not the river in its dry state. He recalls a time when he witnessed a flood himself, and instead of sorrow, people discussed the exact water level and how many steps were submerged. The real tragedy—the destruction of homes and loss of lives—is mentioned casually. Even the cows (Gopi and Brinda) are given names, but the pregnant woman remains unnamed, showing society's lack of concern for human suffering.

Stanza 3:

"The new poets still quoted

the old poets, but no one spoke
in verse
of the pregnant woman
drowned, with perhaps twins in her,
kicking at blank walls
even before birth."

Explanation:

The new poets continue following the old poets, quoting their works instead of creating something new. They fail to write about human tragedy, just like their predecessors. The drowned pregnant woman is a powerful image, symbolizing the suffering that remains unspoken in poetry. The twins "kicking at blank walls" even before birth suggest their helplessness and tragic fate, reinforcing the poet's criticism of literature's selective storytelling.

Stanza 4 (Final Stanza):

"He said:
the river has water enough
to be poetic
about only once a year
and then
it carries away
in the first half-hour
three village houses,
a couple of cows
named Gopi and Brinda
and one pregnant woman
expecting identical twins
with no moles on their bodies,
with different coloured diapers
to tell them apart."

Explanation:

The poet sarcastically comments that the river is only poetic once a year when it floods. However, this poetic moment comes at the cost of destruction and death. The repetition of the losses (houses, cows, and the pregnant woman) emphasizes the tragedy.The final lines about identical twins without moles and diapers to tell them apart show how human life is reduced to small details while poetry ignores the bigger suffering.

Conclusion:

Through A River, A.K. Ramanujan critiques:

Selective Memory in Poetry – Traditional poets romanticize nature while ignoring human pain.

Reality vs. Romanticism – The real, harsh state of the river is never written about.

Neglect of Human Suffering – Tragedies, like the death of the pregnant woman, are not considered poetic subjects. The poet urges modern literature to be more realistic, inclusive, and compassionate, rather than repeating outdated poetic traditions.

<u>Looking for a Cousin on Swing</u>

When she was four or five
she sat on a village swing
and her cousin, six or seven,
sat himself against her;
with every lunge of the swing
By she felt him
in the lunging pits
of her feeling;
and afterwards
we climbed a tree, she said,
not very tall, but full of leaves
like those of a fig tree,
and we were very innocent
about it.
Now she looks for the swing
in cities with fifteen suburbs
and tries to be innocent
about it.
not only on the crotch of a tree
that looked as if it would burst
under every leaf
into a brood of scarlet figs
if someone suddenly sneezed.

A.K. Ramanujan's poem Looking for a Cousin on a Swing explores themes of childhood innocence, early experiences of sensuality, and the longing for lost moments. The poem narrates a girl's memory of childhood play that subtly hints at her first experience of desire, which later transforms into an unfulfilled longing in adulthood.

Stanza 1:

"When she was four or five
she sat on a village swing
and her cousin, six or seven,
sat himself against her;
with every lunge of the swing
she felt him
in the lunging pits
of her feeling;
and afterwards
we climbed a tree, she said,"

Explanation:

The poet introduces a childhood memory of a girl (possibly the speaker's cousin or a woman he knows). She recalls sitting on a swing in the village, with her older cousin sitting close to her. The movement of the swing creates a physical sensation, making her aware of his presence in a way she doesn't fully understand at that age.The phrase "lunging pits of her feeling" suggests an early, subconscious awareness of physical attraction or desire. Afterward, the two children climb a tree, symbolizing their innocence and natural curiosity.

Stanza 2:

"not very tall, but full of leaves
like those of a fig tree,
and we were very innocent
about it."

Explanation:

The tree they climb is not very tall but full of leaves, similar to a fig tree. The fig tree is often associated with sensuality and fertility in literature, subtly reinforcing the idea of awakening desire. However, at that time, the girl and her cousin were completely innocent about their experience, unaware of any deeper meaning.

Stanza 3:

"Now she looks for the swing
in cities with fifteen suburbs
and tries to be innocent
about it"

Explanation:

The poem shifts to the present, where the girl, now an adult, searches for the same feeling she once experienced on the swing. Instead of a village swing, she now lives in a modern city with many suburbs—a stark contrast to her childhood setting. The phrase "tries to be innocent about it" suggests that she is aware of her desires now but struggles to reclaim the innocence of her childhood.

Stanza 4 (Final Stanza):
"not only on the crotch of a tree
that looked as if it would burst
under every leaf
into a brood of scarlet figs
if someone suddenly sneezed."

Explanation:

The phrase "crotch of a tree" carries both literal and symbolic meanings—it refers to the branching part of a tree but also hints at sensuality.

The fig tree imagery intensifies here, suggesting fertility, suppressed desires, and passion.

The phrase "burst under every leaf into a brood of scarlet figs" conveys a sense of overwhelming, repressed desire that might explode at any moment.

The final line—"if someone suddenly sneezed"—adds a sense of fragility, as if the suppressed emotions or desires could be released unexpectedly.

Conclusion:

Through Looking for a Cousin on a Swing, A.K. Ramanujan explores: Childhood Innocence vs. Adult Desire – The poem contrasts a child's innocent experiences with the same emotions resurfacing in adulthood, now laden with awareness.

Memory and Longing – The girl's search for the swing represents a desire to relive the past and recapture lost feelings.

Symbolism of the Fig Tree – The fig tree represents sensuality, suppressed emotions, and the inevitability of desire.

The poem subtly captures the transition from childhood playfulness to adult yearning, showing how memories shape our understanding of emotions.

CHAPTER THIRTY-SIX

Arun Koltakar

Arun Balkrishna Kolatkar (1 November 1932 – 25 September 2004) was an Indian poet who wrote in both Marathi and English. His poems often highlight the humor in everyday life. Kolatkar is the only Indian poet, besides Kabir, to be featured in the World Classics series by the New York Review of Books.

His first collection of English poetry, Jejuri, won the Commonwealth Poetry Prize in 1977. His Marathi poetry collection, Bhijki Vahi, won the Sahitya Akademi Award in 2005. An anthology of his works, Collected Poems in English, edited by Arvind Krishna Mehrotra, was published in Britain by Bloodaxe Books in 2010.

Kolatkar studied art at the J. J. School of Art and also worked as a graphic designer.

The Bus

The tarpaulin flaps are buttoned down
on the windows of the state transport bus.
all the way up to jejuri.
a cold wind keeps whipping
and slapping a corner of tarpaulin at your elbow.
you look down to the roaring road.
you search for the signs of daybreak in what little light spills out of bus.
your own divided face in the pair of glasses
on an oldman`s nose
is all the countryside you get to see.
you seem to move continually forward.
toward a destination
just beyond the castemark beyond his eyebrows.
outside, the sun has risen quitely
it aims through an eyelet in the tarpaulin.

and shoots at the oldman`s glasses.

a sawed off sunbeam comes to rest gently against the driver`s right temple.

the bus seems to change direction.

at the end of bumpy ride with your own face on the either side

when you get off the bus.

you dont step inside the old man`s head

This poem is from Jejuri, a collection by Arun Kolatkar, which captures the poet's journey to the pilgrimage town of Jejuri in Maharashtra. Kolatkar's poetry is known for its vivid imagery, keen observation, and ironic tone. The Bus describes the poet's journey on a state transport bus, portraying not just the physical movement but also the deeper existential themes of perception, identity, and travel as a metaphor for self-discovery.

Stanza-wise Explanation

Stanza 1:

"The tarpaulin flaps are buttoned down
on the windows of the state transport bus.
all the way up to jejuri."

The poem begins by setting the scene inside the bus. The "tarpaulin flaps" covering the windows suggest an enclosed, restricted view of the outside world. The mention of "state transport bus" indicates an ordinary, mundane journey, not a luxurious one. "All the way up to Jejuri" tells us that this is a pilgrimage journey, but the tone remains neutral, not devotional.

Stanza 2:

"a cold wind keeps whipping
and slapping a corner of tarpaulin at your elbow."

The poet adds sensory details here. The cold wind creates discomfort, reinforcing the rough, everyday nature of the journey. The flapping tarpaulin, which constantly "whips" and "slaps," symbolizes the unpredictability of travel and life.

Stanza 3:

"you look down to the roaring road.
you search for the signs of daybreak in what little light spills out of bus."

The road is described as "roaring," emphasizing movement, noise, and energy. The poet looks for daybreak, symbolizing anticipation or the search for meaning. The phrase "what little light spills out" suggests that the view is limited, reinforcing the theme of restricted perception.

Stanza 4:

"your own divided face in the pair of glasses
on an old man's nose
is all the countryside you get to see."

The poet sees his reflection in the glasses of an old man sitting nearby.His "divided face" (split into two reflections) suggests fragmentation—perhaps a metaphor for duality in identity or perception.The phrase "all the countryside you get to see" is ironic. Instead of the actual landscape, the poet only sees himself, suggesting introspection or self-absorption.

Stanza 5:

"you seem to move continually forward.
toward a destination
just beyond the castemark beyond his eyebrows."

The poet's journey is described as continuous and inevitable. The phrase "destination just beyond the castemark" is significant. The old man's caste mark (a religious or social identifier on the forehead) symbolizes tradition and societal divisions. The poet's movement towards a destination "beyond" it suggests that the journey might also be a metaphor for transcending social or religious boundaries.

Stanza 6:

"outside, the sun has risen quietly
it aims through an eyelet in the tarpaulin.
and shoots at the old man's glasses."

The sun, a symbol of enlightenment or awareness, has risen "quietly," contrasting with the roughness of the bus ride. The "eyelet" in the tarpaulin allows a narrow beam of sunlight, which metaphorically represents a limited view of reality. The sunbeam reflecting off the old man's glasses could symbolize knowledge, clarity, or a moment of realization.

Stanza 7:

"a sawed-off sunbeam comes to rest gently against the driver's right temple.
the bus seems to change direction."

The sunbeam now touches the driver's temple, a part of the head associated with thought and decision-making.

The "sawed-off sunbeam" suggests a cut or fragmented ray of light, continuing the theme of partial vision or incomplete understanding.

The phrase "the bus seems to change direction" can be taken literally (a turn in the road) or metaphorically (a shift in perception or destiny).

Final Stanza:
"at the end of bumpy ride with your own face on either side
when you get off the bus.
you don't step inside the old man's head"

The journey comes to an end, described as "bumpy," reinforcing the rough, unromantic nature of travel. The repetition of the divided face ("on either side") suggests that self-reflection continues. The final line, "you don't step inside the old man's head," implies that the poet does not fully understand or enter the world of the old man. This could reflect a failure to bridge the gap between generations, traditions, or perspectives.

Conclusion:

Arun Kolatkar's The Bus captures an ordinary journey with extraordinary depth. The imagery, symbolism, and minimalist style make it a subtle yet profound reflection on perception, identity, and the nature of travel. Instead of a grand spiritual awakening, the poet ends with a quiet realization—one can journey through landscapes, but understanding another person's world (or head) remains elusive.

<u>Chaitanya</u>

a herd of legends
on the hill slope
looked up from its grazing
when chaitanya came into sight
and the hills remained still
when chaitanya
was passing by
a cowbell tinkeled
when he disappeared from view
and the herd of legends
returned to its grazing

This poem is from Jejuri, Arun Kolatkar's celebrated poetry collection that explores themes of faith, mythology, and everyday reality. The poem refers to Chaitanya Mahaprabhu, a 15th-century saint and spiritual leader of the Bhakti movement. Kolatkar presents Chaitanya's presence as a fleeting moment in the landscape, blending mythology with reality in his signature minimalist style.

Stanza 1:
"A herd of legends
on the hill slope

looked up from its grazing
when Chaitanya came into sight."

The phrase "herd of legends" is metaphorical. It suggests that the landscape itself is steeped in mythology, as if legends exist like grazing cattle. The hills symbolize permanence, history, and tradition. Chaitanya's arrival is depicted as a significant event—something so profound that even the "legends" (possibly symbols of ancient faith) momentarily acknowledge his presence.

This creates a contrast between spiritual movement (Chaitanya) and static tradition (the hills and legends).

Stanza 2:

"And the hills remained still
when Chaitanya
was passing by."

The hills, symbols of endurance and immutability, remain unmoved by Chaitanya's passing. This can be interpreted in multiple ways: Chaitanya's presence is gentle, leaving no disruption in nature. The hills, representing tradition, remain unaffected by new spiritual movements. Spiritual figures like Chaitanya pass through time, but history remains unchanged.

Stanza 3:

"A cowbell tinkled
when he disappeared from view."
The "cowbell" represents the return to ordinary life.

The moment of spiritual presence is transient—Chaitanya appears, and then he is gone.

The sound of the bell suggests a shift from the mystical back to the mundane, reinforcing the idea that spirituality is momentary and fleeting.

Final Stanza:

"And the herd of legends
returned to its grazing."

Once Chaitanya is gone, the mythical "herd of legends" returns to its routine. This suggests that faith, myth, and spirituality coexist with daily life, but their impact is momentary. The cyclic nature of belief and routine is highlighted—spiritual moments come and go, but life continues as usual.

Conclusion

Chaitanya is a short but profound poem that questions the impact of spiritual figures and moments on the world. Arun Kolatkar's detached, minimalist style avoids glorification, instead presenting spirituality as a passing presence—acknowledged briefly, but not transformative. The poem leaves the reader with a sense of quiet reflection on the nature of belief and its place in everyday life.

CHAPTER THIRTY-SEVEN

Jayanta Mahapatra

Jayanta Mahapatra (22 October 1928 – 27 August 2023) was a renowned Indian poet and the first to receive the Sahitya Akademi Award for English poetry. His works, including Indian Summer and Hunger, are considered classics in modern Indian English literature. In recognition of his contributions, he was honored with the Padma Shri, India's fourth-highest civilian award, in 2009. However, in 2015, he returned the award as a mark of protest against the growing intolerance in the country.

Dawn at Puri

Endless crow noises
A skull in the holy sands
tilts its empty country towards hunger.
White-clad widowed Women
past the centers of their lives
are waiting to enter the Great Temple
Their austere eyes
stare like those caught in a net
hanging by the dawn's shining strands of faith.
The fail early light catches
ruined, leprous shells leaning against one another,
a mass of crouched faces without names,
and suddenly breaks out of my hide
into the smoky blaze of a sullen solitary pyre
that fills my aging mother:
her last wish to be cremated here
twisting uncertainly like light
on the shifting sands

The poem Dawn at Puri by Jayanta Mahapatra captures the atmosphere of Puri, a sacred pilgrimage site in India, especially around the Jagannath

Temple and the cremation grounds near the sea. The poem blends personal emotions with broader social realities, highlighting themes of death, faith, and human suffering. The poet presents stark imagery of the holy site, contrasting its spiritual significance with the harsh realities of life and death.

Stanza 1:

"Endless crow noises

A skull in the holy sands

tilts its empty country towards hunger."

The poem opens with the unsettling image of "endless crow noises," which create a sense of disturbance. Crows, often associated with death and decay, set a somber tone. The image of a skull in the holy sands suggests death and mortality, reinforcing the idea that even in a sacred place like Puri, death is ever-present. The phrase "tilts its empty country towards hunger" symbolizes both physical and spiritual emptiness—perhaps the hunger for life, fulfillment, or liberation.

Stanza 2:

"White-clad widowed Women

past the centers of their lives

are waiting to enter the Great Temple"

Here, the poet describes widowed women, dressed in white (a traditional color of mourning in India), who have moved beyond the "centers of their lives"—indicating that they have lost their social significance after their husbands' deaths. They are waiting to enter the Jagannath Temple, likely seeking solace or redemption. Their presence highlights the rigid traditions in Indian society, where widows are often marginalized.

Stanza 3:

"Their austere eyes

stare like those caught in a net

hanging by the dawn's shining strands of faith."

The poet describes the widows' eyes as "austere," reflecting their suffering and emotional restraint. Their gaze is compared to those "caught in a net," suggesting entrapment—perhaps by fate, tradition, or religious beliefs. The "dawn's shining strands of faith" indicate that they still cling to their devotion, even amid personal loss.

Stanza 4:

"The frail early light catches

ruined, leprous shells leaning against one another,
a mass of crouched faces without names,"

The early morning light reveals bleak images: "ruined, leprous shells" might refer to the deteriorating temple walls or the physical decay of people suffering from disease. The "crouched faces without names" symbolize the anonymity of the poor and marginalized, who blend into the crowd, unnoticed.

Stanza 5:

"and suddenly breaks out of my hide
into the smoky blaze of a sullen solitary pyre
that fills my aging mother:"

The scene shifts from external observations to a deeply personal moment. The poet envisions a funeral pyre burning alone, symbolizing the inevitability of death. This thought fills his mind, reminding him of his aging mother and her mortality.

Stanza 6:

"her last wish to be cremated here
twisting uncertainly like light
on the shifting sands"

The poem concludes with the poet reflecting on his mother's last wish—to be cremated in Puri, a holy site believed to grant spiritual liberation. However, the phrase "twisting uncertainly like light on the shifting sands" suggests instability and doubt, hinting at the transient nature of human desires and the uncertainty of fulfillment.

Conclusion

Dawn at Puri juxtaposes the sacred with the grim realities of life—death, suffering, and social constraints. The poet uses vivid imagery to highlight the contradictions in Indian society, where deep faith coexists with human misery. Through personal reflection, he also questions the significance of rituals and the inevitability of death, making this poem both poignant and thought-provoking.

<u>Hunger</u>

It was hard to believe the flesh was heavy on my back.
The fisherman said: Will you have her, carelessly,
trailing his nets and his nerves, as though his words
sanctified the purpose with which he faced himself.
I saw his white bone thrash his eyes.
I followed him across the sprawling sands,

my mind thumping in the flesh's sling.
Hope lay perhaps in burning the house I lived in.
Silence gripped my sleeves; his body clawed at the froth
his old nets had only dragged up from the seas.
In the flickering dark his lean-to opened like a wound.
The wind was I, and the days and nights before.
Palm fronds scratched my skin. Inside the shack
an oil lamp splayed the hours bunched to those walls.
Over and over the sticky soot crossed the space of my mind.
I heard him say: My daughter, she's just turned fifteen...
Feel her. I'll be back soon, your bus leaves at nine.
The sky fell on me, and a father's exhausted wile.
Long and lean, her years were cold as rubber.
She opened her wormy legs wide. I felt the hunger there,
the other one, the fish slithering, turning inside.

Jayanta Mahapatra's poem Hunger is a stark and unsettling exploration of human desires—both the physical hunger for survival and the deeper, more disturbing hunger of exploitation. The poem presents a bleak scenario where poverty forces people into acts of desperation, raising questions about morality, objectification, and the dehumanizing effects of poverty. The poet uses vivid imagery, metaphor, and symbolism to highlight the painful realities of survival.

Stanza 1:

"It was hard to believe the flesh was heavy on my back.
The fisherman said: Will you have her, carelessly,
trailing his nets and his nerves, as though his words
sanctified the purpose with which he faced himself.
I saw his white bone thrash his eyes."

Explanation:

The opening line, "It was hard to believe the flesh was heavy on my back," suggests a deep discomfort within the speaker, as if he is weighed down by guilt, desire, or moral conflict. The fisherman's question, "Will you have her, carelessly," reveals a shocking proposition—he is offering his own daughter in exchange for money. The word "carelessly" suggests how routine and normalized such transactions have become in his world.

The fisherman's actions—"trailing his nets and his nerves,"—connect his economic hardship with his moral compromise. His "white bone thrashing his eyes" is a striking image of his desperation, perhaps a reference to his internal suffering or the harshness of his life.

Stanza 2:

"I followed him across the sprawling sands,
my mind thumping in the flesh's sling.
Hope lay perhaps in burning the house I lived in.
Silence gripped my sleeves; his body clawed at the froth
his old nets had only dragged up from the seas."

Explanation:

The act of "following him across the sprawling sands" suggests the speaker's transition from hesitation to action, moving toward a morally ambiguous space. The phrase "my mind thumping in the flesh's sling" implies inner turmoil, as his conscience wrestles with his bodily urges. The line "Hope lay perhaps in burning the house I lived in" indicates a desperate longing for escape or transformation. The speaker may feel that only through destruction can he free himself from his desires or guilt. The fisherman's "body clawing at the froth" paints a haunting picture of someone struggling to survive. His nets "only dragged up from the seas" may symbolize how his attempts at making an honest living have failed, pushing him toward more desperate means.

Stanza 3:

"In the flickering dark his lean-to opened like a wound.
The wind was I, and the days and nights before.
Palm fronds scratched my skin. Inside the shack
an oil lamp splayed the hours bunched to those walls.
Over and over the sticky soot crossed the space of my mind."

Explanation:

The fisherman's "lean-to opened like a wound" suggests that the place is a site of suffering, exposing pain and vulnerability. The speaker's statement, "The wind was I, and the days and nights before," implies a loss of self, as though he is blending into the environment, losing his moral bearings. The phrase "an oil lamp splayed the hours bunched to those walls" suggests a suffocating sense of time, where past and present are trapped in a cycle of suffering. The "sticky soot" represents moral filth, tainting the speaker's conscience. He is aware of the wrongness of what is happening but seems powerless to resist.

Stanza 4:

"I heard him say: My daughter, she's just turned fifteen...
Feel her. I'll be back soon, your bus leaves at nine.

The sky fell on me, and a father's exhausted wile.
Long and lean, her years were cold as rubber.
She opened her wormy legs wide. I felt the hunger there,
the other one, the fish slithering, turning inside."

Explanation:

The fisherman's words, "My daughter, she's just turned fifteen," make the horror explicit—he is offering a child for sexual exploitation, likely out of economic desperation. The phrase "Feel her. I'll be back soon, your bus leaves at nine." dehumanizes the girl, treating her as an object to be used. The mention of the bus departure emphasizes how routine and systematic this act has become. The speaker feels crushed under the weight of this reality—"The sky fell on me,"—as if the enormity of the situation finally overwhelms him. The father's "exhausted wile" suggests that he is neither proud nor ashamed; he is merely trying to survive. His weariness signals a world where morality has been eroded by necessity. The girl is described as "cold as rubber," implying numbness—whether due to trauma, detachment, or sheer survival instinct.The grotesque image of her "wormy legs" reinforces the dehumanization and decay.

The final lines,"*I felt the hunger there, the other one, the fish slithering, turning inside*," present hunger as both physical and metaphorical. The "other one" refers to a different kind of hunger—one that is driven by desperation, power, and exploitation. The "fish slithering inside" is a haunting image, reinforcing the idea that this entire situation is driven by a cycle of need and consumption—whether it be for food, money, or physical gratification.

Conclusion

Jayanta Mahapatra's Hunger is a disturbing yet powerful poem that forces readers to confront uncomfortable truths about poverty, exploitation, and human nature. The speaker's journey reflects not only an individual moral crisis but also a broader societal decay, where hunger—both literal and figurative—drives people into dark, inescapable corners of survival.

CHAPTER THIRTY-EIGHT

Keki Nasserwanji Daruwalla

Keki Nasserwanji Daruwalla was born in Lahore in 1937. He spent his childhood in different places, including Junagadh, where his father worked for the Nawab. He later studied in Ludhiana and earned an M.A. degree. After that, he joined the Indian Police Service and held various government positions, including some postings abroad, until his retirement.

Daruwalla has written several poetry collections, such as Under Orion (1970), Apparition in April (1971), Crossing of Rivers (1976), Winter Poems (1980), The Keeper of the Dead (1982), and Landscapes (1987). He won the Sahitya Akademi Award for The Keeper of the Dead. He has also written two collections of short stories and has edited an anthology called Two Decades of Indian Poetry: 1960-1980.

Daruwalla's Poetry

Daruwalla's poetry is mainly about action and power. Some of his poems, like Hawk and Wolf, focus on predatory animals, while others talk about conquerors and soldiers. He is interested in strength and dominance, and his poems often show history from the perspective of those in power.

In his world, victims of history are seen as just that—victims. While they may deserve sympathy, the reality is that the powerful continue to rule. His poetry suggests that the world operates on the "law of the jungle," where power and violence are natural forces. There is no clear presence of God or justice in his poems—only the reality of how history unfolds.

Some might call Daruwalla a cynic because his poetry does not show much compassion or belief in justice. However, he sees himself as a realist, someone who presents history as it is, without illusions. He does not admire people who give up power unless their renunciation leads to another form of strength, as seen in his poem The King Speaks to the Scribe, based on Ashoka's edicts. For Daruwalla, power, violence, and desire are natural forces that shape human history. The strong will always dominate, and history is a record of this ongoing struggle.

Rumination

I can smell violence in the air
like the lash of coming rain mass hatreds drifting grey
across the moon.
It hovers brooding, poised like a cobra
as I go prodding rat-holes
and sounding caverns
looking for a fang that darts,
a hood that sways
and eyes that squirt a reptile hate.
I watch my wounds but they don't turn green.
Cross-bones I look for you!
Death I am looking
for that bald bone-head of yours!
The drift as it comes to us now
is aroma/stench/nausea
jostling each other!
In the morgue-verandah another queues up,
her nose sliced off, her lung punctured.
(It is a three-word story:
infidelity-irate husband.)
Man is so pliant, adaptable. Bury him
and he is steadfast as the earth.
Burn him and he will ride the flames.
Throw him to the birds and he will
surrender flesh like an ascetic.
Rain comes clamouring down,
But it's in flesh and flesh-tissue
that my destiny lies
and slowly corruption takes a hold.
Over from the mortuary
comes the corpse-drift.
(Death is so soft, put it ten days in a well
and it turns pulpy.)
Rosewater, incense-sticks, flowers–
the relatives have done their bit.
The drift as it comes to us now

is aroma/stench/nausea
jostling each other!
In the morgue-verandah another queues up,
her nose sliced off, her lung punctured.
(It is a three-word story:
infidelity-irate husband.)
Man is so pliant, adaptable. Bury him
and he is steadfast as the earth.
Burn him and he will ride the flames.
Throw him to the birds and he will
surrender flesh like an ascetic.
Rain comes clamouring down,
a blind sheet of water.
Once the blur lifts
colours deepen, the hedge smiles,
the leaf loses its coat of dust,
the scum spills over from the pool.
I look around for a cleansed feeling,
the kind you experience
walking in a temple
after a river-bath.
I cannot find it.
I have misplaced it somewhere
in the caverns of my past.

Explanation of "Rumination" by Keki N. Daruwalla

Daruwalla's poem Rumination presents a dark meditation on violence, death, and decay. Through stark imagery and a detached yet haunting tone, the poem explores how brutality seeps into everyday life, leaving behind an unsettling moral and physical corruption. Below is a stanza-by-stanza analysis:

First Stanza

"I can smell violence in the air
like the lash of coming rain mass hatreds drifting grey
across the moon."

The speaker senses violence as something tangible, comparing it to the way rain arrives with strong winds. "Mass hatreds drifting grey across the moon" suggests an ominous presence, where collective anger and resentment obscure light and clarity. The moon, often a symbol of peace or guidance, is veiled by hatred.

Second Stanza

"It hovers brooding, poised like a cobra
as I go prodding rat-holes
and sounding caverns
looking for a fang that darts,
a hood that sways
and eyes that squirt a reptile hate."

Violence is not just in the air—it is ready to strike, like a cobra coiled in anticipation.

The speaker actively searches for its source, "prodding rat-holes" and "sounding caverns," metaphorically looking for signs of lurking danger or aggression.

The imagery of the snake's fang and hood reinforces the idea that violence is instinctive, waiting to attack.

Third Stanza

"I watch my wounds but they don't turn green."

The speaker acknowledges personal wounds, possibly inflicted by violence, but they do not "turn green"—meaning they do not fester with poison. This could imply resilience or an expectation of corruption that surprisingly does not take hold.

Fourth Stanza

"Cross-bones I look for you!
Death I am looking
for that bald bone-head of yours!"

The speaker directly addresses death, symbolized by crossbones and a "bald bone-head" (perhaps referring to a skull).

There is a sense of confrontation, as if the speaker is actively seeking out death or acknowledging its inescapable presence.

Fifth Stanza

"The drift as it comes to us now
is aroma/stench/nausea
jostling each other!"

Death and decay carry contradictory smells—fragrance (perhaps funeral rites), the stench of rot, and the sickness they cause.

These elements "jostling" indicate the mix of emotions surrounding death—grief, reverence, and disgust.

Sixth Stanza

"In the morgue-verandah another queues up,
her nose sliced off, her lung punctured.
(It is a three-word story:
infidelity-irate husband.)"

A gruesome image of a woman murdered in an honor killing—her body mutilated for alleged infidelity.

The phrase "three-word story" (infidelity, irate husband) brutally reduces her life and suffering to a simplistic cause-and-effect, showing society's casual acceptance of violence.

Seventh Stanza

"Man is so pliant, adaptable. Bury him
and he is steadfast as the earth.
Burn him and he will ride the flames.
Throw him to the birds and he will
surrender flesh like an ascetic."

This stanza reflects on human mortality and adaptability in death.

No matter how the body is disposed of—burial, cremation, or exposure—death transforms it into something else. The comparison to an ascetic suggests that, in death, all human struggle and suffering are surrendered.

Eighth Stanza

"Rain comes clamouring down,
But it's in flesh and flesh-tissue
that my destiny lies
and slowly corruption takes a hold."

The rain, which could symbolize cleansing, falls heavily, but the speaker acknowledges that human fate is tied to decay. "Corruption takes a hold" refers to both physical decomposition and the moral decay evident in violence.

Ninth Stanza

"Over from the mortuary
comes the corpse-drift.
(Death is so soft, put it ten days in a well
and it turns pulpy.)"

The odor of death lingers, emphasizing the inevitability of decomposition.

The grim observation about a body turning pulpy in water highlights the fleeting nature of human existence.

Tenth Stanza

"Rosewater, incense-sticks, flowers—

the relatives have done their bit."

Funeral rituals are performed, showing the contrast between human customs and the relentless process of decay.

"Done their bit" suggests a mechanical, detached approach to mourning.

Eleventh Stanza (Repetition of Fifth Stanza)

"The drift as it comes to us now

is aroma/stench/nausea

jostling each other!"

The repetition reinforces how death and its consequences remain ever-present.

Twelfth Stanza (Repetition of Sixth Stanza)

"In the morgue-verandah another queues up,

her nose sliced off, her lung punctured.

(It is a three-word story:

infidelity-irate husband.)"

The repetition of the murdered woman's story emphasizes the recurrence of such violence.

It shows that these tragedies are not isolated—they are part of an ongoing cycle.

Thirteenth Stanza

"Rain comes clamouring down,

a blind sheet of water.

Once the blur lifts

colours deepen, the hedge smiles,

the leaf loses its coat of dust,

the scum spills over from the pool."

The rain initially blinds but later clears the surroundings.

The world appears refreshed—nature flourishes, dirt is washed away, but...

Final Stanza

"I look around for a cleansed feeling,

the kind you experience

walking in a temple

after a river-bath.

I cannot find it.

I have misplaced it somewhere

in the caverns of my past."

Despite the rain's renewal, the speaker does not feel spiritually cleansed.

He yearns for the purity one feels after a holy bath, but that sense of peace is lost.

The "caverns of my past" suggest that past experiences, especially violent ones, have left a permanent stain on his perception.

Conclusion

Rumination is a powerful meditation on human suffering, exploring how violence, death, and decay shape our world. The speaker seeks meaning and renewal but finds only the unrelenting cycle of brutality. Daruwalla's unflinching realism forces us to confront the darker aspects of life, leaving a lingering sense of unease.

CHAPTER THIRTY-NINE

Rajgopalan Parthasarathy

Rajgopalan Parthasarathy was born in 1934 in Tiruparaitturai, Tamil Nadu. He spent his early years in the temple town of Srirangam before moving to Mumbai for his education. There, he studied at Don Bosco School and Siddharth College, earning a B.A. in English. He later completed his Master's in English from Bombay University. After teaching for some time, he went to England in 1963-64 as a British Council scholar at Leeds University.

Living in England, far from his homeland and mother tongue, deeply influenced his poetry. Although he had privately circulated some poems while in Bombay, his only major poetry collection is Rough Passage (1977), which he revised in 1980. His poems reflect the tension of cultural and linguistic displacement.

Parthasarathy was also an important editor and anthologist. His 1976 anthology, Ten Twentieth Century Indian Poets, published by Oxford University Press, became one of the most widely used collections of modern Indian English poetry. It played a major role in shaping the modernist movement in Indian English poetry. However, some critics argue that his selection of just ten poets and his strict focus on high-modernist poetry made the field narrow and exclusive.

As an editor at Oxford University Press, Parthasarathy maintained high editorial standards and helped publish some of the best-known Indian English modernist poetry. The year 1976 saw several important poetry books released under his supervision. After leaving the publishing house, he moved to the USA, where he completed a PhD at the University of Texas at Austin. He is now a professor at Skidmore College, USA.

Stanza-by-Stanza Explanation of Exile by R. Parthasarathy

This poem from Rough Passage reflects Parthasarathy's experience as an Indian living in England. It explores themes of cultural displacement, exile, identity, and the disillusionment with the West.

Stanza 1-2:

"Through holes in a wall, as it were,

lamps burned in the fog.

In a basement flat, conversation

filled the night, while Ravi Shankar,

cigarette stubs, empty bottles of stout

and crisps provided the necessary pauses."

Explanation:

The poet describes an evening in London, where he and others gather in a basement flat. The reference to "lamps burned in the fog" suggests the dim, hazy environment of the city, symbolizing confusion and alienation. The presence of Indian sitar maestro Ravi Shankar's music, cigarette stubs, and alcohol creates an atmosphere of nostalgia and escapism. This setting shows how expatriates try to hold onto their culture while assimilating into a foreign land.

Stanza 3-4:

"He had spent his youth whoring

after English gods.

There is something to be said for exile:

you learn roots are deep."

Explanation:

The poet reflects on his past, admitting that he once idolized English culture, seeking acceptance in the Western world. The phrase "whoring after English gods" suggests a sense of regret, as if he had betrayed his own culture in pursuit of another. However, exile has taught him the value of his Indian roots, making him realize how deeply connected he is to his homeland.

Stanza 5-6:

"That language is a tree, loses colour

under another sky.

The bark disappears with 'the snow

and branches become hoarse.'"

Explanation:

The poet uses a metaphor to describe how language struggles to survive in a foreign environment. Just as a tree changes when placed in a different climate, a language loses its essence when uprooted. The reference to "snow" suggests England's cold and unfamiliar atmosphere, where his native Tamil and Indian identity weaken, just like a tree losing its bark. The phrase "branches become hoarse" could symbolize how his voice and cultural expression feel strained in a foreign land.

Stanza 7-8:

"However, the most reassuring thing
about the past is that it happened.
Dressed in tweeds or grey flannel,
its suburban pockets
bursting with immigrants—"

Explanation:

The poet finds comfort in the fact that the past is unchangeable. The reference to "tweeds or grey flannel" suggests British clothing, indicating how the past (colonialism, migration) is now woven into England's identity. The line "bursting with immigrants" highlights how England, once the colonizer, is now filled with people from former colonies, reversing historical power dynamics.

Stanza 9-10:

"'Coloureds' is what they call us over
there—the city is no jewel, either:
lanes full of smoke and litter
with puddles of unwashed
English children."

Explanation:

The poet directly addresses racism in Britain, where immigrants are labeled as "coloureds." He challenges the romanticized view of England, showing that the city is not as grand as some might imagine. Instead, it is dirty and filled with neglected English children, highlighting social problems that contradict Britain's image of superiority.

Stanza 11-12:

"On New Year's Eve he heard an old man
at Trafalgar Square, 'It's no use trying to
change people. They'll be what they are.
An empire's last words are heard
on the hot sands of Africa."*

Explanation:

At Trafalgar Square, the poet overhears an old man expressing resignation about human nature, implying that people do not easily change. This could reflect Britain's inability to fully accept its immigrants or move beyond its colonial past. The mention of Africa suggests the crumbling of the British Empire, as nations like Kenya and Rhodesia (Zimbabwe) were fighting for independence around this time.

Stanza 13-14:

"The da Gamas, Clives, Dupleixs are back.

Victoria sleeps on her island

alone, an old hag,

shaking her invincible locks.'"

Explanation:

The poet references historical figures like Vasco da Gama (Portuguese explorer), Robert Clive (British colonial officer in India), and Joseph Dupleix (French colonial governor), suggesting that colonial attitudes still persist. Queen Victoria, once the symbol of British imperial power, is now depicted as an old and powerless figure, showing how the Empire has faded.

Stanza 15-16:

"Standing on Westminster Bridge, it

seemed the Thames had clogged

the chariot wheels of Boadicea to stone.

Under the shadow of poplars

the river divides the city from the night."

Explanation:

Westminster Bridge symbolizes the heart of London, and the poet imagines the Thames turning the wheels of Boadicea's chariot into stone. Boadicea, a Celtic queen who fought against Roman rule, represents resistance. This could symbolize how history weighs down Britain, making it rigid and unchanging. The river acts as a boundary between the bright, modern city and the darkness of its colonial past.

Stanza 17-18:

"The noises reappear,

of early trains, the milkman,

and the events of the day become

vocal in the newsboy."*

Explanation:

As morning arrives, the familiar sounds of London return—trains, milk delivery, and newspaper vendors shouting headlines. This suggests the continuation of daily life, indifferent to personal struggles or historical burdens.

Stanza 19-20:

"A grey sky oppresses the eyes:

porters, rickshaw-pullers, barbers, hawkers,
fortune-tellers, loungers compose the scene.
Above them towers the bridge,
a pale diamond in the water."*
Explanation:
The "grey sky" continues the theme of oppression and bleakness. The poet shifts the setting to India, describing workers and street vendors, emphasizing the vibrancy of everyday life. The bridge, possibly Howrah Bridge in Kolkata, is seen as a "pale diamond," suggesting both its importance and a sense of detachment, as if the poet still feels a gap between himself and his homeland.

Stanza 21-22:
"Trees, big with shade, squat in the maidan
as I walk, my tongue hunchbacked
with words, towards Jadavpur
to your arms."*
Explanation:
The poet now moves towards a more personal moment, possibly returning to a lover in Jadavpur (a locality in Kolkata). The phrase "tongue hunchbacked with words" suggests a struggle with language, possibly due to years of speaking English more than Tamil. This highlights the impact of exile on personal identity.

Stanza 23-24:
"You smell of gin
and cigarette ash. Your breasts,
sharp with desire, hurt my fingers."
Explanation:
The poet describes an intimate reunion, filled with longing and desire. However, the imagery of gin and cigarette ash also suggests exhaustion, world-weariness, or the influence of Western habits.

Stanza 25-26:
"Feelings beggar description,
shiver in dark alleys of the mind,
hungry and alone. Nothing can
really be dispensed with. The heart
needs all."
Explanation:

The poem ends on an emotional note, expressing the depth of feelings that cannot be easily described. The poet acknowledges that exile, love, pain, and longing are all part of him—none can be discarded. His identity is shaped by all these experiences, no matter how conflicting they seem.

Homecoming

In Homecoming, R. Parthasarathy reflects on feelings of exhaustion, failure, and disillusionment. The poem captures the struggles of an individual who feels alienated from himself, overwhelmed by expectations, and uncertain about life.

I am no longer myself as I watch
the evening blur the traffic
to a pair of obese headlights.
I return home, tried,
my face pressed against the window
of expectation . I climb the steps
to my f lat, only to trip over the mat
Outside the door. The key
goes to sleep in my palm.
I fear I have bungled again.
That last refinement of speech
terrifies me. The balloon.
Of poetry has grown red in the face
with repeated blowing. For scriptures
I, therefore, recommend
the humble newspaper: I find
My prayers occasionally answered there.
I shall, perhaps, go on.
Like this, unmindful of day
melting into the night.
My heart I have turned inside out.
Hereafter, I should be content,
I think, to go through life
with the small change of uncertainties.

Stanza 1:

"I am no longer myself as I watch the evening
blur the traffic to a pair of obese headlights."

Explanation:

The poem begins with a sense of detachment. The poet states that he is "no longer himself," suggesting that he feels lost or disconnected. The evening blurs the traffic, reducing it to just two "obese headlights," symbolizing how the outside world appears vague and overwhelming, mirroring his own blurred sense of identity.

Stanza 2:

"I return home, tired, my face pressed against

the window of expectation."

Explanation:

The speaker returns home feeling exhausted, both physically and emotionally. His face is "pressed against the window of expectation," indicating that he is burdened by societal or personal pressures. This could refer to the expectations placed upon him as a poet, as an individual, or as an expatriate who struggles to reconcile different aspects of his identity.

Stanza 3:

"I climb the steps to my flat, only to trip

over the mat outside the door."

Explanation:

This seemingly simple act of tripping over the mat symbolizes repeated failure or mistakes. The poet's struggle is not just mental but also reflected in his everyday actions, reinforcing his sense of inadequacy and frustration.

Stanza 4:

"The key goes to sleep in my palm.

I fear I have bungled again."

Explanation:

The poet hesitates while holding the key, as if even the simple task of unlocking his door feels overwhelming. The phrase "bungled again" suggests a recurring sense of failure, reinforcing his lack of confidence and inner turmoil.

Stanza 5:

"That last refinement of speech terrifies me.

The balloon of poetry has grown red in the face

with repeated blowing."

Explanation:

Here, the poet expresses his frustration with poetry itself. The phrase "refinement of speech" refers to the pressure to perfect his language, but it intimidates him. He compares poetry to a balloon that has been blown up too much—overinflated and exhausted. This could suggest his frustration with literary expectations, writer's block, or a loss of inspiration.

Stanza 6:

"For scriptures I, therefore, recommend

the humble newspaper:

I find my prayers occasionally answered there."

Explanation:

Instead of looking for wisdom in religious texts, the poet turns to something as ordinary as a newspaper. This could reflect a shift towards practicality—seeking truth in everyday life rather than in grand philosophical or poetic ideals. The mention of "prayers occasionally answered" might hint at small moments of hope or connection found in mundane realities.

Stanza 7:

"I shall, perhaps, go on.

Like this, unmindful of day melting into the night."

Explanation:

The poet resigns himself to continuing with life, even in its monotonous, uncertain state. The transition from day to night symbolizes the passing of time, which he accepts without resistance, indicating a sense of surrender or quiet endurance.

Stanza 8:

"My heart I have turned inside out.

Hereafter, I should be content, I think,

to go through life with the small change of uncertainties."

Explanation:

The poet reveals that he has already exposed his emotions and inner struggles—perhaps through poetry or personal reflection. Now, he decides to accept life as it is, with its "small change of uncertainties." This suggests a shift from striving for perfection or certainty to a state of acceptance, where he learns to live with doubt and imperfection.

Overall Analysis:

Homecoming is a deeply introspective poem about self-doubt, exhaustion, and the struggle for meaning. The poet reflects on his failures, his relationship with poetry, and the uncertainties of life. However, by the end, he seems to accept these struggles rather than resist them. The poem captures the emotional weight of returning home—not just physically, but metaphorically, as the poet seeks to reconcile his inner conflicts.

Block 8 - Tara

Scan the QR code to watch video

CHAPTER FORTY

About Mahesh Dattani: Career and Works

Mahesh Dattani was born on August 7, 1958 in Bangalore, Karnataka. He was educated at Baldwin's Boys High School followed by St. Joseph's College, Bangalore. After graduation, he briefly worked as a copywriter for an advertising firm. In 1986, his first play, "Where There is a Will" surfaced. After the resounding success of his first play, Dattani began to concentrate on his writing and came up with an impressive oeuvre comprising "Dance Like a Man" (1989), "Tara" (1990), "Bravely Fought the Queen" (1991), "Final Solutions" (1993), "On a Muggy Night in Mumbai" (1998),"Thirty Days in September" (2001) and others. Since 1995, he has concentrated exclusively on theatre. He is the only English playwright to be awarded the Sahitya Akademi Award. He got this award in 1998. He also writes plays for BBC Radio and he was also one of the 21 playwrights chosen by BBC to write plays to commemorate Chaucer's 600th anniversary in 2000.

Dattani's "Dance Like a Man" was adapted into a film in 2003 and won the award for Best Picture in English at the National Panorama. Mahesh Dattani himself directed Mango Soufflé in 2002. He also wrote and directed Morning Raga in 2004. Starring Shabana Azmi, this movie is about a Carnatic singer whose life has been traumatized by the loss of her son and her best friend in an accident. It earned Dattani an award for Best Artistic Contribution at the Cairo Film Festival.

CHAPTER FORTY-ONE

Overview of "TARA"

About Story :

The play starts with Chandan, now called Dan, feverishly typing a play "Twinke Tara: a Play in Two Acts", about his long deceased sister Tara in his London bedsitter. He talks about his memories and a fanatic urge to record them to commemorate his twin sister, and how he finds himself unable to find words to write.

The play begins with the story of Tara's parents, Bharti and Mr. Patel, who had a love marriage. Mr. Patel comes from a Gujarati family that opposed his relationship with Bharti, but he married her anyway, going against his family's wishes. After the marriage, Mr. Patel moved into Bharti's family home and became financially dependent on her father, a powerful politician in Karnataka.

When Bharti became pregnant, she gave birth to conjoined twins, Tara and Chandan, who were joined at the lower body and shared three legs instead of four. Tara had two legs, while Chandan had one. However, Bharti's husband and father decided to give Chandan two legs because he was a boy, even though the middle leg was better suited to Tara's body. They bribed Dr. Thakkar, the surgeon, to perform the surgery against his better judgment. As a result, Chandan lost the extra leg soon after the surgery because his body couldn't accept it, and Tara became very weak, needing help for even the simplest tasks.

Tara eventually died after undergoing many operations and surgeries. Chandan, feeling guilty about his sister's death, moved to London, changed his name to Dan, and became a writer. Six years later, he decided to write a story about his sister called "Twinkling Tara" to share her life and their family's story.

The story within "Twinkling Tara" begins in Mumbai, with young Chandan and Tara playing cards. Tara, who is very smart, easily beats her brother. Chandan playfully teases her, and their mother, Bharti, enters after finishing her prayers. Seeing that Tara hasn't finished her milk, Bharti lovingly feeds her. Mr. Patel then asks Chandan to join him at the office, but Chandan refuses, suggesting that Tara should go instead because she is very intelligent and could help with the business. Mr. Patel scolds Chandan but agrees to bring Tara along when Chandan insists.

Later, a neighbor named Roopa comes over to visit. She often makes fun of Tara and Chandan, but Bharti asks her to be friends with Tara, even offering a bribe. Roopa agrees to the arrangement.

One day, Mr. Patel finds Chandan doing some sewing work with his mother, which angers him because he believes it's a "woman's job." He scolds both Chandan and Bharti. Tara enters, and Mr. Patel tells her that Chandan will soon be going abroad for his education. Bharti asks about Tara's future, and an argument ensues between Bharti and Mr. Patel. During the argument, Tara suddenly faints and is rushed to the hospital, where it's discovered that she has a serious kidney problem. Bharti decides to donate her kidney to save Tara's life, but after the operation, Bharti has a nervous breakdown and is hospitalized. When Tara returns home, Mr. Patel tells her about her mother's condition, but he refuses to let Tara visit her, which makes Tara very sad.

Frustrated, Tara decides to stop going to physiotherapy and refuses to go to college. Chandan supports her decision by also refusing to attend college without his sister. One day, while watching a movie with Roopa and Chandan, they discuss a character who had to choose between saving her son or daughter. Roopa taunts Tara and Chandan by saying that she would sacrifice her daughter, just like the Patels did. Tara becomes angry and tells Roopa to leave.

Later, Tara questions why her parents are spending so much money on her treatment, expressing that all she wants is to see her mother. She eventually skips physiotherapy to visit her mother at the hospital, where her father reveals the truth about how she and Chandan were born and how they forced the doctor to give Chandan her leg. Meanwhile, Dan receives a call from his father, informing him that his mother has passed away.

CHAPTER FORTY-TWO

Questions & Answers

Question and Answer

Q.1) What are the major themes of Tara ? Discuss what you think is the most important of them.

Ans: Introduction: Tara is a play written by Mahesh Dattani. Mahesh Dattani is an Indian playwright and writer, born in August 1958. He has significantly contributed to Indian English theatre with his unique and original vision. Dattani made history by becoming the first Indian playwright in English to receive the prestigious Sahitya Akademi Award for his collection Final Solutions and Other Plays. Alyque Padamsee, a renowned theatre personality, has praised Dattani for his contributions. Mahesh Dattani's Tara was written in the year of 1990. It was first performed as Twinkle Tara in Bangalore in 1990 by Playpen Performing Arts Group. Later, it was subsequently performed as Tara. It is the story about India's social problem of gender discrimination through the central character of Tara. Mahesh Dattani was awarded Sahitya Kala Award for Tara in 2000.

Main Content: Mahesh Dattani's plays address social and contemporary issues that are often overlooked in our society. He uses various forms of drama to capture the true depth and vibrancy of human experience. Dattani views theatre as a way to highlight the struggles of marginalized groups in society. His plays bring to light the problems and suppressed emotions of those who are often unheard, such as homosexuals, HIV victims, eunuchs, and people with physical disabilities. These bold and unconventional themes set him apart from traditional Indian playwrights.

Gender Discrimination

Mahesh Dattani's plays are celebrated for their social realism, especially in their portrayal of uncomfortable truths, including the persistent belief that women should be subordinate to men. While many Indian novelists have explored female subordination, Dattani was one of the first playwrights to tackle this issue seriously, particularly in his plays "Tara" and "Bravely Fought the Queen." These works highlight that, despite claims of modernity and liberalization, women in India are still often considered secondary.

In "Tara," the injustice comes from the victim's own mother, who favors a healthy male child at the expense of the female conjoined twin. This decision adds depth to the play by showing that it is not just men who perpetuate gender discrimination, but women under the influence of patriarchal values who continue the cycle of injustice. In "Bravely Fought the Queen," the women are largely confined to their homes, where they care for their aging mother-in-law, Baa, and their husbands. The play reveals the cruelty Baa suffered at the hands of her husband and suggests how the two women are trapped by societal expectations. The recurring image of the bonsai symbolizes the stunted condition of the women in the household.

However, Dattani does not treat gender discrimination one-sidedly. In "Dance Like a Man," he explores how societal ideas of "masculinity" restrict men's options, a concept enforced by both men and women in society.

The patriarchy takes the primary theme:
More than the gender prejudice the patriarchy takes the primary theme. It determines the real power - play in the family or the society at large. Both Chandan and Tara are born Siamese twins. Dr. Thakkar separates the two infants and as an expert knows that the third leg with Tara's blood could survive with Tara and so Tara could lead a normal life. But Chandan; the male child could survive with only with natural disability. It is not necessary for the doctor, as a specialist to seek the advice of Bharati or her politically powerful father to perform the operation. But he is bribed by Bharati and her influential father to give the leg to the male - child. The gender prejudice forces a doctor to perform an unethical operation to give the leg to the male child. The result is disastrous for all in the family. Both the children grow up as invalids, and cause concern to the parents and society. The relation between Bharati and Patel suffer. The guilty conscience makes Bharati abnormal and she tries to cover her guilt by her over - zealousness for Tara's well-being. Roopa represents the social angle.

Family Dynamics and Secrets
Tara explores the complexities of family dynamics, particularly the roles of parents in shaping their children's lives. The play uncovers deep family secrets, such as the truth about the twins' surgery, which reveal the

underlying tensions and moral compromises within the family. These secrets contribute to the characters' internal conflicts and drive the narrative towards its tragic conclusion.

Guilt and Redemption

Guilt is a significant theme in Tara, especially for Chandan, who carries the burden of his sister's suffering and eventual death. His decision to change his name to Dan and move to London reflects his attempt to escape this guilt. However, his writing of "Twinkling Tara" suggests a desire for redemption, as he tries to come to terms with the past and honor his sister's memory.

The Role of Fate and Choice

Tara examines the tension between fate and choice, particularly in the decisions made by the twins' parents regarding their surgery. While the parents' choice to prioritize Chandan's life over Tara's is a deliberate act, the consequences of that choice are portrayed as inevitable, leading to questions about the role of fate in shaping human lives.

The Burden of Expectations

The play also explores the theme of societal and familial expectations, particularly how these expectations can constrain and define individuals' lives. Both Tara and Chandan are burdened by the expectations placed on them by their parents and society, leading to feelings of inadequacy and frustration.

Conclusion:

Through these themes, Tara offers a powerful critique of societal norms and challenges the audience to reflect on issues of gender, identity, and the impact of family decisions on individual lives.

Q.2 Discuss the use of English in Dattani's play Tara.

Ans: Introduction: "for this section refer answer 1 of this chapter"

Main Content: Mahesh Dattani is a well known craftsman of contemporary Indian English Drama. English is a link language or contact language. At national and international level, it unites larger sections of society or civilization. About the use of English, he explains, "You've got to be true to your expressions. English is for me a sort of given. It's my language as it is to a lot of Indians here and abroad". Dattani intends to develop theatre which can be understood and enjoyed by multilingual community of India and abroad. The most significant contribution of Dattani is perhaps his use of language. Dattani uses in his plays the kind of English as spoken by people in India. Mahesh Dattani's use of English in his play Tara plays a crucial role in shaping the narrative, character dynamics, and thematic exploration.

Dattani defends using English the way people in India speak it but also makes another important point. He says that his characters "would love to speak in Gujarati," and his challenge as a writer is to show their Gujarati culture in English without changing it. His play Where There's a Will is like a Gujarati play, but it's written in English and set in Bangalore. Dattani's characters speak the kind of English that most middle-class Indians do, and they would naturally speak it in the same situations we would. Dattani's challenge is to ensure the audience doesn't feel that using English limits the expression of his characters. He aims to achieve the same authenticity, depth, and subtlety as a Gujarati playwright writing about the middle class.

Here's how he incorporates English:

Realistic Dialogue: The English spoken in Tara mirrors the way many middle-class Indians speak English in real life. It captures the nuances and inflections of Indian English, making the characters' speech feel authentic and relatable.

Cultural Context: Dattani uses English to convey the cultural identity of the characters. By using English in a way that reflects their everyday speech, he highlights the characters' backgrounds and the socio-economic context they come from.

Character Development: The way characters speak English helps in developing their personalities and social status. For instance, the use of English can indicate their level of education, social class, and their aspirations.

Play's Setting: The play is set in an Indian context, and the use of English is appropriate for this setting. It helps in depicting the social dynamics and family interactions within the context of contemporary Indian society.

Language and Power: Dattani also explores the theme of language as a tool of power and identity. In Tara, English serves as a medium through which characters navigate their personal and social conflicts, highlighting the complexities of language in their lives.

Overall, Dattani's use of English in Tara is both functional and symbolic, reflecting the real-world use of the language in Indian society and contributing to the play's thematic depth.

Q.3) How do Dattani's techniques help to highlight his thematic concerns?

Or

Discuss the use of stage levels and lighting by Dattani in Tara.

Ans: Introduction: "for this section refer answer 1 of this chapter"

Main Content: In Tara, Dattani skillfully uses multi-level sets, flashbacks, voiceovers, and thoughts to enhance the play. He focuses on the family unit and the home as the main setting, dividing it into different parts or levels. Just as modern life and relationships are fragmented, Dattani's stage design reflects this fragmentation. The different stage levels reveal the complicated mindsets of urban people and the challenges of living in a mechanical world.

The lowest level represents the Patel family's house and takes up most of the stage. The next level is the only realistic one, showing Dan's small apartment in a London suburb. At the highest level, Dr. Thakkar is seen seated in a chair throughout the play.

Dan plays a tri role; he is the narrator organizer of action and character in the play. Dattani through Dan brilliantly uses the flashback technique; there is proper blending of past and present. The role of dan can be compared on a level to Harry of The Family Reunion by T S Eliot. Both are suffering from guilt consciousness and are expiating in their own way.

Dattani through his artistic measures brings forward and deals with various issues such as the 'invisible issue of gender discrimination and subaltern issue in Tara. Dattani brings an authorial note through his character Dan by voiceover technique. Voice-over is used to create the effect of storytelling by character or narrator. Sometimes it's also used to create ironic counterpoint.

Another innovation which makes Dattani's plays unique is the use of language especially regional language such as Gujarati. Roopa the girl next door speaks Gujarati words frequently. She says "Prema! Prema-a (no response) Prema-a! Oh, Hello Aunty. (in broken Gujarati) kemchcho? majhjha ma...?"

The title Tara is emblematic in itself as it suggests that a girl child cannot shine because she was not allowed to twinkle in an Indian society. The hypocrisy of the society is brought out by the dramatist where a male child is preferred over female

Dattani transitions between different levels of the stage with incredible speed using lighting and music. At the beginning of the play, a spotlight focuses on Dan. As he starts to remember the past, soft music begins, and another spotlight lights up a different stage level where Tara and Chandan enter. The lights then fade into the Patel's living room, shifting the action there. When Dr. Thakkar is introduced, a spotlight focuses on him while Dan fades into darkness, but Dan continues to speak from his level as the interviewer. This clever use of lighting allows the action to move smoothly between different levels without any pauses for scene changes. This technique creates a sense of continuous action throughout the play, and you can see how Dattani skillfully maintains this throughout the performance.

Dattani uses music as well to both create a certain mood as well as to make a point about certain characters.

Or

Ans: In Tara, Mahesh Dattani employs several narrative techniques that contribute to the play's depth and complexity. These techniques include:

1. Multi-Level Stage Design

Dattani uses a multi-level stage to physically separate different aspects of the narrative. Each level represents different locations and psychological spaces:

The lowest level is the Patel household, where most of the family interactions take place.

The middle level represents Dan's small apartment in London, where he reflects on the past and serves as the narrator of the story.

The highest level features Dr. Thakkar, who is seated on a chair throughout the play, symbolizing his distance from the central family drama and his clinical detachment.

This physical separation of spaces reflects the fragmented nature of the characters' lives and their relationships, underscoring the theme of divided identities.

2. Flashbacks

The play frequently shifts between the present and the past, using flashbacks to reveal key events and relationships. These flashbacks help the audience understand the backstory and the reasons behind the characters' current behavior. They are often triggered by Dan's memories, making the audience experience the past as he does.

3. Voiceover and Thought Technique

Dattani uses voiceovers to give the audience access to the inner thoughts and emotions of the characters, particularly Dan. This technique allows the audience to hear what the characters are thinking, even when they are not speaking aloud, adding depth to their personalities and making their internal conflicts more apparent.

4. Lighting and Music

Lighting and music are essential narrative tools in Tara. Dattani uses lighting to transition smoothly between different levels of the stage and different time periods. For example, a spotlight might pick up a character on one level while another fades into darkness, indicating a shift in focus or time. Music is used to underscore the emotional tone of a scene, often signaling a transition from the present to a flashback.

5. Narration by Dan

Dan serves as the narrator of the play, guiding the audience through the story. As an adult looking back on his childhood, Dan's narration is colored by his memories and emotions, making him both a character in the story and an observer of it. His role as narrator also adds a layer of introspection to the play, as the audience sees events from his perspective, which may be biased or incomplete.

6. Fragmented Structure

The structure of the play is non-linear, with scenes from the past and present interwoven. This fragmented approach mirrors the characters' fractured lives and the divided nature of their identities. It also reflects the theme of duality that runs throughout the play, particularly in the lives of the twin siblings, Tara and Chandan.

7. Symbolism

The play is rich in symbolism, much of which is conveyed through the narrative techniques mentioned above. For example, the use of different stage levels symbolizes the various social, psychological, and emotional layers of the characters' lives. The fragmented narrative structure symbolizes the fractured identities and relationships within the family.

8. Use of Dialogue

Dattani's dialogue is realistic and reflective of middle-class Indian life, particularly in the way it captures the bilingual nature of the characters' speech. The use of English mixed with regional languages (like Gujarati) adds authenticity and helps to convey the characters' cultural identities.

Conclusion:

In Tara, these narrative techniques work together to create a rich, layered exploration of identity, family dynamics, and the impact of societal expectations. They allow Dattani to tell a complex story in a way that is both engaging and thought-provoking, making Tara a powerful example of modern Indian theater.

Q.4) Discuss Dattani's treatment of gender in the play Tara.
Or

What according to you, are the main themes of Tara ?

Ans: Introduction: "for this section refer answer 1 of this chapter"

Main Content: In Tara, Mahesh Dattani explores the theme of gender through a sharp critique of how society treats boys and girls differently, especially within a family setting. His treatment of gender in the play sheds light on the deep-seated patriarchal attitudes that shape the lives and identities of the characters.

Tara is about Siamese twins, Tara and Chandan, who were joined at the hip and had three legs. After surgery, one of them could have two legs. The legs were more suited for Tara because her body supplied most of the blood to them, but they were given to Chandan. However, one of the legs eventually had to be removed because it could not survive. The main idea of the play is the emotional distance that grows between the twins after their mother and grandfather interfere with their surgery to favor the boy, Chandan, over the girl, Tara.

It is often seen that boys are given more chances to survive than girls. When a choice must be made between a boy and a girl, the boy is usually preferred. Society has always given more importance and power to men over women. In Tara, Dattani skillfully shows how patriarchal attitudes, strict behavior, and social norms control and limit girls. Tara would have had a better chance of surviving with two legs, but since there was no male heir in the family, the patriarchal system chose to favor Chandan, the boy, over Tara, the girl.

Santwana Halder explains: "This is a society where an influential politician makes a corrupt deal with a well-known doctor, who forgets all about professional ethics for personal gain. It is also a society where girl children are given equal opportunities, such as the same education and medical care as boys, but the girl is never seen as the true heir of the family. Planning for her future is seen as unnecessary."

Dattani is an experienced and expert dramatist to mirror us to see the deep-rooted face of gender discrimination in society that is very difficult to shrug off. Rome cannot make it in one day; therefore, it is not easy to crack the shackles of discrimination against girls based on gender where they are born, live, and die. It is not only the notion of contemporary society but it has existed since ancient. Gender discrimination is the notion that men do but women have an equal part in this- women also discriminate women from men.

The play illustrates how women's lives and choices are controlled by patriarchal norms. Tara, despite being strong and capable, is denied the chance to thrive because of societal expectations that place men above women. Even Bharati, Tara's mother, who seems to love her daughter, plays a role in this injustice by supporting the decision to favor Chandan. This shows how deeply ingrained patriarchal values can be, even among women.

Bharati's character is complex because she is both a victim and a participant in the patriarchal system. Although she tries to care for Tara and expresses guilt over the surgery, she is complicit in the decision to prioritize Chandan's future. Her actions reflect how women, even when they recognize the injustice, often uphold the system that oppresses them.

Dattani's portrayal of Tara's story is a strong feminist critique of the gender inequalities in Indian society. The play challenges the notion that men are inherently more valuable than women and questions the societal structures that reinforce this belief. Dattani exposes the hypocrisy of a society that claims The play also explores the power dynamics within the family and society at large. The men in the family, especially the grandfather, wield significant influence over critical decisions, while the women, including Tara, have little control over their own lives. This power imbalance is a reflection of the broader patriarchal system that governs societal interactions.to care for both genders equally while systematically favoring boys.

Chandan's guilt over the surgery and his preferential treatment shows that gender discrimination affects not only the victims but also those who benefit from it. As he grows older, Chandan realizes the unfairness of the situation and struggles with the burden of having been given opportunities at Tara's expense. This emotional conflict adds depth to the play's exploration of gender. Tara's awareness of the injustice she faces creates emotional pain and bitterness. She knows that her life could have been different if she were a boy, and this knowledge leads to a sense of helplessness and anger. Dattani uses Tara's emotional journey to show the psychological toll that gender discrimination takes on women.

Conclusion: Dattani's Tara offers a poignant critique of gender discrimination and the patriarchy that governs society. Through Tara's story, Dattani explores the emotional, psychological, and societal impact of gender bias, highlighting how deeply it affects both men and women. The play challenges societal norms and calls for a reevaluation of how gender is viewed and valued.

Q.5) How important is family in Mahesh Dattani's play Tara? Explain.

Ans: Introduction: "for this section refer answer 1 of this chapter"

Main Content: In Mahesh Dattani's play Tara, the theme of family is central to the narrative. The family not only provides the setting for the story but also plays a critical role in shaping the lives and identities of the characters. The dynamics within the family reveal deep-seated issues of gender bias, emotional manipulation, and the burden of societal expectations. Here's an exploration of how important family is in Tara:

1. Family as the Source of Conflict

Medical Decision Based on Gender: The Patel family's decision to prioritize Chandan's future over Tara's is the primary conflict in the play. The family's choice to give Chandan the legs, even though they biologically belonged to Tara, reflects their deep-rooted preference for the male child. This decision, driven by the parents and influenced by societal pressures, becomes the source of both physical and emotional pain for Tara. It shows how family decisions can profoundly impact the lives of children, especially when influenced by gender discrimination.

Patriarchal Influence: The influence of Tara's grandfather, a powerful figure in the family, is another important aspect. His control over the decision-making process highlights the patriarchal values that govern the family. The family's actions are not just personal but reflect broader societal norms that favor boys over girls. The family becomes a microcosm of the larger patriarchal society, where gender dictates the treatment of children.

2. Family as a Site of Emotional Struggles

Parental Guilt and Manipulation: The emotional struggles of the parents, particularly Bharati (the mother), play a crucial role in the story. Bharati's guilt over the decision to prioritize Chandan over Tara leads her to overcompensate in her relationship with Tara. She becomes overprotective and tries to make up for the wrong done to Tara by giving her excessive attention, even to the point of trying to donate her kidney to Tara. Bharati's actions, while stemming from guilt, create further emotional complications within the family.

Father's Emotional Distance: Mr. Patel, the father, represents the more detached, pragmatic side of the family. He appears distant and emotionally unavailable, especially to Tara. His cold demeanor and refusal to openly acknowledge the injustice done to Tara reveal the lack of emotional support in the family. This emotional distance contributes to the overall dysfunction within the household.

3. Family as a Reflection of Social Norms

Gender Roles within the Family: The family dynamics in Tara reflect the traditional gender roles prevalent in Indian society. Chandan, as the male child, is automatically given more importance, even when it comes at the expense of Tara's well-being. This preference for the boy reflects the societal expectation that boys will carry on the family name and legacy, while girls are seen as less important.

Impact on Tara's Identity: Tara's sense of self and identity is shaped by her family's actions. She is constantly aware that she was denied the chance to live a full life because her family prioritized her brother. This realization deeply affects Tara's emotional well-being and self-worth, leading her to question her value in the family and society. The family's treatment of Tara, and the underlying gender bias, serves as a commentary on how families can reinforce societal norms that limit the potential of girls.

4. Family and Emotional Manipulation

Bharati's Relationship with Tara: Bharati's guilt-driven relationship with Tara is complex. While she tries to show love and care for Tara, her actions are often manipulative. Her desire to donate her kidney to Tara can be seen as a way to ease her own guilt rather than a genuine act of love. This manipulation creates emotional tension between mother and daughter, revealing how family relationships can be complicated by past wrongs and unresolved guilt.

Chandan's Guilt and Distance: Chandan, the favored child, is also emotionally affected by the family dynamics. He carries the burden of guilt for having been given the legs that were meant for Tara. This guilt causes him to distance himself from Tara and the family, which leads to his own emotional struggles. The family's decisions not only affect Tara but also create emotional conflict for Chandan.

5. The Family as a Source of Tragedy

Tara's Tragic Fate: The family's decisions ultimately lead to Tara's tragic fate. Her life is cut short, not just physically but emotionally, as she is denied opportunities that could have allowed her to thrive. The family, particularly her mother and grandfather, are responsible for this tragedy, making the family a central force in shaping the outcome of Tara's life.

Breakdown of Relationships: The family's relationships break down over the course of the play. Bharati's mental instability, Mr. Patel's emotional distance, and Chandan's guilt all contribute to the disintegration of the family unit. The family, which should be a source of support and love, becomes a place of emotional turmoil and tragedy.

6. The Family as a Mirror of Society

Social Expectations and Family Dynamics: Dattani uses the family to mirror the broader societal expectations that prioritize boys over girls. The Patel family's decision to favor Chandan reflects the values of the patriarchal society they live in. The family's actions are not isolated but are part of a larger social system that places higher value on men. Dattani critiques this system by showing how it plays out within the family, leading to the emotional and physical suffering of Tara.

Cultural and Social Pressures: The family in Tara is also shaped by cultural and social pressures. The desire to have a male heir, the influence of the grandfather, and the need to conform to societal expectations all play a role in the decisions the family makes. The family becomes a battleground where personal desires conflict with societal norms, and ultimately, the societal pressures win, leading to Tara's marginalization.

7. Chandan's Attempt to Reconcile with the Family History

Writing as a Means of Redemption: In the play, an older Chandan tries to write Tara's story as a way of dealing with his guilt and the family's history. His attempt to give voice to Tara's suffering is a reflection of his need to come to terms with the family's past. However, his inability to finish the story suggests that the emotional wounds caused by the family's decisions are too deep to fully heal.

Conclusion: Family is a crucial element in Dattani's Tara. It is the source of both the physical and emotional conflict in the play, driving the narrative and shaping the characters' identities. The family's choices, influenced by gender bias and societal expectations, lead to the tragic outcome of Tara's life. Through the family, Dattani explores the themes of gender discrimination, emotional manipulation, and the lasting impact of patriarchal values on both men and women. The family in Tara reflects the larger social structures that perpetuate inequality, making it a powerful force in the play's critique of society.

Q.6) Discuss Mahesh Dattani's Tara as a play with social purpose.

Or

Discuss Mahesh Dattani's play Tara as a social tragedy.

Ans: Introduction: "for this section refer answer 1 of this chapter"

Main Content:

Mahesh Dattani's play Tara can be seen as a social tragedy because it highlights the devastating effects of societal norms and prejudices on individuals, particularly in the context of gender discrimination. The tragedy in Tara is not only personal but also social, as it reflects the broader inequalities and injustices that exist in patriarchal societies. Dattani uses the story of conjoined twins, Tara and Chandan, to expose how deeply ingrained societal biases, particularly against women, can lead to emotional and physical suffering. Below are key aspects that explain why Tara can be considered a social tragedy:

1. Gender Discrimination as the Root of Tragedy

Preference for Boys Over Girls: The central tragedy in Tara stems from the societal preference for boys over girls. This bias is reflected in the family's decision to give the second leg to Chandan, even though biologically, Tara had a better chance of survival with both legs. This decision, motivated by the family's and society's patriarchal values, results in Tara being physically and emotionally disadvantaged. The tragedy lies in the fact that Tara's potential is sacrificed simply because she is a girl, exposing how gender discrimination can have tragic consequences on individual lives.

Missed Opportunities for Tara: Throughout the play, Tara is portrayed as a bright and capable individual who could have thrived if given the same opportunities as her brother. However, societal expectations dictate that the boy's future is more important, and this leads to Tara being denied a full life. This missed opportunity for Tara becomes a key element of the tragedy, as the audience witnesses how unfair societal norms limit her potential and lead to her untimely death.

2. Family as the Vehicle of Social Prejudices

Family's Role in Perpetuating Patriarchal Values: The Patel family, particularly Tara's mother Bharati and grandfather, plays a significant role in perpetuating the gender biases that ultimately lead to the tragic outcome. Bharati's decision to favor Chandan over Tara is influenced by societal pressures to prioritize the male child, even though she later feels immense guilt for her actions. The family becomes a reflection of the larger patriarchal society, where boys are seen as the future and girls are sidelined. This tragic flaw in the family's thinking leads to the emotional and physical destruction of Tara.

Emotional Manipulation and Guilt: The family dynamics in Tara are marked by guilt and emotional manipulation, especially between Bharati and Tara. Bharati's overprotectiveness and guilt-driven behavior stem from her role in the surgery decision, but her attempts to make amends only create more tension. The family's inability to confront their guilt and address the injustice they inflicted on Tara becomes another tragic element, as it prevents any form of healing or redemption.

3. Social Critique of Patriarchy

Patriarchal Control over Women's Lives: Tara is a powerful critique of how patriarchal societies control and limit women's lives. Tara's tragic fate is not just the result of family decisions but a reflection of the broader societal belief that men are more valuable than women. Dattani uses Tara's story to critique the ways in which women are systematically denied opportunities and agency. The tragedy in the play is not just personal but social, as it exposes how the entire system works to oppress and marginalize women.

Symbolism of the Legs: The decision to give Chandan the legs, which rightfully belonged to Tara, becomes a symbol of how women are deprived of their rights and opportunities in a patriarchal society. The legs, in this sense, represent Tara's potential and her future, which is taken away from her simply because she is a girl. This symbolic act of injustice is at the heart of the social tragedy in the play.

4. Tara's Struggle for Identity and Acceptance

Tara's Awareness of Injustice: A key tragic element in the play is Tara's awareness of the unfair treatment she receives because of her gender. She knows that she was denied the chance to live a full life because of societal and familial biases, and this knowledge creates deep emotional pain and resentment. Tara's struggle to accept her identity as a girl in a society that undervalues her becomes a central theme in the play, adding to the sense of tragedy.

Chandan's Guilt and Denial: Chandan, who benefits from the family's decision, also experiences guilt and emotional turmoil. His inability to fully accept the injustice done to Tara and his attempts to distance himself from the family's history reflect the emotional cost of gender discrimination on both men and women. Chandan's guilt and denial contribute to the tragic tone of the play, as he too becomes a victim of the same social system that favored him over his sister.

5. Tragic Ending and Emotional Consequences

Tara's Death: The play ends with the tragic death of Tara, whose life was cut short by both the physical consequences of the surgery and the emotional toll of being treated as less important than her brother. Tara's death is the culmination of the societal and familial failures to recognize her worth as an individual. It is a powerful reminder of how deeply ingrained social norms can lead to the destruction of lives, particularly those of women.

Emotional Fallout for the Family: The tragedy in Tara extends beyond Tara's death to the emotional fallout experienced by the entire family. Bharati's mental breakdown, Chandan's guilt, and Mr. Patel's emotional distance all contribute to the sense of loss and devastation that permeates the play. The family's inability to come to terms with the decisions they made, and the resulting consequences, adds to the overall sense of tragedy.

6. Critique of Medical and Professional Ethics

Corruption in the Medical Profession: The play also touches on the corruption in the medical profession, as the doctor involved in Tara and Chandan's surgery agrees to perform the operation in a way that favors the boy, despite knowing that Tara would have benefited more. This aspect of the play critiques how societal biases can infiltrate even the most respected professions, leading to unethical decisions that reinforce gender discrimination. The medical profession, which is supposed to act in the best interest of the patient, instead becomes complicit in the tragedy of Tara's life.

7. A Broader Social Commentary

Representation of Indian Society: Tara serves as a broader commentary on Indian society and its treatment of women. Dattani uses the Patel family as a microcosm of the larger social system that values boys over girls, and this is reflected in the choices they make. The play highlights how social norms, family pressures, and institutionalized gender discrimination work together to create tragic outcomes for women like Tara.

Universal Themes of Injustice: While Tara is set in the context of Indian society, the themes of gender discrimination and social injustice are universal. Dattani's portrayal of how a family and society prioritize male children over female children resonates with broader global issues of gender inequality. The play's tragic elements reflect the universal consequences of a world where women are denied equal opportunities and recognition.

Conclusion:

Tara is a powerful social tragedy that explores the devastating effects of gender discrimination and patriarchal values on the lives of individuals. Through Tara's story, Dattani critiques the deep-seated biases that exist within families and society at large, showing how these biases lead to physical and emotional suffering. The play's tragic elements, from the unfair medical decision to Tara's untimely death, highlight the consequences of a system that values men over women. Ultimately, Tara is a poignant commentary on the social injustices that continue to shape the lives of women in patriarchal societies, making it a deeply moving and tragic play.

Q.7) Discuss the relationship between Tara and Chandan in Dattani's play 'Tara'

Ans: Introduction: "for this section refer answer 1 of this chapter"

In Mahesh Dattani's play Tara, the relationship between the twins, Tara and Chandan, is central to the narrative and deeply complex. Their bond is shaped by both their unique physical connection and the emotional turmoil caused by the gender bias within their family and society. The play explores how love, guilt, and societal pressures intertwine in their sibling relationship, leading to both closeness and eventual estrangement. Here are the key aspects of their relationship:

1. Inseparable Bond as Conjoined Twins

Physical Connection: Tara and Chandan were born conjoined at the hip, which forms the foundation of their relationship. This physical bond highlights their deep emotional connection, as they have shared not only their bodies but also their early experiences of life. As conjoined twins, their relationship is marked by mutual dependence, and this forms the core of their attachment to each other.

Emotional Connection: Their emotional bond is strong, with both siblings sharing a deep affection for one another. Despite the surgery that physically separates them, Tara and Chandan continue to care for and support each other emotionally. Tara, in particular, is shown to be protective of Chandan, while Chandan also shares a sense of responsibility toward his sister. This closeness is a result of their shared experience of being different from the rest of the world.

2. Impact of Gender Bias on Their Relationship

Family's Preference for Chandan: The critical turning point in their relationship comes from the family's decision to give Chandan the second leg, which biologically should have been Tara's. This act of favoritism toward the male child is a manifestation of societal gender bias, and it creates an unspoken tension between the twins. Tara, who realizes that she was sacrificed for Chandan's benefit, experiences feelings of hurt and injustice, though she never directly blames Chandan for it. This decision, driven by the patriarchal values of their family, alters the dynamics of their relationship.

Chandan's Guilt: Chandan, who benefits from the surgery, carries a deep sense of guilt for having received the leg that should have belonged to Tara. He is aware that his sister was wronged, and this guilt creates a distance between them as he struggles to reconcile his love for her with the knowledge that he was unfairly favored. Chandan's guilt prevents him from fully embracing his relationship with Tara, as he feels responsible for her suffering, even though the decision was not his own. This guilt becomes a barrier to their emotional closeness.

3. Tara's Resentment and Pain

Awareness of Injustice: Tara is acutely aware of the injustice she has suffered due to the family's decision to prioritize Chandan's future over hers. While she does not directly express anger toward her brother, this awareness affects her self-esteem and her sense of worth. Tara's pain and frustration are directed more at the societal norms and the family's decisions rather than Chandan himself, but this does impact how she relates to her brother. She feels that her life was unfairly limited because of her gender, which creates an emotional distance between her and Chandan, despite their love for each other.

Sacrificial Love: Despite her awareness of the injustice, Tara never holds Chandan responsible. In fact, she continues to show love and concern for him. Her sacrificial love is evident in how she supports Chandan emotionally, even when she is suffering herself. This reflects Tara's deep sense of loyalty and affection toward her brother, even in the face of the gender discrimination she experiences.

4. Chandan's Escape and Denial

Chandan's Flight to London: After Tara's death, Chandan moves to London and attempts to distance himself from the past. He changes his name to Dan and tries to escape the guilt and pain associated with Tara's death. His physical and emotional escape from India symbolizes his inability to come to terms with the family's decisions and his role in Tara's suffering. This flight is not only a way to avoid the family's history but also a means of distancing himself from the deep emotional connection he shared with Tara.

Writing as Redemption: Chandan's attempt to write Tara's story is an effort to come to terms with the guilt he feels over her fate. By trying to tell her story, Chandan seeks to give voice to Tara and acknowledge the injustice she faced. However, his inability to complete the story reflects his unresolved emotional conflict. He is still haunted by his role in Tara's life and death, and this unresolved guilt prevents him from finding closure. This aspect of their relationship reveals how deeply Chandan's identity is tied to Tara's and how her loss continues to affect him long after her death.

5. Symbol of Gender Disparity

Chandan and Tara as Representations of Gender Roles: The relationship between Tara and Chandan can be seen as a symbolic representation of the gender disparities that exist in society. Chandan, as the male child, is given more opportunities and is favored by the family, while Tara, as the girl, is seen as less important. The surgery that physically separates them and gives Chandan the leg meant for Tara is a metaphor for how society divides opportunities between men and women, often to the detriment of women. Their relationship is thus shaped by the larger societal forces of patriarchy, which favor boys over girls.

Tara's Strength vs. Chandan's Guilt: Throughout the play, Tara is shown to be emotionally stronger and more resilient than Chandan, despite the fact that she is the one who suffers more from the family's decisions. Chandan, on the other hand, is emotionally fragile and struggles with guilt. This contrast in their personalities highlights the different ways in which gender roles affect individuals. Tara, though marginalized by society, shows inner strength, while Chandan, who benefits from societal favoritism, is emotionally burdened by the consequences.

6. Tragic Nature of Their Relationship

Mutual Love but Unavoidable Distance: The tragedy of Tara and Chandan's relationship lies in the fact that, despite their deep love for each other, they are separated by forces beyond their control. The gender bias that shapes their lives creates a rift between them, even though neither of them is directly responsible for it. Their relationship, marked by love, guilt, and societal pressure, is ultimately tragic because they cannot overcome the emotional and psychological barriers created by the family's decisions and the broader societal expectations.

Tara's Death and Chandan's Emotional Burden: Tara's premature death is the ultimate tragedy in their relationship. Chandan is left to carry the emotional burden of her death, knowing that his life was prioritized over hers. His inability to fully confront this guilt and find closure means that the emotional distance between them continues even after Tara's death. Chandan's ongoing struggle with his identity and his relationship with Tara reflects the lasting impact of the tragedy on his life.

Conclusion:

The relationship between Tara and Chandan in Dattani's *Tara* is complex and multifaceted, shaped by love, guilt, and the societal pressures of gender bias. As conjoined twins, they share a deep emotional bond, but the family's decision to prioritize Chandan over Tara introduces an element of tragedy into their relationship. While they love and care for each other, the weight of societal expectations and familial choices creates a distance between them. Tara's strength and Chandan's guilt form the emotional core of their relationship, making it both a reflection of the personal cost of gender discrimination and a powerful commentary on the impact of societal norms on individual lives. Ultimately, their relationship is a tragic one, defined by love and loss, and shaped by the larger forces of patriarchy and injustice.

IGNOU Previous years' Question papers

CHAPTER FORTY-THREE

June 2020

Q.1. Explain with reference to the context any four of the following passages in about 150 words each:

(a) "These hands are cold-but if thy notes divine May be by mortal wakened once again, Harp of my country, let me strike the strain!"

(b) "For your sakes shall the tree be ever dear! Blent with your images, it shall arise In memory, till the hot tears blind mine eyes!"

(c) "Beauty of the light, surround my life, Beauty of the light! I have sacrificed longing and parted from grief, I can bear thy delight."

(d) "O Love, I dreamed my soul had ransomed thee, In thy lone, dread, incalculable hour From those pale hands at which all mortals cower, And conquered Death by Love, like Savitri."

(e) "It started as a pilgrimage, Exalting minds and making all The burdens light. The second stage Explored but did not test the call."

(f) "I who have lost My way and beg now at stranger's door to Receive love, at least in small change?"

(g) "He had spent his youth whoring after English gods. There is something to be said for exile: You learn roots are deep."

Q.2. Discuss Mulk Raj Anand's novel Untouchable as a Gandhian novel. (500 words)

Or

Discuss the use of various Myths and Symbolism in Raja Rao's novel Kanthapura. (500 words)

Q.3. Discuss the salient features of Swami Vivekananda's "Addresses at the Parliament of Religions". (500 words)

Or

Discuss the political dimensions in Anita Desai's novel Clear Light of Day. (500 words)

Q.4. Discuss Amitav Ghosh as a short story writer with reference to his stories in your syllabus. (500 words).

Or

Discuss Githa Hariharan as a short story writer with reference to her stories in your syllabus. (500 words)

Q.5. Discuss the narrative technique or Salman Rushdie's novel Midnight's Children. (500 words)

Or

Discuss the plot of Mahesh Dattani's play Tara. (500 words)

CHAPTER FORTY-FOUR

Dec 2020

Q.1. Explain with reference to the context any four of the following passages in about 150 words each:

(a) "Neglected, mute, and desolate art thou, Like ruined monument on desert plain."

(b) "Love came to Flora asking for a flower That would of flowers be undisputed queen, The lily and the rose, long, long had been Rivals for that high honour."

(c) "Voice of infinity, sound in my heart, – Call of the One! Stamp there thy radiance, never to part, O living Sun."

(d) "A poet-rascal-clown was born, The frightened child who would not eat Or sleep, a boy of meagre bone."

(e) "Dress in sarees, be girl Be wife, they said. Be embroiderer, be cook, Be a quarreller with servants."

(f) "The new poets still quoted the old poets, but no one spoke in verse of the pregnant woman drowned, with perhaps twins in her kicking at blank walls even before birth."

(g) "Her last wish to be cremated here twisting uncertainly like light on the shifting sands."

Q.2. Discuss Mulk Raj Anand's Untouchable as a Gandhian novel. (500 words)

OR

Discuss the narrative technique of Raja Rao's Kanthapura. (500 words)

Q.3. Comment upon the importance of the character of Raja in Desai's Clear Light of Day. (500 words)

OR

Write a critical essay on your understanding of Hind Swaraj. What is the relevance of the Hind Swaraj in the modern day context? (500 words)

Q.4. Discuss R.K. Narayan as a short story writer. (500 words)

OR

Discuss Ruskin Bond as a short story writer with special reference to "No Room for a Leopard"? (500 words)

Q.5. Discuss Rushdie's novel Midnight's Children as a postcolonial novel. (500 words)

OR

Comment on the plot of Mahesh Dattani's Tara. (500 words)

CHAPTER FORTY-FIVE

June 2021

Q.1. Explain with reference to the context any four of the following passages in about 150 words each:

(a) "My country! In thy day of glory Past A beauteous halo circled round thy brow, And worshipped as a deity thou wast."

(b) "Like a huge Python, winding round and round The rugged trunk, indented deep with scars Up to its very summit near the stars, A creeper climbs, in whose embraces bound No other tree could live."

(c) "This is the soul of man. Body and brain Hungry for earth our heavenly flight detain."

(d) "I have made my commitments now. This is one: to stay where I am, And others choose to give themselves In some remote and backward place. My backward place is where I am."

(e) "You cannot believe, darling Can you, that I lived in such a house and Was proud, and loved ...."

(f) "The good wife lies in my bed through the long afternoon; dreaming still, unexhausted by the deep roar of funeral pyres."

(g) "I can smell violence in the air like the lash of coming rain— mass hatreds drifting grey across the moon."

Q.2.Discuss the narrative technique of Mulk Raj Anand's Untouchable. (500 words)

Or

Discuss Raja Rao's Kanthapura as a Gandhian novel. (500 words)

Q.3. Comment upon the relationship between Bim and Tara in Desai's novel Clear Light of Day. (500 words)

Or

"An Autobiography of an Unknown Indian transcends the framework of an autobiography and contributes significantly to contemporary history." Discuss. (500 words)

Q.4. Write a critical appreciation of Subhadra Sen Gupta's The Fourth Girl. (500 words)

Or

Comment upon Shashi Deshpande's Miracle. (500 words)

Q.5. Discuss the character of Saleem in Rushdie's novel Midnight's Children. (500 words)

Or

Discuss Mahesh Dattan's Tara as a feminist play. (500 words)

CHAPTER FORTY-SIX

Dec 2021

Q.1. Explain with reference to the context any four of the following passages in about 150 words each:

(a) "Those hands are cold-but if thy notes divine May be by mortal wakened once again, Harp of my country, let me strike the strain!"

(b) "Image of ecstasy, thrill and enlace,- Image of bliss! I would see only thy marvellous face, Feel only thy kiss."

(c) "The London seasons passed me by I lay in bed two years alone. And then a woman came to tell My willing ears I was the son Of man. I knew that I had failed."

(d) "There is a house now far away where once I received love. That woman died, The house withdrew into silence, Snakes moved among books."

(e) "In Madurai City of temples and poets, Who sang of cities and temples; every summer a river dries to a trickle in the sand."

(f) "Her last wish to be cremated here twisting uncertainly like light on the shifting sands."

(g) "Your own divided face in a Pair of glasses On an old man's nose is all the countryside you get to see."

Q.2. Discuss the plot and structure of Mulk Raj Anand's novel Untouchable. (500 words)

Or

Discuss the role of Moorthy in Raja Rao's novel Kanthapura. (500 words)

Q.3. Discuss the importance of Bim and Tara relationship in Anita Desai's novel Clear Light of Day. (500 words)

Or

Comment on the prose style of Nirad C. Chaudhari's The Autobiography of an Unknown Indian. (500 words)

Q.4. Discuss the theme of R.K. Narayan's An Astrologer's Day. (500 words)

Or

Discuss Ruskin Bond as a short story writer. (500 words)

Q.5. Discuss the role of Saleem as a narrator in Salman Rushdie's Midnight's Children. (500 words)

Or

Discuss the language and techniques in Mahesh Dattani's play Tara. (500 words)

CHAPTER FORTY-SEVEN

June 2022

Q.1. Explain with reference to the context any four of the following passages in about 150 words each:

(a) "My Country! In thy day of glory past A beauteous halo circled round thy brow, And worshipped as a deity thou wast."

(b) "Beauty of thy Light, Surround my Life—Beauty of the Light! I have sacrificed longing and parted from grief, I can bear thy delight."

(c) "The trip had darkened every face, Our deeds were neither great nor rare Home is where we have to earn our grace."

(d) "Why not Leave Me alone, Critics, friends, visiting cousins, Every one of you? Why not let me Speak in Any language I like?"

(e) "Now she looks for the swing in cities with fifteen suburbs and tries to be innocent about it."

(f) "Mortal as I am, I face the end with unspeakable relief, knowing how I should feel if I were stopped and cut off."

(g) "Somewhere along that stretch of silt a cry goes up as someone spots you, your head bobbing along the waters like a coconut."

Q.2. Discuss the role of Bakha in Mulk Raj Anand's novel Untouchable. (500 words)

Or

Discuss the importance of Harikatha in Raja Rao's novel Kanthapura. (500 words)

Q.3. Discuss the significance of the title of Anita Desai's novel Clear Light of Day. (500 words)

Or

Discuss the post-colonial elements in Mahatma Gandhi's Hind Swaraj. (500 words)

Q.4. Comment upon the diasporic elements in Arun Joshi's The Only American from Our Village. (500 words)

Or

Discuss Subhadra Sengupta's The Fourth Daughter as a Feminist Story. (500 words)

Q.5. Discuss Salman Rushdie's Midnight's Children as a post-colonial novel. (500 words)

Or

Discuss the relationship of Chandan and Tara in Mahesh Dattani's play Tara. (500 words)

CHAPTER FORTY-EIGHT

Dec 2022

Q.1. Explain with reference to the context any four of the following passages in about 150 words each:

(a) "Silence hath bound thee with her fatal chain; Neglected, mute, and desolate art thou, Like ruined monument on desert plain."

(b) "Life only is, or death is life disguised– Life a short death until by life we are surprised."

(c) "Eyes ravished with rapture, celestially panting, What passionate bosoms affaming with fire Drink deep of the hush of the hyacinth heavens that glimmer around them in fountains of light."

(d) "We stood it very well, I thought, Observed and put down copious notes On things the peasants sold and bought The way of serpents and of goats, Three cities where a sage had taught."

(e) "I don't know politics but I know the names Of those in power, and can repeat them like Days of week, or names of months, beginning with Nehru."

(f) "Now she looks for the swing in cities with fifteen suburbs and tries to be innocent about it."

(g) "Endless crow noises. A skull on the holy sands tilts its empty country towards hunger."

Q.2. Discuss in brief the influence of Gandhi on Mulk Raj Anand's novel Untouchable. (500 words)

Or

Discuss the significance of Harikatha in Raja Rao's Kanthapura. (500 words)

Q.3. Comment upon Anita Desai's use of Imagery in Clear Light of Day. (500 words)

Or

Discuss the autobiographical elements in Nehru's Autobiography. (500 words)

Q.4. Comment upon the theme of A Toast to Herself. (500 words)

Or

Comment upon the prose style used by Arun Joshi in The only American from our Village. (500 words)

Q.5. Comment upon the use of language and techniques used in Rushdie's Midnight's Children. (500 words)

Or

Discuss the relationship between Tara and Chandan in Dattani's play Tara. (500 words)

CHAPTER FORTY-NINE

June 2023

Q.1. Explain with reference to the context any four of the following passages in about 150 words each:

(a) "Silence hath bound thee with her fatal chain; Neglected, mute, and desolate art thou, Like ruined monument on desert plain."

(b) "Life only is, or death is life disguised– Life a short death until by life we are surprised."

(c) "Eyes ravished with rapture, celestially panting, What passionate bosoms affaming with fire Drink deep of the hush of the hyacinth heavens that glimmer around them in fountains of light."

(d) "We stood it very well, I thought, Observed and put down copious notes On things the peasants sold and bought The way of serpents and of goats, Three cities where a sage had taught."

(e) "I don't know politics but I know the names Of those in power, and can repeat them like Days of week, or names of months, beginning with Nehru."

(f) "Now she looks for the swing in cities with fifteen suburbs and tries to be innocent about it."

(g) "Endless crow noises. A skull on the holy sands tilts its empty country towards hunger."

Q.2. Discuss in brief the influence of Gandhi on Mulk Raj Anand's novel Untouchable. (500 words)

OR

Discuss the significance of Harikatha in Raja Rao's Kanthapura. (500 words)

Q.3. Comment upon Anita Desai's use of Imagery in Clear Light of Day. (500 words)

OR

Discuss the autobiographical elements in Nehru's An Autobiography. (500 words)

Q.4. Comment upon the theme of A Toast to Herself. (500 words)

OR

Comment upon the prose style used by Arun Joshi in The only American from our Village. (500 words)

Q.5. Comment upon the use of language and techniques used in Rushdie's Midnight's Children. (500 words)

OR

Discuss the relationship between Tara and Chandan in Dattani's play Tara. (500 words)

CHAPTER FIFTY

Dec 2023

Q.1 Explain with reference to the context any four of the following passages in about 150 words each:

(a) "A few small fragments of those wrecks sublime
Which human eye may never more behold;
And let the guerdon of my labor be
My fallen country! One kind wish from thee!"

(b) "That would thy beauty fain, oh fain rehearse,
May Love defend thee from Oblivion's curse."

(c) "Thy golden light came down into my feet;
My earth is now thy playfield and thy seat."

(d) "A poet-rascal-clown was born,
The frightened child who would not eat
Or sleep, a boy of meagre bone."

(e) "I am Indian, very brown, born in Malabar, I speak three languages,
Write in two, dream in one."

(f) "I resemble everyone
but myself, and sometimes see
in shop-windows,
despite the well known laws,
of optics
the portrait of a stranger."

(g) "Fishermen's broken shacks by the river
Let even starlight slip out
From their weak roofs.
A temple stands frail and still
In the distance, as though lost in reverie."

Q.2. Comment upon the role of Bakha in Mulk Raj Anand's novel Untouchable. (500 words)

OR

Discuss the narrative technique of Raja Rao's Kanthapura. (500 words)

Q.3. Comment upon the structure of Anita Desai's novel Clear Light of Day. (500 words)

OR

Discuss Gandhi's Hind Swaraj as a post-colonial text. (500 words)

Q.4. Write a critical appreciation of A trip into the Jungle. (500 words)

OR

Comment upon Gita Hariharan's Gajar Halwa. (500 words)

Q.5. Discuss Rushdie's novel Midnight's Children as a post-colonial novel. (500 words)

OR

Comment upon the plot of Mahesh Dattani's play Tara. (500 words)

CHAPTER FIFTY-ONE

June 2024

Q.1 Explain with reference to the context any four of the following passages in about 150 words each:

(a) "Three happy children in a darkened room! What do they gaze on with wide-open eyes?"

(b) "O Love, alas, that love could not assuage The burden of thy human heritage, Or save thee from the swift decrees of Death."

(c) "It is I who laugh, It is I who make love And then, feel shame, It is I who lie dying With a rattle in my throat."

(d) "The golden Light came down into my feet; My earth is now thy playfield and thy seat."

(e) "Really what keeps us apart at the end of year is unshared Childhood. You cannot, for instance, meet my father."

(f) "Life only is, or death is life disguised, Life a short death until by life we are surprised."

Q.2. Discuss the solutions Mulk Raj Anand offers for the eradication of untouchability. Answer with reference to his novel.

Q.3. Critically evaluate the structure of Clear Light of Day.

OR

Do you prefer stories that are open-ended or those stories which offer clear resolutions? Answer with reference to the stories you have read in this course.

Q.4. Discuss Salmon Rushdie's use of magic realism in his novel Midnight's Children.

OR

What are the major themes of Dattani's Tara? Discuss what you think is most important of them.

Q.5. Discuss Ruskin Bond's techniques of characterization in the stories you have read.

OR

Enunciate Anita Desai's great contribution to the Indian-English novel.

Thank you for choosing this book! We hope this book has provided you with valuable insights and knowledge in Indian English Literature. As you embark in your academic journey, we understand the importance of comprehensive preparation, not only for exams but for a deeper understanding of the subject.

If you are interested in delving further into the realm of literature, we recommend exploring our companion books,

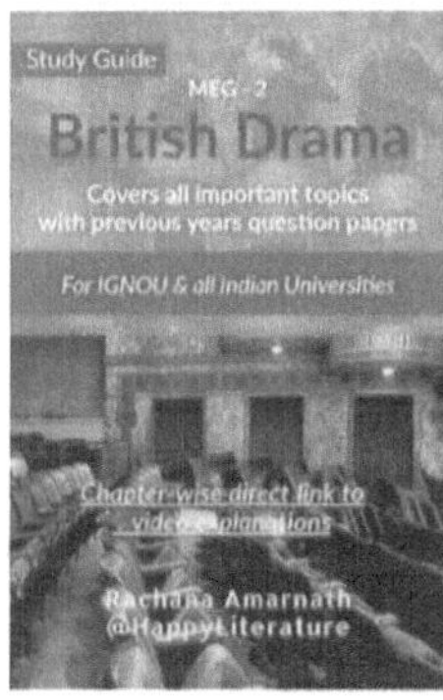

These books available in all leading marketplace & Online platforms

(for a 21% discount on MRP you can buy it on notion press website by using coupon code "SPECIAL")

Remember, diligent preparation, proper time management, and a positive mindset are key to success in exams.

Best regards,

Rachana Amarnath

For any feedbacks, please get in touch by email at happyliterature2021@gmail.com